Alpha
Architecture
Reference
Manual

Alpha
Architecture
Reference
Manual

Contributing Authors

Richard Witek
   Alpha co-architect

and
Ellen M. Batbouta
Richard A. Brunner
Wayne M. Cardoza
Daniel W. Dobberpuhl
Robert A. Giggi
Henry N. Grieb
Richard B. Grove
Robert H. Halstead, Jr.
Michael S. Harvey
Nancy P. Kronenberg
Raymond J. Lanza
Stephen J. Morris
William B. Noyce
Charles G. Nylander
Mary H. Payne
Audrey R. Reith
Robert M. Supnik
Benjamin J. Thomas
Catharine Van Ingen

Edited by
Richard L. Sites
Alpha co-architect

digital   DIGITAL PRESS

Printed in the United States of America.

9 8 7 6 5 4 3 2 1

Order number EY-L520E-DP
ISBN 1-55558-098-X

Technical Writer: Charles Greenman
Production Editor: Kathe Rhoades
Technical Illustrator: Lynne Kenison
Cover Design: Marshall Henrichs

Contents

Foreword
Preface

Part I / Common Architecture

1   Introduction
2   Basic Architecture
3   Instruction Formats
4   Instruction Descriptions
5   System Architecture and Programming Implications
6   Common PALcode Architecture
7   Console Subsystem Overview
8   Input/Output

Part II / OpenVMS Alpha Software

1   Introduction to OpenVMS Alpha
2   OpenVMS PALcode Instruction Descriptions
3   OpenVMS Memory Management
4   OpenVMS Process Structure
5   OpenVMS Internal Processor Registers
6   OpenVMS Exceptions, Interrupts, and Machine Checks

Part III / DEC OSF/1 Alpha Software

1   Introduction to DEC OSF/1 Alpha
2   OSF/1 PALcode Instruction Descriptions
3   OSF/1 Memory Management
4   OSF/1 Process Structure
5   OSF/1 Exceptions and Interrupts

Appendixes

A   Software Considerations
B   IEEE Floating-Point Conformance
C   Instruction Encodings

Index

Foreword

In the foreword to the *VAX Architecture Reference Manual*, Sam Fuller, Digital's Vice President for Research and Architecture, wrote, "Computer design continues to be a dynamic field; I expect we will see more rather than less change and innovation in the decades ahead." *The Alpha Architecture Reference Manual* demonstrates the accuracy of that prediction.

Alpha follows VAX by about fifteen years. Those fifteen years have witnessed a torrent of change in computer technology, one that shows no sign of abating:

- More than a 1000-fold increase in the performance of microprocessors
- More than a 1000-fold increase in the density of semiconductor memories
- More than a 500-fold increase in the density of magnetic storage devices
- More than a 100-fold increase in the speed of network connections

During the same period, the internal organization of computer systems has changed as well, based on developments such as RISC architecture, symmetric multiprocessing, and coherent distributed systems. Moreover, the fundamental paradigms of computing have changed not once, but several times, with the introduction of personal computers, graphics workstations, local area networks, and client/server computing.

These developments present an enormous challenge for computing in the 21st century. Future computers will be called upon to solve problems of great scale and complexity, worldwide, in a distributed manner. They will have to provide unprecedented performance, flexibility, reliability, and scalability in order to implement a global infrastructure of information, and to give users an untrammeled window on the world.

Alpha is Digital's response to the challenges of 21st-century computing. It represents the culmination of the company's knowledge and belief about how the next generations of computers should be built. Alpha is based on a decade's experimental and engineering work in RISC architecture, high-speed implementation, software compatibility and migration, and system serviceability. It provides the foundation for implementations ranging from mobile computing units to massively parallel supercomputers.

Alpha is designed to handle the largest computing problems of today and tomorrow. When the Alpha architecture is compared to its predecessor, the VAX architecture, two differences stand out immediately. First, Alpha is a 64-bit architecture; VAX is a 32-bit architecture. This means that Alpha's virtual address extends to a 64-bit linear range of bytes in memory. Supporting this extended virtual address space are an extended maximum physical address range (up to 48 bits) and larger pages (8KB to 64KB). Alpha's extended virtual address range allows direct manipulation of the gigabytes and terabytes of data produced in electrical and mechanical design, database and transaction processing, and imaging.

Second, Alpha is a RISC architecture; VAX is a CISC architecture. RISC stands for Reduced Instruction Set Computer, CISC for Complex Instruction Set Computer. RISC architectures are characterized by simple, fixed-length instruction formats; a small number of addressing modes; large register files; a load-store instruction set model; and direct hardware execution of instructions. CISC architectures are characterized by variable-length instruction formats; a large number of addressing modes; small-to-medium-sized register files; a full set of register-to-memory (or even memory-to-memory) instructions; and microcoded execution of instructions. Alpha's streamlined organization facilitates high-speed implementation in a variety of technologies, while providing strong compatibility with today's programs and data.

The following tabulation contrasts the architectural differences between VAX and Alpha:

	VAX	**Alpha**
Architecture	CISC	RISC
Virtual address range	32 bits	Up to 64 bits
Physical address range	Up to 32 bits	Up to 48 bits
Page size	512 bytes	8KB–64KB
Instruction lengths	1–51 bytes	4 bytes
General registers	16×32 bits	64×64 bits
Addressing modes	21	3
Instruction set architecture	General	Load-store
Directly supported data types	Integer, floating, bit field, queue, character string, decimal string	Integer, floating

This book is the culmination of an effort begun three years ago. In that time, Alpha has grown from a paper specification to a cohesive set of chips, systems, and software, spanning the computer spectrum. This achievement is due to the efforts of many hundreds of people in Engineering, Marketing, Sales, Service, and Manufacturing. This book is documentation of, and a tribute to, the outstanding work they have done.

Bob Supnik
Corporate Consultant,
Vice President

Preface

The Alpha architecture is a RISC architecture that was designed for high performance and longevity. Following Amdahl, Blaauw, and Brooks,[1] we distinguish between architecture and implementation:

- Computer architecture is defined as the attributes of a computer seen by a machine-language programmer. This definition includes the instruction set, instruction formats, operation codes, addressing modes, and all registers and memory locations that may be directly manipulated by a machine-language programmer.

- Implementation is defined as the actual hardware structure, logic design, and data-path organization.

This architecture book describes the required behavior of all Alpha implementations, as seen by the machine-language programmer. The architecture does not speak to implementation considerations such has how fast a program runs, what specific bit pattern is left in a hardware register after an unpredictable operation, how to schedule code for a particular chip, or how to wire up a given chip; those considerations are described in implementation-specific documents.

Various Alpha implementations are expected over the coming years, starting with the Digital 21064 chip.

Goals

When we started the Alpha project in the fall of 1988, we had a small number of goals:

1. High performance

2. Longevity

3. Run VMS and UNIX

4. Easy migration from VAX (and soon-to-be MIPS) customer base

As principal architects, Rich Witek and I made design decisions that were driven directly by these goals.

We assumed that high performance was needed to make a new architecture attractive in the marketplace, and to keep Digital competitive.

We set a 15–25 year design horizon (longevity) and tried to avoid any design elements that we thought would become limitations during this time. The design horizon led directly to the conclusion that Alpha could not be a 32-bit architecture: 32-bit addresses will be too small within 10 years. We thus adopted a full 64-bit

---

1. Amdahl, G.M., G.A. Blaauw, and F.P. Brooks, Jr. "Architecture of the IBM System/360." *IBM Journal of Research and Development*, vol. 8, no. 2 (April 1964): 87–101.

architecture, with a minimal number of 32-bit operations for backward compatibility. Wherever possible, 32-bit operands are put in registers in a 64-bit canonical form and operated upon with 64-bit operations.

The longevity goal also caused us to examine how the performance of implementations would scale up over 25 years. Over the past 25 years, computers have become about 1000 times faster. This suggested to us that Alpha implementations would need to do the same, or we would have to bet that the industry would fall off the historical performance curve. We were unwilling to bet against the industry, and were unwilling to ignore the issue, so we seriously examined the consequences of longevity.

We thought that it would be realistic for implementors to improve clock speeds by a factor of 10 over 25 years, but not by a factor of 100 or 1000. (Clock speeds have improved by about a factor of 100 over the past 25 years, but physical limits are now slowing down the rate of increase.)

We concluded that the remaining factor of 100 would have to come from other design dimensions. If you cannot make the clock faster, the next dimension is to do more work per clock cycle. So the Alpha architecture is focused on allowing implementations that issue many instructions every clock cycle. We thought that it would be realistic for implementors to achieve about a factor of 10 over 25 years by using multiple instruction issue, but not a factor of 100. Even a factor of 10 will require perhaps a decade of compiler research.

We concluded that the remaining factor of 10 would have to come from some other design dimension. If you cannot make the clock faster, and cannot do more work per clock, the next dimension is to have multiple clocked instruction streams, that is, multiple processors. So the Alpha architecture is focused on allowing implementations that apply multiple processors to a single problem. We thought that it would be realistic for implementors to achieve the remaining factor of 10 over 25 years by using multiple processors.

Overall, the factor-of-1000 increase in performance looked reasonable, but required factor-of-10 increases in three different dimensions. These three dimensions therefore formed part of our design framework:

• Gracefully allow fast cycle-time implementations

• Gracefully allow multiple-instruction-issue implementations

• Gracefully allow multiple-processor implementations

The cycle-time goal encouraged us to keep the instruction definitions very simple, and to keep the interactions between instructions very simple. The multiple-instruction-issue goal encouraged us to eliminate specialized registers, architected delay slots, precise arithmetic traps, and byte writes (with their embedded read-modify-write bottleneck). The multiple-processor goal encouraged us to consider the memory model and atomic-update primitives carefully. We adopted load-locked/store-conditional sequences as the atomic-update primitive, and eliminated strict read-write ordering between processors.

All of the above design decisions were driven directly by the performance and longevity goals. The lack of byte writes, precise arithmetic traps, and multiprocessor read/write ordering have been the most controversial decisions, so far.

Clean Sheet of Paper

To run both OpenVMS and UNIX without burdening the hardware implementations with elaborate (and sometimes conflicting) operating system underpinnings, we adopted an idea from a previous Digital RISC design. Alpha places the underpinnings for interrupt delivery and return, exceptions, context switching, memory management, and error handling in a set of privileged software subroutines called PALcode (privileged architecture library code). PALcode subroutines have controlled entries, run with interrupts turned off, and have access to real hardware (implementation) registers. By having different sets of PALcode for different operating systems, the architecture itself is not biased toward a specific operating system or computing style.

PALcode allowed us to design an architecture that could run OpenVMS gracefully without elaborate hardware and without massively rewriting the VMS synchronization and protection mechanisms. PALcode lets the Alpha architecture support some complex VAX primitives (such as the interlocked queue instructions) that are heavily used by OpenVMS, without burdening a UNIX implementation in any way.

Finally, we also considered how to move VAX and MIPS code to Alpha. We rejected various forms of "compatibility mode" hardware, because they would have severely compromised the performance and time-to-market of the first implementation. After some experimentation, we adopted the strategy of running existing binary code by building software translators. One translator converts OpenVMS VAX images to functionally identical OpenVMS Alpha images. A second translator converts MIPS ULTRIX images to functionally identical DEC OSF/1 Alpha images.

Fundamentally, PALcode gave us a migration path for existing operating systems, and the translators (and native compilers) gave us a migration path for existing user-mode code. PALcode and the translators provided a clean sheet of design paper for the bulk of the Alpha architecture. Other than an extra set of VAX floating-point formats (included for good business reasons, but subsettable later), no specific VAX or MIPS features are carried directly into the Alpha architecture for compatibility reasons.

These considerations substantially shaped the architecture described in the rest of this book.

Organization

The first part of this book describes the instruction-set architecture, and is largely self-contained for readers who are involved with compilers or with assembly language programming. The second and third parts describe the supporting PALcode routines for each operating system—the specific operating system PALcode architecture.

Acknowledgments

My collaboration with Rich Witek over the past few years has been extremely rewarding, both personally and professionally. By combining our backgrounds and viewpoints, we have produced an architecture that is substantially better than either of us could have produced alone. Thank you, Rich.

A work of this magnitude cannot be done on a shoestring or in isolation. Rich and I were blessed with a rich environment of dozens and later hundreds of bright, thoughtful, and outspoken professional peers. I thank the management of Digital Equipment Corporation for providing that rich environment, and those peers for making the architecture so much more robust and well-considered.

Three people have especially influenced my views of computer architecture, through personal interaction and landmark machine design: Fred Brooks, John Cocke, and Seymour Cray. This work is built directly upon theirs, and could not exist without them.

The organization, editing, and production of this text in final form is largely the work of Charlie Greenman, whose clear writing is much appreciated.

Richard L. Sites
May 1992

A Note on the Structure of This Book

The *Alpha Architecture Reference Manual* is divided into three parts, three appendixes, and an index. Each part describes a major portion of the Alpha architecture. Each contains its own table of contents.

The following tabulation outlines the book's contents:

Name	Contents
Name	**Contents**
Part I	Common Architecture
	This part describes the instruction-set architecture that is common to and required by all implementations.
Part II	OpenVMS Alpha Software
	This part describes how the OpenVMS operating system relates to the Alpha architecture.
Part III	DEC OSF/1 Alpha Software
	This part describes how the DEC OSF/1 operating system relates to the Alpha architecture.
Appendixes	The appendixes describe implementation considerations, IEEE floating-point conformance, and instruction encodings.
Index	Index entries are called out by the symbol (I), (II), or (III). Each symbol is associated with the corresponding Part. Index entries for the appendixes are called out by appendix name and page number.

Part I

Common Architecture

This part describes the common Alpha architecture and contains the following chapters:

1. Introduction
2. Basic Architecture
3. Instruction Formats
4. Instruction Descriptions
5. System Architecture and Programming Implications
6. Common PALcode Architecture
7. Console Subsystem Overview
8. Input/Output

Contents

Common Architecture (I)

Chapter 1   Introduction (I)

1.1	The Alpha Approach to RISC Architecture	1–1
1.2	Data Format Overview	1–3
1.3	Instruction Format Overview	1–4
1.4	Instruction Overview	1–5
1.5	Instruction Set Characteristics	1–6
1.6	Terminology and Conventions	1–7
1.6.1	Numbering	1–7
1.6.2	Security Holes	1–7
1.6.3	UNPREDICTABLE and UNDEFINED	1–7
1.6.4	Ranges and Extents	1–8
1.6.5	ALIGNED and UNALIGNED	1–8
1.6.6	Must Be Zero (MBZ)	1–9
1.6.7	Read As Zero (RAZ)	1–9
1.6.8	Should Be Zero (SBZ)	1–9
1.6.9	Ignore (IGN)	1–9
1.6.10	Implementation Dependent (IMP)	1–9
1.6.11	Figure Drawing Conventions	1–9
1.6.12	Macro Code Example Conventions	1–9

Chapter 2   Basic Architecture (I)

2.1	Addressing	2–1
2.2	Data Types	2–1
2.2.1	Byte	2–1
2.2.2	Word	2–1
2.2.3	Longword	2–2
2.2.4	Quadword	2–2
2.2.5	VAX Floating-Point Formats	2–3
2.2.5.1	F_floating	2–3
2.2.5.2	G_floating	2–5
2.2.5.3	D_floating	2–6
2.2.6	IEEE Floating-Point Formats	2–7
2.2.6.1	S_Floating	2–8
2.2.6.2	T_floating	2–10

2.2.7	Longword Integer Format in Floating-Point Unit	2–11
2.2.8	Quadword Integer Format in Floating-Point Unit	2–12
2.2.9	Data Types with No Hardware Support	2–13

Chapter 3 Instruction Formats (I)

3.1	Alpha Registers	3–1
3.1.1	Program Counter	3–1
3.1.2	Integer Registers	3–1
3.1.3	Floating-Point Registers	3–2
3.1.4	Lock Registers	3–2
3.1.5	Optional Registers	3–2
3.1.5.1	Memory Prefetch Registers	3–2
3.1.5.2	VAX Compatibility Register	3–2
3.2	Notation	3–2
3.2.1	Operand Notation	3–3
3.2.2	Instruction Operand Notation	3–4
3.2.3	Operators	3–5
3.2.4	Notation Conventions	3–8
3.3	Instruction Formats	3–8
3.3.1	Memory Instruction Format	3–9
3.3.1.1	Memory Format Instructions with a Function Code	3–9
3.3.1.2	Memory Format Jump Instructions	3–10
3.3.2	Branch Instruction Format	3–10
3.3.3	Operate Instruction Format	3–10
3.3.4	Floating-Point Operate Instruction Format	3–12
3.3.4.1	Floating-Point Convert Instructions	3–12
3.3.5	PALcode Instruction Format	3–13

Chapter 4 Instruction Descriptions (I)

4.1	Instruction Set Overview	4–1
4.1.1	Subsetting Rules	4–2
4.1.1.1	Floating-Point Subsets	4–2
4.1.2	Software Emulation Rules	4–2
4.1.3	Opcode Qualifiers	4–3
4.2	Memory Integer Load/Store Instructions	4–4
4.2.1	Load Address	4–5
4.2.2	Load Memory Data into Integer Register	4–6
4.2.3	Load Unaligned Memory Data into Integer Register	4–7
4.2.4	Load Memory Data into Integer Register Locked	4–8
4.2.5	Store Integer Register Data into Memory Conditional	4–11
4.2.6	Store Integer Register Data into Memory	4–13
4.2.7	Store Unaligned Integer Register Data into Memory	4–14
4.3	Control Instructions	4–15

4.3.1   Conditional Branch   4–17

4.3.2   Unconditional Branch   4–19

4.3.3   Jumps   4–20

4.4   Integer Arithmetic Instructions   4–22

4.4.1   Longword Add   4–23

4.4.2   Scaled Longword Add   4–24

4.4.3   Quadword Add   4–25

4.4.4   Scaled Quadword Add   4–26

4.4.5   Integer Signed Compare   4–27

4.4.6   Integer Unsigned Compare   4–28

4.4.7   Longword Multiply   4–29

4.4.8   Quadword Multiply   4–30

4.4.9   Unsigned Quadword Multiply High   4–31

4.4.10   Longword Subtract   4–32

4.4.11   Scaled Longword Subtract   4–33

4.4.12   Quadword Subtract   4–34

4.4.13   Scaled Quadword Subtract   4–35

4.5   Logical and Shift Instructions   4–36

4.5.1   Logical Functions   4–37

4.5.2   Conditional Move Integer   4–38

4.5.3   Shift Logical   4–40

4.5.4   Shift Arithmetic   4–41

4.6   Byte-Manipulation Instructions   4–42

4.6.1   Compare Byte   4–44

4.6.2   Extract Byte   4–46

4.6.3   Byte Insert   4–50

4.6.4   Byte Mask   4–52

4.6.5   Zero Bytes   4–55

4.7   Floating-Point Instructions   4–56

4.7.1   Floating Subsets and Floating Faults   4–56

4.7.2   Definitions   4–57

4.7.3   Encodings   4–58

4.7.4   Floating-Point Rounding Modes   4–59

4.7.5   Floating-Point Trapping Modes   4–60

4.7.5.1   Imprecise /Software Completion Trap Modes   4–62

4.7.5.2   Invalid Operation Arithmetic Trap   4–63

4.7.5.3   Division by Zero Arithmetic Trap   4–63

4.7.5.4   Overflow Arithmetic Trap   4–63

4.7.5.5   Underflow Arithmetic Trap   4–63

4.7.5.6   Inexact Result Arithmetic Trap   4–64

4.7.5.7   Integer Overflow Arithmetic Trap   4–64

4.7.6   Floating-Point Single-Precision Operations   4–64

4.7.7   FPCR Register and Dynamic Rounding Mode   4–64

4.7.7.1   Accessing the FPCR   4–66

4.7.7.2   Default Values of the FPCR   4–67

4.7.7.3   Saving and Restoring the FPCR 4–67

4.7.8   IEEE Standard 4–67

4.8   Memory Format Floating-Point Instructions 4–68

4.8.1   Load F_floating 4–69

4.8.2   Load G_floating 4–70

4.8.3   Load S_floating 4–71

4.8.4   Load T_floating 4–72

4.8.5   Store F_floating 4–73

4.8.6   Store G_floating 4–74

4.8.7   Store S_floating 4–75

4.8.8   Store T_floating 4–76

4.9   Branch Format Floating-Point Instructions 4–77

4.9.1   Conditional Branch 4–78

4.10   Floating-Point Operate Format Instructions 4–80

4.10.1   Copy Sign 4–83

4.10.2   Convert Integer to Integer 4–84

4.10.3   Floating-Point Conditional Move 4–85

4.10.4   Move from/to Floating-Point Control Register 4–87

4.10.5   VAX Floating Add 4–88

4.10.6   IEEE Floating Add 4–89

4.10.7   VAX Floating Compare 4–91

4.10.8   IEEE Floating Compare 4–92

4.10.9   Convert VAX Floating to Integer 4–94

4.10.10   Convert Integer to VAX Floating 4–95

4.10.11   Convert VAX Floating to VAX Floating 4–96

4.10.12   Convert IEEE Floating to Integer 4–98

4.10.13   Convert Integer to IEEE Floating 4–99

4.10.14   Convert IEEE Floating to IEEE Floating 4–100

4.10.15   VAX Floating Divide 4–102

4.10.16   IEEE Floating Divide 4–104

4.10.17   VAX Floating Multiply 4–106

4.10.18   IEEE Floating Multiply 4–107

4.10.19   VAX Floating Subtract 4–109

4.10.20   IEEE Floating Subtract 4–111

4.11   Miscellaneous Instructions 4–113

4.11.1   Call Privileged Architecture Library 4–114

4.11.2   Prefetch Data 4–115

4.11.3   Memory Barrier 4–117

4.11.4   Read Process Cycle Counter 4–118

4.11.5   Trap Barrier 4–120

4.12   VAX Compatibility Instructions 4–121

4.12.1   VAX Compatibility Instructions 4–122

Chapter 5 System Architecture and Programming Implications (I)

5.1	Introduction	5–1
5.2	Physical Memory Behavior	5–1
5.2.1	Coherency of Memory Access	5–1
5.2.2	Granularity of Memory Access	5–2
5.2.3	Width of Memory Access	5–2
5.2.4	Memory-Like Behavior	5–3
5.3	Translation Buffers and Virtual Caches	5–3
5.4	Caches and Write Buffers	5–4
5.5	Data Sharing	5–5
5.5.1	Atomic Change of a Single Datum	5–5
5.5.2	Atomic Update of a Single Datum	5–6
5.5.3	Atomic Update of Data Structures	5–6
5.5.4	Ordering Considerations for Shared Data Structures	5–8
5.6	Read/Write Ordering	5–9
5.6.1	Alpha Shared Memory Model	5–9
5.6.1.1	Architectural Definition of Processor Issue Sequence	5–10
5.6.1.2	Definition of Processor Issue Order	5–11
5.6.1.3	Definition of Memory Access Sequence	5–11
5.6.1.4	Definition of Location Access Order	5–11
5.6.1.5	Definition of Storage	5–12
5.6.1.6	Relationship Between Issue Order and Access Order	5–12
5.6.1.7	Definition of Before	5–12
5.6.1.8	Definition of After	5–13
5.6.1.9	Timeliness	5–13
5.6.2	Litmus Tests	5–13
5.6.2.1	Litmus Test 1 (Impossible Sequence)	5–13
5.6.2.2	Litmus Test 2 (Impossible Sequence)	5–13
5.6.2.3	Litmus Test 3 (Impossible Sequence)	5–14
5.6.2.4	Litmus Test 4 (Sequence Okay)	5–14
5.6.2.5	Litmus Test 5 (Sequence Okay)	5–14
5.6.2.6	Litmus Test 6 (Sequence Okay)	5–14
5.6.2.7	Litmus Test 7 (Impossible Sequence)	5–15
5.6.2.8	Litmus Test 8 (Impossible Sequence)	5–15
5.6.2.9	Litmus Test 9 (Impossible Sequence)	5–15
5.6.3	Implied Barriers	5–16
5.6.4	Implications for Software	5–16
5.6.4.1	Single-Processor Data Stream	5–16
5.6.4.2	Single-Processor Instruction Stream	5–16
5.6.4.3	Multiple-Processor Data Stream (Including Single Processor with DMA I/O)	5–16
5.6.4.4	Multiple-Processor Instruction Stream (Including Single Processor with DMA I/O)	5–17
5.6.4.5	Multiple-Processor Context Switch	5–17
5.6.4.6	Multiple-Processor Send/Receive Interrupt	5–20
5.6.5	Implications for Hardware	5–20

5.7   Arithmetic Traps   5–21

Chapter 6   Common PALcode Architecture (I)

6.1   PALcode   6–1
6.2   PALcode Instructions and Functions   6–1
6.3   PALcode Environment   6–2
6.4   Special Functions Required for PALcode   6–2
6.5   PALcode Effects on System Code   6–3
6.6   PALcode Replacement   6–3
6.7   Required PALcode Instructions   6–4
6.7.1   Drain Aborts   6–5
6.7.2   Halt   6–6
6.7.3   Instruction Memory Barrier   6–7

Chapter 7   Console Subsystem Overview (I)

Chapter 8   Input/Output (I)

8.1   Introduction   8–1
8.2   Local I/O Space Access   8–2
8.2.1   Read/Write Ordering   8–2
8.3   Remote I/O Space Access   8–2
8.3.1   Mailbox Posting   8–3
8.3.2   Mailbox Pointer Register (MBPR)   8–4
8.3.3   Mailbox Structure   8–5
8.3.4   Mailbox Access Synchronization   8–6
8.3.5   Mailbox Read/Write Ordering   8–7
8.3.6   Remote I/O Space Access Granularity   8–7
8.3.7   Remote I/O Space Read Accesses   8–8
8.3.8   Remote I/O Space Write Accesses   8–9
8.4   Direct Memory Accesss (DMA)   8–10
8.4.1   Access Granularity   8–10
8.4.2   Read/Write Ordering   8–11
8.4.3   Device Address Translation   8–12
8.5   Interrupts   8–12
8.6   I/O Bus-Specific Mailbox Usage   8–12
8.6.1   Mailbox Field Checking   8–12
8.6.2   CMD Field   8–13
8.6.3   Special Commands   8–13

Figures

1–1	Instruction Format Overview	1–4
2–1	Byte Format	2–1
2–2	Word Format	2–2
2–3	Longword Format	2–2
2–4	Quadword Format	2–3
2–5	F_floating Datum	2–3
2–6	F_floating Register Format	2–4
2–7	G_floating Datum	2–5
2–8	G_floating Format	2–5
2–9	D_floating Datum	2–6
2–10	D_floating Register Format	2–6
2–11	S_floating Datum	2–8
2–12	S_floating Register Format	2–8
2–13	T_floating Datum	2–10
2–14	T_floating Register Format	2–10
2–15	Longword Integer Datum	2–11
2–16	Longword Integer Floating-Register Format	2–11
2–17	Quadword Integer Datum	2–12
2–18	Quadword Integer Floating-Register Format	2–12
3–1	Memory Instruction Format	3–9
3–2	Memory Instruction with Function Code Format	3–9
3–3	Branch Instruction Format	3–10
3–4	Operate Instruction Format	3–11
3–5	Floating-Point Operate Instruction Format	3–12
3–6	PALcode Instruction Format	3–13
4–1	Floating-Point Control Register (FPCR) Format	4–65
8–1	Alpha System Overview	8–1
8–2	Mailbox Pointer Register Format	8–4
8–3	Mailbox Data Structure Format	8–5

Tables

2–1	F_floating Load Exponent Mapping	2–4
2–2	S_floating Load Exponent Mapping	2–9
3–1	Operand Notation	3–3
3–2	Operand Value Notation	3–3
3–3	Expression Operand Notation	3–3
3–4	Operators	3–5
4–1	Opcode Qualifiers	4–3
4–2	Memory Integer Load/Store Instructions	4–4
4–3	Control Instructions Summary	4–16
4–4	Jump Instructions Branch Prediction	4–21
4–5	Integer Arithmetic Instructions Summary	4–22
4–6	Logical and Shift Instructions Summary	4–36

4–7   Byte-Manipulation Instructions Summary   4–42

4–8   Floating-Point Control Register (FPCR) Bit Descriptions   4–65

4–9   Memory Format Floating-Point Instructions Summary   4–68

4–10   Floating-Point Branch Instructions Summary   4–77

4–11   Floating-Point Operate Instructions Summary   4–80

4–12   Miscellaneous Instructions Summary   4–113

4–13   VAX Compatibility Instructions Summary   4–121

5–1   Processor Issue Order   5–11

5–2   Location Access Order   5–12

6–1   PALcode Instructions that Require Recognition   6–4

6–2   Required PALcode Instructions   6–4

8–1   Mailbox Pointer Register Format   8–4

8–2   Mailbox Data Structure Format   8–5

Chapter 1

Introduction (I)

Alpha is a 64-bit load/store RISC architecture that is designed with particular emphasis on the three elements that most affect performance: clock speed, multiple instruction issue, and multiple processors.

The Alpha architects examined and analyzed current and theoretical RISC architecture design elements and developed high-performance alternatives for the Alpha architecture. The architects adopted only those design elements that appeared valuable for a projected 25-year design horizon. Thus, Alpha becomes the first 21st century computer architecture.

The Alpha architecture is designed to avoid bias toward any particular operating system or programming language. Alpha initially supports the OpenVMS Alpha and DEC OSF/1 operating systems, and supports simple software migration from applications that run on those operating systems.

This manual describes in detail how Alpha is designed to be the leadership 64-bit architecture of the computer industry.

1.1 The Alpha Approach to RISC Architecture

Alpha Is a True 64-Bit Architecture

Alpha was designed as a 64-bit architecture. All registers are 64 bits in length and all operations are performed between 64-bit registers. It is not a 32-bit architecture that was later expanded to 64 bits.

Alpha Is Designed for Very High-Speed Implementations

The instructions are very simple. All instructions are 32 bits in length. Memory operations are either loads or stores. All data manipulation is done between registers.

The Alpha architecture facilitates pipelining multiple instances of the same operations because there are no special registers and no condition codes.

The instructions interact with each other only by one instruction writing a register or memory and another instruction reading from the same place. That makes it particularly easy to build implementations that issue multiple instructions every CPU cycle. (The first implementation issues two instructions per cycle.)

Alpha makes it easy to maintain binary compatibility across multiple implementations and easy to maintain full speed on multiple-issue implementations. For example, there are no implementation-specific pipeline timing hazards, no load-delay slots, and no branch-delay slots.

Alpha's Approach to Byte Manipulation

The Alpha architecture does byte shifting and masking with normal 64-bit register-to-register instructions, crafted to keep instruction sequences short.

Alpha does not include single-byte store instructions. This has several advantages:

- Cache and memory implementations need not include byte shift-and-mask logic, and sequencer logic need not perform read-modify-write on memory locations. Such logic is awkward for high-speed implementation and tends to slow down cache access to normal 32-bit or 64-bit aligned quantities.

- Alpha's approach to byte manipulation makes it easier to build a high-speed error-correcting write-back cache, which is often needed to keep a very fast RISC implementation busy.

- Alpha's approach can make it easier to pipeline multiple byte operations.

Alpha's Approach to Arithmetic Traps

Alpha lets the software implementor determine the precision of arithmetic traps. With the Alpha architecture, arithmetic traps (such as overflow and underflow) are imprecise—they can be delivered an arbitrary number of instructions after the instruction that triggered the trap. Also, traps from many different instructions can be reported at once. That makes implementations that use pipelining and multiple issue substantially easier to build.

However, if precise arithmetic exceptions are desired, trap barrier instructions can be explicitly inserted in the program to force traps to be delivered at specific points.

Alpha's Approach to Multiprocessor Shared Memory

As viewed from a second processor (including an I/O device), a sequence of reads and writes issued by one processor may be arbitrarily reordered by an implementation. This allows implementations to use multibank caches, bypassed write buffers, write merging, pipelined writes with retry on error, and so forth. If strict ordering between two accesses must be maintained, explicit memory barrier instructions can be inserted in the program.

The basic multiprocessor interlocking primitive is a RISC-style load_locked, modify, store_conditional sequence. If the sequence runs without interrupt, exception, or an interfering write from another processor, then the conditional store succeeds. Otherwise, the store fails and the program eventually must branch back and retry the sequence. This style of interlocking scales well with very fast caches, and makes Alpha an especially attractive architecture for building multiple-processor systems.

Alpha Instructions Include Hints for Achieving Higher Speed

A number of Alpha instructions include hints for implementations, all aimed at achieving higher speed.

- Calculated jump instructions have a target hint that can allow much faster subroutine calls and returns.

- There are prefetching hints for the memory system that can allow much higher cache hit rates.

- There are granularity hints for the virtual-address mapping that can allow much more effective use of translation lookaside buffers for large contiguous structures.

PALcode—Alpha's Very Flexible Privileged Software Library

A Privileged Architecture Library (PALcode) is a set of subroutines that are specific to a particular Alpha operating system implementation. These subroutines provide operating-system primitives for context switching, interrupts, exceptions, and memory management. PALcode is similar to the BIOS libraries that are provided in personal computers.

PALcode subroutines are invoked by implementation hardware or by software CALL_PAL instructions.

PALcode is written in standard machine code with some implementation-specific extensions to provide access to low-level hardware.

One version of PALcode lets Alpha implementations run the full OpenVMS operating system by mirroring many of the OpenVMS VAX features. The OpenVMS PALcode instructions let Alpha run OpenVMS with little more hardware than that found on a conventional RISC machine: the PAL mode bit itself, plus 4 extra protection bits in each Translation Buffer entry.

Another version of PALcode lets Alpha implementations run the OSF/1 operating system by mirroring many of the RISC ULTRIX features. Other versions of PALcode can be developed for real-time, teaching, and other applications.

PALcode makes Alpha an especially attractive architecture for multiple operating systems.

Alpha and Programming Languages

Alpha is an attractive architecture for compiling a large variety of programming languages. Alpha has been carefully designed to avoid bias toward one or two programming languages. For example:

- Alpha does not contain a subroutine call instruction that moves a register window by a fixed amount. Thus, Alpha is a good match for programming languages with many parameters and programming languages with no parameters.

- Alpha does not contain a global integer overflow enable bit. Such a bit would need to be changed at every subroutine boundary when a FORTRAN program calls a C program.

1.2 Data Format Overview

Alpha is a load/store RISC architecture with the following data characteristics:

- All operations are done between 64-bit registers.

- Memory is accessed via 64-bit virtual little-endian byte addresses.

- There are 32 integer registers and 32 floating-point registers.

- Longword (32-bit) and quadword (64-bit) integers are supported.

- Four floating-point data types are supported:
    - VAX F_floating (32-bit)
    - VAX G_floating (64-bit)
    - IEEE single (32-bit)
    - IEEE double (64-bit)

1.3 Instruction Format Overview

As shown in Figure 1–1, Alpha instructions are all 32 bits in length. As represented in Figure 1–1, there are four major instruction format classes that contain 0, 1, 2, or 3 register fields. All formats have a 6-bit opcode.

Figure 1–1: Instruction Format Overview

31	26 25	21 20	16 15	5 4	0	
Opcode		Number				PALcode Format
Opcode	RA	Disp				Branch Format
Opcode	RA	RB	Disp			Memory Format
Opcode	RA	RB	Function		RC	Operate Format

- **PALcode instructions** specify, in the function code field, one of a few dozen complex operations to be performed.

- **Conditional branch instructions** test register Ra and specify a signed 21-bit PC-relative longword target displacement. Subroutine calls put the return address in register Ra.

- **Load and store instructions** move longwords or quadwords between register Ra and memory, using Ra plus a signed 16-bit displacement as the memory address.

- **Operate instructions** for floating-point and integer operations are both represented in Figure 1–1 by the operate format illustration and are as follows:

    - Floating-point operations use Ra and Rb as source registers, and write the result in register Rc. There is an 11-bit extended opcode in the function field.

    - Integer operations use Ra and Rb or an 8-bit literal as the source operand, and write the result in register Rc.

    Integer operate instructions can use the Rb field and part of the function field to specify an 8-bit literal. There is a 7-bit extended opcode in the function field.

1.4 Instruction Overview

PALcode Instructions

As described above, a Privileged Architecture Library (PALcode) is a set of subroutines that is specific to a particular Alpha operating-system implementation. These subroutines can be invoked by hardware or by software CALL_PAL instructions, which use the function field to vector to the specified subroutine.

Branch Instructions

Conditional branch instructions can test a register for positive/negative or for zero /nonzero. They can also test integer registers for even/odd.

Unconditional branch instructions can write a return address into a register.

There is also a calculated jump instruction that branches to an arbitrary 64-bit address in a register.

Load/Store Instructions

Load and store instructions move either 32-bit or 64-bit aligned quantities from and to memory. Memory addresses are flat 64-bit virtual addresses, with no segmentation.

The VAX floating-point load/store instructions swap words to give a consistent register format for floating-point operations.

A 32-bit integer datum is placed in a register in a canonical form that makes 33 copies of the high bit of the datum. A 32-bit floating-point datum is placed in a register in a canonical form that extends the exponent by 3 bits and extends the fraction with 29 low-order zeros. The 32-bit operates preserve these canonical forms.

There are facilities for doing byte manipulation in registers, eliminating the need for 8-bit or 16-bit load/store instructions.

Compilers, as directed by user declarations, can generate any mixture of 32-bit and 64-bit operations. The Alpha architecture has no 32/64 mode bit.

Integer Operate Instructions

The integer operate instructions manipulate full 64-bit values, and include the usual assortment of arithmetic, compare, logical, and shift instructions.

There are just three 32-bit integer operates: add, subtract, and multiply. They differ from their 64-bit counterparts only in overflow detection and in producing 32-bit canonical results.

There is no integer divide instruction.

The Alpha architecture also supports the following additional operations:

- Scaled add/subtract instructions for quick subscript calculation

- 128-bit multiply for division by a constant, and multiprecision arithmetic

- Conditional move instructions for avoiding branch instructions

- An extensive set of in-register byte and word manipulation instructions

Integer overflow trap enable is encoded in the function field of each instruction, rather than kept in a global state bit. Thus, for example, both ADDQ/V and ADDQ opcodes exist for specifying 64-bit ADD with and without overflow checking. That makes it easier to pipeline implementations.

Floating-Point Operate Instructions

The floating-point operate instructions include four complete sets of VAX and IEEE arithmetic instructions, plus instructions for performing conversions between floating-point and integer quantities.

In addition to the operations found in conventional RISC architectures, Alpha includes conditional move instructions for avoiding branches and merge sign /exponent instructions for simple field manipulation.

The arithmetic trap enables and rounding mode are encoded in the function field of each instruction, rather then kept in global state bits. That makes it easier to pipeline implementations.

1.5 Instruction Set Characteristics

Alpha instruction set characteristics are as follows:

- All instructions are 32 bits long and have a regular format.

- There are 32 integer registers (R0 through R31), each 64 bits wide. R31 reads as zero, and writes to R31 are ignored.

- There are 32 floating-point registers (F0 through F31), each 64 bits wide. F31 reads as zero, and writes to F31 are ignored.

- All integer data manipulation is between integer registers, with up to two variable register source operands (one may be an 8-bit literal), and one register destination operand.

- All floating-point data manipulation is between floating-point registers, with up to two register source operands and one register destination operand.

- All memory reference instructions are of the load/store type that move data between registers and memory.

- There are no branch condition codes. Branch instructions test an integer or floating-point register value, which may be the result of a previous compare.

- Integer and logical instructions operate on quadwords.

- Floating-point instructions operate on G_floating, F_floating, IEEE double, and IEEE single operands. D_floating "format compatibility," in which binary files of D_floating numbers may be processed, but without the last 3 bits of fraction precision, is also provided.

- A minimal number of VAX compatibility instructions are included.

1.6 Terminology and Conventions

The following sections describe the terminology and conventions used in this book.

1.6.1 Numbering

All numbers are decimal unless otherwise indicated. Where there is ambiguity, numbers other than decimal are indicated with the name of the base in subscript form, for example, 10_{16}.

1.6.2 Security Holes

A security hole is an error of commission, omission, or oversight in a system that allows protection mechanisms to be bypassed.

Security holes exist when unprivileged software (that is, software running outside of kernel mode) can:

- Affect the operation of another process without authorization from the operating system;

- Amplify its privilege without authorization from the operating system; or

- Communicate with another process, either overtly or covertly, without authorization from the operating system.

The Alpha architecture has been designed to contain no architectural security holes. Hardware (processors, buses, controllers, and so on) and software should likewise be designed to avoid security holes.

1.6.3 UNPREDICTABLE and UNDEFINED

The terms UNPREDICTABLE and UNDEFINED are used throughout this book. Their meanings are quite different and must be carefully distinguished.

In particular, only privileged software (software running in kernel mode) can trigger UNDEFINED operations. Unprivileged software cannot trigger UNDEFINED operations. However, either privileged or unprivileged software can trigger UNPREDICTABLE results or occurences.

UNPREDICTABLE results or occurences do not disrupt the basic operation of the processor; it continues to execute instructions in its normal manner. In contrast, UNDEFINED operation can halt the processor or cause it to lose information.

The terms UNPREDICTABLE and UNDEFINED can be further described as follows:

UNPREDICTABLE

- Results or occurrences specified as UNPREDICTABLE may vary from moment to moment, implementation to implementation, and instruction to instruction within implementations. Software can never depend on results specified as UNPREDICTABLE.

- An UNPREDICTABLE result may acquire an arbitrary value subject to a few constraints. Such a result may be an arbitrary function of the input operands or of any state information that is accessible to the process in its current access mode. UNPREDICTABLE results may be unchanged from their previous values.

Operations that produce UNPREDICTABLE results may also produce exceptions.

- An occurrence specified as UNPREDICTABLE may happen or not based on an arbitrary choice function. The choice function is subject to the same constraints as are UNPREDICTABLE results and, in particular, must not constitute a security hole.

  Specifically, UNPREDICTABLE results must not depend upon, or be a function of, the contents of memory locations or registers which are inaccessible to the current process in the current access mode.

  Also, operations that may produce UNPREDICTABLE results must not:

  - Write or modify the contents of memory locations or registers to which the current process in the current access mode does not have access, or

  - Halt or hang the system or any of its components.

  For example, a security hole would exist if some UNPREDICTABLE result depended on the value of a register in another process, on the contents of processor temporary registers left behind by some previously running process, or on a sequence of actions of different processes.

UNDEFINED

- Operations specified as UNDEFINED may vary from moment to moment, implementation to implementation, and instruction to instruction within implementations. The operation may vary in effect from nothing, to stopping system operation.

- UNDEFINED operations may halt the processor or cause it to lose information. However, UNDEFINED operations must not cause the processor to hang, that is, reach an unhalted state from which there is no transition to a normal state in which the machine executes instructions.

1.6.4 Ranges and Extents

Ranges are specified by a pair of numbers separated by a ".." and are inclusive. For example, a range of integers 0..4 includes the integers 0, 1, 2, 3, and 4.

Extents are specified by a pair of numbers in angle brackets separated by a colon and are inclusive. For example, bits <7:3> specify an extent of bits including bits 7, 6, 5, 4, and 3.

1.6.5 ALIGNED and UNALIGNED

In this document the terms ALIGNED and NATURALLY ALIGNED are used interchangeably to refer to data objects that are powers of two in size. An aligned datum of size $2**N$ is stored in memory at a byte address that is a multiple of $2**N$, that is, one that has N low-order zeros. Thus, an aligned 64-byte stack frame has a memory address that is a multiple of 64.

If a datum of size 2**N is stored at a byte address that is not a multiple of 2**N, it is called UNALIGNED.

1.6.6 Must Be Zero (MBZ)

Fields specified as Must be Zero (MBZ) must never be filled by software with a non-zero value. These fields may be used at some future time. If the processor encounters a non-zero value in a field specified as MBZ, an Illegal Operand exception occurs.

1.6.7 Read As Zero (RAZ)

Fields specified as Read as Zero (RAZ) return a zero when read.

1.6.8 Should Be Zero (SBZ)

Fields specified as Should be Zero (SBZ) should be filled by software with a zero value. Non-zero values in SBZ fields produce UNPREDICTABLE results and may produce extraneous instruction-issue delays.

1.6.9 Ignore (IGN)

Fields specified as Ignore (IGN) are ignored when written.

1.6.10 Implementation Dependent (IMP)

Fields specified as Implementation Dependent (IMP) may be used for implementation-specific purposes. Each implementation must document fully the behavior of all fields marked as IMP by the Alpha specification.

1.6.11 Figure Drawing Conventions

Figures that depict registers or memory follow the convention that increasing addresses run right to left and top to bottom.

1.6.12 Macro Code Example Conventions

All instructions in macro code examples are either listed in Chapter 4 or *OpenVMS Section, Chapter 2*, or are stylized code forms found in *Appendix A*.

Chapter 2

Basic Architecture (I)

2.1 Addressing

The basic addressable unit in Alpha is the 8-bit byte. Virtual addresses are 64 bits long. An implementation may support a smaller virtual address space. The minimum virtual address size is 43 bits.

Virtual addresses as seen by the program are translated into physical memory addresses by the memory management mechanism.

2.2 Data Types

Following are descriptions of the Alpha architecture data types.

2.2.1 Byte

A byte is 8 contiguous bits starting on an addressable byte boundary. The bits are numbered from right to left, 0 through 7, as shown in Figure 2–1.

Figure 2–1: Byte Format

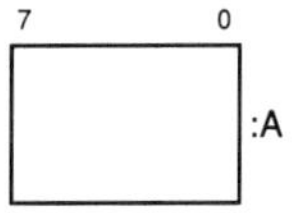

A byte is specified by its address A. A byte is an 8-bit value. The byte is only supported in Alpha by the extract, mask, insert, and zap instructions.

2.2.2 Word

A word is 2 contiguous bytes starting on an arbitrary byte boundary. The bits are numbered from right to left, 0 through 15, as shown in Figure 2–2.

Figure 2–2: Word Format

A word is specified by its address, the address of the byte containing bit 0.

A word is a 16-bit value. The word is only supported in Alpha by the extract, mask, and insert instructions.

2.2.3 Longword

A longword is 4 contiguous bytes starting on an arbitrary byte boundary. The bits are numbered from right to left, 0 through 31, as shown in Figure 2–3.

Figure 2–3: Longword Format

A longword is specified by its address A, the address of the byte containing bit 0. A longword is a 32-bit value.

When interpreted arithmetically, a longword is a two's-complement integer with bits of increasing significance from 0 through 30. Bit 31 is the sign bit. The longword is only supported in Alpha by sign-extended load and store instructions and by longword arithmetic instructions.

> **NOTE**
> Alpha implementations will impose a significant performance penalty when accessing longword operands that are not naturally aligned. (A naturally aligned longword has zero as the low-order two bits of its address.)

2.2.4 Quadword

A quadword is 8 contiguous bytes starting on an arbitrary byte boundary. The bits are numbered from right to left, 0 through 63, as shown in Figure 2–4.

Figure 2–4: Quadword Format

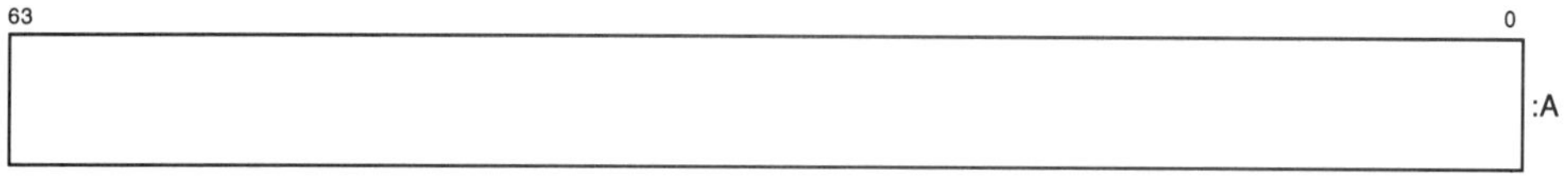

A quadword is specified by its address A, the address of the byte containing bit 0. A quadword is a 64-bit value. When interpreted arithmetically, a quadword is either a two's-complement integer with bits of increasing significance from 0 through 62 and bit 63 as the sign bit, or an unsigned integer with bits of increasing significance from 0 through 63.

> **NOTE**
>
> Alpha implementations will impose a significant performance penalty when accessing quadword operands that are not naturally aligned. (A naturally aligned quadword has zero as the low-order three bits of its address.)

2.2.5 VAX Floating-Point Formats

VAX floating-point numbers are stored in one set of formats in memory and in a second set of formats in registers. The floating-point load and store instructions convert between these formats purely by rearranging bits; no rounding or range-checking is done by the load and store instructions.

2.2.5.1 F_floating

An F_floating datum is 4 contiguous bytes in memory starting on an arbitrary byte boundary. The bits are labeled from right to left, 0 through 31, as shown in Figure 2–5.

Figure 2–5: F_floating Datum

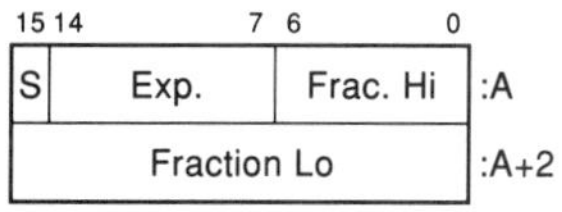

An F_floating operand occupies 64 bits in a floating register, left-justified in the 64-bit register, as shown in Figure 2–6.

Figure 2–6: F_floating Register Format

63 62		52 51	45 44		29 28		0	
S	Exp.		Frac. Hi	Fraction Lo		0		:Fx

The F_floating load instruction reorders bits on the way in from memory, expands the exponent from 8 to 11 bits, and sets the low-order fraction bits to zero. This produces in the register an equivalent G_floating number suitable for either F_floating or G_floating operations. The mapping from 8-bit memory-format exponents to 11-bit register-format exponents is shown in Table 2–1.

Table 2–1: F_floating Load Exponent Mapping

Memory <14:7>	Register <62:52>	
1 1111111	1 000 1111111	
1 xxxxxxx	1 000 xxxxxxx	(xxxxxxx not all 1's)
0 xxxxxxx	0 111 xxxxxxx	(xxxxxxx not all 0's)
0 0000000	0 000 0000000	

This mapping preserves both normal values and exceptional values.

The F_floating store instruction reorders register bits on the way to memory and does no checking of the low-order fraction bits. Register bits <61:59> and <28:0> are ignored by the store instruction.

An F_floating datum is specified by its address A, the address of the byte containing bit 0. The memory form of an F_floating datum is sign magnitude with bit 15 the sign bit, bits <14:7> an excess-128 binary exponent, and bits <6:0> and <31:16> a normalized 24-bit fraction with the redundant most significant fraction bit not represented. Within the fraction, bits of increasing significance are from 16 through 31 and 0 through 6. The 8-bit exponent field encodes the values 0 through 255. An exponent value of 0, together with a sign bit of 0, is taken to indicate that the F_floating datum has a value of 0.

If the result of a VAX floating-point format instruction has a value of zero, the instruction always produces a datum with a sign bit of 0, an exponent of 0, and all fraction bits of 0. Exponent values of 1..255 indicate true binary exponents of –127..127. An exponent value of 0, together with a sign bit of 1, is taken as a reserved operand. Floating-point instructions processing a reserved operand take an arithmetic exception. The value of an F_floating datum is in the approximate range $0.29*10**–38..1.7*10**38$. The precision of an F_floating datum is approximately one part in $2**23$, typically 7 decimal digits.

NOTE

Alpha implementations will impose a significant performance penalty when accessing F_floating operands that are not naturally aligned. (A naturally aligned F_floating datum has zero as the low-order two bits of its address.)

2.2.5.2 G_floating

A G_floating datum in memory is 8 contiguous bytes starting on an arbitrary byte boundary. The bits are labeled from right to left, 0 through 63, as shown in Figure 2–7.

Figure 2–7: G_floating Datum

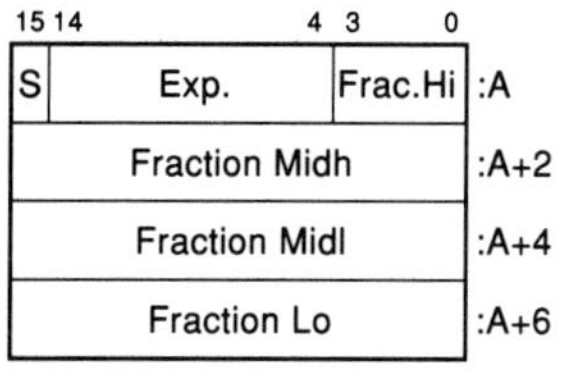

15 14
4 3
0
S
Exp.
Frac.Hi
:A
Fraction Midh
:A+2
Fraction Midl
:A+4
Fraction Lo
:A+6

A G_floating operand occupies 64 bits in a floating register, arranged as shown in Figure 2–8.

Figure 2–8: G_floating Format

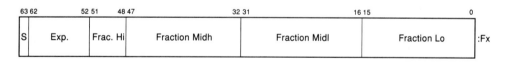

63 62
52 51
48 47
32 31
16 15
0
S
Exp.
Frac. Hi
Fraction Midh
Fraction Midl
Fraction Lo
:Fx

A G_floating datum is specified by its address A, the address of the byte containing bit 0. The form of a G_floating datum is sign magnitude with bit 15 the sign bit, bits <14:4> an excess-1024 binary exponent, and bits <3:0> and <63:16> a normalized 53-bit fraction with the redundant most significant fraction bit not represented. Within the fraction, bits of increasing significance are from 48 through 63, 32 through 47, 16 through 31, and 0 through 3. The 11-bit exponent field encodes the values 0 through 2047. An exponent value of 0, together with a sign bit of 0, is taken to indicate that the G_floating datum has a value of 0.

If the result of a floating-point instruction has a value of zero, the instruction always produces a datum with a sign bit of 0, an exponent of 0, and all fraction bits of 0. Exponent values of 1..2047 indicate true binary exponents of

–1023..1023. An exponent value of 0, together with a sign bit of 1, is taken as a reserved operand. Floating-point instructions processing a reserved operand take a user-visible arithmetic exception. The value of a G_floating datum is in the approximate range 0.56*10**–308..0.9*10**308. The precision of a G_floating datum is approximately one part in 2**52, typically 15 decimal digits.

NOTE

Alpha implementations will impose a significant per-formance penalty when accessing G_floating operands that are not naturally aligned. (A naturally aligned G_floating datum has zero as the low-order three bits of its address.)

2.2.5.3 D_floating

A D_floating datum in memory is 8 contiguous bytes starting on an arbitrary byte boundary. The bits are labeled from right to left, 0 through 63, as shown in Figure 2–9.

Figure 2–9: D_floating Datum

15 14	7 6	0	
S	Exp.	Frac.Hi	:A
Fraction Midh			:A+2
Fraction Midl			:A+4
Fraction Lo			:A+6

A D_floating operand occupies 64 bits in a floating register, arranged as shown in Figure 2–10.

Figure 2–10: D_floating Register Format

63 62	55 54	48 47	32 31	16 15	0	
S	Exp.	Frac. Hi	Fraction Midh	Fraction Midl	Fraction Lo	:Fx

The reordering of bits required for a D_floating load or store are identical to those required for a G_floating load or store. The G_floating load and store instructions are therefore used for loading or storing D_floating data.

A D_floating datum is specified by its address A, the address of the byte containing bit 0. The memory form of a D_floating datum is identical to an F_floating datum except for 32 additional low significance fraction bits. Within the fraction, bits of increasing significance are from 48 through 63, 32 through 47, 16 through 31, and 0 through 6. The exponent conventions and approximate range of values is the same for D_floating as F_floating. The precision of a D_floating datum is approximately one part in 2**55, typically 16 decimal digits.

NOTE

D_floating is not a fully supported data type; no D_floating arithmetic operations are provided in the architecture. For backward compatibility, exact D_ floating arithmetic may be provided via software emulation. D_floating "format compatibility" in which binary files of D_floating numbers may be processed, but without the last 3 bits of fraction precision, can be obtained via conversions to G_floating, G arithmetic operations, then conversion back to D_floating.

NOTE

Alpha implementations will impose a significant performance penalty on access to D_floating operands that are not naturally aligned. (A naturally aligned D_ floating datum has zero as the low-order three bits of its address.)

2.2.6 IEEE Floating-Point Formats

The IEEE standard for binary floating-point arithmetic, ANSI/IEEE 754-1985, defines four floating-point formats in two groups, basic and extended, each having two widths, single and double. The Alpha architecture supports the basic single and double formats, with the basic double format serving as the extended single format. The values representable within a format are specified by using three integer parameters:

1. P—the number of fraction bits

2. Emax—the maximum exponent

3. Emin—the minimum exponent

Within each format, only the following entities are permitted:

1. Numbers of the form $(-1)^{**}S \times 2^{**}E \times b(0).b(1)b(2)..b(P-1)$ where:

   a. S = 0 or 1

   b. E = any integer between Emin and Emax, inclusive

   c. b(n) = 0 or 1

2. Two infinities—positive and negative

3. At least one Signaling NaN
4. At least one Quiet NaN

NaN is an acronym for Not-a-Number. A NaN is an IEEE floating-point bit pattern that represents something other than a number. NaNs come in two forms: Signaling NaNs and Quiet NaNs. Signaling NaNs are used to provide values for uninitialized variables and for arithmetic enhancements. Quiet NaNs provide retrospective diagnostic information regarding previous invalid or unavailable data and results. Signaling NaNs signal an invalid operation when they are an operand to an arithmetic instruction, and may generate an arithmetic exception. Quiet NaNs propagate through almost every operation without generating an arithmetic exception.

Arithmetic with the infinities is handled as if the operands were of arbitrarily large magnitude. Negative infinity is less than every finite number; positive infinity is greater than every finite number.

2.2.6.1 S_Floating

An IEEE single-precision, or S_floating, datum occupies 4 contiguous bytes in memory starting on an arbitrary byte boundary. The bits are labeled from right to left, 0 through 31, as shown in Figure 2–11.

Figure 2–11: S_floating Datum

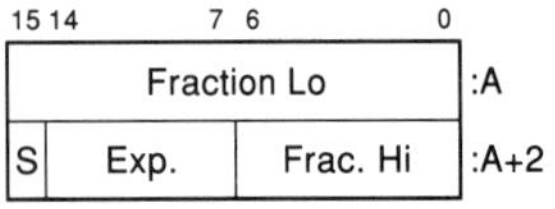

15 14
7 6
0
Fraction Lo
:A
S
Exp.
Frac. Hi
:A+2

An S_floating operand occupies 64 bits in a floating register, left-justified in the 64-bit register, as shown in Figure 2–12.

Figure 2–12: S_floating Register Format

63 62
52 51
45 44
29 28
0
S
Exp.
Frac. Hi
Fraction Lo
0
:Fx

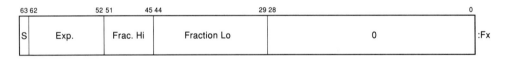

The S_floating load instruction reorders bits on the way in from memory, expanding the exponent from 8 to 11 bits, and sets the low-order fraction bits to zero. This produces in the register an equivalent T_floating number, suitable for either S_floating or T_floating operations. The mapping from 8-bit memory-format exponents to 11-bit register-format exponents is shown in Table 2–2.

Table 2–2: S_floating Load Exponent Mapping

Memory <30:23>	Register <62:52>	
1 1111111	1 111 1111111	
1 xxxxxxx	1 000 xxxxxxx	(xxxxxx not all 1's)
0 xxxxxxx	0 111 xxxxxxx	(xxxxxx not all 0's)
0 0000000	0 000 0000000	

This mapping preserves both normal values and exceptional values. Note that the mapping for all 1's differs from that of F_floating load, since for S_floating all 1's is an exceptional value and for F_floating all 1's is a normal value.

The S_floating store instruction reorders register bits on the way to memory and does no checking of the low-order fraction bits. Register bits <61:59> and <28:0> are ignored by the store instruction. The S_floating load instruction does no checking of the input.

The S_floating store instruction does no checking of the data; the preceding operation should have specified an S_floating result.

An S_floating datum is specified by its address A, the address of the byte containing bit 0. The memory form of an S_floating datum is sign magnitude with bit 31 the sign bit, bits <30:23> an excess-127 binary exponent, and bits <22:0> a 23-bit fraction.

The value (V) of an S_floating number is inferred from its constituent sign (S), exponent (E), and fraction (F) fields as follows:

1. If E=255 and F<>0, then V is NaN, regardless of S.

2. If E=255 and F=0, then $V = (-1)^{**}S \times$ Infinity.

3. If $0 < E < 255$, then $V = (-1)^{**}S \times 2^{**}(E-127) \times (1.F)$.

4. If E=0 and F<>0, then $V = (-1)^{**}S \times 2^{**}(-126) \times (0.F)$.

5. If E=0 and F=0, then $V = (-1)^{**}S \times 0$ (zero).

Floating-point operations on S_floating numbers may take an arithmetic exception for a variety of reasons, including invalid operations, overflow, underflow, division by zero, and inexact results.

NOTE

Alpha implementations will impose a significant performance penalty when accessing S_floating operands that are not naturally aligned. (A naturally aligned S_floating datum has zero as the low-order two bits of its address.)

2.2.6.2 T_floating

An IEEE double-precision, or T_floating, datum occupies 8 contiguous bytes in memory starting on an arbitrary byte boundary. The bits are labeled from right to left, 0 through 63, as shown in Figure 2–13.

Figure 2–13: T_floating Datum

15 14
4 3
0
Fraction Lo
:A
Fraction Midl
:A+2
Fraction Midh
:A+4
S
Exponent
Frac.Hi
:A+6

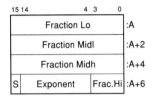

A T_floating operand occupies 64 bits in a floating register, arranged as shown in Figure 2–14.

Figure 2–14: T_floating Register Format

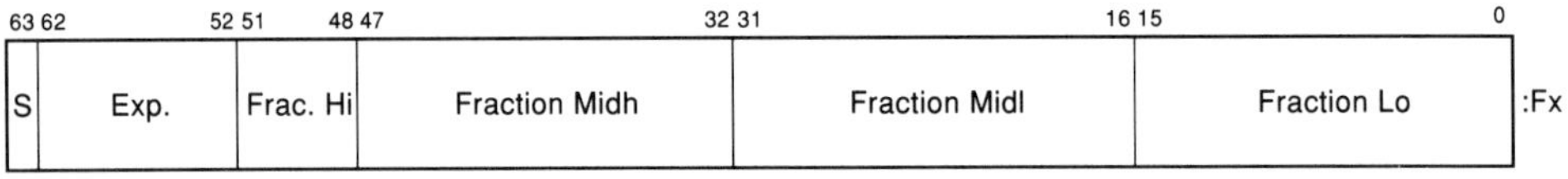

63 62
52 51
48 47
32 31
16 15
0
S
Exp.
Frac. Hi
Fraction Midh
Fraction Midl
Fraction Lo
:Fx

The T_floating load instruction performs no bit reordering on input, nor does it perform checking of the input data.

The T_floating store instruction performs no bit reordering on output. This instruction does no checking of the data; the preceding operation should have specified a T_floating result.

A T_floating datum is specified by its address A, the address of the byte containing bit 0. The form of a T_floating datum is sign magnitude with bit 63 the sign bit, bits <62:52> an excess-1023 binary exponent, and bits <51:0> a 52-bit fraction.

The value (V) of a T_floating number is inferred from its constituent sign (S), exponent (E), and fraction (F) fields as follows:

1. If E=2047 and F<>0, then V is NaN, regardless of S.
2. If E=2047 and F=0, then V = (–1)**S x Infinity.
3. If 0 < E < 2047, then V = (–1)**S x 2**(E–1023) x (1.F).
4. If E=0 and F<>0, then V = (–1)**S x 2**(–1022) x (0.F).

5. If E=0 and F=0, then V = (–1)**S x 0 (zero).

Floating-point operations on T_floating numbers may take an arithmetic exception for a variety of reasons, including invalid operations, overflow, underflow, division by zero, and inexact results.

NOTE
Alpha implementations will impose a significant performance penalty when accessing T_floating operands that are not naturally aligned. (A naturally aligned T_floating datum has zero as the low-order three bits of its address.)

2.2.7 Longword Integer Format in Floating-Point Unit

A longword integer operand occupies 32 bits in memory, arranged as shown in Figure 2–15.

Figure 2–15: Longword Integer Datum

A longword integer operand occupies 64 bits in a floating register, arranged as shown in Figure 2–16.

Figure 2–16: Longword Integer Floating-Register Format

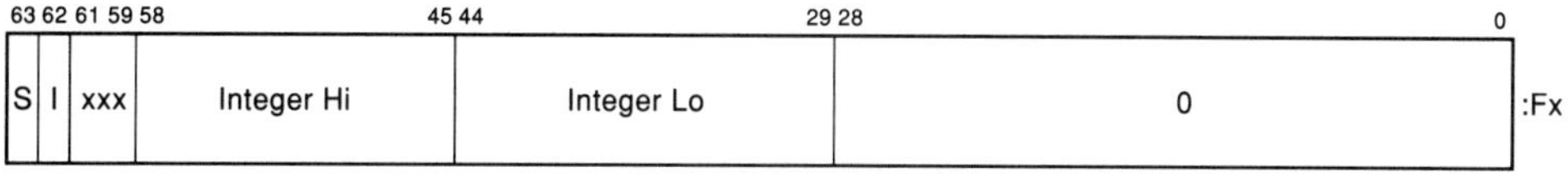

63 62 61 59 58			45 44	29 28		0
S	I	xxx	Integer Hi	Integer Lo	0	:Fx

There is no explicit longword load or store instruction; the S_floating load/store instructions are used to move longword data into or out of the floating registers. The register bits <61:59> are set by the S_floating load exponent mapping. They are ignored by S_floating store. They are also ignored in operands of a longword integer operate instruction, and they are set to 000 in the result of a longword operate instruction.

The register format bit <62>, "I", in Figure 2–16 is part of the Integer Hi field in Figure 2–15 and represents the high-order bit of that field. Bits <58:45> of Figure 2–16 are the remaining bits of the Integer Hi field of Figure 2–15.

2.2.8 Quadword Integer Format in Floating-Point Unit

A quadword integer operand occupies 64 bits in memory, arranged as shown in
Figure 2–17.

Figure 2–17: Quadword Integer Datum

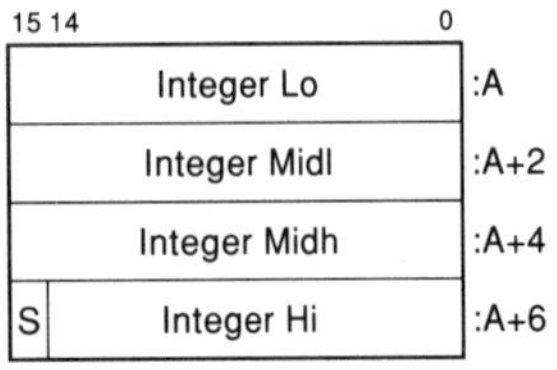

```
15 14                  0
┌───┬────────────────┐
│   │  Integer Lo    │ :A
├───┴────────────────┤
│     Integer Midl   │ :A+2
├────────────────────┤
│     Integer Midh   │ :A+4
├───┬────────────────┤
│ S │  Integer Hi    │ :A+6
└───┴────────────────┘
```

A quadword integer operand occupies 64 bits in a floating register, arranged as
shown in Figure 2–18.

Figure 2–18: Quadword Integer Floating-Register Format

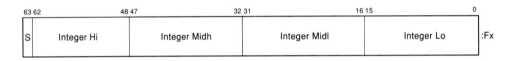

```
63 62              48 47              32 31              16 15                 0
┌───┬──────────────┬──────────────────┬──────────────────┬─────────────────┐
│ S │  Integer Hi  │   Integer Midh   │   Integer Midl   │   Integer Lo    │ :Fx
└───┴──────────────┴──────────────────┴──────────────────┴─────────────────┘
```

There is no explicit quadword load or store instruction; the T_floating load/store
instructions are used to move quadword data into or out of the floating registers.

The T_floating load instruction performs no bit reordering on input. The T_floating
store instruction performs no bit reordering on output. This instruction does no
checking of the data; when used to store quadwords, the preceding operation should
have specified a quadword result.

2.2.9 Data Types with No Hardware Support

The following VAX data types are not directly supported in Alpha hardware.

- Octaword
- H_floating
- D_floating (except load/store and convert to/from G_floating)
- Variable-Length Bit Field
- Character String
- Trailing Numeric String
- Leading Separate Numeric String
- Packed Decimal String

Chapter 3

Instruction Formats (I)

3.1 Alpha Registers

Each Alpha processor has a set of registers that hold the current processor state. If an Alpha system contains multiple Alpha processors, there are multiple per-processor sets of these registers.

3.1.1 Program Counter

The Program Counter (PC) is a special register that addresses the instruction stream. As each instruction is decoded, the PC is advanced to the next sequential instruction. This is referred to as the *updated PC*. Any instruction that uses the value of the PC will use the updated PC. The PC includes only bits <63:2> with bits <1:0> treated as RAZ/IGN. This quantity is a longword-aligned byte address. The PC is an implied operand on conditional branch and subroutine jump instructions. The PC is not accessible as an integer register.

3.1.2 Integer Registers

There are 32 integer registers (R0 through R31), each 64 bits wide.

Register R31 is assigned special meaning by the Alpha architecture. When R31 is specified as a register source operand, a zero-valued operand is supplied.

For all cases except the Unconditional Branch and Jump instructions, results of an instruction that specifies R31 as a destination operand are discarded. Also, it is UNPREDICTABLE whether the other destination operands (implicit and explicit) are changed by the instruction. It is implementation dependent to what extent the instruction is actually executed once it has been fetched. It is also UNPREDICTABLE whether exceptions are signaled during the execution of such an instruction. Note, however, that exceptions associated with the instruction fetch of such an instruction are always signaled.

There are some interesting cases involving R31 as a destination:

- STx_C R31,disp(Rb)

  Although this might seem like a good way to zero out a shared location and reset the lock_flag, this instruction causes the lock_flag and virtual location {Rbv + SEXT(disp)} to become UNPREDICTABLE.

- LDx_L R31,disp(Rb)

  This instruction produces no useful result since it causes both lock_flag and locked_physical_address to become UNPREDICTABLE.

Unconditional Branch (BR and BSR) and Jump (JMP, JSR, RET, and JSR_COROUTINE) instructions, when R31 is specified as the Ra operand, execute normally and update the PC with the target virtual address. Of course, no PC value can be saved in R31.

3.1.3 Floating-Point Registers

There are 32 floating-point registers (F0 through F31), each 64 bits wide.

When F31 is specified as a register source operand, a true zero-valued operand is supplied. See Section 4.7.2 for a definition of true zero.

Results of an instruction that specifies F31 as a destination operand are discarded and it is UNPREDICTABLE whether the other destination operands (implicit and explicit) are changed by the instruction. In this case, it is implementation-dependent to what extent the instruction is actually executed once it has been fetched. It is also UNPREDICTABLE whether exceptions are signaled during the execution of such an instruction. Note, however, that exceptions associated with the instruction fetch of such an instruction are always signaled.

A floating-point instruction that operates on single-precision data reads all bits <63:0> of the source floating-point register. A floating-point instruction that produces a single-precision result writes all bits <63:0> of the destination floating-point register.

3.1.4 Lock Registers

There are two per-processor registers associated with the LDx_L and STx_C instructions, the lock_flag and the locked_physical_address register. The use of these registers is described in Section 4.2.

3.1.5 Optional Registers

Some Alpha implementations may include optional memory prefetch or VAX compatibility processor registers.

3.1.5.1 Memory Prefetch Registers

If the prefetch instructions FETCH and FETCH_M are implemented, an implementation will include two sets of state prefetch registers used by those instructions. The use of these registers is described in Section 4.11. These registers are not directly accessible by software and are listed for completeness.

3.1.5.2 VAX Compatibility Register

The VAX compatibility instructions RC and RS include the intr_flag register, as described in Section 4.12.

3.2 Notation

The notation used to describe the operation of each instruction is given as a sequence of control and assignment statements in an ALGOL-like syntax.

3.2.1 Operand Notation

Tables 3–1, 3–2, and 3–3 list the notation for the operands, the operand values, and the other expression operands.

Table 3–1: Operand Notation

Notation	Meaning
Ra	An integer register operand in the Ra field of the instruction.
Rb	An integer register operand in the Rb field of the instruction.
#b	An integer literal operand in the Rb field of the instruction.
Rc	An integer register operand in the Rc field of the instruction.
Fa	A floating-point register operand in the Ra field of the instruction.
Fb	A floating-point register operand in the Rb field of the instruction.
Fc	A floating-point register operand in the Rc field of the instruction.

Table 3–2: Operand Value Notation

Notation	Meaning
Rav	The value of the Ra operand. This is the contents of register Ra.
Rbv	The value of the Rb operand. This could be the contents of register Rb, or a zero-extended 8-bit literal in the case of an Operate format instruction.
Fav	The value of the floating point Fa operand. This is the contents of register Fa.
Fbv	The value of the floating point Fb operand. This is the contents of register Fb.

Table 3–3: Expression Operand Notation

Notation	Meaning
IPR_x	Contents of Internal Processor Register x
IPR_SP[mode]	Contents of the per-mode stack pointer selected by mode
PC	Updated PC value
Rn	Contents of integer register n
Fn	Contents of floating-point register n
X[m]	Element m of array X

3.2.2 Instruction Operand Notation

The notation used to describe instruction operands follows from the operand specifier notation used in the *VAX Architecture Standard*. Instruction operands are described as follows:

<name>.<access type><data type>

<name>

Specifies the instruction field (Ra, Rb, Rc, or disp) and register type of the operand (integer or floating). It can be one of the following:

Name	Meaning
disp	The displacement field of the instruction.
fnc	The PAL function field of the instruction.
Ra	An integer register operand in the Ra field of the instruction.
Rb	An integer register operand in the Rb field of the instruction.
#b	An integer literal operand in the Rb field of the instruction.
Rc	An integer register operand in the Rc field of the instruction.
Fa	A floating-point register operand in the Ra field of the instruction.
Fb	A floating-point register operand in the Rb field of the instruction.
Fc	A floating-point register operand in the Rc field of the instruction.

<access type>

Is a letter denoting the operand access type:

Access Type	Meaning
a	The operand is used in an address calculation to form an effective address. The data type code that follows indicates the units of addressability (or scale factor) applied to this operand when the instruction is decoded. For example: ".al" means scale by 4 (longwords) to get byte units (used in branch displacements); ".ab" means the operand is already in byte units (used in load/store instructions).
i	The operand is an immediate literal in the instruction.
r	The operand is read only.
m	The operand is both read and written.

Access Type	Meaning
w	The operand is write only.

\<data type\>

Is a letter denoting the data type of the operand:

Data Type	Meaning
b	Byte
f	F_floating
g	G_floating
l	Longword
q	Quadword
s	IEEE single floating (S_floating)
t	IEEE double floating (T_floating)
w	Word
x	The data type is specified by the instruction

3.2.3 Operators

The operators shown in Table 3–4 are used:

Table 3–4: Operators

Operator	Meaning
!	Comment delimiter
+	Addition
-	Subtraction
*	Signed multiplication
*U	Unsigned multiplication
**	Exponentiation (left argument raised to right argument)
/	Division
←	Replacement
| |	Bit concatenation
{}	Indicates explicit operator precedence
(x)	Contents of memory location whose address is x
x\<m:n\>	Contents of bit field of x defined by bits n through m

Table 3–4 (Cont.): Operators

Operator	Meaning
x<m>	M'th bit of x
ACCESS(x,y)	Accessibility of the location whose address is x using the access mode y. Returns a Boolean value TRUE if the address is accessible, else FALSE.
AND	Logical product
ARITH_RIGHT_SHIFT(x,y)	Arithmetic right shift of first operand by the second operand. Y is an unsigned shift value. Bit 63, the sign bit, is copied into vacated bit positions and shifted out bits are discarded.
BYTE_ZAP(x,y)	X is a quadword, y is an 8-bit vector in which each bit corresponds to a byte of the result. The y bit to x byte correspondence is y<n> ↔ x<8n+7:8n>. This correspondence also exists between y and the result.
	For each bit of y from n = 0 to 7, if y <n> is 0 then byte <n> of x is copied to byte <n> of result, and if y <n> is 1 then byte <n> of result is forced to all zeros.
CASE	The CASE construct selects one of several actions based on the value of its argument. The form of a case is:

```
CASE argument OF
        argvalue1: action_1
        argvalue2: action_2
        ...
        argvaluen: action_n
        [otherwise: default_action]
ENDCASE
```

	If the value of argument is argvalue1 then action_1 is executed; if argument = argvalue2, then action_2 is executed, and so forth.
	Once a single action is executed, the code stream breaks to the ENDCASE (there is an implicit break as in Pascal). Each action may nonetheless be a sequence of pseudocode operations, one operation per line.
	Optionally, the last argvalue may be the atom 'otherwise'. The associated default action will be taken if none of the other argvalues match the argument.
DIV	Integer division (truncates)
LEFT_SHIFT(x,y)	Logical left shift of first operand by the second operand.
	Y is an unsigned shift value. Zeros are moved into the vacated bit positions, and shifted out bits are discarded.
LOAD_LOCKED	The processor records the target physical address in a per-processor locked_physical_address register and sets the per-processor lock_flag.
lg	Log to the base 2

Table 3–4 (Cont.): Operators

Operator	Meaning
NOT	Logical (ones) complement
OR	Logical sum
x MOD y	x modulo y
Relational Operators	

Operator	Meaning
LT	Less than signed
LTU	Less than unsigned
LE	Less or equal signed
LEU	Less or equal unsigned
EQ	Equal signed and unsigned
NE	Not equal signed and unsigned
GE	Greater or equal signed
GEU	Greater or equal unsigned
GT	Greater signed
GTU	Greater unsigned
LBC	Low bit clear
LBS	Low bit set

MINU(x,y)	Returns the smaller of x and y, with x and y interpreted as unsigned integers
PHYSICAL_ADDRESS	Translation of a virtual address
PRIORITY_ENCODE	Returns the bit position of most significant set bit, interpreting its argument as a positive integer (= int(lg(x))). For example: `priority_encode( 255 ) = 7`
RIGHT_SHIFT(x,y)	Logical right shift of first operand by the second operand. Y is an unsigned shift value. Zeros are moved into vacated bit positions, and shifted out bits are discarded.
SEXT(x)	X is sign-extended to the required size.
STORE_CONDITIONAL	If the lock_flag is set, then do the indicated store and clear the lock_flag.

Table 3–4 (Cont.): Operators

Operator	Meaning
TEST(x,cond)	The contents of register x are tested for branch condition (cond) true. TEST returns a Boolean value TRUE if x bears the specified relation to 0, else FALSE is returned. Integer and floating test conditions are drawn from the preceding list of relational operators.
XOR	Logical difference
ZEXT(x)	X is zero-extended to the required size.

3.2.4 Notation Conventions

The following conventions are used:

1. Only operands that appear on the left side of a replacement operator are modified.

2. No operator precedence is assumed other than that replacement (←) has the lowest precedence. Explicit precedence is indicated by the use of "{}".

3. All arithmetic, logical, and relational operators are defined in the context of their operands. For example, "+" applied to G_floating operands means a G_floating add, whereas "+" applied to quadword operands is an integer add. Similarly, "LT" is a G_floating comparison when applied to G_floating operands and an integer comparison when applied to quadword operands.

3.3 Instruction Formats

There are five basic Alpha instruction formats:

- Memory
- Branch
- Operate
- Floating-point Operate
- PALcode

All instruction formats are 32 bits long with a 6-bit major opcode field in bits <31:26> of the instruction.

Any unused register field (Ra, Rb, Fa, Fb) of an instruction must be set to a value of 31.

There are several instructions, each formatted as a memory instruction, that do not use the Ra and/or Rb fields. These instructions are: Memory Barrier, Fetch, Fetch_M, Read Process Cycle Counter, Read and Clear, Read and Set, and Trap Barrier.

3.3.1 Memory Instruction Format

The Memory format is used to transfer data between registers and memory, to load an effective address, and for subroutine jumps. It has the format shown in Figure 3–1.

Figure 3–1: Memory Instruction Format

```
 31        26 25    21 20    16 15                         0
┌───────────┬───────┬───────┬───────────────────────────┐
│  Opcode   │  Ra   │  Rb   │       Memory_disp          │
└───────────┴───────┴───────┴───────────────────────────┘
```

A Memory format instruction contains a 6-bit opcode field, two 5-bit register address fields, Ra and Rb, and a 16-bit signed displacement field.

The displacement field is a byte offset. It is sign-extended and added to the contents of register Rb to form a virtual address. Overflow is ignored in this calculation.

The virtual address is used as a memory load/store address or a result value, depending on the specific instruction. The virtual address (va) is computed as follows for all memory format instructions except the load address high (LDAH):

        va ← {Rbv + SEXT(Memory_disp)}

For LDAH the virtual address (va) is computed as follows:

        va ← {Rbv + SEXT(Memory_disp*65536)}

3.3.1.1 Memory Format Instructions with a Function Code

Memory format instructions with a function code replace the memory displacement field in the memory instruction format with a function code that designates a set of miscellaneous instructions. The format is shown in Figure 3–2.

Figure 3–2: Memory Instruction with Function Code Format

```
 31        26 25    21 20    16 15                         0
┌───────────┬───────┬───────┬───────────────────────────┐
│  Opcode   │  Ra   │  Rb   │         Function           │
└───────────┴───────┴───────┴───────────────────────────┘
```

The memory instruction with function code format contains a 6-bit opcode field and a 16-bit function field. Unused function encodings produce UNPREDICTABLE but not UNDEFINED results; they are not security holes.

There are two fields, Ra and Rb. The usage of those fields depends on the instruction. See Section 4.11.

3.3.1.2 Memory Format Jump Instructions

For computed branch instructions (CALL, RET, JMP, JSR_COROUTINE) the displacement field is used to provide branch-prediction hints as described in Section 4.3.

3.3.2 Branch Instruction Format

The Branch format is used for conditional branch instructions and for PC-relative subroutine jumps. It has the format shown in Figure 3–3.

Figure 3–3: Branch Instruction Format

```
31        26 25    21 20                            0
┌──────────┬───────┬──────────────────────────────┐
│          │       │                              │
│ Opcode   │  Ra   │       Branch_disp            │
│          │       │                              │
└──────────┴───────┴──────────────────────────────┘
```

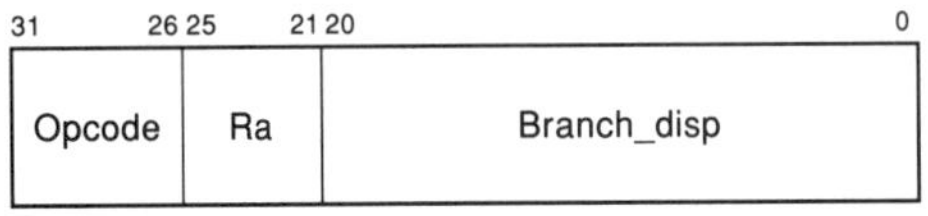

A Branch format instruction contains a 6-bit opcode field, one 5-bit register address field (Ra), and a 21-bit signed displacement field.

The displacement is treated as a longword offset. This means it is shifted left two bits (to address a longword boundary), sign-extended to 64 bits and added to the updated PC to form the target virtual address. Overflow is ignored in this calculation. The target virtual address (va) is computed as follows:

```
va ← PC + {4*SEXT(Branch_disp)}
```

3.3.3 Operate Instruction Format

The Operate format is used for instructions that perform integer register to integer register operations. The Operate format allows the specification of one destination operand and two source operands. One of the source operands can be a literal constant. The Operate format in Figure 3–4 shows the two cases when bit <12> of the instruction is 0 and 1.

Figure 3–4:   Operate Instruction Format

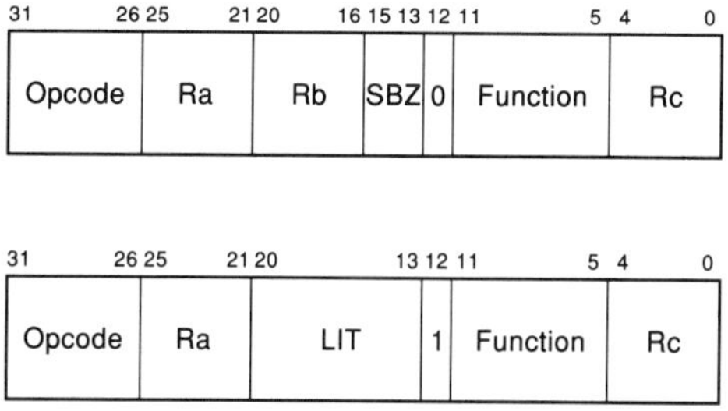

```
31        26 25    21 20   16 15 13 12 11       5 4      0
┌─────────┬──────┬───────┬────┬─┬──────────┬────────┐
│ Opcode  │  Ra  │  Rb   │SBZ │0│ Function │   Rc   │
└─────────┴──────┴───────┴────┴─┴──────────┴────────┘

31        26 25    21 20           13 12 11       5 4      0
┌─────────┬──────┬──────────────┬─┬──────────┬────────┐
│ Opcode  │  Ra  │     LIT      │1│ Function │   Rc   │
└─────────┴──────┴──────────────┴─┴──────────┴────────┘
```

An Operate format instruction contains a 6-bit opcode field and a 7-bit function field. Unused function encodings produce UNPREDICTABLE but not UNDEFINED results; they are not security holes.

There are three operand fields, Ra, Rb, and Rc.

The Ra field specifies a source operand. Symbolically, the integer Rav operand is formed as follows:

```
IF inst<25:21> EQ 31 THEN
    Rav ←  0
ELSE
    Rav ←  Ra
END
```

The Rb field specifies a source operand. Integer operands can specify a literal or an integer register using bit <12> of the instruction.

If bit <12> of the instruction is 0, the Rb field specifies a source register operand.

If bit <12> of the instruction is 1, an 8-bit zero-extended literal constant is formed by bits <20:13> of the instruction. The literal is interpreted as a positive integer between 0 and 255 and is zero-extended to 64 bits. Symbolically, the integer Rbv operand is formed as follows:

```
IF inst<12> EQ 1 THEN
    Rbv ←  ZEXT(inst<20:13>)
ELSE
    IF inst<20:16> EQ 31 THEN
        Rbv ←  0
    ELSE
        Rbv ←  Rb
    END
END
```

The Rc field specifies a destination operand.

3.3.4 Floating-Point Operate Instruction Format

The Floating-point Operate format is used for instructions that perform floating-point register to floating-point register operations. The Floating-point Operate format allows the specification of one destination operand and two source operands. The Floating-point Operate format is shown in Figure 3–5.

Figure 3–5: Floating-Point Operate Instruction Format

A Floating-point Operate format instruction contains a 6-bit opcode field and an 11-bit function field. Unused function encodings produce UNPREDICTABLE results, as defined in Section 1.6.3.

There are three operand fields, Fa, Fb, and Fc. Each operand field specifies either an integer or floating-point operand as defined by the instruction.

The Fa field specifies a source operand. Symbolically, the Fav operand is formed as follows:

```
IF inst<25:21> EQ 31 THEN
     Fav ←  0
ELSE
     Fav ←  Fa
END
```

The Fb field specifies a source operand. Symbolically, the Fbv operand is formed as follows:

```
IF inst<20:16> EQ 31 THEN
     Fbv ←  0
ELSE
     Fbv ←  Fb
END
```

NOTE

Neither Fa nor Fb can be a literal in Floating-point Operate instructions.

The Fc field specifies a destination operand.

3.3.4.1 Floating-Point Convert Instructions

Floating-point Convert instructions use a subset of the Floating-point Operate format and perform register-to-register conversion operations. The Fb operand specifies the source; the Fa field must be F31.

The floating-point register to be used is specified by the Fa, Fb, and Fc fields all pointing to the same floating-point register. If the Fa, Fb, and Fc fields do not all point to the same floating-point register, then it is UNPREDICTABLE which register is used.

3.3.5 PALcode Instruction Format

The Privileged Architecture Library (PALcode) format is used to specify extended processor functions. It has the format shown in Figure 3–6.

Figure 3–6: PALcode Instruction Format

```
31      26 25                                    0
┌────────┬──────────────────────────────────────┐
│ Opcode │        PALcode Function              │
│        │                                      │
└────────┴──────────────────────────────────────┘
```

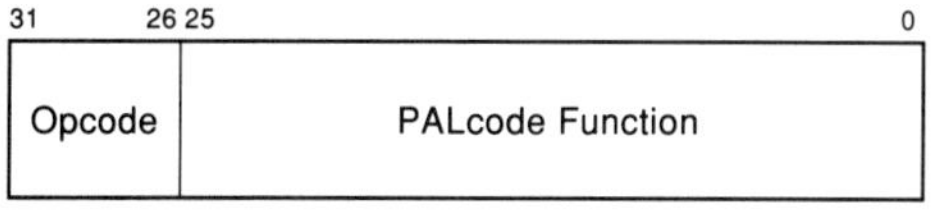

The 26-bit PALcode function field specifies the operation.

The source and destination operands for PALcode instructions are supplied in fixed registers that are specified in the individual instruction descriptions.

An opcode of zero and a PALcode function of zero specify the HALT instruction.

Chapter 4
Instruction Descriptions (I)

4.1 Instruction Set Overview

This chapter describes the instructions implemented by the Alpha architecture. The instruction set is divided into the following sections:

Instruction Type	Section
Integer load and store	4.2
Integer control	4.3
Integer arithmetic	4.4
Logical and shift	4.5
Byte manipulation	4.6
Floating-point load and store	4.8
Floating-point control	4.9
Floating-point operate	4.10
Miscellaneous	4.11

Within each major section, closely related instructions are combined into groups and described together. The instruction group description is composed of the following:

- The group name
- The format of each instruction in the group, which includes the name, access type, and data type of each instruction operand
- The operation of the instruction
- Exceptions specific to the instruction
- The instruction mnemonic and name of each instruction in the group
- Qualifiers specific to the instructions in the group
- A description of the instruction operation
- Optional programming examples and optional notes on the instruction

4.1.1 Subsetting Rules

An instruction that is omitted in a subset implementation of the Alpha architecture is not performed in either hardware or PALcode. System software may provide emulation routines for subsetted instructions.

4.1.1.1 Floating-Point Subsets

Floating-point support is optional on an Alpha processor. An implementation that supports floating-point must implement the 32 floating-point registers, the Floating-point Control Register (FPCR) and the instructions to access it, floating-point branch instructions, floating-point copy sign (CPYSx) instructions, floating-point convert instructions, floating-point conditional move instruction (FCMOV), and the S_floating and T_floating memory operations.

> **SOFTWARE NOTE**
>
> A system that will not support floating-point operations is still required to provide the 32 floating-point registers, the Floating-point Control Register (FPCR) and the instructions to access it, and the T_floating memory operations if the system intends to support the OpenVMS Alpha operating system. This requirement facilitates the implementation of a floating-point emulator and simplifies context-switching.

In addition, floating-point support requires at least one of the following subset groups:

1. VAX Floating-point Operate and Memory instructions (F_ and G_floating).

2. IEEE Floating-point Operate instructions (S_ and T_floating). Within this group, an implementation can choose to include or omit separately the ability to perform IEEE rounding to plus infinity and minus infinity.

Note: if one instruction in a group is provided, all other instructions in that group must be provided. An implementation with full floating-point support includes both groups; a subset floating-point implementation supports only one of these groups. The individual instruction descriptions indicate whether an instruction can be subsetted.

4.1.2 Software Emulation Rules

General-purpose layered and application software that executes in User mode may assume that certain loads (LDL, LDQ, LDF, LDG, LDS, and LDT) and certain stores (STL, STQ, STF, STG, STL and STT) of unaligned data are emulated by system software. General-purpose layered and application software that executes in User mode may assume that subsetted instructions are emulated by system software. Frequent use of emulation may be significantly slower than using alternative code sequences.

Emulation of loads and stores of unaligned data and subsetted instructions need not be provided in privileged access modes. System software that supports special-purpose dedicated applications need not provide emulation in User mode if emulation is not needed for correct execution of the special-purpose applications.

4.1.3 Opcode Qualifiers

Some Operate format and Floating-point Operate format instructions have several variants. For example, for the VAX formats, Add F_floating (ADDF) is supported with and without floating underflow enabled, and with either chopped or VAX rounding. For IEEE formats, IEEE unbiased rounding, chopped, round toward plus infinity, and round toward minus infinity can be selected.

The different variants of such instructions are denoted by opcode qualifiers, which consist of a slash (/) followed by a string of selected qualifiers. Each qualifier is denoted by a single character as shown in Table 4–1. The opcodes for each qualifier are listed in *Appendix C*.

Table 4–1: Opcode Qualifiers

Qualifier	Meaning
C	Chopped rounding
D	Rounding mode dynamic
M	Round toward minus infinity
I	Inexact result enable
S	Software completion enable
U	Floating underflow enable
V	Integer overflow enable

The default values are normal rounding, software completion disabled, inexact result disabled, floating underflow disabled, and integer overflow disabled.

4.2 Memory Integer Load/Store Instructions

The instructions in this section move data between the integer registers and memory.

They use the Memory instruction format. The instructions are summarized in Table 4–2.

Table 4–2: Memory Integer Load/Store Instructions

Mnemonic	Operation
LDA	Load Address
LDAH	Load Address High
LDL	Load Sign-Extended Longword
LDL_L	Load Sign-Extended Longword Locked
LDQ	Load Quadword
LDQ_L	Load Quadword Locked
LDQ_U	Load Quadword Unaligned
STL	Store Longword
STL_C	Store Longword Conditional
STQ	Store Quadword
STQ_C	Store Quadword Conditional
STQ_U	Store Quadword Unaligned

4.2.1 Load Address

Format:

    LDAx   Ra.wq,disp.ab(Rb.ab)   !Memory format

Operation:

```
Ra ←  Rbv + SEXT(disp)              !LDA
Ra ←  Rbv + SEXT(disp*65536)        !LDAH
```

Exceptions:

    None

Instruction mnemonics:

    LDA   Load Address
    LDAH   Load Address High

Qualifiers:

    None

Description:

The virtual address is computed by adding register Rb to the sign-extended 16-bit displacement for LDA, and 65536 times the sign-extended 16-bit displacement for LDAH. The 64-bit result is written to register Ra.

4.2.2 Load Memory Data into Integer Register

Format:

LDx   Ra.wq,disp.ab(Rb.ab)   !Memory format

Operation:

```
va  ←  {Rbv + SEXT(disp)}
Ra  ←  SEXT((va)<31:0>)              !LDL
Ra  ←  (va)<63:0>                    !LDQ
```

Exceptions:

Access Violation

Alignment

Fault on Read

Translation Not Valid

Instruction mnemonics:

LDL   Load Sign-Extended Longword from Memory to Register

LDQ   Load Quadword from Memory to Register

Qualifiers:

None

Description:

The virtual address is computed by adding register Rb to the sign-extended 16-bit displacement. The source operand is fetched from memory, sign-extended, and written to register Ra. If the data is not naturally aligned, an alignment exception is generated.

4.2.3 Load Unaligned Memory Data into Integer Register

Format:

LDQ_U   Ra.wq,disp.ab(Rb.ab)   !Memory format

Operation:

```
va ←  {{Rbv + SEXT(disp)} AND NOT 7}
Ra ←  (va)<63:0>
```

Exceptions:

Access Violation

Fault on Read

Translation Not Valid

Instruction mnemonics:

LDQ_U   Load Unaligned Quadword from Memory to Register

Qualifiers:

None

Description:

The virtual address is computed by adding register Rb to the sign-extended 16-bit displacement, then the low-order three bits are cleared. The source operand is fetched from memory and written to register Ra.

4.2.4 Load Memory Data into Integer Register Locked

Format:

LDx_L Ra.wq,disp.ab(Rb.ab)   !Memory format

Operation:

```
va ← {Rbv + SEXT(disp)}

lock_flag ← 1
locked_physical_address ← PHYSICAL_ADDRESS(va)
Ra ← SEXT((va)<31:0>)                !LDL_L
Ra ← (va)<63:0>                      !LDQ_L
```

Exceptions:

Access Violation

Alignment

Fault on Read

Translation Not Valid

Instruction mnemonics:

LDL_L Load Sign-Extended Longword from Memory to Register Locked

LDQ_L Load Quadword from Memory to Register Locked

Qualifiers:

None

Description:

The virtual address is computed by adding register Rb to the sign-extended 16-bit displacement. The source operand is fetched from memory, sign-extended for LDL_ L, and written to register Ra.

When a LDx_L instruction is executed without faulting, the processor records the target physical address in a per-processor locked_physical_address register and sets the per-processor lock_flag.

If the per-processor lock_flag is (still) set when a STx_C instruction is executed, the store occurs; otherwise, it does not occur, as described for the STx_C instructions.

If processor A's lock_flag is set and processor B successfully does a store within A's locked range of physical addresses, then A's lock_flag is cleared. A processor's locked range is the aligned block of 2**N bytes that includes the locked_physical_address. The 2**N value is implementation dependent. It is at least 8 (minimum lock range is an aligned quadword) and is at most the page size for that implementation (maximum lock range is one physical page).

A processor's lock_flag is also cleared if that processor encounters a CALL_PAL REI instruction. It is UNPREDICTABLE whether or not a processor's lock_flag is cleared on any other CALL_PAL instruction. It is UNPREDICTABLE whether a processor's lock_flag is cleared by that processor's executing a normal load or store instruction. It is UNPREDICTABLE whether a processor's lock_flag is cleared by that processor's executing a taken branch (including BR, BSR, and Jumps); conditional branches that fall through do not clear the lock_flag.

The sequence LDx_L, modify, STx_C, BEQ xxx executed on a given processor does an atomic read-modify-write of a datum in shared memory if the branch falls through; if the branch is taken, the store did not modify memory and the sequence may be repeated until it succeeds.

Notes:

- LDx_L instructions do not check for write access; hence a matching STx_C may take an access-violation or fault-on-write exception.

  Executing a LDx_L instruction on one processor does not affect any architecturally visible state on another processor, and in particular cannot cause a STx_C on another processor to fail.

  LDx_L and STx_C instructions need not be paired. In particular, an LDx_L may be followed by a conditional branch: on the fall-through path an STx_C is done, whereas on the taken path no matching STx_C is done.

  If two LDx_L instructions execute with no intervening STx_C, the second one overwrites the state of the first one. If two STx_C instructions execute with no intervening LDx_L, the second one always fails because the first clears lock_flag.

- Software will not emulate unaligned LDx_L instructions.

- If any other memory access (LDx, LDQ_U, STx, STQ_U) is done on the given processor between the LDx_L and the STx_C, the sequence above may always fail on some implementations; hence, no useful program should do this.

- If a branch is taken between the LDx_L and the STx_C, the sequence above may always fail on some implementations; hence, no useful program should do this. (CMOVxx may be used to avoid branching.)

- If a subsetted instruction (for example, floating-point) is done between the LDx_L and the STx_C, the sequence above may always fail on some implementations, because of the Illegal Instruction Trap; hence, no useful program should do this.

- If a large number of instructions are executed between the LDx_L and the STx_C, the sequence above may always fail on some implementations, because of a timer interrupt always clearing the lock_flag before the sequence completes; hence, no useful program should do this.

- Hardware implementations are encouraged to lock no more than 128 bytes. Software implementations are encouraged to separate locked locations by at least 128 bytes from other locations that could potentially be written by another processor while the first location is locked.

IMPLEMENTATION NOTES

Implementations that impede the mobility of a cache block on LDx_L, such as that which may occur in a Read for Ownership cache coherency protocol, may release the cache block and make the subsequent STx_C fail if a branch-taken or memory instruction is executed on that processor.

All implementations should guarantee that at least 40 non-subsetted operate instructions can be executed between timer interrupts.

4.2.5 Store Integer Register Data into Memory Conditional

Format:

STx_C   Ra.mq,disp.ab(Rb.ab)   !Memory format

Operation:

```
va ←  {Rbv + SEXT(disp)}
IF lock_flag EQ 1 THEN
    (va)<31:0> ←  Rav<31:0>         !STL_C
    (va) ←  Rav                     !STQ_C
Ra ←  lock_flag
lock_flag ←  0
```

Exceptions:

Access Violation

Fault on Write

Alignment

Translation Not Valid

Instruction mnemonics:

STL_C   Store Longword from Register to Memory Conditional

STQ_C   Store Quadword from Register to Memory Conditional

Qualifiers:

None

Description:

The virtual address is computed by adding register Rb to the sign-extended 16-bit displacement. If the lock_flag is set, the Ra operand is written to memory at this address. (See the LDx_L description for conditions that clear the lock_flag.) The lock_flag is returned in RA and then set to a zero.

Notes:

- Software will not emulate unaligned STx_C instructions.

- Each implementation must do the test and store atomically, so that if two processors execute store conditionals within the same lock range, exactly one of the stores succeeds.

- The following sequence should not be used:

```
try_again: LDQ_L    R1,x
           <modify R1>
           STQ_C    R1,x
           BEQ      R1, try_again
           .
           .
           .
```

That sequence penalizes performance when the STQ_C succeeds, because the sequence contains a backward branch, which is predicted to be taken in the Alpha architecture. In the case where the STQ_C succeeds and the branch will actually fall through, that sequence incurs unnecessary delay due to a mispredicted backward branch. Instead, a forward branch should be used to handle the failure case as shown in Section 5.5.2.

SOFTWARE NOTE

The address specified by a STx_C instruction need not match that given in a preceding LDx_L. Specifying unmatched addresses for those instructions requires an MB in between to guarantee ordering.

IMPLEMENTATION NOTES

A STx_C must propagate to the point of coherency, where it is guaranteed to prevent any other store from changing the state of the lock bit, before its outcome can be determined.

If an implementation could encounter a TB or cache miss on the data reference of the STx_C in the sequence above (as might occur in some shared I- and D-stream direct-mapped TBs/caches), it must be able to resolve the miss and complete the store without always failing.

4.2.6 Store Integer Register Data into Memory

Format:

STx   Ra.rq,disp.ab(Rb.ab)   !Memory format

Operation:

```
va ←  {Rbv + SEXT(disp)}
(va)<31:0> ←  Rav<31:0>              !STL
(va) ←  Rav                          !STQ
```

Exceptions:

Access Violation

Fault on Write

Alignment

Translation Not Valid

Instruction mnemonics:

STL   Store Longword from Register to Memory

STQ   Store Quadword from Register to Memory

Qualifiers:

None

Description:

The virtual address is computed by adding register Rb to the sign-extended 16-bit displacement. The Ra operand is written to memory at this address. If the data is not naturally aligned, an alignment exception is generated.

4.2.7 Store Unaligned Integer Register Data into Memory

Format:

STQ_U   Ra.rq,disp.ab(Rb.ab)   !Memory format

Operation:

```
va ←  {{Rbv + SEXT(disp)} AND NOT 7}
(va)<63:0> ←  Rav<63:0>
```

Exceptions:

Access Violation

Fault on Write

Translation Not Valid

Instruction mnemonics:

STQ_U   Store Unaligned Quadword from Register to Memory

Qualifiers:

None

Description:

The virtual address is computed by adding register Rb to the sign-extended 16-bit displacement, then clearing the low order three bits. The Ra operand is written to memory at this address.

4.3 Control Instructions

Alpha provides integer conditional branch, unconditional branch, branch to subroutine, and jump instructions. The PC used in these instructions is the updated PC, as described in Section 3.1.1.

To allow implementations to achieve high performance, the Alpha architecture includes explicit hints based on a branch-prediction model:

1. For many implementations of computed branches (JSR/RET/JMP), there is a substantial performance gain in forming a good guess of the expected target I-cache address before register Rb is accessed.

2. For many implementations, the first-level (or only) I-cache is no bigger than a page (8 KB to 64 KB).

3. Correctly predicting subroutine returns is important for good performance. Some implementations will therefore keep a small stack of predicted subroutine return I-cache addresses.

The Alpha architecture provides three kinds of branch-prediction hints: likely target address, return-address stack action, and conditional branch-taken.

For computed branches, the otherwise unused displacement field contains a function code (JMP/JSR/RET/JSR_COROUTINE), and, for JSR and JMP, a field that statically specifies the 16 low bits of the most likely target address. The PC-relative calculation using these bits can be exactly the PC-relative calculation used in unconditional branches. The low 16 bits are enough to specify an I-cache block within the largest possible Alpha page and hence are expected to be enough for branch-prediction logic to start an early I-cache access for the most likely target.

For all branches, hint or opcode bits are used to distinguish simple branches, subroutine calls, subroutine returns, and coroutine links. These distinctions allow branch-predict logic to maintain an accurate stack of predicted return addresses.

For conditional branches, the sign of the target displacement is used as a taken /fall-through hint. The instructions are summarized in Table 4–3.

Table 4–3: Control Instructions Summary

Mnemonic	Operation
BEQ	Branch if Register Equal to Zero
BGE	Branch if Register Greater Than or Equal to Zero
BGT	Branch if Register Greater Than Zero
BLBC	Branch if Register Low Bit Is Clear
BLBS	Branch if Register Low Bit Is Set
BLE	Branch if Register Less Than or Equal to Zero
BLT	Branch if Register Less Than Zero
BNE	Branch if Register Not Equal to Zero
BR	Unconditional Branch
BSR	Branch to Subroutine
JMP	Jump
JSR	Jump to Subroutine
RET	Return from Subroutine
JSR_COROUTINE	Jump to Subroutine Return

4.3.1 Conditional Branch

Format:

Bxx   Ra.rq,disp.al   !Branch format

Operation:

```
{update PC}
va ←  PC + {4*SEXT(disp)}
IF  TEST(Rav, Condition_based_on_Opcode)  THEN
    PC ←  va
```

Exceptions:

None

Instruction mnemonics:

BEQ	Branch if Register Equal to Zero
BGE	Branch if Register Greater Than or Equal to Zero
BGT	Branch if Register Greater Than Zero
BLBC	Branch if Register Low Bit Is Clear
BLBS	Branch if Register Low Bit Is Set
BLE	Branch if Register Less Than or Equal to Zero
BLT	Branch if Register Less Than Zero
BNE	Branch if Register Not Equal to Zero

Qualifiers:

None

Description:

Register Ra is tested. If the specified relationship is true, the PC is loaded with the target virtual address; otherwise, execution continues with the next sequential instruction.

The displacement is treated as a signed longword offset. This means it is shifted left two bits (to address a longword boundary), sign-extended to 64 bits, and added to the updated PC to form the target virtual address.

The conditional branch instructions are PC-relative only. The 21-bit signed displacement gives a forward/backward branch distance of +/– 1M instructions.

The test is on the signed quadword integer interpretation of the register contents; all 64 bits are tested.

Notes:

- Forward conditional branches (positive displacement) are predicted to fall through. Backward conditional branches (negative displacement) are predicted to be taken. Conditional branches do not affect a predicted return address stack.

4.3.2 Unconditional Branch

Format:

BxR   Ra.wq,disp.al   !Branch format

Operation:

```
{update PC}
Ra  ←   PC
PC  ←   PC + {4*SEXT(disp)}
```

Exceptions:

None

Instruction mnemonics:

BR   Unconditional Branch
BSR   Branch to Subroutine

Qualifiers:

None

Description:

The PC of the following instruction (the updated PC) is written to register Ra, and then the PC is loaded with the target address.

The displacement is treated as a signed longword offset. This means it is shifted left two bits (to address a longword boundary), sign-extended to 64 bits, and added to the updated PC to form the target virtual address.

The unconditional branch instructions are PC-relative. The 21-bit signed displacement gives a forward/backward branch distance of +/– 1M instructions.

PC-relative addressability can be established by:

```
        BR  Rx,L1
    L1:
```

Notes:

- BR and BSR do identical operations. They only differ in hints to possible branch-prediction logic. BSR is predicted as a subroutine call (pushes the return address on a branch-prediction stack), whereas BR is predicted as a branch (no push).

4.3.3 Jumps

Format:

mnemonic   Ra.wq,(Rb.ab),hint   !Memory format

Operation:

```
{update PC}
va ← Rbv AND {NOT 3}
Ra ← PC
PC ← va
```

Exceptions:

None

Instruction mnemonics:

JMP	Jump
JSR	Jump to Subroutine
RET	Return from Subroutine
JSR_COROUTINE	Jump to Subroutine Return

Qualifiers:

None

Description:

The PC of the instruction following the Jump instruction (the updated PC) is written to register Ra, and then the PC is loaded with the target virtual address.

The new PC is supplied from register Rb. The low two bits of Rb are ignored. Ra and Rb may specify the same register; the target calculation using the old value is done before the new value is assigned.

All Jump instructions do identical operations. They only differ in hints to possible branch-prediction logic. The displacement field of the instruction is used to pass this information. The four different "opcodes" set different bit patterns in disp<15:14>, and the hint operand sets disp<13:0>.

These bits are intended to be used as shown in Table 4–4.

Table 4–4: Jump Instructions Branch Prediction

disp<15:14>	Meaning	Predicted Target<15:0>	Prediction Stack Action
00	JMP	PC + {4*disp<13:0>}	–
01	JSR	PC + {4*disp<13:0>}	Push PC
10	RET	Prediction stack	Pop
11	JSR_COROUTINE	Prediction stack	Pop, push PC

The design in Table 4–4 allows specification of the low 16 bits of a likely longword target address (enough bits to start a useful I-cache access early), and also allows distinguishing call from return (and from the other two less frequent operations).

Note that the above information is used only as a hint; correct setting of these bits can improve performance but is not needed for correct operation. See *Appendix A* for more information on branch prediction.

An unconditional long jump can be performed by:

```
JMP   R31,(Rb),hint
```

Coroutine linkage can be performed by specifying the same register in both the Ra and Rb operands. When disp<15:14> equals '10' (RET) or '11' (JSR_COROUTINE) (that is, the target address prediction, if any, would come from a predictor implementation stack), then bits <13:0> are reserved for software and must be ignored by all implementations. All encodings for bits <13:0> are used by Digital software or Reserved to Digital, as follows:

Encoding	Meaning
0000_{16}	Indicates non-procedure return
0001_{16}	Indicates procedure return
	All other encodings are reserved to Digital.

4.4 Integer Arithmetic Instructions

The integer arithmetic instructions perform add, subtract, multiply, and signed and unsigned compare operations.

The integer instructions are summarized in Table 4–5.

Table 4–5: Integer Arithmetic Instructions Summary

Mnemonic	Operation
ADD	Add Quadword/Longword
S4ADD	Scaled Add by 4
S8ADD	Scaled Add by 8
CMPEQ	Compare Signed Quadword Equal
CMPLT	Compare Signed Quadword Less Than
CMPLE	Compare Signed Quadword Less Than or Equal
CMPULT	Compare Unsigned Quadword Less Than
CMPULE	Compare Unsigned Quadword Less Than or Equal
MUL	Multiply Quadword/Longword
UMULH	Multiply Quadword Unsigned High
SUB	Subtract Quadword/Longword
S4SUB	Scaled Subtract by 4
S8SUB	Scaled Subtract by 8

There is no integer divide instruction. Division by a constant can be done via UMULH; division by a variable can be done via a subroutine. See *Appendix A*.

4.4.1 Longword Add

Format:

ADDL	Ra.rq,Rb.rq,Rc.wq	!Operate format
ADDL	Ra.rq,#b.ib,Rc.wq	!Operate format

Operation:

```
Rc ←  SEXT( (Rav + Rbv)<31:0>)
```

Exceptions:

Integer Overflow

Instruction mnemonics:

ADDL   Add Longword

Qualifiers:

Integer Overflow Enable (/V)

Description:

Register Ra is added to register Rb or a literal, and the sign-extended 32-bit sum is written to Rc.

The high order 32 bits of Ra and Rb are ignored. Rc is a proper sign extension of the truncated 32-bit sum. Overflow detection is based on the longword sum Rav<31:0> + Rbv<31:0>.

4.4.2 Scaled Longword Add

Format:

SxADDL	Ra.rq,Rb.rq,Rc.wq	!Operate format
SxADDL	Ra.rq,#b.ib,Rc.wq	!Operate format

Operation:

```
CASE
    S4ADDL:  Rc ←  SEXT (((LEFT_SHIFT(Rav,2)) + Rbv)<31:0>)
    S8ADDL:  Rc ←  SEXT (((LEFT_SHIFT(Rav,3)) + Rbv)<31:0>)
ENDCASE
```

Exceptions:

None

Instruction mnemonics:

S4ADDL	Scaled Add Longword by 4
S8ADDL	Scaled Add Longword by 8

Qualifiers:

None

Description:

Register Ra is scaled by 4 (for S4ADDL) or 8 (for S8ADDL) and is added to register Rb or a literal, and the sign-extended 32-bit sum is written to Rc.

The high 32 bits of Ra and Rb are ignored. Rc is a proper sign extension of the truncated 32-bit sum.

4.4.3 Quadword Add

Format:

ADDQ	Ra.rq,Rb.rq,Rc.wq	!Operate format
ADDQ	Ra.rq,#b.ib,Rc.wq	!Operate format

Operation:

Rc ← Rav + Rbv

Exceptions:

Integer Overflow

Instruction mnemonics:

ADDQ   Add Quadword

Qualifiers:

Integer Overflow Enable (/V)

Description:

Register Ra is added to register Rb or a literal, and the 64-bit sum is written to Rc.

On overflow, the least significant 64 bits of the true result are written to the destination register.

The unsigned compare instructions can be used to generate carry. After adding two values, if the sum is less unsigned than either one of the inputs, there was a carry out of the most significant bit.

4.4.4 Scaled Quadword Add

Format:

SxADDQ	Ra.rq,Rb.rq,Rc.wq	!Operate format
SxADDQ	Ra.rq,#b.ib,Rc.wq	!Operate format

Operation:

```
CASE
   S4ADDQ:  Rc ←  LEFT_SHIFT(Rav,2) + Rbv
   S8ADDQ:  Rc ←  LEFT_SHIFT(Rav,3) + Rbv
ENDCASE
```

Exceptions:

None

Instruction mnemonics:

S4ADDQ	Scaled Add Quadword by 4
S8ADDQ	Scaled Add Quadword by 8

Qualifiers:

None

Description:

Register Ra is scaled by 4 (for S4ADDQ) or 8 (for S8ADDQ) and is added to register Rb or a literal, and the 64-bit sum is written to Rc.

On overflow, the least significant 64 bits of the true result are written to the destination register.

4.4.5 Integer Signed Compare

Format:

CMPxx	Ra.rq,Rb.rq,Rc.wq	!Operate format
CMPxx	Ra.rq,#b.ib,Rc.wq	!Operate format

Operation:

```
IF  Rav SIGNED_RELATION Rbv  THEN
    Rc ←  1
ELSE
    Rc ←  0
```

Exceptions:

None

Instruction mnemonics:

CMPEQ	Compare Signed Quadword Equal
CMPLE	Compare Signed Quadword Less Than or Equal
CMPLT	Compare Signed Quadword Less Than

Qualifiers:

None

Description:

Register Ra is compared to Register Rb or a literal. If the specified relationship is true, the value one is written to register Rc; otherwise, zero is written to Rc.

Notes:

* Compare Less Than A,B is the same as Compare Greater Than B,A; Compare Less Than or Equal A,B is the same as Compare Greater Than or Equal B,A. Therefore, only the less-than operations are included.

4.4.6 Integer Unsigned Compare

Format:

CMPUxx	Ra.rq,Rb.rq,Rc.wq	!Operate format
CMPUxx	Ra.rq,#b.ib,Rc.wq	!Operate format

Operation:

```
IF  Rav UNSIGNED_RELATION Rbv  THEN
    Rc ←  1
ELSE
    Rc ←  0
```

Exceptions:

None

Instruction mnemonics:

CMPULE	Compare Unsigned Quadword Less Than or Equal
CMPULT	Compare Unsigned Quadword Less Than

Qualifiers:

None

Description:

Register Ra is compared to Register Rb or a literal. If the specified relationship is true, the value one is written to register Rc; otherwise, zero is written to Rc.

4.4.7 Longword Multiply

Format:

MULL	Ra.rq,Rb.rq,Rc.wq	!Operate format
MULL	Ra.Rq,#b.ib,Rc.wq	!Operate format

Operation:

```
Rc ←  SEXT ((Rav * Rbv)<31:0>)
```

Exceptions:

Integer Overflow

Instruction mnemonics:

MULL   Multiply Longword

Qualifiers:

Integer Overflow Enable (/V)

Description:

Register Ra is multiplied by register Rb or a literal, and the sign-extended 32-bit product is written to Rc.

The high 32 bits of Ra and Rb are ignored. Rc is a proper sign extension of the truncated 32-bit product. Overflow detection is based on the longword product Rav<31:0> * Rbv<31:0>. On overflow, the proper sign extension of the least significant 32 bits of the true result are written to the destination register.

The MULQ instruction can be used to return the full 64-bit product.

4.4.8 Quadword Multiply

Format:

MULQ	Ra.rq,Rb.rq,Rc.wq	!Operate format
MULQ	Ra.Rq,#b.ib,Rc.wq	!Operate format

Operation:

```
Rc  ←  Rav * Rbv
```

Exceptions:

Integer Overflow

Instruction mnemonics:

MULQ   Multiply Quadword

Qualifiers:

Integer Overflow Enable (/V)

Description:

Register Ra is multiplied by register Rb or a literal, and the 64-bit product is written to register Rc. Overflow detection is based on considering the operands and the result as signed quantities. On overflow, the least significant 64 bits of the true result are written to the destination register.

The UMULH instruction can be used to generate the upper 64 bits of the 128-bit result when an overflow occurs.

4.4.9 Unsigned Quadword Multiply High

Format:

UMULH	Ra.rq,Rb.rq,Rc.wq	!Operate format
UMULH	Ra.Rq,#b.ib,Rc.wq	!Operate format

Operation:

```
Rc  ←  {Rav *U Rbv}<127:64>
```

Exceptions:

None

Instruction mnemonics:

UMULH   Unsigned Multiply Quadword High

Qualifiers:

None

Description:

Register Ra and Rb or a literal are multiplied as unsigned numbers to produce a 128-bit result. The high-order 64-bits are written to register Rc.

The UMULH instruction can be used to generate the upper 64 bits of a 128-bit result as follows:

Ra and Rb are unsigned: result of UMULH

Ra and Rb are signed: (result of UMULH) − Ra<63>*Rb − Rb<63>*Ra

The MULQ instruction gives the low 64 bits of the result in either case.

4.4.10 Longword Subtract

Format:

SUBL	Ra.rq,Rb.rq,Rc.wq	!Operate format
SUBL	Ra.rq,#b.ib,Rc.wq	!Operate format

Operation:

$$Rc \leftarrow SEXT((Rav - Rbv)<31:0>)$$

Exceptions:

Integer Overflow

Instruction mnemonics:

SUBL   Subtract Longword

Qualifiers:

Integer Overflow Enable (/V)

Description:

Register Rb or a literal is subtracted from register Ra, and the sign-extended 32-bit difference is written to Rc.

The high 32 bits of Ra and Rb are ignored. Rc is a proper sign extension of the truncated 32-bit difference. Overflow detection is based on the longword difference Rav<31:0> – Rbv<31:0>.

4.4.11 Scaled Longword Subtract

Format:

SxSUBL	Ra.rq,Rb.rq,Rc.wq	!Operate format
SxSUBL	Ra.rq,#b.ib,Rc.wq	!Operate format

Operation:

```
CASE
  S4SUBL:  Rc ←  SEXT (((LEFT_SHIFT(Rav,2)) - Rbv)<31:0>)
  S8SUBL:  Rc ←  SEXT (((LEFT_SHIFT(Rav,3)) - Rbv)<31:0>)
ENDCASE
```

Exceptions:

None

Instruction mnemonics:

S4SUBL	Scaled Subtract Longword by 4
S8SUBL	Scaled Subtract Longword by 8

Qualifiers:

None

Description:

Register Rb or a literal is subtracted from the scaled value of register Ra, which is scaled by 4 (for S4SUBL) or 8 (for S8SUBL), and the sign-extended 32-bit difference is written to Rc.

The high 32 bits of Ra and Rb are ignored. Rc is a proper sign extension of the truncated 32-bit difference.

4.4.12 Quadword Subtract

Format:

SUBQ	Ra.rq,Rb.rq,Rc.wq	!Operate format
SUBQ	Ra.rq,#b.ib,Rc.wq	!Operate format

Operation:

Rc ← Rav – Rbv

Exceptions:

Integer Overflow

Instruction mnemonics:

SUBQ   Subtract Quadword

Qualifiers:

Integer Overflow Enable (/V)

Description:

Register Rb or a literal is subtracted from register Ra, and the 64-bit difference is written to register Rc. On overflow, the least significant 64 bits of the true result are written to the destination register.

The unsigned compare instructions can be used to generate borrow. If the minuend (Rav) is less unsigned than the subtrahend (Rbv), there will be a borrow.

4.4.13 Scaled Quadword Subtract

Format:

SxSUBQ	Ra.rq,Rb.rq,Rc.wq	!Operate format
SxSUBQ	Ra.rq,#b.ib,Rc.wq	!Operate format

Operation:

```
CASE
  S4SUBQ:  Rc ←  LEFT_SHIFT(Rav,2) - Rbv
  S8SUBQ:  Rc ←  LEFT_SHIFT(Rav,3) - Rbv
ENDCASE
```

Exceptions:

None

Instruction mnemonics:

S4SUBQ	Scaled Subtract Quadword by 4
S8SUBQ	Scaled Subtract Quadword by 8

Qualifiers:

None

Description:

Register Rb or a literal is subtracted from the scaled value of register Ra, which is scaled by 4 (for S4SUBQ) or 8 (for S8SUBQ), and the 64-bit difference is written to Rc.

4.5 Logical and Shift Instructions

The logical instructions perform quadword Boolean operations. The conditional move integer instructions perform conditionals without a branch. The shift instructions perform left and right logical shift and right arithmetic shift. These are summarized in Table 4–6.

Table 4–6: Logical and Shift Instructions Summary

Mnemonic	Operation
AND	Logical Product
BIC	Logical Product with Complement
BIS	Logical Sum (OR)
EQV	Logical Equivalence (XORNOT)
ORNOT	Logical Sum with Complement
XOR	Logical Difference
CMOVxx	Conditional Move Integer
SLL	Shift Left Logical
SRA	Shift Right Arithmetic
SRL	Shift Right Logical

SOFTWARE NOTE

There is no arithmetic left shift instruction. Where an arithmetic left shift would be used, a logical shift will do. For multiplying by a small power of two in address computations, logical left shift is acceptable.

Integer multiply should be used to perform an arithmetic left shift with overflow checking.

Bit field extracts can be done with two logical shifts. Sign extension can be done with left logical shift and a right arithmetic shift.

4.5.1 Logical Functions

Format:

mnemonic	Ra.rq,Rb.rq,Rc.wq	!Operate format
mnemonic	Ra.rq,#b.ib,Rc.wq	!Operate format

Operation:

```
Rc ← Rav AND Rbv          ! AND
Rc ← Rav OR  Rbv          ! BIS
Rc ← Rav XOR Rbv          ! XOR
Rc ← Rav AND {NOT Rbv}    ! BIC
Rc ← Rav OR  {NOT Rbv}    ! ORNOT
Rc ← Rav XOR {NOT Rbv}    ! EQV
```

Exceptions:

None

Instruction mnemonics:

AND	Logical Product
BIC	Logical Product with Complement
BIS	Logical Sum (OR)
EQV	Logical Equivalence (XORNOT)
ORNOT	Logical Sum with Complement
XOR	Logical Difference

Qualifiers:

None

Description:

These instructions perform the designated Boolean function between register Ra and register Rb or a literal. The result is written to register Rc.

The "NOT" function can be performed by doing an ORNOT with zero (Ra = R31).

4.5.2 Conditional Move Integer

Format:

CMOVxx	Ra.rq,Rb.rq,Rc.wq	!Operate format
CMOVxx	Ra.rq,#b.ib,Rc.wq	!Operate format

Operation:

```
IF TEST(Rav, Condition_based_on_Opcode) THEN
    Rc ← Rbv
```

Exceptions:

None

Instruction mnemonics:

CMOVEQ	CMOVE if Register Equal to Zero
CMOVGE	CMOVE if Register Greater Than or Equal to Zero
CMOVGT	CMOVE if Register Greater Than Zero
CMOVLBC	CMOVE if Register Low Bit Clear
CMOVLBS	CMOVE if Register Low Bit Set
CMOVLE	CMOVE if Register Less Than or Equal to Zero
CMOVLT	CMOVE if Register Less Than Zero
CMOVNE	CMOVE if Register Not Equal to Zero

Qualifiers:

None

Description:

Register Ra is tested. If the specified relationship is true, the value Rbv is written to register Rc.

Notes:

Except that it is likely in many implementations to be substantially faster, the instruction:

```
CMOVEQ Ra,Rb,Rc
```

is exactly equivalent to:

```
       BNE   Ra,label
       OR    Rb,Rb,Rc
label: ...
```

For example, a branchless sequence for:

```
R1=MAX(R1,R2)
```

is:

```
CMPLT   R1,R2,R3        ! R3=1 if R1<R2
CMOVNE  R3,R2,R1        ! Move R2 to R1 if R1<R2
```

4.5.3 Shift Logical

Format:

SxL	Ra.rq,Rb.rq,Rc.wq	!Operate format
SxL	Ra.rq,#b.ib,Rc.wq	!Operate format

Operation:

```
Rc ← LEFT_SHIFT(Rav,  Rbv<5:0>)     !SLL
Rc ← RIGHT_SHIFT(Rav,  Rbv<5:0>)    !SRL
```

Exceptions:

None

Instruction mnemonics:

SLL	Shift Left Logical
SRL	Shift Right Logical

Qualifiers:

None

Description:

Register Ra is shifted logically left or right 0 to 63 bits by the count in register Rb or a literal. The result is written to register Rc. Zero bits are propagated into the vacated bit positions.

4.5.4 Shift Arithmetic

Format:

SRA	Ra.rq,Rb.rq,Rc.wq	!Operate format
SRA	Ra.rb,#b.ib,Rc.wq	!Operate format

Operation:

```
Rc ← ARITH_RIGHT_SHIFT(Rav, Rbv<5:0>)
```

Exceptions:

None

Instruction mnemonics:

SRA   Shift Right Arithmetic

Qualifiers:

None

Description:

Register Ra is right shifted arithmetically 0 to 63 bits by the count in register Rb or a literal. The result is written to register Rc. The sign bit (Rav<63>) is propagated into the vacated bit positions.

4.6 Byte-Manipulation Instructions

Alpha provides instructions for operating on byte operands within registers. These instructions allow full-width memory accesses in the load/store instructions combined with powerful in-register byte manipulation.

The instructions are summarized in Table 4–7.

Table 4–7: Byte-Manipulation Instructions Summary

Mnemonic	Operation
CMPBGE	Compare Byte
EXTBL	Extract Byte Low
EXTWL	Extract Word Low
EXTLL	Extract Longword Low
EXTQL	Extract Quadword Low
EXTWH	Extract Word High
EXTLH	Extract Longword High
EXTQH	Extract Quadword High
INSBL	Insert Byte Low
INSWL	Insert Word Low
INSLL	Insert Longword Low
INSQL	Insert Quadword Low
INSWH	Insert Word High
INSLH	Insert Longword High
INSQH	Insert Quadword High
MSKBL	Mask Byte Low
MSKWL	Mask Word Low
MSKLL	Mask Longword Low
MSKQL	Mask Quadword Low
MSKWH	Mask Word High
MSKLH	Mask Longword High
MSKQH	Mask Quadword High

Table 4–7 (Cont.): Byte-Manipulation Instructions Summary

Mnemonic	Operation
ZAP	Zero Bytes
ZAPNOT	Zero Bytes Not

4.6.1 Compare Byte

Format:

CMPBGE Ra.rq,Rb.rq,Rc.wq	!Operate format
CMPBGE Ra.rq,#b.ib,Rc.wq	!Operate format

Operation:

```
FOR i FROM 0 TO 7
   temp<8:0> ←  {0 ||      Rav<i*8+7:i*8>} +
                {0|| NOT Rbv<i*8+7:i*8>} + 1
   Rc<i> ←  temp<8>
END
Rc<63:8> ←   0
```

Exceptions:

None

Instruction mnemonics:

CMPBGE   Compare Byte

Qualifiers:

None

Description:

CMPBGE does eight parallel unsigned byte comparisons between corresponding bytes of Rav and Rbv, storing the eight results in the low eight bits of Rc. The high 56 bits of Rc are set to zero. Bit 0 of Rc corresponds to byte 0, bit 1 of Rc corresponds to byte 1, and so forth. A result bit is set in Rc if the corresponding byte of Rav is greater than or equal to Rbv (unsigned).

Notes:

The result of CMPBGE can be used as an input to ZAP and ZAPNOT.

To scan for a byte of zeros in a character string:

```
        <initialize R1 to aligned QW address of string>
LOOP:
        LDQ     R2,0(R1)        ; Pick up 8 bytes
        LDA     R1,8(R1)        ; Increment string pointer
        CMPBGE  R31,R2,R3       ; If NO bytes of zero, R3<7:0>=0
        BEQ     R3,LOOP         ; Loop if no terminator byte found
        ...                     ; At this point, R3 can be used to
                                ; determine which byte terminated
```

To compare two character strings for greater/less:

```
        <initialize R1 to aligned QW address of string1>
        <initialize R2 to aligned QW address of string2>
LOOP:
        LDQ     R3,0(R1)        ; Pick up 8 bytes of string1
        LDA     R1,8(R1)        ; Increment string1 pointer
        LDQ     R4,0(R2)        ; Pick up 8 bytes of string2
        LDA     R2,8(R2)        ; Increment string2 pointer
        XOR     R3,R4,R5        ; Test for all equal bytes
        BEQ     R5,LOOP         ; Loop if all equal
        CMPBGE  R31,R5,R5       ;
        ...                     ; At this point, R5 can be used to
                                ; determine the first not-equal
                                ; byte position.
```

To range-check a string of characters in R1 for '0'..'9':

```
        LDQ     R2,lit0s        ; Pick up 8 bytes of the character
                                ; BELOW '0'  '////////'
        LDQ     R3,lit9s        ; Pick up 8 bytes of the character
                                ; ABOVE '9'  ':::::::::'
        CMPBGE  R2,R1,R4        ; Some R4<i>=1 if character is LT '0'
        CMPBGE  R1,R3,R5        ; Some R5<i>=1 if character is GT '9'
        BNE     R4,ERROR        ; Branch if some char too low
        BNE     R5,ERROR        ; Branch if some char too high
```

4.6.2 Extract Byte

Format:

EXTxx	Ra.rq,Rb.rq,Rc.wq	!Operate format
EXTxx	Ra.rq,#b.ib,Rc.wq	!Operate format

Operation:

```
CASE
        EXTBL: byte_mask ←  0000 0001₂
        EXTWx: byte_mask ←  0000 0011₂
        EXTLx: byte_mask ←  0000 1111₂
        EXTQx: byte_mask ←  1111 1111₂
ENDCASE

CASE
        EXTxL:
            byte_loc ←  Rbv<2:0>*8
            temp ←  RIGHT_SHIFT(Rav, byte_loc<5:0>)
            Rc ←  BYTE_ZAP(temp, NOT(byte_mask) )

        EXTxH:
            byte_loc ←  64 - Rbv<2:0>*8
            temp ←  LEFT_SHIFT(Rav, byte_loc<5:0>)
            Rc ←  BYTE_ZAP(temp, NOT(byte_mask) )
ENDCASE
```

Exceptions:

None

Instruction mnemonics:

EXTBL	Extract Byte Low
EXTWL	Extract Word Low
EXTLL	Extract Longword Low
EXTQL	Extract Quadword Low
EXTWH	Extract Word High
EXTLH	Extract Longword High
EXTQH	Extract Quadword High

Qualifiers:

None

Description:

EXTxL shifts register Ra right by 0 to 7 bytes, inserts zeros into vacated bit positions, and then extracts 1, 2, 4, or 8 bytes into register Rc. EXTxH shifts register Ra left by 0 to 7 bytes, inserts zeros into vacated bit positions, and then extracts 2, 4, or 8 bytes into register Rc. The number of bytes to shift is specified by Rbv<2:0>. The number of bytes to extract is specified in the function code. Remaining bytes are filled with zeros.

Notes:

The comments in the examples below assume that the effective address (ea) of X(R11) is such that (ea mod 8) = 5, the value of the aligned quadword containing X(R11) is CBAx xxxx, and the value of the aligned quadword containing X+7(R11) is yyyH GFED.

The examples below are the most general case unless otherwise noted; if more information is known about the value or intended alignment of X, shorter sequences can be used.

The intended sequence for loading a quadword from unaligned address X(R11) is:

```
LDQ_U    R1,X(R11)       ; Ignores va<2:0>, R1 = CBAx xxxx
LDQ_U    R2,X+7(R11)     ; Ignores va<2:0>, R2 = yyyH GFED
LDA      R3,X(R11)       ; R3<2:0> = (X mod 8) = 5
EXTQL    R1,R3,R1        ; R1 = 0000 0CBA
EXTQH    R2,R3,R2        ; R2 = HGFE D000
OR       R2,R1,R1        ; R1 = HGFE DCBA
```

The intended sequence for loading and zero-extending a longword from unaligned address X is:

```
LDQ_U    R1,X(R11)       ; Ignores va<2:0>, R1 = CBAx xxxx
LDQ_U    R2,X+3(R11)     ; Ignores va<2:0>, R2 = yyyy yyyD
LDA      R3,X(R11)       ; R3<2:0> = (X mod 8) = 5
EXTLL    R1,R3,R1        ; R1 = 0000 0CBA
EXTLH    R2,R3,R2        ; R2 = 0000 D000
OR       R2,R1,R1        ; R1 = 0000 DCBA
```

The intended sequence for loading and sign-extending a longword from unaligned address X is:

```
LDQ_U    R1,X(R11)       ; Ignores va<2:0>, R1 = CBAx xxxx
LDQ_U    R2,X+3(R11)     ; Ignores va<2:0>, R2 = yyyy yyyD
LDA      R3,X(R11)       ; R3<2:0> = (X mod 8) = 5
EXTLL    R1,R3,R1        ; R1 = 0000 0CBA
EXTLH    R2,R3,R2        ; R2 = 0000 D000
OR       R2,R1,R1        ; R1 = 0000 DCBA
SLL      R1,#32,R1       ; R1 = DCBA 0000
SRA      R1,#32,R1       ; R1 = ssss DCBA
```

The intended sequence for loading and zero-extending a word from unaligned address X is:

```
LDQ_U   R1,X(R11)       ; Ignores va<2:0>, R1 = yBAx xxxx
LDQ_U   R2,X+1(R11)     ; Ignores va<2:0>, R2 = yBAx xxxx
LDA     R3,X(R11)       ; R3<2:0> = (X mod 8) = 5
EXTWL   R1,R3,R1        ; R1 = 0000 00BA
EXTWH   R2,R3,R2        ; R2 = 0000 0000
OR      R2,R1,R1        ; R1 = 0000 00BA
```

The intended sequence for loading and sign-extending a word from unaligned address X is:

```
LDQ_U   R1,X(R11)       ; Ignores va<2:0>, R1 = yBAx xxxx
LDQ_U   R2,X+1(R11)     ; Ignores va<2:0>, R2 = yBAx xxxx
LDA     R3,X(R11)       ; R3<2:0> = (X mod 8) = 5
EXTWL   R1,R3,R1        ; R1 = 0000 00BA
EXTWH   R2,R3,R2        ; R2 = 0000 0000
OR      R2,R1,R1        ; R1 = 0000 00BA
SLL     R1,#48,R1       ; R1 = BA00 0000
SRA     R1,#48,R1       ; R1 = ssss ssBA
```

The intended sequence for loading and zero-extending a byte from address X is:

```
LDQ_U   R1,X(R11)       ; Ignores va<2:0>, R1 = yyAx xxxx
LDA     R3,X(R11)       ; R3<2:0> = (X mod 8) = 5
EXTBL   R1,R3,R1        ; R1 = 0000 000A
```

The intended sequence for loading and sign-extending a byte from address X is:

```
LDQ_U   R1, X(R11)      ; Ignores va<2:0>, R1 = yyAx xxxx
LDA     R3, X+1(R11)    ; R3<2:0> = (X + 1) mod 8, i.e.,
                        ; convert byte position within
                        ; quadword to one-origin based
EXTQH   R1, R3, R1      ; Places the desired byte into byte 7
                        ; of R1.final by left shifting
                        ; R1.initial by ( 8 - R3<2:0> ) byte
                        ; positions
SRA     R1, #56, R1     ; Arithmetic Shift of byte 7 down
                        ; into byte 0,
```

Optimized examples:

Assume that a word fetch is needed from 10(R3), where R3 is intended to contain a longword-aligned address. The optimized sequences below take advantage of the known constant offset, and the longword alignment (hence a single aligned longword contains the entire word). The sequences generate a Data Alignment Fault if R3 does not contain a longword-aligned address.

The intended sequence for loading and zero-extending an aligned word from 10(R3) is:

```
LDL     R1,8(R3)        ; R1 = ssss BAxx
                        ; Faults if R3 is not longword aligned
EXTWL   R1,#2,R1        ; R1 = 0000 00BA
```

The intended sequence for loading and sign-extending an aligned word from 10(R3) is:

```
LDL     R1,8(R3)        ; R1 = ssss BAxx
                        ; Faults if R3 is not longword aligned
SRA     R1,#16,R1       ; R1 = ssss ssBA
```

4.6.3 Byte Insert

Format:

INSxx	Ra.rq,Rb.rq,Rc.wq	!Operate format
INSxx	Ra.rq,#b.ib,Rc.wq	!Operate format

Operation:

```
CASE
    INSBL: byte_mask ←  0000 0000 0000 0001₂
    INSWx: byte_mask ←  0000 0000 0000 0011₂
    INSLx: byte_mask ←  0000 0000 0000 1111₂
    INSQx: byte_mask ←  0000 0000 1111 1111₂
ENDCASE
byte_mask ←  LEFT_SHIFT(byte_mask, rbv<2:0>)

CASE

    INSxL:
        byte_loc ←  Rbv<2:0>*8
        temp ←  LEFT_SHIFT(Rav, byte_loc<5:0>)
        Rc ←  BYTE_ZAP(temp, NOT(byte_mask<7:0>))
    INSxH:
        byte_loc ←  64 - Rbv<2:0>*8
        temp ←  RIGHT_SHIFT(Rav, byte_loc<5:0>)
        Rc ←  BYTE_ZAP(temp, NOT(byte_mask<15:8>))

ENDCASE
```

Exceptions:

None

Instruction mnemonics:

INSBL	Insert Byte Low
INSWL	Insert Word Low
INSLL	Insert Longword Low
INSQL	Insert Quadword Low
INSWH	Insert Word High
INSLH	Insert Longword High
INSQH	Insert Quadword High

Qualifiers:

None

Description:

INSxL and INSxH shift bytes from register Ra and insert them into a field of zeros, storing the result in register Rc. Register Rb<2:0> selects the shift amount, and the function code selects the maximum field width: 1, 2, 4, or 8 bytes. The instructions can generate a byte, word, longword, or quadword datum that is spread across two registers at an arbitrary byte alignment.

4.6.4 Byte Mask

Format:

MSKxx	Ra.rq,Rb.rq,Rc.wq	!Operate format
MSKxx	Ra.rq,#b.ib,Rc.wq	!Operate format

Operation:

```
CASE
    MSKBL: byte_mask ←   0000 0000 0000 0001₂
    MSKWx: byte_mask ←   0000 0000 0000 0011₂
    MSKLx: byte_mask ←   0000 0000 0000 1111₂
    MSKQx: byte_mask ←   0000 0000 1111 1111₂
ENDCASE
byte_mask ←   LEFT_SHIFT(byte_mask, rbv<2:0>)

CASE
    MSKxL:
        Rc ←   BYTE_ZAP(Rav, byte_mask<7:0>)

    MSKxH:
        Rc ←   BYTE_ZAP(Rav, byte_mask<15:8>)

ENDCASE
```

Exceptions:

None

Instruction mnemonics:

MSKBL	Mask Byte Low
MSKWL	Mask Word Low
MSKLL	Mask Longword Low
MSKQL	Mask Quadword Low
MSKWH	Mask Word High
MSKLH	Mask Longword High
MSKQH	Mask Quadword High

Qualifiers:

None

Description:

MSKxL and MSKxH set selected bytes of register Ra to zero, storing the result in register Rc. Register Rb<2:0> selects the starting position of the field of zero bytes, and the function code selects the maximum width: 1, 2, 4, or 8 bytes. The instructions generate a byte, word, longword, or quadword field of zeros that can spread across two registers at an arbitrary byte alignment.

Notes:

The comments in the examples below assume that the effective address (ea) of X(R11) is such that (ea mod 8) = 5, the value of the aligned quadword containing X(R11) is CBAx xxxx, the value of the aligned quadword containing X+7(R11) is yyyH GFED, and the value to be stored from R5 is hgfe dcba.

The examples below are the most general case; if more information is known about the value or intended alignment of X, shorter sequences can be used.

The intended sequence for storing an unaligned quadword R5 at address X(R11) is:

```
LDA     R6,X(R11)       ; R6<2:0> = (X mod 8) = 5
LDQ_U   R2,X+7(R11)     ; Ignores va<2:0>, R2 = yyyH GFED
LDQ_U   R1,X(R11)       ; Ignores va<2:0>, R1 = CBAx xxxx
INSQH   R5,R6,R4        ; R4 = 000h gfed
INSQL   R5,R6,R3        ; R3 = cba0 0000
MSKQH   R2,R6,R2        ; R2 = yyy0 0000
MSKQL   R1,R6,R1        ; R1 = 000x xxxx
OR      R2,R4,R2        ; R2 = yyyh gfed
OR      R1,R3,R1        ; R1 = cbax xxxx
STQ_U   R2,X+7(R11)     ; Must store high then low for
STQ_U   R1,X(R11)       ; degenerate case of aligned QW
```

The intended sequence for storing an unaligned longword R5 at X is:

```
LDA     R6,X(R11)       ; R6<2:0> = (X mod 8) = 5
LDQ_U   R2,X+3(R11)     ; Ignores va<2:0>, R2 = yyyy yyyD
LDQ_U   R1,X(R11)       ; Ignores va<2:0>, R1 = CBAx xxxx
INSLH   R5,R6,R4        ; R4 = 0000 000d
INSLL   R5,R6,R3        ; R3 = cba0 0000
MSKLH   R2,R6,R2        ; R2 = yyyy yyy0
MSKLL   R1,R6,R1        ; R1 = 000x xxxx
OR      R2,R4,R2        ; R2 = yyyy yyyd
OR      R1,R3,R1        ; R1 = cbax xxxx
STQ_U   R2,X+3(R11)     ; Must store high then low for
STQ_U   R1,X(R11)       ; degenerate case of aligned
```

The intended sequence for storing an unaligned word R5 at X is:

```
LDA     R6,X(R11)       ; R6<2:0> = (X mod 8) = 5
LDQ_U   R2,X+1(R11)     ; Ignores va<2:0>, R2 = yBAx xxxx
LDQ_U   R1,X(R11)       ; Ignores va<2:0>, R1 = yBAx xxxx
INSWH   R5,R6,R4        ; R4 = 0000 0000
INSWL   R5,R6,R3        ; R3 = 0ba0 0000
MSKWH   R2,R6,R2        ; R2 = yBAx xxxx
MSKWL   R1,R6,R1        ; R1 = y00x xxxx
OR      R2,R4,R2        ; R2 = yBAx xxxx
OR      R1,R3,R1        ; R1 = ybax xxxx
STQ_U   R2,X+1(R11)     ; Must store high then low for
STQ_U   R1,X(R11)       ; degenerate case of aligned
```

The intended sequence for storing a byte R5 at X is:

```
LDA     R6,X(R11)       ; R6<2:0> = (X mod 8) = 5
LDQ_U   R1,X(R11)       ; Ignores va<2:0>, R1 = yyAx xxxx
INSBL   R5,R6,R3        ; R3 = 00a0 0000
MSKBL   R1,R6,R1        ; R1 = yy0x xxxx
OR      R1,R3,R1        ; R1 = yyax xxxx
STQ_U   R1,X(R11)       ;
```

4.6.5 Zero Bytes

Format:

ZAPx	Ra.rq,Rb.rq,Rc.wq	!Operate format
ZAPx	Ra.rq,#b.ib,Rc.wq	!Operate format

Operation:

```
CASE
    ZAP:
         Rc ←  BYTE_ZAP(Rav, rbv<7:0>)
    ZAPNOT:
         Rc ←  BYTE_ZAP(Rav, NOT rbv<7:0>)
ENDCASE
```

Exceptions:

None

Instruction mnemonics:

ZAP	Zero Bytes
ZAPNOT	Zero Bytes Not

Qualifiers:

None

Description:

ZAP and ZAPNOT set selected bytes of register Ra to zero, and store the result in register Rc. Register Rb<7:0> selects the bytes to be zeroed; bit 0 of Rbv corresponds to byte 0, bit 1 of Rbv corresponds to byte 1, and so on. A result byte is set to zero if the corresponding bit of Rbv is a one for ZAP and a zero for ZAPNOT.

4.7 Floating-Point Instructions

Alpha provides instructions for operating on floating-point operands in each of four data formats:

- F_floating (VAX single)

- G_floating (VAX double, 11-bit exponent)

- S_floating (IEEE single)

- T_floating (IEEE double, 11-bit exponent)

Data conversion instructions are also provided to convert operands between floating-point and quadword integer formats, between double and single floating, and between quadword and longword integers.

NOTE

D_floating is a partially supported datatype; no D_ floating arithmetic operations are provided in the architecture. For backward compatibility, exact D_ floating arithmetic may be provided via software emulation. D_floating "format compatibility," in which binary files of D_floating numbers may be processed but without the last 3 bits of fraction precision, can be obtained via conversions to G_floating, G arithmetic operations, then conversion back to D_floating.

The choice of data formats is encoded in each instruction. Each instruction also encodes the choice of rounding mode and the choice of trapping mode.

All floating-point operate instructions (that is, *not* including loads or stores) that yield an F_ or G_floating zero result must materialize a true zero.

4.7.1 Floating Subsets and Floating Faults

All floating-point operations may take floating disabled faults. Any subsetted floating-point instruction may take an Illegal Instruction Trap. These faults are not explicitly listed in the description of each instruction.

All floating-point loads and stores may take memory management faults (access control violation, translation not valid, fault on read/write, data alignment).

The Floating-point Enable (FEN) internal processor register (IPR) allows system software to restrict access to the floating registers.

If a floating instruction is implemented and FEN = 0, attempts to execute the instruction cause a floating disabled fault.

If a floating instruction is not implemented, attempts to execute the instruction cause an Illegal Instruction Trap. This rule holds regardless of the value of FEN.

An Alpha implementation may provide both VAX and IEEE floating-point operations, either, or none.

Some floating-point instructions are common to the VAX and IEEE subsets, some are VAX only, and some are IEEE only. These are designated in the descriptions that follow. If either subset is implemented, all the common instructions must be implemented.

An implementation including IEEE floating-point may subset the ability to perform rounding to plus infinity and minus infinity. If not implemented, instructions requesting these rounding modes take Illegal Instruction Trap.

4.7.2 Definitions

The following definitions apply to Alpha floating-point support.

true result
The mathematically correct result of an operation, assuming that the input operand values are exact. The true result is typically rounded to the nearest representable result.

representable result
a real number that can be represented exactly as a VAX or IEEE floating-point number, with finite precision and bounded exponent range.

LSB
The least significant bit. For a positive representable number A whose fraction is not all ones, A + 1 LSB is the next larger representable number, and A + 1/2 LSB is exactly halfway between A and the next larger representable number.

true zero
The value +0, represented as exactly 64 zeros in a floating-point register.

Alpha finite number
A floating-point number with a definite, in-range value. Specifically, all numbers in the inclusive ranges –MAX..–MIN, zero, +MIN..+MAX, where MAX is the largest non-infinite representable floating-point number and MIN is the smallest non-zero representable normalized floating-point number.

For VAX floating-point, finites do not include reserved operands or dirty zeros (this differs from the usual VAX interpretation of dirty zeros as finite). For IEEE floating-point, finites do not include infinites, NaNs, or denormals, but do include minus zero.

Not-a-Number
An IEEE floating-point bit pattern that represents something other than a number. This comes in two forms: signaling NaNs (for Alpha, those with an initial fraction bit of 1) and quiet NaNs (for Alpha, those with initial fraction bit of 0).

infinity
An IEEE floating-point bit pattern that represents plus or minus infinity.

denormal

An IEEE floating-point bit pattern that represents a number whose magnitude lies between zero and the smallest finite number.

dirty zero

A VAX floating-point bit pattern that represents a zero value, but not in true-zero form.

reserved operand

A VAX floating-point bit pattern that represents an illegal value.

trap shadow

The set of instructions potentially executed after an instruction that signals an arithmetic trap but before the trap is actually taken.

4.7.3 Encodings

Floating-point numbers are represented with three fields: sign, exponent, and fraction. The sign is 1 bit; the exponent is 8 or 11 bits; and the fraction is 23, 52, or 55 bits. Some encodings represent special values:

Sign	Exponent	Fraction	Vax Meaning	VAX Finite	IEEE Meaning	IEEE Finite
x	All-1's	Non-zero	Finite	Yes	+/–NaN	No
x	All-1's	0	Finite	Yes	+/–Infinity	No
0	0	Non-zero	Dirty zero	No	+Denormal	No
1	0	Non-zero	Resv. operand	No	–Denormal	No
0	0	0	True zero	Yes	+0	Yes
1	0	0	Resv. operand	No	–0	Yes
x	Other	x	Finite	Yes	finite	Yes

The values of MIN and MAX for each of the four floating-point data formats are:

Data Format	MIN	MAX
F_floating	$2**-127 * 0.5$ (0.294e–38)	$2**127 * (1.0 - 2**-24)$ (1.70e38)
G_floating	$2**-1023 * 0.5$ (0.56e–308)	$2**1023 * (1.0 - 2**-53)$ (0.899e308)
S_floating	$2**-126 * 1.0$ (1.175e–38)	$2**127 * (2.0 - 2**-23)$ (3.40e38)

Data Format	MIN	MAX
T_floating	$2{**}{-}1022 * 1.0$	$2{**}1023 * (2.0 - 2{**}{-}52)$
	$(2.225e{-}308)$	$(1.798e308)$

4.7.4 Floating-Point Rounding Modes

All rounding modes map a true result that is exactly representable to that representable value.

VAX Rounding Modes

For VAX floating-point operations, two rounding modes are provided and are specified in each instruction: normal (biased) rounding and chopped rounding.

Normal VAX rounding maps the true result to the nearest of two representable results, with true results exactly halfway between mapped to the larger in absolute value (sometimes called biased rounding away from zero); maps true results $\geq$ MAX + 1/2 LSB in magnitude to an overflow; maps true results < MIN − 1/2 LSB in magnitude to an underflow.

Chopped VAX rounding maps the true result to the smaller in magnitude of two surrounding representable results; maps true results $\geq$ MAX + 1 LSB in magnitude to an overflow; maps true results < MIN in magnitude to an underflow.

IEEE Rounding Modes

For IEEE floating-point operations, four rounding modes are provided: normal rounding (unbiased round to nearest), rounding toward minus infinity, round toward zero, and rounding toward plus infinity. The first three can be specified in the instruction. Rounding toward plus infinity can be obtained by setting the Floating-point Control Register (FPCR) to select it and then specifying dynamic rounding mode in the instruction (See Section 4.7.7). Alpha IEEE arithmetic does rounding before detecting overflow/underflow.

Normal IEEE rounding maps the true result to the nearest of two representable results, with true results exactly halfway between mapped to the one whose fraction ends in 0 (sometimes called unbiased rounding to even); maps true results $\geq$ MAX + 1/2 LSB in magnitude to an overflow; maps true results < MIN − 1/2 LSB in magnitude to an underflow.

Plus infinity IEEE rounding maps the true result to the larger of two surrounding representable results; maps true results > MAX in magnitude to an overflow; maps positive true results $\leq$ +MIN − 1 LSB to an underflow; and maps negative true results > −MIN to an underflow.

Minus infinity IEEE rounding maps the true result to the smaller of two surrounding representable results; maps true results > MAX in magnitude to an overflow; maps positive true results < +MIN to an underflow; and maps negative true results $\geq$ −MIN + 1 LSB to an underflow.

Chopped IEEE rounding maps the true result to the smaller in magnitude of two surrounding representable results; maps true results $\geq$ MAX + 1 LSB in magnitude to an overflow; and maps non-zero true results < MIN in magnitude to an underflow.

Dynamic rounding mode uses the IEEE rounding mode selected by the FPCR register and is described in more detail in Section 4.7.7.

The following tables summarize the floating-point rounding modes:

VAX Rounding Mode	Instruction Notation
Normal rounding	(No modifier)
Chopped	/C

IEEE Rounding Mode	Instruction Notation
Normal rounding	(No modifier)
Dynamic rounding	/D
Plus infinity	/D and ensure that FPCR<DYN> = '11'
Minus infinity	/M
Chopped	/C

4.7.5 Floating-Point Trapping Modes

There are six exceptions that can be generated by floating-point operate instructions, all signaled by an arithmetic exception trap. These exceptions are:

- Invalid operation

- Division by zero

- Overflow

- Underflow, may be disabled

- Inexact result, may be disabled

- Integer overflow (conversion to integer only), may be disabled

For more detail on the information passed to an arithmetic exception handler, see *Part II, Operating Systems*.

VAX Trapping Modes

For VAX floating-point operations other than CVTxQ, four trapping modes are provided. They specify software completion and whether traps are enabled for underflow.

For VAX conversions from floating-point to integer, four trapping modes are provided. They specify software completion and whether traps are enabled for integer overflow.

IEEE Trapping Modes

For IEEE floating-point operations other than CVTxQ, four trapping modes are provided. They specify software completion and whether traps are enabled for underflow and inexact results.

For IEEE conversions from floating-point to integer, four trapping modes are provided. They specify software completion, and whether traps are enabled for integer overflow and inexact results.

The modes and instruction notation are:

VAX Trap Mode	Instruction Notation
Imprecise, underflow disabled	(No modifier)
Imprecise, underflow enabled	/U
Software, underflow disabled	/S
Software, underflow enabled	/SU

VAX Convert-to-Integer Trap Mode	Instruction Notation
Imprecise, integer overflow disabled	(No modifier)
Imprecise, integer overflow enabled	/V
Software, integer overflow disabled	/S
Software, integer overflow enabled	/SV

IEEE Trap Mode	Instruction Notation
Imprecise, unfl disabled, inexact disabled	(No modifier)
Imprecise, unfl enabled, inexact disabled	/U
Software, unfl enabled, inexact disabled	/SU
Software, unfl enabled, inexact enabled	/SUI

IEEE Convert-to-Integer Trap Mode	Instruction Notation
Imprecise, int.ovfl disabled, inexact disabled	(No modifier)
Imprecise, int.ovfl enabled, inexact disabled	/V
Software, int.ovfl enabled, inexact disabled	/SV
Software, int.ovfl enabled, inexact enabled	/SVI

4.7.5.1 Imprecise /Software Completion Trap Modes

Floating-point instructions may be pipelined, and all exceptions are imprecise traps:

- The trapping instruction may write an UNPREDICTABLE result value.

- The trap PC is an arbitrary number of instructions past the one triggering the trap. The trigger instruction plus all intervening executed instructions are collectively referred to as the *trap shadow* of the trigger instruction.

- The extent of the trap shadow is bounded only by a TRAPB instruction (or the implicit TRAPB within a CALL_PAL instruction).

- Input operand values may have been overwritten in the trap shadow.

- Result values may have been overwritten in the trap shadow.

- An UNPREDICTABLE result value may have been used as an input operand in the trap shadow.

- Additional traps may occur in the trap shadow.

- In general, it is not feasible to fix up the result value or to continue from the trap.

This behavior is ideal for operations on finite operands that give finite results. For programs that deliberately operate outside the overflow/underflow range, or use IEEE NaNs, software assistance is required to complete floating-point operations correctly. This assistance can be provided by a software arithmetic trap handler, plus constraints on the instructions surrounding the trap.

For a trap handler to complete non-finite arithmetic, the following conditions must hold:

1. On entry to the trap shadow, if any Alpha register or memory location contains a value that is used as an operand value by some instruction in the trap shadow (live on entry), then no instruction in the trap shadow may modify the register or memory location.

2. Within the trap shadow, the computation of the base register for a memory load or store instruction may not involve using the result of an instruction that might generate an UNPREDICTABLE result.

3. Within the trap shadow, no register may be used more than once as a destination register.

4. The trap shadow may not include any branch instructions.

5. Each floating instruction to be completed must be so marked, by specifying the /S software completion modifier.

The first condition allows a software trap handler to emulate the trigger instruction with its original input operand values and then to reexecute the rest of the trap shadow.

The second condition prevents memory accesses at unpredictable addresses.

The remaining conditions make it possible for a software trap handler to find the trigger instruction via a linear scan backwards from the trap PC.

NOTE

The /S modifier does not affect instruction operation or trap behavior; it is an informational bit passed to a software trap handler. It allows a trap handler to test easily whether an instruction is intended to be completed. (The /S bits of instructions signaling traps are carried into the trap summary.) The handler may then assume that the other conditions are met without examining the code stream.

If a software trap handler is provided, it must handle the completion of all floating-point operations marked /S that follow the rules above. In effect, one TRAPB instruction per basic block can be used.

4.7.5.2 Invalid Operation Arithmetic Trap

An invalid operation arithmetic trap is signaled if any operand of a floating arithmetic-operate instruction is non-finite. (CMPTxy is an exception to the rule and operates normally with plus and minus infinity and does not trap in this case.) This trap is always enabled. If this trap occurs, an UNPREDICTABLE value is stored in the result register. (IEEE-compliant system software must also supply an invalid operation indication to the user for SQRT of a negative non-zero number, 0/0, x REM 0, and conversions to integer that take an integer overflow trap.)

4.7.5.3 Division by Zero Arithmetic Trap

A division by zero arithmetic trap is taken if the numerator does not cause an invalid operation trap and the denominator is zero. This trap is always enabled. If this trap occurs, an UNPREDICTABLE value is stored in the result register.

4.7.5.4 Overflow Arithmetic Trap

An overflow arithmetic trap is signaled if the rounded result exceeds in magnitude the largest finite number of the destination format. This trap is always enabled. If this trap occurs, an UNPREDICTABLE value is stored in the result register.

4.7.5.5 Underflow Arithmetic Trap

An underflow occurs if the rounded result is smaller in magnitude than the smallest finite number of the destination format.

If an underflow occurs, a true zero (64 bits of zero) is always stored in the result register, even if the proper IEEE result would have been –0 (underflow below the negative denormal range).

If an underflow occurs and underflow traps are enabled by the instruction, an underflow arithmetic trap is signaled.

4.7.5.6 Inexact Result Arithmetic Trap

An inexact result occurs if the infinitely precise result differs from the rounded result.

If an inexact result occurs, the normal rounded result is still stored in the result register.

If an inexact result occurs and inexact result traps are enabled by the instruction, an inexact result arithmetic trap is signaled.

4.7.5.7 Integer Overflow Arithmetic Trap

In conversions from floating to quadword integer, an integer overflow occurs if the rounded result is outside the range $-2**63..2**63-1$. In conversions from quadword integer to longword integer, an integer overflow occurs if the result is outside the range $-2**31..2**31-1$.

If an integer overflow occurs in CVTxQ or CVTQL, the true result truncated to the low-order 64 or 32 bits respectively is stored in the result register.

If an integer overflow occurs and integer overflow traps are enabled by the instruction, an integer overflow arithmetic trap is signaled.

4.7.6 Floating-Point Single-Precision Operations

Single-precision values (F_floating or S_floating) are stored in the floating registers in canonical form, as subsets of double-precision values, with 11-bit exponents restricted to the corresponding single-precision range, and with the 29 low-order fraction bits restricted to be all zero.

Single-precision operations applied to canonical single-precision values give single-precision results. Single-precision operations applied to non-canonical operands give UNPREDICTABLE results.

Longword integer values in floating registers are stored in bits <63:62,58:29>, with bits <61:59> ignored and zeros in bits <28:0>.

4.7.7 FPCR Register and Dynamic Rounding Mode

When an IEEE floating-point operate instruction specifies dynamic mode (/D) in its function field (function code bits <7:6> = 11), the rounding mode to be used for the instruction is derived from the FPCR register. The layout of the rounding mode bits and their assignments matches exactly the format used in the 11-bit function field of the floating-point operate instructions.

In addition, the FPCR gives a summary for each exception type of the exceptions conditions detected by all IEEE floating-point operates thus far as well as an overall summary bit that indicates whether any of these exception conditions has been detected. The individual exception bits match exactly in purpose and order the exceptions bits found in the exception summary quadword that is pushed for arithmetic traps. However, for each instruction, these exceptions bits are set independent of the trapping mode specified for the instruction. Therefore, even though trapping may be disabled for a certain exceptional condition, the fact that the exceptional condition was encountered by an instruction will still be recorded in the FPCR.

Floating-point operates that belong to the IEEE subset and CVTQL, which belongs to both VAX and IEEE subsets, appropriately set the FPCR exception bits. It is UNPREDICTABLE whether floating-point operates that belong only to the VAX floating-point subset set the FPCR exception bits.

Alpha floating-point hardware only transitions these exception bits from zero to one. Once set to one, these exception bits are only cleared when software writes zero into these bits by writing a new value into the FPCR.

The format of the FPCR is shown in Figure 4–1 and described in Table 4–8.

Figure 4–1: Floating-Point Control Register (FPCR) Format

63 62	60 59 58 57 56 55 54 53 52 51								0
S U M	RAZ/ IGN	D Y N	I O N V	I N E F	U N F	O V F	D Z E	I N V	RAZ/IGN

Table 4–8: Floating-Point Control Register (FPCR) Bit Descriptions

Bit	Description
63	Summary Bit (SUM). Records bitwise OR of FPCR exception bits. Equal to (FPCR[57] | FPCR[56] | FPCR[55] | FPCR[54] | FPCR[53] | FPCR[52]).
62–60	Reserved. Read As Zero; Ignored when written.
59–58	Dynamic Rounding Mode (DYN). Indicates the rounding mode to be used by an IEEE floating-point operate instruction when the instruction's function field specifies dynamic mode (/D). Assignments are:

DYN	IEEE Rounding Mode Selected
00	Chopped rounding mode
01	Minus infinity
10	Normal rounding
11	Plus infinity

Bit	Description
57	Integer Overflow (IOV). An integer arithmetic operation or a conversion from floating to integer overflowed the destination precision.
56	Inexact Result (INE). A floating arithmetic or conversion operation gave a result that differed from the mathematically exact result.

Table 4–8 (Cont.): Floating-Point Control Register (FPCR) Bit Descriptions

Bit	Description
55	Underflow (UNF). A floating arithmetic or conversion operation underflowed the destination exponent.
54	Overflow (OVF). A floating arithmetic or conversion operation overflowed the destination exponent.
53	Division by Zero (DZE). An attempt was made to perform a floating divide operation with a divisor of zero.
52	Invalid Operation (INV). An attempt was made to perform a floating arithmetic, conversion, or comparison operation, and one or more of the operand values were illegal.
51–0	Reserved. Read As Zero; Ignored when written.

FPCR is read from and written to the floating-point registers by the MT_FPCR and MF_FPCR instructions respectively, which are described in Section 4.7.7.1.

FPCR and the instructions to access it are required for an implementation that supports floating-point (see Section 4.1.1.1). On implementations that do not support floating-point, the instructions that access FPCR (MF_FPCR and MT_FPCR) take an Illegal Instruction Trap.

SOFTWARE NOTE

As noted in Section 4.1.1.1, support for FPCR is required on a system that supports the OpenVMS Alpha operating system even if that system does not support floating-point.

4.7.7.1 Accessing the FPCR

Because Alpha floating-point hardware can overlap the execution of a number of floating-point instructions, accessing the FPCR must be synchronized with other floating-point instructions. A TRAPB must be issued both prior to and after accessing the FPCR to ensure that the FPCR access is synchronized with the execution of previous and subsequent floating-point instructions; otherwise synchronization is not ensured.

Issuing a TRAPB followed by an MT_FPCR followed by another TRAPB ensures that only floating-point instructions issued after the second TRAPB are affected by and affect the new value of the FPCR. Issuing a TRAPB followed by an MF_FPCR followed by another TRAPB ensures that the value read from the FPCR only records the exception information for floating-point instructions issued prior to the first TRAPB.

Consider the following example:

```
ADDT/D
TRAPB                    ;1
MT_FPCR F1,F1,F1
TRAPB                    ;2
SUBT/D
```

Without the first TRAPB, it is possible in an implementation for the ADDT/D to execute in parallel with the MT_FPCR. Thus, it would be UNPREDICTABLE whether the ADDT/D was affected by the new rounding mode set by the MT_FPCR and whether fields cleared by the MT_FPCR in the exception summary were subsequently set by the ADDT/D.

Without the second TRAPB, it is possible in an implementation for the MT_FPCR to execute in parallel with the SUBT/D. Thus, it would be UNPREDICTABLE whether the SUBT/D was affected by the new rounding mode set by the MT_FPCR and whether fields cleared by the MT_FPCR in the exception summary field of FPCR were previously set by the SUBT/D.

4.7.7.2 Default Values of the FPCR

Processor initialization leaves the value of FPCR UNPREDICTABLE.

> **SOFTWARE NOTE**
>
> Digital software should initialize FPCR<DYN> = 11 during program activation. Using this default, interval arithmetic code can switch from plus to minus infinity rounding with no penalty in performance by using /M and /D qualifiers.
>
> Program activation should clear all other fields of the FPCR.

4.7.7.3 Saving and Restoring the FPCR

The FPCR must be saved and restored across context switches so that the FPCR value of one process does not affect the rounding behavior and exception summary of another process.

The dynamic rounding mode put into effect by the programmer (or initialized by image activation) is valid for the entirety of the program and remains in effect until subsequently changed by the programmer or until image run-down occurs.

> **SOFTWARE NOTE**
>
> The IEEE standard precludes saving and restoring the FPCR across subroutine calls.

4.7.8 IEEE Standard

The IEEE Standard for Binary Floating-Point Arithmetic (ANSI/IEEE Standard 754-1985) is included by reference.

4.8 Memory Format Floating-Point Instructions

The instructions in this section move data between the floating-point registers and memory. They use the Memory instruction format. They do not interpret the bits moved in any way; specifically, they do not trap on non-finite values.

The instructions are summarized in Table 4–9.

Table 4–9: Memory Format Floating-Point Instructions Summary

Mnemonic	Operation	Subset
LDF	Load F_floating	VAX
LDG	Load G_floating (Load D_floating)	VAX
LDS	Load S_floating (Load Longword Integer)	Both
LDT	Load T_floating (Load Quadword Integer)	Both
STF	Store F_floating	VAX
STG	Store G_floating (Store D_floating)	VAX
STS	Store S_floating (Store Longword Integer)	Both
STT	Store T_floating (Store Quadword Integer)	Both

4.8.1 Load F_floating

Format:

LDF   Fa.wf,disp.ab(Rb.ab)   !Memory format

Operation:

```
va  ←   {Rbv + SEXT(disp)}
Fa  ←   (va)<15>  ||  MAP_F((va)<14:7>)  ||
        (va)<6:0>  ||  (va)<31:16>  ||  0<28:0>
```

Exceptions:

Access Violation

Fault on Read

Alignment

Translation Not Valid

Instruction mnemonics:

LDF   Load F_floating

Qualifiers:

None

Description:

LDF fetches an F_floating datum from memory and writes it to register Fa. If the data is not naturally aligned, an alignment exception is generated.

The 8-bit memory-format exponent is expanded to an 11-bit register-format exponent according to Table 2–1.

The virtual address is computed by adding register Rb to the sign-extended 16-bit displacement. The source operand is fetched from memory and the bytes are reordered to conform to the F_floating register format. The result is then zero-extended in the low-order longword and written to register Fa.

4.8.2 Load G_floating

Format:

LDG   Fa.wg,disp.ab(Rb.ab)   !Memory format

Operation:

```
va ←  {Rbv + SEXT(disp)}
Fa ←  (va)<15:0>  ||  (va)<31:16> ||
      (va)<47:32> ||  (va)<63:48>
```

Exceptions:

Access Violation

Fault on Read

Alignment

Translation Not Valid

Instruction mnemonics:

LDG   Load G_floating (Load D_floating)

Qualifiers:

None

Description:

LDG fetches a G_floating (or D_floating) datum from memory and writes it to register Fa. If the data is not naturally aligned, an alignment exception is generated.

The virtual address is computed by adding register Rb to the sign-extended 16-bit displacement. The source operand is fetched from memory, the bytes are reordered to conform to the G_floating register format (also conforming to the D_floating register format), and the result is then written to register Fa.

4.8.3 Load S_floating

Format:

LDS   Fa.ws,disp.ab(Rb.ab)   !Memory format

Operation:

```
va ←   {Rbv + SEXT(disp)}
Fa ←   (va)<31>      || MAP_S((va)<30:23>) ||
       (va)<22:0>    || 0<28:0>
```

Exceptions:

Access Violation

Fault on Read

Alignment

Translation Not Valid

Instruction mnemonics:

LDS   Load S_floating (Load Longword Integer)

Qualifiers:

None

Description:

LDS fetches a longword (integer or S_floating) from memory and writes it to register Fa. If the data is not naturally aligned, an alignment exception is generated.

The 8-bit memory-format exponent is expanded to an 11-bit register-format exponent according to Table 2–2.

The virtual address is computed by adding register Rb to the sign-extended 16-bit displacement. The source operand is fetched from memory, is zero-extended in the low-order longword, and then written to register Fa.

Notes:

• Longword integers in floating registers are stored in bits <63:62,58:29>, with bits <61:59> ignored and zeros in bits <28:0>.

4.8.4 Load T_floating

Format:

> LDT   Fa.wt,disp.ab(Rb.ab)   !Memory format

Operation:

```
va ←  {Rbv + SEXT(disp)}
Fa ←  (va)<63:0>
```

Exceptions:

> Access Violation
>
> Fault on Read
>
> Alignment
>
> Translation Not Valid

Instruction mnemonics:

> LDT   Load T_floating (Load Quadword Integer)

Qualifiers:

> None

Description:

LDT fetches a quadword (integer or T_floating) from memory and writes it to register Fa. If the data is not naturally aligned, an alignment exception is generated.

The virtual address is computed by adding register Rb to the sign-extended 16-bit displacement. The source operand is fetched from memory and written to register Fa.

4.8.5 Store F_floating

Format:

STF	Fa.rf,disp.ab(Rb.ab)	!Memory format

Operation:

```
va ←  {Rbv + SEXT(disp)}
(va)<31:0> ←  Fav<44:29> || Fav<63:62>|| Fav<58:45>
```

Exceptions:

Access Violation

Fault on Write

Alignment

Translation Not Valid

Instruction mnemonics:

STF	Store F_floating

Qualifiers:

None

Description:

STF stores an F_floating datum from Fa to memory. If the data is not naturally aligned, an alignment exception is generated.

The virtual address is computed by adding register Rb to the sign-extended 16-bit displacement. The bits of the source operand are fetched from register Fa, the bits are reordered to conform to F_floating memory format, and the result is then written to memory. Bits <61:59> and <28:0> of Fa are ignored. No checking is done.

4.8.6 Store G_floating

Format:

> STG Fa.rg,disp.ab(Rb.ab)   !Memory format

Operation:

```
va ←  {Rbv + SEXT(disp)}
(va)<63:0> ←  Fav<15:0>  || Fav<31:16> ||
              Fav<47:32> || Fav<63:48>
```

Exceptions:

> Access Violation
>
> Fault on Write
>
> Alignment
>
> Translation Not Valid

Instruction mnemonics:

> STG Store G_floating (Store D_floating)

Qualifiers:

> None

Description:

STG stores a G_floating (or D_floating) datum from Fa to memory. If the data is not naturally aligned, an alignment exception is generated.

The virtual address is computed by adding register Rb to the sign-extended 16-bit displacement. The source operand is fetched from register Fa, the bytes are reordered to conform to the G_floating memory format (also conforming to the D_floating memory format), and the result is then written to memory.

4.8.7 Store S_floating

Format:

STS   Fa.rs,disp.ab(Rb.ab)   !Memory format

Operation:

```
va ←  {Rbv + SEXT(disp)}
(va)<31:0> ←  Fav<63:62>||Fav<58:29>
```

Exceptions:

Access Violation

Fault on Write

Alignment

Translation Not Valid

Instruction mnemonics:

STS   Store S_floating (Store Longword Integer)

Qualifiers:

None

Description:

STS stores a longword (integer or S_floating) datum from Fa to memory. If the data is not naturally aligned, an alignment exception is generated.

The virtual address is computed by adding register Rb to the sign-extended 16-bit displacement. The bits of the source operand are fetched from register Fa, the bits are reordered to conform to S_floating memory format, and the result is then written to memory. Bits <61:59> and <28:0> of Fa are ignored. No checking is done.

4.8.8 Store T_floating

Format:

> STT   Fa.rt,disp.ab(Rb.ab)   !Memory format

Operation:

```
va ← {Rbv + SEXT(disp)}
(va)<63:0> ← Fav<63:0>
```

Exceptions:

> Access Violation
> Fault on Write
> Alignment
> Translation Not Valid

Instruction mnemonics:

> STT   Store T_floating (Store Quadword Integer)

Qualifiers:

> None

Description:

STT stores a quadword (integer or T_floating) datum from Fa to memory. If the data is not naturally aligned, an alignment exception is generated.

The virtual address is computed by adding register Rb to the sign-extended 16-bit displacement. The source operand is fetched from register Fa and written to memory.

4.9 Branch Format Floating-Point Instructions

Alpha provides six floating conditional branch instructions. These branch-format instructions test the value of a floating-point register and conditionally change the PC.

They do not interpret the bits tested in any way; specifically, they do not trap on non-finite values.

The test is based on the sign bit and whether the rest of the register is all zero bits. All 64 bits of the register are tested. The test is independent of the format of the operand in the register. Both plus and minus zero are equal to zero. A non-zero value with a sign of zero is greater than zero. A non-zero value with a sign of one is less than zero. No reserved operand or non-finite checking is done.

The floating-point branch operations are summarized in Table 4–10.

Table 4–10: Floating-Point Branch Instructions Summary

Mnemonic	Operation	Subset
FBEQ	Floating Branch Equal	Both
FBGE	Floating Branch Greater Than or Equal	Both
FBGT	Floating Branch Greater Than	Both
FBLE	Floating Branch Less Than or Equal	Both
FBLT	Floating Branch Less Than	Both
FBNE	Floating Branch Not Equal	Both

4.9.1 Conditional Branch

Format:

FBxx   Fa.rq,disp.al   !Branch format

Operation:

```
{update PC}
va ←  PC + {4*SEXT(disp)}
IF  TEST(Fav, Condition_based_on_Opcode)  THEN
    PC ←  va
```

Exceptions:

None

Instruction mnemonics:

FBEQ	Floating Branch Equal
FBGE	Floating Branch Greater Than or Equal
FBGT	Floating Branch Greater Than
FBLE	Floating Branch Less Than or Equal
FBLT	Floating Branch Less Than
FBNE	Floating Branch Not Equal

Qualifiers:

None

Description:

Register Fa is tested. If the specified relationship is true, the PC is loaded with the target virtual address; otherwise, execution continues with the next sequential instruction.

The displacement is treated as a signed longword offset. This means it is shifted left two bits (to address a longword boundary), sign-extended to 64 bits, and added to the updated PC to form the target virtual address.

The conditional branch instructions are PC-relative only. The 21-bit signed displacement gives a forward/backward branch distance of +/– 1M instructions.

Notes:

- To branch properly on non-finite operands, compare to F31, then branch on the result of the compare.

- The largest negative integer ($8000\ 0000\ 0000\ 0000_{16}$) is the same bit pattern as floating minus zero, so it is treated as equal to zero by the branch instructions. To branch properly on the largest negative integer, convert it to floating or move it to an integer register and do an integer branch.

4.10 Floating-Point Operate Format Instructions

The floating-point bit-operate instructions perform copy and integer convert operations on 64-bit register values. The bit-operate instructions do not interpret the bits moved in any way; specifically, they do not trap on non-finite values.

The floating-point arithmetic-operate instructions perform add, subtract, multiply, divide, compare, and floating convert operations on 64-bit register values in one of the four specified floating formats.

Each instruction specifies the source and destination formats of the values, as well as the rounding mode and trapping mode to be used. These instructions use the Floating-point Operate format.

The floating-point operate instructions are summarized in Table 4–11.

Table 4–11: Floating-Point Operate Instructions Summary

Mnemonic	Operation	Subset
Bit and FPCR Operations		
CPYS	Copy Sign	Both
CPYSE	Copy Sign and Exponent	Both
CPYSN	Copy Sign Negate	Both
CVTLQ	Convert Longword to Quadword	Both
CVTQL	Convert Quadword to Longword	Both
FCMOVxx	Floating Conditional Move	Both
MF_FPCR	Move from Floating-point Control Register	Both
MT_FPCR	Move to Floating-point Control Register	Both

Table 4–11 (Cont.): Floating-Point Operate Instructions Summary

Mnemonic	Operation	Subset
Arithmetic Operations		
ADDF	Add F_floating	VAX
ADDG	Add G_floating	VAX
ADDS	Add S_floating	IEEE
ADDT	Add T_floating	IEEE
CMPGxx	Compare G_floating	VAX
CMPTxx	Compare T_floating	IEEE
CVTDG	Convert D_floating to G_floating	VAX
CVTGD	Convert G_floating to D_floating	VAX
CVTGF	Convert G_floating to F_floating	VAX
CVTGQ	Convert G_floating to Quadword	VAX
CVTQF	Convert Quadword to F_floating	VAX
CVTQG	Convert Quadword to G_floating	VAX
CVTQS	Convert Quadword to S_floating	IEEE
CVTQT	Convert Quadword to T_floating	IEEE
CVTTQ	Convert T_floating to Quadword	IEEE
CVTTS	Convert T_floating to S_floating	IEEE
DIVF	Divide F_floating	VAX
DIVG	Divide G_floating	VAX
DIVS	Divide S_floating	IEEE
DIVT	Divide T_floating	IEEE
MULF	Multiply F_floating	VAX
MULG	Multiply G_floating	VAX
MULS	Multiply S_floating	IEEE
MULT	Multiply T_floating	IEEE
SUBF	Subtract F_floating	VAX

Table 4–11 (Cont.): Floating-Point Operate Instructions Summary

Mnemonic	Operation	Subset
Arithmetic Operations		
SUBG	Subtract G_floating	VAX
SUBS	Subtract S_floating	IEEE
SUBT	Subtract T_floating	IEEE

4.10.1 Copy Sign

Format:

CPYSy   Fa.rq,Fb.rq,Fc.wq   !Floating-point Operate format

Operation:

```
CASE
    CPYS:   Fc ←  Fav<63> || Fbv<62:0>
    CPYSN:  Fc ←  NOT(Fav<63>) || Fbv<62:0>
    CPYSE:  Fc ←  Fav<63:52> || Fbv<51:0>
ENDCASE
```

Exceptions:

None

Instruction mnemonics:

CPYS   Copy Sign

CPYSE   Copy Sign and Exponent

CPYSN   Copy Sign Negate

Qualifiers:

None

Description:

For CPYS and CPYSN, the sign bit of Fa is fetched (and complemented in the case of CPYSN) and concatenated with the exponent and fraction bits from Fb; the result is stored in Fc.

For CPYSE, the sign and exponent bits from Fa are fetched and concatenated with the fraction bits from Fb; the result is stored in Fc.

No checking of the operands is performed.

Notes:

- Register moves can be performed using CPYS Fx,Fx,Fy. Floating-point absolute value can be done using CPYS F31,Fx,Fy. Floating-point negation can be done using CPYSN Fx,Fx,Fy. Floating values can be scaled to a known range by using CPYSE.

4.10.2 Convert Integer to Integer

Format:

CVTxy   Fb.rq,Fc.wx   !Floating-point Operate format

Operation:

```
CASE
     CVTQL: Fc ←   Fbv<31:30> || 0<2:0> ||
                   Fbv<29:0>  || 0<28:0>
     CVTLQ: Fc ←   SEXT(Fbv<63:62> || Fbv<58:29>)
ENDCASE
```

Exceptions:

Integer Overflow, CVTQL only

Instruction mnemonics:

CVTLQ   Convert Longword to Quadword

CVTQL   Convert Quadword to Longword

Qualifiers:

Trapping: Software (/S)

Integer Overflow Enable (/V) (CVTQL only)

Description:

The two's-complement operand in register Fb is converted to a two's-complement result and written to register Fc.

The conversion from quadword to longword is a repositioning of the low 32 bits of the operand, with zero fill and optional integer overflow checking. Integer overflow occurs if Fb is outside the range $-2**31..2**31-1$. If integer overflow occurs, the truncated result is stored in Fc, and an arithmetic trap is taken if enabled.

The conversion from longword to quadword is a repositioning of 32 bits of the operand, with sign extension.

4.10.3 Floating-Point Conditional Move

Format:

FCMOVxx Fa.rq,Fb.rq,Fc.wq   !Floating-point Operate format

Operation:

```
IF  TEST(Fav, Condition_based_on_Opcode)  THEN
    Fc ← Fbv
```

Exceptions:

None

Instruction mnemonics:

FCMOVEQ   FCMOVE if Register Equal to Zero
FCMOVGE   FCMOVE if Register Greater Than or Equal to Zero
FCMOVGT   FCMOVE if Register Greater Than Zero
FCMOVLE   FCMOVE if Register Less Than or Equal to Zero
FCMOVLT   FCMOVE if Register Less Than Zero
FCMOVNE   FCMOVE if Register Not Equal to Zero

Qualifiers:

None

Description:

Register Fa is tested. If the specified relationship is true, register Fb is written to register Fc; otherwise, the move is suppressed and register Fc is unchanged. The test is based on the sign bit and whether the rest of the register is all zero bits, as described for floating branches in Section 4.9.

Notes:

Except that it is likely in many implementations to be substantially faster, the instruction:

```
FCMOVxx Fa,Fb,Fc
```

is exactly equivalent to:

```
        FByy Fa,label    ; yy = NOT xx
        CPYS Fb,Fb,Fc
label:  ...
```

For example, a branchless sequence for:

```
F1=MAX(F1,F2)
```

is:

```
CMPxLT  F1,F2,F3         ! F3=one if F1<F2; x=F/G/S/T
FCMOVNE F3,F2,F1         ! Move F2 to F1 if F1<F2
```

4.10.4 Move from/to Floating-Point Control Register

Format:

Mx_FPCR   Fa.rq,Fa.rq,Fa.wq   !Floating-point Operate format

Operation:

```
CASE
    MT_FPCR:  FPCR ←  Fav
    MF_FPCR:  Fa   ←  FPCR
ENDCASE
```

Exceptions:

None

Instruction mnemonics:

MF_FPCR   Move from Floating-point Control Register

MT_FPCR   Move to Floating-point Control Register

Qualifiers:

None

Description:

The Floating-point Control Register (FPCR) is read from (MF_FPCR) or written to (MT_FPCR), a floating-point register. The floating-point register to be used is specified by the Fa, Fb, and Fc fields all pointing to the same floating-point register. If the Fa, Fb, and Fc fields do not all point to the same floating-point register, then it is UNPREDICTABLE which register is used.

The use of these instructions and the FPCR are described in Section 4.7.7.

4.10.5 VAX Floating Add

Format:

    ADDx   Fa.rx,Fb.rx,Fc.wx   !Floating-point Operate format

Operation:

    Fc ← Fav + Fbv

Exceptions:

    Invalid Operation
    Overflow
    Underflow

Instruction mnemonics:

ADDF	Add F_floating
ADDG	Add G_floating

Qualifiers:

Rounding:	Chopped (/C)
Trapping:	Software (/S)
	Underflow Enable (/U)

Description:

Register Fa is added to register Fb, and the sum is written to register Fc.

The sum is rounded or chopped to the specified precision, and then the corresponding range is checked for overflow/underflow. The single-precision operation on canonical single-precision values produces a canonical single-precision result.

An invalid operation trap is signaled if either operand has exp=0 and is not a true zero (that is, VAX reserved operands *and* dirty zeros trap). The contents of Fc are UNPREDICTABLE if this occurs. See Section 4.7.5 for details of the stored result on overflow or underflow.

4.10.6 IEEE Floating Add

Format:

ADDx   Fa.rx,Fb.rx,Fc.wx   !Floating-point Operate format

Operation:

Fc ← Fav + Fbv

Exceptions:

Invalid Operation
Overflow
Underflow
Inexact Result

Instruction mnemonics:

ADDS   Add S_floating
ADDT   Add T_floating

Qualifiers:

Rounding: Dynamic (/D)
               Minus infinity (/M)
               Chopped (/C)
Trapping: Software (/S)
               Underflow Enable (/U)
               Inexact Enable (/I)

Description:

Register Fa is added to register Fb, and the sum is written to register Fc.

The sum is rounded to the specified precision, and then the corresponding range is checked for overflow/underflow. The single-precision operation on canonical single-precision values produces a canonical single-precision result.

An invalid operation trap is signaled if either operand has exp=0 and a non-zero fraction (IEEE denormals trap), or if exp=all-ones (IEEE NaNs and infinities trap).

The contents of Fc are UNPREDICTABLE if this occurs.

See Section 4.7.5 for details of the stored result on overflow, underflow, or inexact result.

4.10.7 VAX Floating Compare

Format:

CMPGyy   Fa.rg,Fb.rg,Fc.wq   !Floating-point Operate format

Operation:

```
IF  Fav SIGNED_RELATION Fbv  THEN
     Fc ←   4000 0000 0000 0000₁₆
ELSE
     Fc ←   0000 0000 0000 0000₁₆
```

Exceptions:

Invalid Operation

Instruction mnemonics:

CMPGEQ	Compare G_floating Equal
CMPGLE	Compare G_floating Less Than or Equal
CMPGLT	Compare G_floating Less Than

Qualifiers:

Trapping: Software (/S)

Description:

The two operands in Fa and Fb are compared. If the relationship specified by the qualifier is true, a non-zero floating value (0.5) is written to register Fc; otherwise, a true zero is written to Fc.

Comparisons are exact and never overflow or underflow. Three mutually exclusive relations are possible: less than, equal, and greater than.

An invalid operation trap is signaled if either operand has exp=0 and is not a true zero (that is, VAX reserved operands *and* dirty zeros trap). The contents of Fc are UNPREDICTABLE if this occurs.

Notes:

- Compare Less Than A,B is the same as Compare Greater Than B,A; Compare Less Than or Equal A,B is the same as Compare Greater Than or Equal B,A. Therefore, only the less-than operations are included.

4.10.8 IEEE Floating Compare

Format:

    CMPTyy   Fa.rx,Fb.rx,Fc.wq   !Floating-point Operate format

Operation:

```
IF  Fav SIGNED_RELATION Fbv  THEN
     Fc ←  4000 0000 0000 0000₁₆
ELSE
     Fc ←  0000 0000 0000 0000₁₆
```

Exceptions:

Invalid Operation

Instruction mnemonics:

CMPTEQ	Compare T_floating Equal
CMPTLE	Compare T_floating Less Than or Equal
CMPTLT	Compare T_floating Less Than
CMPTUN	Compare T_floating Unordered

Qualifiers:

Trapping: Software (/S)

Description:

The two operands in Fa and Fb are compared. If the relationship specified by the qualifier is true, a non-zero floating value (2.0) is written to register Fc; otherwise, a true zero is written to Fc.

Comparisons are exact and never overflow or underflow. Four mutually exclusive relations are possible: less than, equal, greater than, and unordered. The unordered relation is true if one or both operands are NaN. (This behavior must be provided by a software trap handler, since NaNs trap.) Comparisons ignore the sign of zero, so $+0 = -0$.

An invalid operation trap is signaled if either operand has exp=0 and a non-zero fraction (IEEE denormals trap), or if exp=all-ones and a non-zero fraction (IEEE NaNs). The contents of Fc are UNPREDICTABLE if this occurs.

Comparisons with plus and minus infinity execute normally and do not take an invalid operation trap.

Notes:

- Compare Less Than A,B is the same as Compare Greater Than B,A; Compare Less Than or Equal A,B is the same as Compare Greater Than or Equal B,A. Therefore, only the less-than operations are included.

4.10.9 Convert VAX Floating to Integer

Format:

CVTGQ   Fb.rx,Fc.wq   !Floating-point Operate format

Operation:

```
Fc ← {conversion of Fbv}
```

Exceptions:

Invalid Operation

Integer Overflow

Instruction mnemonics:

CVTGQ   Convert G_floating to Quadword

Qualifiers:

Rounding: Chopped (/C)

Trapping: Software (/S)

             Integer Overflow Enable (/V)

Description:

The floating operand in register Fb is converted to a two's-complement quadword number and written to register Fc. The conversion aligns the operand fraction with the binary point just to the right of bit zero, rounds as specified, and complements the result if negative.

An invalid operation trap is signaled if the operand has exp=0 and is not a true zero (that is, VAX reserved operands *and* dirty zeros trap). The contents of Fc are UNPREDICTABLE if this occurs.

See Section 4.7.5 for details of the stored result on integer overflow.

4.10.10 Convert Integer to VAX Floating

Format:

CVTQy   Fb.rq,Fc.wx   !Floating-point Operate format

Operation:

Fc ←   {conversion of Fbv<63:0>}

Exceptions:

None

Instruction mnemonics:

CVTQF   Convert Quadword to F_floating
CVTQG   Convert Quadword to G_floating

Qualifiers:

Rounding: Chopped (/C)

Description:

The two's-complement quadword operand in register Fb is converted to a single-
or double-precision floating result and written to register Fc. The conversion
complements a number if negative, normalizes it, rounds to the target precision,
and packs the result with an appropriate sign and exponent field.

4.10.11 Convert VAX Floating to VAX Floating

Format:

> CVTxy   Fb.rx,Fc.wx   !Floating-point Operate format

Operation:

> Fc ← {conversion of Fbv}

Exceptions:

> Invalid Operation
>
> Overflow
>
> Underflow

Instruction mnemonics:

> CVTDG   Convert D_floating to G_floating
>
> CVTGD   Convert G_floating to D_floating
>
> CVTGF   Convert G_floating to F_floating

Qualifiers:

> Rounding: Chopped (/C)
>
> Trapping: Software (/S)
>
>   Underflow Enable (/U)

Description:

The floating operand in register Fb is converted to the specified alternate floating format and written to register Fc.

An invalid operation trap is signaled if the operand has exp=0 and is not a true zero (that is, VAX reserved operands *and* dirty zeros trap). The contents of Fc are UNPREDICTABLE if this occurs.

See Section 4.7.5 for details of the stored result on overflow or underflow.

Notes:

- The only arithmetic operations on D_floating values are conversions to and from G_floating. The conversion to G_floating rounds or chops as specified, removing three fraction bits. The conversion from G_floating to D_floating adds three low-order zeros as fraction bits, then the 8-bit exponent range is checked for overflow /underflow.

- The conversion from G_floating to F_floating rounds or chops to single precision, then the 8-bit exponent range is checked for overflow/underflow.

- No conversion from F_floating to G_floating is required, since F_floating values are always stored in registers as equivalent G_floating values.

4.10.12 Convert IEEE Floating to Integer

Format:

CVTTQ   Fb.rx,Fc.wq   !Floating-point Operate format

Operation:

```
Fc ←  {conversion of Fbv}
```

Exceptions:

Invalid Operation
Inexact Result
Integer Overflow

Instruction mnemonics:

CVTTQ   Convert T_floating to Quadword

Qualifiers:

Rounding: Dynamic (/D)

Minus infinity (/M)

Chopped (/C)

Trapping: Software (/S)

Integer Overflow Enable (/V)

Inexact Enable (/I)

Description:

The floating operand in register Fb is converted to a two's-complement number and written to register Fc. The conversion aligns the operand fraction with the binary point just to the right of bit zero, rounds as specified, and complements the result if negative.

An invalid operation trap is signaled if either operand has exp=0 and a non-zero fraction (IEEE denormals trap), or if exp=all-ones (IEEE NaNs and infinities trap).

The contents of Fc are UNPREDICTABLE if this occurs.

See Section 4.7.5 for details of the stored result on integer overflow and inexact result.

4.10.13 Convert Integer to IEEE Floating

Format:

CVTQy Fb.rq,Fc.wx   !Floating-point Operate format

Operation:

```
Fc ← {conversion of Fbv<63:0>}
```

Exceptions:

Inexact Result

Instruction mnemonics:

CVTQS   Convert Quadword to S_floating
CVTQT   Convert Quadword to T_floating

Qualifiers:

Rounding: Dynamic (/D)
      Minus infinity (/M)
      Chopped (/C)
Trapping: Software (/S)
      Inexact Enable (/I)

Description:

The two's-complement operand in register Fb is converted to a single- or double-precision floating result and written to register Fc. The conversion complements a number if negative, normalizes it, rounds to the target precision, and packs the result with an appropriate sign and exponent field.

See Section 4.7.5 for details of the stored result on inexact result.

4.10.14 Convert IEEE Floating to IEEE Floating

Format:

CVTTS   Fb.rx,Fc.wx   !Floating-point Operate format

Operation:

```
Fc ← {conversion of Fbv}
```

Exceptions:

Invalid Operation
Overflow
Underflow
Inexact Result

Instruction mnemonics:

CVTTS   Convert T_floating to S_floating

Qualifiers:

Rounding:	Dynamic (/D)
	Minus infinity (/M)
	Chopped (/C)
Trapping:	Software (/S)
	Underflow Enable (/U)
	Inexact Enable (/I)

Description:

The floating operand in register Fb is converted to the specified alternate floating format and written to register Fc.

An invalid operation trap is signaled if either operand has exp=0 and a non-zero fraction (IEEE denormals trap), or if exp=all-ones (IEEE NaNs and infinities trap).

The contents of Fc are UNPREDICTABLE if this occurs.

See Section 4.7.5 for details of the stored result on overflow, underflow, or inexact result.

Notes:

- No conversion from S_floating to T_floating is required, since S_floating values are always stored in registers as equivalent T_floating values.

4.10.15 VAX Floating Divide

Format:

DIVx   Fa.rx,Fb.rx,Fc.wx   !Floating-point Operate format

Operation:

Fc ← Fav / Fbv

Exceptions:

Invalid Operation
Division by Zero
Overflow
Underflow

Instruction mnemonics:

DIVF   Divide F_floating
DIVG   Divide G_floating

Qualifiers:

Rounding: Chopped (/C)
Trapping: Software (/S)
               Underflow Enable (/U)

Description:

The dividend operand in register Fa is divided by the divisor operand in register Fb, and the quotient is written to register Fc.

The quotient is rounded or chopped to the specified precision and then the corresponding range is checked for overflow/underflow. The single-precision operation on canonical single-precision values produces a canonical single-precision result.

An invalid operation trap is signaled if either operand has exp=0 and is not a true zero (that is, VAX reserved operands *and* dirty zeros trap). The contents of Fc are UNPREDICTABLE if this occurs.

A division by zero trap is signaled if Fbv is zero. The contents of Fc are UNPREDICTABLE if this occurs.

See Section 4.7.5 for details of the stored result on overflow or underflow.

4.10.16 IEEE Floating Divide

Format:

DIVx   Fa.rx,Fb.rx,Fc.wx   !Floating-point Operate format

Operation:

Fc ← Fav / Fbv

Exceptions:

Invalid Operation
Division by Zero
Overflow
Underflow
Inexact Result

Instruction mnemonics:

DIVS   Divide S_floating
DIVT   Divide T_floating

Qualifiers:

Rounding: Dynamic (/D)
               Minus infinity (/M)
               Chopped (/C)
Trapping: Software (/S)
               Underflow Enable (/U)
               Inexact Enable (/I)

Description:

The dividend operand in register Fa is divided by the divisor operand in register Fb, and the quotient is written to register Fc.

The quotient is rounded to the specified precision, and then the corresponding range is checked for overflow/underflow. The single-precision operation on canonical single-precision values produces a canonical single-precision result.

An invalid operation trap is signaled if either operand has exp=0 and a non-zero fraction (IEEE denormals trap), or if exp=all-ones (IEEE NaNs and infinities trap).

The contents of Fc are UNPREDICTABLE if this occurs.

A division by zero trap is signaled if Fbv is zero. The contents of Fc are UNPREDICTABLE if this occurs.

See Section 4.7.5 for details of the stored result on overflow, underflow, or inexact result.

4.10.17 VAX Floating Multiply

Format:

> MULx   Fa.rx,Fb.rx,Fc.wx   !Floating-point Operate format

Operation:

> Fc ← Fav * Fbv

Exceptions:

> Invalid Operation
> Overflow
> Underflow

Instruction mnemonics:

> MULF   Multiply F_floating
> MULG   Multiply G_floating

Qualifiers:

> Rounding: Chopped (/C)
> Trapping: Software (/S)
>   Underflow Enable (/U)

Description:

The multiplicand operand in register Fb is multiplied by the multiplier operand in register Fa, and the product is written to register Fc.

The product is rounded or chopped to the specified precision, and then the corresponding range is checked for overflow/underflow. The single-precision operation on canonical single-precision values produces a canonical single-precision result.

An invalid operation trap is signaled if either operand has exp=0 and is not a true zero (that is, VAX reserved operands *and* dirty zeros trap). The contents of Fc are UNPREDICTABLE if this occurs.

See Section 4.7.5 for details of the stored result on overflow or underflow.

4.10.18 IEEE Floating Multiply

Format:

MULx   Fa.rx,Fb.rx,Fc.wx   !Floating-point Operate format

Operation:

Fc ← Fav * Fbv

Exceptions:

Invalid Operation
Overflow
Underflow
Inexact Result

Instruction mnemonics:

MULS   Multiply S_floating
MULT   Multiply T_floating

Qualifiers:

Rounding: Dynamic (/D)
             Minus infinity (/M)
             Chopped (/C)
Trapping: Software (/S)
             Underflow Eenable (/U)
             Inexact Enable (/I)

Description:

The multiplicand operand in register Fb is multiplied by the multiplier operand in register Fa, and the product is written to register Fc.

The product is rounded to the specified precision, and then the corresponding range is checked for overflow/underflow. The single-precision operation on canonical single-precision values produces a canonical single-precision result.

An invalid operation trap is signaled if either operand has exp=0 and a non-zero fraction (IEEE denormals trap), or if exp=all-ones (IEEE NaNs and infinities trap).

The contents of Fc are UNPREDICTABLE if this occurs.

See Section 4.7.5 for details of the stored result on overflow, underflow, or inexact result.

4.10.19 VAX Floating Subtract

Format:

    SUBx   Fa.rx,Fb.rx,Fc.wx   !Floating-point Operate format

Operation:

    Fc ← Fav - Fbv

Exceptions:

    Invalid Operation
    Overflow
    Underflow

Instruction mnemonics:

SUBF	Subtract F_floating
SUBG	Subtract G_floating

Qualifiers:

Rounding:	Chopped (/C)
Trapping:	Software (/S)
	Underflow Enable (/U)

Description:

The subtrahend operand in register Fb is subtracted from the minuend operand in register Fa, and the difference is written to register Fc.

The difference is rounded or chopped to the specified precision, and then the corresponding range is checked for overflow/underflow. The single-precision operation on canonical single-precision values produces a canonical single-precision result.

An invalid operation trap is signaled if either operand has exp=0 and is not a true zero (that is, VAX reserved operands *and* dirty zeros trap). The contents of Fc are UNPREDICTABLE if this occurs.

See Section 4.7.5 for details of the stored result on overflow or underflow.

4.10.20 IEEE Floating Subtract

Format:

SUBx   Fa.rx,Fb.rx,Fc.wx   !Floating-point Operate format

Operation:

Fc ← Fav - Fbv

Exceptions:

Invalid Operation
Overflow
Underflow
Inexact Result

Instruction mnemonics:

SUBS   Subtract S_floating
SUBT   Subtract T_floating

Qualifiers:

Rounding: Dynamic (/D)
              Minus infinity (/M)
              Chopped (/C)
Trapping: Software (/S)
              Underflow Enable (/U)
              Inexact Enable (/I)

Description:

The subtrahend operand in register Fb is subtracted from the minuend operand in register Fa, and the difference is written to register Fc.

The difference is rounded to the specified precision, and then the corresponding range is checked for overflow/underflow. The single-precision operation on canonical single-precision values produces a canonical single-precision result.

An invalid operation trap is signaled if either operand has exp=0 and a non-zero fraction (IEEE denormals trap), or if exp=all-ones (IEEE NaNs and infinities trap).

The contents of Fc are UNPREDICTABLE if this occurs.

See Section 4.7.5 for details of the stored result on overflow, underflow, or inexact result.

4.11 Miscellaneous Instructions

Alpha provides the miscellaneous instructions shown in Table 4–12.

Table 4–12: Miscellaneous Instructions Summary

Mnemonic	Operation
CALL_PAL	Call Privileged Architecture Library Routine
FETCH	Prefetch Data
FETCH_M	Prefetch Data, Modify Intent
MB	Memory Barrier
RPCC	Read Process Cycle Counter
TRAPB	Trap Barrier

4.11.1 Call Privileged Architecture Library

Format:

CALL_PAL   fnc.ir   !PAL format

Operation:

```
{Stall instruction issuing until all
prior instructions are guaranteed to
complete without incurring exceptions.}
{Trap to PALcode.}
```

Exceptions:

None

Instruction mnemonics:

CALL_PAL   Call Privileged Architecture Library

Qualifiers:

None

Description:

The CALL_PAL instruction is not issued until all previous instructions are guaranteed to complete without exceptions. If an exception occurs, the continuation PC in the exception stack frame points to the CALL_PAL instruction. The CALL_PAL instruction causes a trap to PALcode.

4.11.2 Prefetch Data

Format:

FETCHx   0(Rb.ab)   !Memory format

Operation:

```
va ← {Rbv}
{Optionally prefetch aligned 512-byte block surrounding va.}
```

Exceptions:

None

Instruction mnemonics:

FETCH   Prefetch Data
FETCH_M   Prefetch Data, Modify Intent

Qualifiers:

None

Description:

The virtual address is given by Rbv. This address is used to designate an aligned 512-byte block of data. An implementation may optionally attempt to move all or part of this block (or a larger surrounding block) of data to a faster-access part of the memory hierarchy, in anticipation of subsequent Load or Store instructions that access that data.

The FETCH instruction is a hint to the implementation that may allow faster execution. An implementation is free to ignore the hint. If prefetching is done in an implementation, the order of fetch within the designated block is UNPREDICTABLE.

The FETCH_M instruction gives the additional hint that modifications (stores) to some or all of the data block are anticipated.

No exceptions are generated by FETCHx. If a Load (or Store in the case of FETCH_ M) that uses the same address would fault, the prefetch request is ignored. It is UNPREDICTABLE whether a TB-miss fault is ever taken by FETCHx.

IMPLEMENTATION NOTE

Implementations are encouraged to take the TB-miss fault, then continue the prefetch.

The programming model for effective use of FETCH and FETCH_M is given in *Appendix A*.

SOFTWARE NOTE

FETCH is intended to help software overlap memory latencies on the order of 100 cycles. FETCH is unlikely to help (or be implemented) for memory latencies on the order of 10 cycles. Code scheduling should be used to overlap such short latencies.

4.11.3 Memory Barrier

Format:

    MB   !Memory format

Operation:

```
{Guarantee that all subsequent loads or stores
will not access memory until after all previous
loads and stores have accessed memory, as
observed by other processors.}
```

Exceptions:

    None

Instruction mnemonics:

    MB   Memory Barrier

Qualifiers:

    None

Description:

The use of the Memory Barrier (MB) instruction is required only in multiprocessor systems.

In the absence of an MB instruction, loads and stores to different physical locations are allowed to complete out of order on the issuing processor as observed by other processors. The MB instruction allows memory accesses to be serialized on the issuing processor as observed by other processors. See Chapter 5 for details on using the MB instruction to serialize these accesses. Chapter 5 also details coordinating memory accesses across processors.

Note that MB ensures serialization only; it does not necessarily accelerate the progress of memory operations.

4.11.4 Read Process Cycle Counter

Format:

> RPCC   Ra.wq   !Memory format

Operation:

> Ra ← {cycle counter}

Exceptions:

> None

Instruction mnemonics:

> RPCC   Read Process Cycle Counter

Qualifiers:

> None

Description:

Register Ra is written with the process cycle counter (PCC).

The low-order 32 bits of the process cycle counter is an unsigned 32-bit integer that increments once per N CPU cycles, where N is an implementation-specific integer in the range 1..16. The cycle counter frequency is the number of times the process cycle counter gets incremented per second, rounded to a 64-bit integer. The integer count wraps to 0 from a count of $FFFF\ FFFF_{16}$. The counter wraps no more frequently than 1.5 times the implementation's interval clock interrupt period (which is two thirds of the interval clock interrupt frequency). The high-order 32 bits of the process cycle counter are an offset that when added to the low-order 32 bits gives the cycle count for this process.

The process cycle counter is suitable for timing intervals on the order of nanoseconds and may be used for detailed performance characterization. It is required on all implementations. PCC is required for every processor, and each processor in a multiprocessor system has its own private, independent PCC.

As an example, consider the following code that returns in R0 the current cycle count MOD 2**32.

```
RPCC    R0               ; Read the process cycle counter
SLL     R0, #32, R1      ; line up the offset and count fields
ADDQ    R0, R1, R0       ; do add
SRL     R0, #32, R0      ; zero extend the cycle count to 64 bits
```

4.11.5 Trap Barrier

Format:

TRAPB   !Memory format

Operation:

```
{Stall instruction issuing until all prior instructions are
guaranteed to complete without incurring arithmetic traps.}
```

Exceptions:

None

Instruction mnemonics:

TRAPB   Trap Barrier

Qualifiers:

None

Description:

The TRAPB instruction allows software to guarantee that in a pipelined implementation, all previous arithmetic instructions will complete without incurring any arithmetic traps before any instructions after the TRAPB are issued. For example, TRAPB should be used before changing an exception handler to ensure that all exceptions on previous instructions are processed in the current exception-handling environment.

4.12 VAX Compatibility Instructions

Alpha provides the instructions shown in Table 4–13 for use in translated VAX code. These instructions are not a permanent part of the architecture and will not be available in some future implementations. They are intended to preserve customer assumptions about VAX instruction atomicity in porting code from VAX to Alpha.

These instructions should be generated only by the VAX-to-Alpha software translator; they should never be used in native Alpha code. Any native code that uses them may cease to work.

Table 4–13: VAX Compatibility Instructions Summary

Mnemonic	Operation
RC	Read and Clear
RS	Read and Set

4.12.1 VAX Compatibility Instructions

Format:

Rx   Ra.wq   !Memory format

Operation:

```
Ra ←  intr_flag
intr_flag ←  0                    !RC
intr_flag ←  1                    !RS
```

Exceptions:

None

Instruction mnemonics:

RC   Read and Clear

RS   Read and Set

Qualifiers:

None

Description:

The intr_flag is returned in Ra and then cleared to zero (RC) or set to one (RS).

These instructions may be used to determine whether the sequence of Alpha instructions between RS and RC (corresponding to a single VAX instruction) was executed without interruption or exception.

Intr_flag is a per-processor state bit. The intr_flag is cleared if that processor encounters a CALL_PAL REI instruction.

It is UNPREDICTABLE whether a processor's intr_flag is affected when that processor executes an LDx_L or STx_C instruction. A processor's intr_flag is not affected when that processor executes a normal load or store instruction.

A processor's intr_flag is not affected when that processor executes a taken branch.

NOTE
These instructions are intended *only* for use by the VAX-to-Alpha software translator; they should never be used by native code.

Chapter 5

System Architecture and Programming Implications (I)

5.1 Introduction

Portions of the Alpha architecture have implications for programming, and the system structure, of both uniprocessor and multiprocessor implementations. Architectural implications considered in the following sections are:

- Physical memory behavior

- Caches and write buffers

- Translation buffers and virtual caches

- Data sharing

- Read/write ordering

- Stacks

- Arithmetic traps

To meet the requirements of the Alpha architecture, software and hardware implementors need to take these issues into consideration.

5.2 Physical Memory Behavior

Alpha physical memory space is divided into four regions, based on the two most significant, implemented, physical address bits. Each region's behavior can be described in terms of its coherency, granularity, width, and memory-like behavior.

5.2.1 Coherency of Memory Access

Alpha implementations must provide a coherent view of memory, in which each write by a processor or I/O device (hereafter, called "processor") becomes visible to all other processors. No distinction is made between coherency of "memory space" and "I/O space".

Memory coherency may be provided in different ways, for each of the four physical address regions.

Possible per-region policies include, but are not restricted to:

1. No caching

    No copies are kept of data in a region; all reads and writes access the actual data location (memory or I/O register).

2. Write-through caching

   Copies are kept of any data in the region; reads may use the copies, but writes update the actual data location and either update or invalidate all copies.

3. Write-back caching

   Copies are kept of any data in the region; reads and writes may use the copies, and writes use additional state to determine whether there are other copies to invalidate or update.

Part of the coherency policy implemented for a given physical address region may include restrictions on excess data transfers (performing more accesses to a location than is necessary to acquire or change the location's value), or may specify data transfer widths (the granularity used to access a location).

Independent of coherency policy, a processor may use different hardware or different hardware resource policies for caching or buffering different physical address regions.

5.2.2 Granularity of Memory Access

For each region, an implementation must support aligned quadword access and may optionally support aligned longword access.

For a quadword access region, accesses to physical memory must be implemented such that independent accesses to adjacent aligned quadwords produce the same results regardless of the order of execution. Further, an access to an aligned quadword must be done in a single atomic operation.

For a longword access region, accesses to physical memory must be implemented such that independent accesses to adjacent aligned longwords produce the same results regardless of the order of execution. Further, an access to an aligned longword must be done in a single atomic operation, and an access to an aligned quadword must also be done in a single atomic operation.

In this context, "atomic" means that if different processors do simultaneous reads and writes of the same data, it must not be possible to observe a partial write of the subject longword or quadword.

5.2.3 Width of Memory Access

Subject to the granularity, ordering, and coherency constraints given in Sections 5.2.1, 5.2.2, and 5.6, accesses to physical memory may be freely cached, buffered, and prefetched.

A processor may read more physical memory data (such as a full cache block) than is actually accessed, writes may trigger reads, and writes may write back more data than is actually updated. A processor may elide multiple reads and/or writes to the same data.

5.2.4 Memory-Like Behavior

A memory-like region obeys the following rules:

- Each page frame in the region either exists in its entirety or does not exist in its entirety; there are no holes within a page frame.

- All locations that exist are read/write.

- A write to a location followed by a read from that location returns precisely the bits written; all bits act as memory.

- A write to one location does not change any other location.

- Reads have no side effects.

- Longword access granularity is provided.

- Instruction-fetch is supported.

- Load-locked and store-conditional are supported.

Non-memory-like regions may have much more arbitrary behavior:

- Unimplemented locations or bits may exist anywhere.

- Some locations or bits may be read-only and others write-only.

- Address ranges may overlap, such that a write to one location changes the bits read from a different location.

- Reads may have side effects, although this is strongly discouraged.

- Longword granularity need not be supported.

- Instruction-fetch need not be supported.

- Load-locked and store-conditional need not be supported.

> **HARDWARE/SOFTWARE COORDINATION NOTE**
> The details of such behavior are outside the scope of the Alpha architecture. Specific processor and I/O device implementations may choose and document whatever behavior they need. It is the responsibility of system designers to impose enough consistency to allow processors successfully to access matching non-memory devices in a coherent way.

5.3 Translation Buffers and Virtual Caches

A system may choose to include a a virtual instruction cache (virtual I-cache) or a virtual data cache (virtual D-cache). A system may also choose to include either a combined data and instruction Translation Buffer (TB) or separate data and instruction TBs (DTB and ITB). The contents of these caches and/or translation buffers may become invalid, depending on what operating system activity is being performed.

Whenever a nonsoftware field of a valid Page Table Entry (PTE) is modified, copies of that PTE must be made coherent. PALcode mechanisms are available to clear all TBs, both DTB and ITB entries for a given VA, either DTB or ITB entries for a given VA, or all entries with the Address Space Match (ASM) bit clear. Virtual D-cache entries are made coherent whenever the corresponding DTB entry is requested to be cleared by any of the appropriate PALcode mechanisms. Virtual I-cache entries can be made coherent via the CALL_PALL IMB instruction.

If a processor implements address space numbers (ASNs), and the old PTE has the address space match (ASM) bit clear (ASNs in use) and the valid bit set, then entries can also effectively be made coherent by assigning a new, unused ASN to the currently running process and not reusing the previous ASN before calling the appropriate PALcode routine to invalidate the Translation Buffer (TB).

In a multiprocessor environment, making the TBs and/or caches coherent on only one processor is not always sufficient. An operating system must arrange to perform the above actions on each processor that could possibly have copies of the PTE or data for any affected page.

5.4 Caches and Write Buffers

A hardware implementation may include mechanisms to reduce memory access time by making local copies of recently used memory contents (or those expected to be used) or by buffering writes to complete at a later time. Caches and write buffers are examples of these mechanisms. They must be implemented so that their existence is transparent to software (except for timing, error reporting/control/recovery, and modification to the I-stream).

The following requirements must be met by all cache/write-buffer implementations. All processors must provide a coherent view of memory.

1. Write buffers may be used to delay and aggregate writes. From the viewpoint of another processor, buffered writes appear not to have happened yet. (Write buffers must not delay writes indefinitely. See Section 5.6.1.9.)

2. Write-back caches must be able to detect a later write from another processor and invalidate or update the cache contents.

3. A processor must guarantee that a data store to a location followed by a data load from the same location must read the updated value.

4. Cache prefetching is allowed, but virtual caches must not prefetch from invalid pages.

5. A processor must guarantee that all of its previous writes are visible to all other processors before a HALT instruction completes. A processor must guarantee that its caches are coherent with the rest of the system before continuing from a HALT.

6. If battery backup is supplied, a processor must guarantee that the memory system remains coherent across a powerfail/recovery sequence. Data that was written by the processor before the powerfail may not be lost, and any caches must be in a valid state before (and if) normal instruction processing is continued after power is restored.

7. Virtual instruction caches are not required to notice modifications of the virtual I-stream (they need not be coherent with the rest of memory). Software that creates or modifies the instruction stream must execute a CALL_PAL IMB before trying to execute the new instructions.

   For example, if two different virtual addresses, VA1 and VA2, map to the same page frame, a store to VA1 modifies the virtual I-stream fetched via VA2.

   However, the sequence:

   1. Change the mapping of an I-stream page from valid to invalid, then

   2. Copy the corresponding page frame to a new page frame, then

   3. Change the original mapping to be valid and point to the new page frame

   does not modify the virtual I-stream (this might happen in soft page faults).

8. Physical instruction caches are not required to notice modifications of the physical I-stream (they need not be coherent with the rest of memory), except for certain paging activity. (See Section 5.6.1.9.) Software that creates or modifies the instruction stream must execute a CALL_PAL IMB before trying to execute the new instructions.

   In this context, to "modify the physical I-stream" means any Store to the same physical address that is subsequently fetched as an instruction.

In this context, to "modify the virtual I-stream" means any Store to the same physical address that is subsequently fetched as an instruction via some corresponding (virtual address, ASN) pair, or to change the virtual-to-physical address mapping so that different values are fetched.

5.5 Data Sharing

In a multiprocessor environment, writes to shared data must be synchronized by the programmer.

5.5.1 Atomic Change of a Single Datum

The ordinary STL and STQ instructions can be used to perform an atomic change of a shared aligned longword or quadword. ("Change" means that the new value is not a function of the old value.) In particular, an ordinary STL or STQ instruction can be used to change a variable that could be simultaneously accessed via an LDx_L/STx_C sequence.

5.5.2 Atomic Update of a Single Datum

The load-locked/store-conditional instructions may be used to perform an atomic update of a shared aligned longword or quadword. ("Update" means that the new value is a function of the old value.)

The following sequence performs a read-modify-write operation on location x. Only register-to-register operate instructions and branch fall-throughs may occur in the sequence:

```
try_again:
        LDQ_L   R1,x
        <modify R1>
        STQ_C   R1,x
        BEQ     R1,no_store
        :
        :
no_store:
        <code to check for excessive iterations>
        BR      try_again
```

If this sequence runs with no exceptions or interrupts, and no other processor writes to location x (more precisely, the locked range including x) between the LDQ_L and STQ_C instructions, then the STQ_C shown in the example stores the modified value in x and sets R1 to 1. If, however, the sequence encounters exceptions or interrupts that eventually continue the sequence, or another processor writes to x, then the STQ_C does not store and sets R1 to 0. In this case, the sequence is repeated via the branches to no_store and try_again. This repetition continues until the reasons for exceptions or interrupts are removed, and no interfering store is encountered.

To be useful, the sequence must be constructed so that it can be replayed an arbitrary number of times, giving the same result values each time. A sufficient (but not necessary) condition is that, within the sequence, the set of operand destinations and the set of operand sources are disjoint.

NOTE
A sufficiently long instruction sequence between LDQ_ L and STQ_C will never complete, because periodic timer interrupts will always occur before the sequence completes. The rules in *Appendix A* describe sequences that will eventually complete in *all* Alpha implementations.

This load-locked/store-conditional paradigm may be used whenever an atomic update of a shared aligned quadword is desired, including getting the effect of atomic byte writes.

5.5.3 Atomic Update of Data Structures

Before accessing shared writable data structures (those that are not a single aligned longword or quadword), the programmer can acquire control of the data structure by using an atomic update to set a software lock variable. Such a software lock can be cleared with an ordinary store instruction.

A software-critical section, therefore, may look like the sequence:

```
stq_c_loop:
spin_loop:
        LDQ_L  R1,lock_variable    \
        BLBS   R1,already_set      \
        OR     R1,#1,R2              > Set lock bit
        STQ_C  R2,lock_variable    /
        BEQ    R2,stq_c_fail       /

        MB
        <critical section: updates various data structures>
        MB

        STQ    R31,lock_variable    ; Clear lock bit
        :
        :
already_set:
        <code to block or reschedule or test for too many iterations>
        BR     spin_loop
stq_c_fail:
        <code to test for too many iterations>
        BR     stq_c_loop
```

This code has a number of subtleties:

1. If the lock_variable is already set, the spin loop is done without doing any stores. This avoidance of stores improves memory subsystem performance and avoids the deadlock described below.

2. If the lock_variable is actually being changed from 0 to 1, and the STQ_C fails (due to an interrupt, or because another processor simultaneously changed lock_variable), the entire process starts over by reading the lock_variable again.

3. Only the fall-through path of the BLBS does a STx_C; some implementations may not allow a successful STx_C after a branch-taken.

4. Only register-to-register operate instructions are used to do the modify.

5. Both conditional branches are forward branches, so they are properly predicted not to be taken (to match the common case of no contention for the lock).

6. The OR writes its result to a second register; this allows the OR and the BLBS to be interchanged if that would give a faster instruction schedule.

7. Other operate instructions (from the critical section) may be scheduled into the LDQ_L..STQ_C sequence, so long as they do not fault or trap, and they give correct results if repeated; other memory or operate instructions may be scheduled between the STQ_C and BEQ.

8. The MB instructions are discussed in Section 5.5.4.

9. An ordinary STQ instruction is used to clear the lock_variable.

It would be a performance mistake to spin-wait by repeating the full LDQ_L..STQ_C sequence (to move the BLBS after the BEQ) because that sequence may repeatedly change the software lock_variable from "locked" to "locked," with each write causing extra access delays in all other caches that contain the lock_variable. In the extreme, spin-waits that contain writes may deadlock as follows:

If, when one processor spins with writes, another processor is modifying (not changing) the lock_variable, then the writes on the first processor may cause the STx_C of the modify on the second processor always to fail.

This deadlock situation is avoided by:

- Having only one processor do a store (no STx_C), or

- Having no write in the spin loop, or

- Doing a write *only* if the shared variable actually changes state ($1 \rightarrow 1$ does not change state).

5.5.4 Ordering Considerations for Shared Data Structures

A critical section sequence, such as shown in Section 5.5.3, is conceptually only three steps:

1. Acquire software lock

2. Critical section—read/write shared data

3. Clear software lock

In the absence of explicit instructions to the contrary, the Alpha architecture allows reads and writes to be reordered. While this may allow more implementation speed and overlap, it can also create undesired side effects on shared data structures. Normally, the critical section just described would have two instructions added to it:

```
<acquire software lock>
MB (memory barrier #1)
<critical section -- read/write shared data>
MB (memory barrier #2)
<clear software lock>
```

The first memory barrier prevents any reads (from within the critical section) from being prefetched before the software lock is acquired; such prefetched reads would potentially contain stale data.

The second memory barrier prevents any reads or writes (from within the critical section) from being delayed past the clearing of the software lock; such delayed accesses could interact with the next user of the shared data, defeating the purpose of the software lock entirely.

SOFTWARE NOTE

In the VAX architecture, many instructions provide non-interruptable read-modify-write sequences to memory variables. Most programmers never regard data sharing as an issue.

In the Alpha architecture, programmers must pay more attention to synchronizing access to shared data; for example, to AST routines. In the VAX, a programmer can use an ADDL2 to update a variable that is shared between a "MAIN" routine and an AST routine, if running on a single processor. In the Alpha architecture, a programmer must deal with AST shared data by using multiprocessor shared data sequences.

5.6 Read/Write Ordering

This section does not apply to programs that run on a single processor and do not write to the instruction stream. On a single processor, all memory accesses appear to happen in the order specified by the programmer. This section deals entirely with predictable read/write ordering across multiple processors.

The order of reads and writes done in an Alpha implementation may differ from that specified by the programmer.

For any two memory references A and B, either A must occur before B in all Alpha implementations, B must occur before A, or they are UNORDERED. In the last case, software cannot depend upon one occurring first: the order may vary from implementation to implementation, and even from run to run or moment to moment on a single implementation.

If two references cannot be shown to be ordered by the rules given, they are UNORDERED and implementations are free to do them in any order that is convenient. Implementations may take advantage of this freedom to deliver substantially higher performance.

The discussion that follows first defines the architectural issue sequence of memory references on a single processor, then defines the (partial) ordering on this issue sequence that *all* Alpha implementations are required to maintain.

The individual issue sequences on multiple processors are merged into access sequences at each shared memory location. The discussion defines the (partial) ordering on the individual access sequences that *all* Alpha implementations are required to maintain.

The net result is that for any code that executes on multiple processors, one can determine which memory accesses are required to occur before others on *all* Alpha implementations and hence can write useful shared-variable software.

Software writers can force one reference to occur before another by inserting a memory barrier instruction (MB or IMB) between the references.

5.6.1 Alpha Shared Memory Model

An Alpha system consists of a collection of *processors* and shared coherent *memories* that are accessible by all processors. (There may also be unshared memories, but they are outside the scope of this section.)

A *processor* is an Alpha CPU or an I/O device (or anything else that gets added).

A *shared memory* is the primary storage place for one or more locations.

A *location* is an aligned quadword, specified by its physical address. Multiple virtual addresses may map to the same physical address. Ordering considerations are based only on the physical address.

> **IMPLEMENTATION NOTE**
>
> An implementation may allow a location to have multiple physical addresses, but the rules for accesses via mixtures of the addresses are implementation-specific and outside the scope of this section. Accesses via exactly one of the physical addresses follow the rules described next.

Each processor may generate *accesses* to shared memory locations. There are five types of accesses:

1. Instruction fetch by processor i to location x, returning value a, denoted Pi:I(x,a).

2. Data read by processor i to location x, returning value a, denoted Pi:R(x,a).

3. Data write by processor i to location x, storing value a, denoted Pi:W(x,a).

4. Memory barrier instruction issued by processor i, denoted Pi:MB.

5. I-stream memory barrier instruction issued by processor i, denoted Pi:IMB.

The first access type is also called an I-stream access or I-fetch. The next two are also called D-stream accesses. The first three types collectively are called read/write accesses, denoted Pi:*(x,a). The last two types collectively are called barriers.

During actual execution in an Alpha system, each processor has a time-ordered *issue sequence* of all the memory references presented by that processor (to all memory locations), and each location has a time-ordered *access sequence* of all the accesses presented to that location (from all processors).

5.6.1.1 Architectural Definition of Processor Issue Sequence

The issue sequence for a processor is architecturally defined with respect to a hypothetical simple implementation that contains one processor and a single shared memory, with no caches or buffers. This is the instruction execution model:

1. I-fetch: An Alpha instruction is fetched from memory.

2. Read/Write: That instruction is executed and runs to completion, including a single data read from memory for a Load instruction or a single data write to memory for a Store instruction.

3. Update: The PC for the processor is updated.

4. Loop: Repeat the above sequence indefinitely.

If the instruction fetch step gets a memory management fault, the I-fetch is not done and the PC is updated to point to a PALcode fault handler. If the read/write step gets a memory management fault, the read/write is not done and the PC is updated to point to a PALcode fault handler.

All memory references are aligned quadwords. For the purpose of defining ordering, aligned longword references are modeled as quadword references to the containing aligned quadword.

5.6.1.2 Definition of Processor Issue Order

A partial ordering, called processor issue order, is imposed on the issue sequence defined in Section 5.6.1.1.

For two accesses u and v issued by processor Pi, u is said to PRECEDE v IN ISSUE ORDER (<) if u occurs earlier than v in the issue sequence for Pi, and either of the following applies:

1. The access types are of the following issue order:

Table 5–1: Processor Issue Order

1st↓/2nd→	Pi:I(y,b)	Pi:R(y,b)	Pi:W(y,b)	Pi:MB	Pi:IMB
Pi:I(x,a)	< if x=y		< if x=y	<	<
Pi:R(x,a)		< if x=y	< if x=y	<	<
Pi:W(x,a)		< if x=y	< if x=y	<	<
Pi:MB		<	<	<	<
Pi:IMB	<	<	<	<	<

2. Or, u is a TB fill, for example, a PTE read in order to satisfy a TB miss, and v is an I- or D-stream access using that PTE (see Section 5.6.2).

Issue order is thus a partial order imposed on the architecturally specified issue sequence. Implementations are free to do memory accesses from a single processor in any sequence that is consistent with this partial order.

Note that accesses to different locations are ordered only with respect to barriers and TB fill. The table asymmetry for I-fetch allows writes to the I-stream to be incoherent until an IMB is executed.

5.6.1.3 Definition of Memory Access Sequence

The access sequence for a location cannot be observed directly, nor fully predicted before an actual execution, nor reproduced exactly from one execution to another. Nonetheless, some useful ordering properties must hold in all Alpha implementations.

5.6.1.4 Definition of Location Access Order

A partial ordering, called location access order, is imposed on the memory access sequence defined above.

For two accesses u and v to location x, u is said to PRECEDE v IN ACCESS ORDER (≪) if u occurs earlier than v in the access sequence for x, and at least one of them is a write:

Table 5–2: Location Access Order

1st↓/2nd→	Pi:I(x,b)	Pi:R(x,b)	Pi:W(x,b)
Pi:I(x,a)			≪
Pi:R(x,a)			≪
Pi:W(x,a)	≪	≪	≪

Access order is thus a partial order imposed on the actual access sequence for a given location. Each location has a separate access order. There is no direct ordering relationship between accesses to different locations.

Note that reads and I-fetches are ordered only with respect to writes.

5.6.1.5 Definition of Storage

If u is Pi:W(x,a), and v is either Pj:I(x,b) or Pj:R(x,b), and u≪v, and no w Pk:W(x,c) exists such that u≪w≪v, then the value b returned by v is exactly the value a written by u.

Conversely, if u is Pi:W(x,a), and v is either Pj:I(x,b) or Pj:R(x,b), and b=a (and a is distinguishable from values written by accesses other than u), then u≪v and for any other w Pk:W(x,c) either w≪u or v≪w.

The only way to communicate information between different processors is for one to write a shared location and the other to read the shared location and receive the newly written value. (In this context, the sending of an interrupt from processor Pi to processor Pj is modeled as Pi writing to a location INTij, and Pj reading from INTij.)

5.6.1.6 Relationship Between Issue Order and Access Order

If u is Pi:*(x,a), and v is Pi:*(x,b), one of which is a write, and u<v in the issue order for processor Pi, then u≪v in the access order for location x.

In other words, if two accesses to the same location are ordered on a given processor, they are ordered in the same way at the location.

5.6.1.7 Definition of Before

For two accesses u and v, u is said to be BEFORE v (⇐) if:

u < v or
u ≪ v or
there exists an access w such that:

  (u < w and w ⇐ v) or
  (u ≪ w and w ⇐ v).

In other words, "before" is the transitive closure over issue order and access order.

5.6.1.8 Definition of After

If u ⇐ v, then v is said to be AFTER u.

At most one of u ⇐ v and v ⇐ u is true.

5.6.1.9 Timeliness

Even in the absence of a barrier after the write, a write by one processor to a given location may not be delayed indefinitely in the access order for that location.

5.6.2 Litmus Tests

Many issues about writing and reading shared data can be cast into questions about whether a write is before or after a read. These questions can be answered by rigorously applying the ordering rules described previously to demonstrate whether the accesses in question are ordered at all.

Assume, in the litmus tests below, that initially all memory locations contain 1.

5.6.2.1 Litmus Test 1 (Impossible Sequence)

Pi	Pj
[U1] Pi:W(x,2)	[V1] Pj:R(x,2)
	[V2] Pj:R(x,1)

V1 reading 2 implies U1 ≪ V1, by the definition of storage
V2 reading 1 implies V2 ≪ U1, by the definition of storage
V1 < V2, by the definition of issue order

The first two orderings imply that V2 ⇐ V1, whereas the last implies that V1 ⇐ V2.

Both implications cannot be true. Thus, once a processor reads a new value from a location, it must never see an old value—time must not go backward. V2 must read 2.

5.6.2.2 Litmus Test 2 (Impossible Sequence)

Pi	Pj
[U1] Pi:W(x,2)	[V1] Pj:W(x,3)
	[V2] Pj:R(x,2)
	[V3] Pj:R(x,3)

V2 reading 2 implies V1 ⇐ U1
V3 reading 3 implies U1 ⇐ V1

Both implications cannot be true. Thus, once a processor reads a new value written by U1, any other writes that must precede the read must also precede U1. V3 must read 2.

5.6.2.3 Litmus Test 3 (Impossible Sequence)

Pi	Pj	Pk
[U1] Pi:W(x,2)	[V1] Pj:W(x,3)	[W1] Pk:R(x,3)
[U2] Pi:R(x,3)		[W2] Pk:R(x,2)

    U2 reading 3 implies U1 ⇐ V1
    W2 reading 2 implies V1 ⇐ U1

Both implications cannot be true. Again, time cannot go backward. If U2 reads 3 then W2 must read 3. Alternately, if W2 reads 2, then U2 must read 2.

5.6.2.4 Litmus Test 4 (Sequence Okay)

Pi	Pj
[U1] Pi:W(x,2)	[V1] Pj:R(y,2)
[U2] Pi:W(y,2)	[V2] Pj:R(x,1)

There are no conflicts in this sequence. U2 ⇐ V1 and V2 ⇐ U1. U1 and U2 are not ordered with respect to each other. V1 and V2 are not ordered with respect to each other. There is no conflicting implication that U1 ⇐ V2.

5.6.2.5 Litmus Test 5 (Sequence Okay)

Pi	Pj
[U1] Pi:W(x,2)	[V1] Pj:R(y,2)
	[V2] Pj:MB
[U2] Pi:W(y,2)	[V3] Pj:R(x,1)

There are no conflicts in this sequence. U2 ⇐ V1 ⇐ V3 ⇐ U1. There is no conflicting implication that U1 ⇐ U2.

5.6.2.6 Litmus Test 6 (Sequence Okay)

Pi	Pj
[U1] Pi:W(x,2)	[V1] Pj:R(y,2)
[U2] Pi:MB	
[U3] Pi:W(y,2)	[V2] Pj:R(x,1)

There are no conflicts in this sequence. V2 ⇐ U1 ⇐ U3 ⇐ V1. There is no conflicting implication that V1 ⇐ V2.

In scenarios 4, 5, and 6, writes to two different locations x and y are observed (by another processor) to occur in the opposite order than that in which they were performed. An update to y propagates quickly to Pj, but the update to x is delayed, and Pi and Pj do not both have MBs.

5.6.2.7 Litmus Test 7 (Impossible Sequence)

Pi	Pj
[U1] Pi:W(x,2)	[V1] Pj:R(y,2)
[U2] Pi:MB	[V2] Pj:MB
[U3] Pi:W(y,2)	[V3] Pj:R(x,1)

V1 reading 2 implies U3 ← V1
V3 reading 1 implies V3 ← U1
But, by transitivity, U1 ← U3 ← V1 ← V3

Both cannot be true, so if V1 reads 2, then V3 must also read 2.

5.6.2.8 Litmus Test 8 (Impossible Sequence)

Pi	Pj
[U1] Pi:W(x,2)	[V1] Pj:W(y,2)
[U2] Pi:MB	[V2] Pj:MB
[U3] Pi:R(y,1)	[V3] Pj:R(x,1)

U3 reading 1 implies U3 ← V1
V3 reading 1 implies V3 ← U1
But, by transitivity, U1 ← U3 ← V1 ← V3

Both cannot be true, so if U3 reads 1, then V3 must read 2, and vice versa.

5.6.2.9 Litmus Test 9 (Impossible Sequence)

Pi	Pj
[U1] Pi:W(x,2)	[V1] Pj:W(x,3)
[U2] Pi:R(x,2)	[V2] Pj:R(x,3)
[U3] Pi:R(x,3)	[V3] Pj:R(x,2)

V3 reading 2 implies U1 ← V3
V2 ← V3 and V2 reading 3 implies V2 ← U1
V1 ← V2 and V2 ← U1 implies V1 ← U1

U3 reading 3 implies V1 ← U3
U2 ← U3 and U2 reading 2 implies U2 ← V1
U1 ← U2 and U2 ← V1 implies U1 ← V1

Both V1 ← U1 and U1 ← V1 cannot be true. Time cannot go backwards. If V3 reads 2, then U3 must read 2. Alternatively, If U3 reads 3, then V3 must read 3.

5.6.3 Implied Barriers

In Alpha, there are no implied barriers. If an implied barrier is needed for functionally correct access to shared data, it must be written as an explicit instruction. (Software must explicitly include any needed MB or IMB instructions.)

Alpha transitions such as the following have no built-in implied memory barriers:

- Entry to PALcode

- Sending and receiving interrupts

- Returning from exceptions, interrupts, or machine checks

- Swapping context

- Invalidating the Translation Buffer (TB)

Depending on implementation choices for maintaining cache coherency, some PAL /cache implementations may have an implied IMB in the I-stream TB fill routine, but this is transparent to the non-PAL programmer.

5.6.4 Implications for Software

Software must explicitly include MB or IMB instructions in the following circumstances.

5.6.4.1 Single-Processor Data Stream

No barriers are ever needed. A read to physical address x will always return the value written by the immediately preceding write to x in the processor issue sequence.

5.6.4.2 Single-Processor Instruction Stream

An I-fetch from virtual or physical address x does not necessarily return the value written by the immediately preceding write to x in the issue sequence. To make the I-fetch reliably get the newly written instruction, an IMB is needed between the write and the I-fetch.

5.6.4.3 Multiple-Processor Data Stream (Including Single Processor with DMA I/O)

The only way to communicate shared data reliably is to write the shared data on one processor, then do an MB on that processor, then write a flag (equivalently, send an interrupt) signaling the other processor that the shared data is ready. Each receiving processor must read the new flag (equivalently, receive the interrupt), then do an MB, then read or update the shared data.

Leaving out the first MB removes the assurance that the shared data is written before the flag is.

Leaving out the second MB removes the assurance that the shared data is read or updated only after the flag is seen to change; in this case, an early read could see an old value, and an early update could be overwritten.

This implies that after a CPU has prepared some data buffer to be read from memory by a DMA I/O device (such as writing a buffer to disk), it must do an MB before starting the I/O, and the I/O device after receiving the start signal must logically do an MB before reading the data buffer.

This also implies that after a DMA I/O device has written some data to memory (such as paging in a page from disk), the DMA device must logically do an MB before posting a completion interrupt, and the interrupt handler software must do an MB before the data is guaranteed to be visible to the interrupted processor. Other processors must also do MBs before they are guaranteed to see the new data.

An important special case occurs when a write is done (perhaps by an I/O device) to some physical page frame, then an MB, then a previously invalid PTE is changed to be a valid mapping of the physical page frame that was just written. In this case, all processors that access using the newly valid PTE must guarantee to deliver the newly written data after the TB miss, for both I-stream and D-stream accesses.

5.6.4.4 Multiple-Processor Instruction Stream (Including Single Processor with DMA I/O)

The only way to update the I-stream reliably is to write the shared I-stream on one processor, then do an IMB (MB if the writing processor is not going to execute the new I-stream) on that processor, then write a flag (equivalently, send an interrupt) signaling the other processor that the shared I-stream is ready. Each receiving processor must read the new flag (equivalently, receive the interrupt), then do an IMB, then fetch the shared I-stream.

Leaving out the first IMB(MB) removes the assurance that the shared I-stream is written before the flag is.

Leaving out the second IMB removes the assurance that the shared I-stream is read only *after* the flag is seen to change; in this case, an early read could see an old value.

This implies that after a DMA I/O device has written some I-stream to memory (such as paging in a page from disk), the DMA device must logically do an IMB(MB) before posting a completion interrupt, and the interrupt handler software must do an IMB before the I-stream is guaranteed to be visible to the interrupted processor. Other processors must also do IMBs before they are guaranteed to see the new I-stream.

An important special case occurs when a write is done (perhaps by an I/O device) to some physical page frame, then an IMB(MB), then a previously invalid PTE is changed to be a valid mapping of the physical page frame that was just written. In this case, all processors that access using the newly valid PTE must guarantee to deliver the newly written I-stream after the TB miss.

5.6.4.5 Multiple-Processor Context Switch

If a process migrates from executing on one processor to executing on another, the context switch operating system code must include a number of barriers.

A process migrates by having its context stored into memory, then eventually having that context reloaded on another processor. In between, some shared mechanism must be used to communicate that the context saved in memory by the first processor is available to the second processor. This could be done by using an interrupt, by using a flag bit associated with the saved context, or by using a shared-memory multiprocessor data structure, as follows:

First Processor	Second Processor
:	
Save state of current process.	
MB [1]	
Pass ownership of process context data structure memory. ⇒	Pick up ownership of process context data structure memory.
	MB [2]
	Restore state of new process context data structure memory.
	Make I-stream coherent [3].
	Make TB coherent [4].
	:
	Execute code for new process that accesses memory that is not common to all processes.

MB [1] ensures that the writes done to save the state of the current process happen before the ownership is passed.

MB [2] ensures that the reads done to load the state of the new process happen after the ownership is picked up and hence are reliably the values written by the processor saving the old state. Leaving this MB out makes the code fail if an old value of the context remains in the second processor's cache and invalidates from the writes done on the first processor are not delivered soon enough.

The TB on the second processor must be made coherent with any write to the page tables that may have occurred on the first processor just before the save of the process state. This must be done with a series of TB invalidate instructions to remove any nonglobal page mapping for this process, or by assigning an ASN that is unused on the second processor to the process. One of these actions must occur sometime before starting execution of the code for the new process that accesses memory (instruction or data) that is not common to all processes. A common method is to assign a new ASN after gaining ownership of the new process and before loading its context, which includes its ASN.

The D-cache on the second processor must be made coherent with any write to the D-stream that may have occurred on the first processor just before the save of process state. This is ensured by MB [2] and does not require any additional instructions.

The I-cache on the second processor must be made coherent with any write to the I-stream that may have occurred on the first processor just before the save of process state. This can be done with an IMB PAL call sometime before the execution of any code that is not common to all processes, More commonly, this can be done by forcing a TB miss (via the new ASN or via TB invalidate instructions) and using the TB-fill rule (see Section 5.6.4.3). This latter approach does not require any additional instruction.

Combining all these considerations gives:

First Processor	Second Processor
:	
Pick up ownership of process context data structure memory.	
MB	
Assign new ASN or invalidate TBs.	
Save state of current process.	
Restore state of new process.	
MB	:
Pass ownership of process context data structure memory. ⇒	Pickup ownership of new process context data structure memory.
:	MB
:	Assign new ASN or invalidate TBs.
	Save state of current process.
	Restore state of new process.
	MB
	Pass ownership of old process context data structure memory.
	:
	Execute code for new process that accesses memory that is not common to all processes.

Note that on a single processor there is no need for the barriers.

5.6.4.6 Multiple-Processor Send/Receive Interrupt

If one processor writes some shared data, then sends an interrupt to a second processor, and that processor receives the interrupt, then accesses the shared data, the sequence from Section 5.6.4.3 must be used:

First Processor		Second Processor
:		
Write data		
MB		
Send int.	$\Rightarrow$	Receive int.
		MB
		Access data
		:

Leaving out the MB at the beginning of the interrupt-receipt routine makes the code fail if an old value of the context remains in the second processor's cache and invalidates from the writes done on the first processor are not delivered soon enough.

5.6.5 Implications for Hardware

The coherency point for physical address x is the place in the memory subsystem at which accesses to x are ordered. It may be at a main memory board, or at a cache containing x exclusively, or at the point of winning a common bus arbitration.

The coherency point for x may move with time, as exclusive access to x migrates between main memory and various caches.

MB and IMB force all preceding writes to at least reach their respective coherency points. This does not mean that main-memory writes have been done, just that the *order* of the eventual writes is committed. For example, on the XMI with retry, this means getting the writes acknowledged as received with good parity at the inputs to memory board queues; the actual RAM write happens later.

MB and IMB also force all queued cache invalidates to be delivered to the local caches before starting any subsequent reads (that may otherwise cache hit on stale data) or writes (that may otherwise write the cache, only to have the write effectively overwritten by a late-delivered invalidate).

Implementations may allow reads of x to hit (by physical address) on pending writes in a write buffer, even before the writes to x reach the coherency point for x. If this is done, it is still true that no earlier value of x may subsequently be delivered to the processor that took the hit on the write buffer value.

Virtual data caches are allowed to deliver data before doing address translation, but only if there cannot be a pending write under a synonym virtual address. Lack of a write-buffer match on untranslated address bits is sufficient to guarantee this.

Virtual data caches must invalidate or otherwise become coherent with the new value whenever a PALcode routine is executed that affects the validity, fault behavior, protection behavior, or virtual-to-physical mapping specified for one or more pages. Becoming coherent can be delayed until the next subsequent MB instruction or TB fill (using the new mapping), if the implementation of the PALcode routine always forces a subsequent TB fill.

5.7 Arithmetic Traps

Alpha implementations are allowed to execute multiple instructions concurrently and to forward results from one instruction to another. Thus, when an arithmetic trap is detected, the PC may have advanced an arbitrarily large number of instructions past the instruction T (calculating result R) whose execution triggered the trap.

When the trap is detected, any or all of these subsequent instructions may run to completion before the trap is actually taken. Instruction T and the set of instructions subsequent to T that complete before the trap is taken are collectively called the trap shadow of T. The PC pushed on the stack when the trap is taken is the PC of the first instruction past the trap shadow.

The instructions in the trap shadow of T may use the undefined result R of T, they may generate additional traps, and they may completely change the PC (branches, JSR).

Thus, by the time a trap is taken, the PC pushed on the stack may bear no useful relationship to the PC of the trigger instruction T, and the state visible to the programmer may have been updated using the undefined result R. If an instruction in the trap shadow of T uses R to calculate a subsequent register value, that register value is undefined, even though there may be no trap associated with the subsequent calculation. Similarly:

- If an instruction in the trap shadow of T stores R or any subsequent undefined result, the stored value is undefined.

- If an instruction in the trap shadow of T uses R or any subsequent undefined result as the basis of a conditional or calculated branch, the branch target is undefined.

- If an instruction in the trap shadow of T uses R or any subsequent undefined result as the basis of an address calculation, the memory address actually accessed is undefined.

Software that is intended to bound how far the PC may advance before taking a trap, or how far an undefined result may propagate, must insert TRAPB instructions at appropriate points.

Software that is intended to continue from a trap by supplying a well-defined result R within an arithmetic trap handler, can do so reliably by following the rules for software completion code sequences given in Section 4.7.5.

Chapter 6
Common PALcode Architecture (I)

6.1 PALcode

In a family of machines, both users and operating system implementors require functions to be implemented consistently. When functions conform to a common interface, the code that uses those functions can be used on several different implementations without modification.

These functions range from the binary encoding of the instruction and data to the exception mechanisms and synchronization primitives. Some of these functions can be implemented cost effectively in hardware, but others are impractical to implement directly in hardware. These functions include low-level hardware support functions such as Translation Buffer miss fill routines, interrupt acknowledge, and vector dispatch. They also include support for privileged and atomic operations that require long instruction sequences.

In the VAX, these functions are generally provided by microcode. This is not seen as a problem because the VAX architecture lends itself to a microcoded implementation.

One of the goals of Alpha is that microcode will not be necessary for practical implementation. However, it is still desirable to provide an architected interface to these functions that will be consistent across the entire family of machines. The Privileged Architecture Library (PALcode) provides a mechanism to implement these functions without resorting to a microcoded machine.

6.2 PALcode Instructions and Functions

PALcode is used to implement the following functions:

- Instructions that require complex sequencing as an atomic operation
- Instructions that require VAX-style interlocked memory access
- Privileged instructions
- Memory management control (including translation buffer (TB) management)
- Context swapping
- Interrupt and exception dispatching
- Power-up initialization and booting
- Console functions
- Emulation of instructions with no hardware support.

The Alpha architecture lets these functions be implemented in standard machine code that is resident in main memory. PALcode is written in standard machine code with some implementation-specific extensions to provide access to low-level hardware. This lets an Alpha implementation make various design trade-offs based on the hardware technology being used to implement the machine. The PALcode can abstract these differences and make them invisible to system software.

For example, in a MOS VLSI implementation, a small (32 entry) fully associative TB can be the right match to the media, given that chip area is a costly resource. In an ECL version, a large (1024 entry) direct-mapped TB can be used because it will use RAM chips and does not have fast associative memories available. This difference would be handled by implementation-specific versions of the PALcode on the two systems, both versions providing transparent TB miss service routines. The operating system code would not need to know there were any differences.

Part II, Operating Systems describes the Digital-supplied Alpha Privileged Architecture Library (PALcode) routines and environment. Other systems may use the Digital-supplied PALcode library or architect and implement a different library of routines. Alpha systems are required to support the replacement of Digital-defined PALcode with an operating system-specific version.

6.3 PALcode Environment

The PALcode environment differs from the normal environment in the following ways:

- Complete control of the machine state.

- Interrupts are disabled.

- Implementation-specific hardware functions are enabled, as described below.

- I-stream memory management traps are prevented (by disabling I-stream mapping, mapping PALcode with a permanent TB entry, or by other mechanisms).

Complete control of the machine state allows all functions of the machine to be controlled. Disabling interrupts allows the system to provide multi-instruction sequences as atomic operations. Enabling implementation-specific hardware functions allows access to low-level system hardware. Preventing I-stream memory management traps allows PALcode to implement memory management functions such as translation buffer fill.

6.4 Special Functions Required for PALcode

PALcode uses the Alpha instruction set for most of its operations. A small number of additional functions are needed to implement the PALcode. There are five opcodes reserved to implement PALcode functions: PALRES0, PALRES1, PALRES2, PALRES3 and PALRES4. These instructions produce an Illegal Instruction Trap if executed outside the PALcode environment.

- PALcode needs a mechanism to save the current state of the machine and dispatch into PALcode.

- PALcode needs a set of instructions to access hardware control registers.

- PALcode needs a hardware mechanism to transition the machine from the PALcode environment to the non-PALcode environment. This mechanism loads the PC, enables interrupts, enables mapping, and disables PALcode privileges.

An Alpha implementation may also choose to provide additional functions to simplify or improve performance of some PALcode functions. The following are some examples:

- An Alpha implementation may include a read/write virtual function that allows PALcode to perform mapped memory accesses using the mapping hardware rather than providing the virtual-to-physical translation in PALcode routines. PALcode may provide a special function to do physical reads and writes and have the Alpha loads and stores continue to operate on virtual address in the PALcode environment.

- An Alpha implementation may include hardware assists for various functions—for example, saving the virtual address of a reference on a memory management error rather than having to generate it by simulating the effective address calculation in PALcode.

- An Alpha implementation may include private registers so it can function without having to save and restore the native general registers.

6.5 PALcode Effects on System Code

PALcode will have one effect on system code. Because PALcode may be resident in main memory and maintain privileged data structures in main memory, the operating system code that allocates physical memory cannot use all of physical memory.

The amount of memory PALcode requires is small, so the loss to the system is negligible.

6.6 PALcode Replacement

Alpha systems are required to support the replacement of Digital-supplied PALcode with an operating system-specific version. The following functions must be implemented in PALcode, *not* directly in hardware, to facilitate replacement with different versions.

1. Translation Buffer fill. Different operating systems will want to replace the Translation Buffer (TB) fill routines. The replacement routines will use different data structures. The page tables documented in *Part II, Operating Systems* will not be present in these systems. Therefore, no portion of the TB fill flow that would change with a change in page tables may be placed in hardware, unless it is placed in a manner that can be overridden by PALcode.

2. Process structure. Different operating systems might want to replace the process context switch routines. The replacement routines will use different data structures. The HWPCB or PCB documented in *Part II, Operating Systems* will not be present in these systems. Therefore, no portion of the context switching flows that would change with a change in process structure may be placed in hardware.

PALcode must be written in a modular manner that facilitates easy replacement of major subsections. The subsections that need to be simple to replace are:

- Translation Buffer fill

- Process structure and context switch

- Interrupt and exception frame format and routine dispatch

- Privileged PALcode instructions

6.7 Required PALcode Instructions

The PALcode instructions listed in Table 6–1 and *Appendix C* must be recognized by mnemonic and opcode in all operating system implementations, but the effect of each instruction is dependent on the implementation. The operation of these PALcode instructions for Digital-supplied operating system implementations is described in *Part II, Operating Systems*.

Table 6–1: PALcode Instructions that Require Recognition

Mnemonic	Name
BPT	Breakpoint trap
BUGCHK	Bugcheck trap
GENTRAP	Generate trap
RDUNIQUE	Read unique value
WRUNIQUE	Write unique value

The PALcode instructions listed in Table 6–2 and described in the following sections must be supported by all Alpha implementations:

Table 6–2: Required PALcode Instructions

Mnemonic	Type	Operation
DRAINA	Privileged	Drain aborts
HALT	Privileged	Halt processor
IMB	Unprivileged	I-stream memory barrier

6.7.1 Drain Aborts

Format:

CALL_PAL   DRAINA   !PALcode format

Operation:

```
IF  PS<CM> NE 0  THEN
    {privileged instruction exception}

{Stall instruction issuing until all prior
 instructions are guaranteed to complete
 without incurring aborts.}
```

Exceptions:

Privileged Instruction

Instruction Mnemonics:

CALL_PAL   DRAINA   Drain Aborts

Description:

If aborts are deliberately generated and handled (such as non-existent-memory aborts while sizing memory or searching for I/O devices), the DRAINA instruction forces any outstanding aborts to be taken before continuing.

Aborts are necessarily implementation-dependent. DRAINA stalls instruction issue at least until all previously-issued instructions have completed and any associated aborts have been signaled. For operate instructions, this will usually mean stalling until the result register has been written. For branch instructions, this will usually mean stalling until the result register and PC have been written. For load instructions, this will usually mean stalling until the result register has been written. For store instructions, this will usually mean stalling until at least the first level in a potentially multi-level memory hierarchy has been written.

For load instructions, DRAINA does not necessarily guarantee that the unaccessed portions of a cache block have been transferred error-free before continuing.

For store instructions, DRAINA does not necessarily guarantee that the ultimate target location of the store has received error-free data before continuing. An implementation-specific technique must be used to guarantee the ultimate completion of a write in implementations that have multi-level memory hierarchies or store-and-forward bus adapters.

6.7.2 Halt

Format:

CALL_PAL   HALT   !PALcode format

Operation:

```
IF  PS<CM> NE 0  THEN
    {privileged instruction exception}
CASE {halt_action} OF
    halt:                {halt}
    restart/halt:        {restart/halt}
    restart/boot/halt:   {restart/boot/halt}
    boot/halt:           {boot/halt}
ENDCASE
```

Exceptions:

Privileged Instruction

Instruction mnemonics:

CALL_PAL HALT   Halt Processor

Description:

The HALT instruction stops normal instruction processing, and depending on the HALT action setting, the processor may either enter console mode or the restart sequence.

6.7.3 Instruction Memory Barrier

Format:

> CALL_PAL   IMB   !PALcode format

Operation:

> {Make instruction stream coherent with Data stream}

Exceptions:

> None

Instruction mnemonics:

> CALL_PAL IMB   I-stream Memory Barrier

Description:

An IMB instruction must be executed after software or I/O devices write into the instruction stream or modify the instruction stream virtual address mapping, and before the new value is fetched as an instruction. An implementation may contain an instruction cache that does not track either processor or I/O writes into the instruction stream. The instruction cache and memory are made coherent by an IMB instruction.

If the instruction stream is modified and an IMB is not executed before fetching an instruction from the modified location, it is UNPREDICTABLE whether the old or new value is fetched.

The cache coherency and sharing rules are described in Chapter 5.

Chapter 7
Console Subsystem Overview (I)

On an Alpha system, underlying control of the system platform hardware is provided by a *console*. The console:

1. Initializes, tests, and prepares the system platform hardware for Alpha system software.

2. Bootstraps (loads into memory and starts the execution of) system software.

3. Controls and monitors the state and state transitions of each processor in a multiprocessor system.

4. Provides services to system software that simplify system software control of and access to platform hardware.

5. Provides a means for a *console operator* to monitor and control the system.

The console interacts with system platform hardware to accomplish the first three tasks. The actual mechanisms of these interactions are specific to the platform hardware; however, the net effects are common to all systems.

The console interacts with system software once control of the system platform hardware has been transferred to that software.

The console interacts with the console operator through a virtual display device or *console terminal*. The console operator may be a human being or a management application.

Chapter 8

Input/Output (I)

8.1 Introduction

Conceptually, Alpha systems consist of processors, memory, processor-memory interconnect (PMI), I/O buses, bridges, and I/O devices.

Figure 8–1 shows the Alpha system overview.

Figure 8–1: Alpha System Overview

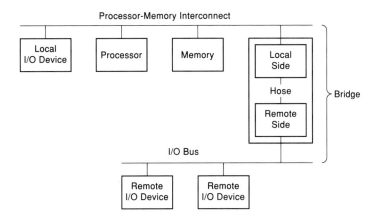

As shown in Figure 8–1, processors and memory are connected by the PMI.

A bridge connects a tightly coupled I/O bus to the system, either directly to the PMI or through another tightly coupled I/O bus. A tightly coupled I/O bus is one whose address space is accessible to the processor either directly or through an I/O mailbox.

A bridge has at least a local side and a remote side, connected by a hose. The local side is electrically closer to the PMI; the remote side is electrically further.

I/O devices can be connected to the PMI or to an I/O bus. A local device connects to the PMI; a remote device connects to an I/O bus.

The following sections discuss Alpha I/O operations:

- Accesses to local I/O space are discussed in Section 8.2.

- Accesses to remote I/O space are discussed in Section 8.3.

- Reads and writes to processor memory-like regions initiated by I/O devices, or "DMAs", are discussed in Section 8.4.

- Processor interrupts requested by devices are discussed in Section 8.5.

- Bus-specific I/O accesses are discussed in Section 8.6.

8.2 Local I/O Space Access

Local I/O space locations may appear in either memory or non-memory-like regions. Local I/O space locations which appear in memory regions may be cached subject to the platform cache coherency scheme. See Chapter 5.

An Alpha platform need only support atomic quadword accesses. The Alpha instruction architecture requires only quadword accesses. Processor implementations may further restrict the access granularity of local I/O space. For example, a given implementation could permit addressing of only cache blocks. To support byte or word accesses to a local device, the device must be mapped into a non-memory-like region with a sparse address space. The necessary mapping is dependent on the implementation of the processor, cache, and PMI protocol. For example, the four individual bytes of a longword device control register could be mapped into the low order byte of each of four contiguous quadwords.

8.2.1 Read/Write Ordering

Access to local I/O space does not cause any implicit read/write ordering; explicit barrier instructions must be used to ensure any desired ordering. Barrier instructions must be used:

- After updating a memory-resident data structure and before writing a local I/O space location to notify the device of the updates.

- Between multiple consecutive direct accesses to local I/O space, e.g. device control registers, if those accesses are expected to be ordered at the device.

Again, note that implementations may cache not only memory-resident data structures, but also local I/O space locations.

8.3 Remote I/O Space Access

Remote I/O space locations are accessed indirectly through a memory-resident "mailbox" data structure. To post an access, the physical address of the mailbox is written into a MailBox Pointer Register (MBPR) on a local bridge side. For remote I/O space writes, the command and data are posted in the mailbox, and status is returned. For remote I/O space reads, the command is posted in the mailbox, and status and data are returned.

An Alpha system may have any number of local bridge sides. Each local side may provide connections for up to 256 hoses. Each hose may connect to a single remote side or may connect to multiple remote sides. A single remote side may connect to one or more hoses. A bridge need not include a hose; the local and remote sides may be implemented as a single entity. A local side or an entire bridge may be incorporated into a processor board.

8.3.1 Mailbox Posting

A remote I/O space access is defined by the contents of the mailbox structure. A remote I/O space access is invoked by writing the base physical address of the mailbox structure into the appropriate bridge MailBox Pointer Register (MBPR). Each I/O bus may be associated with one and only one MBPR. A single MBPR may be associated with one or more remote I/O buses and a single bridge may have multiple MBPR registers. The MBPR appears in local I/O space.

The MBPR is accessed only with the STQ_C instruction. Flow control is achieved by the associated (per-processor) lock_flag as follows:

```
post_mbx:
        <derive PA of mailbox and load R1>
        <derive VA of MBPR and load R0>
        STQ_C  R1,R0
        BEQ    R1,wait_post_mbx
        .
        .
        .

wait_post_mbx:
        <backoff delay>
        BR     post_mbx
```

If the STQ_C lock_flag is set, the mailbox has been posted to the bridge. If the STQ_C lock_flag is clear, all MBPR resources are occupied; the MBPR write must be retried. In multi-processor configurations, this use of the STQ_C instruction affects only the local per-processor lock_flag. The state of the per-processor lock_flag of other processors is unchanged.

HARDWARE/SOFTWARE IMPLEMENTATION NOTE
The use above of the STQ_C instruction is specific to the first Alpha implementations. Future implementations may use a different access mechanism.

A given remote I/O space location is uniformly accessible to all processors in a multi-processor configuration. A given hose, hence a given remote I/O bus, may be accessed via an MBPR at the same physical address from any processor. A software thread need have no knowledge of the specific processor on which it is executing.

A FIFO structure may be implemented behind each MBPR register to permit the posting of multiple outstanding mailbox operations. A set of processor-specific request queues may be implemented behind each MBPR register to ensure fair access to all processors. Any such FIFO or queue is invisible to software.

Bridge implementations must protect against lockout and ensure fair MBPR access to all processors in a multi-processor configuration. Multiple writes to an MBPR by a single processor must not be able to cause the starvation or timeout of competing writes to the same MBPR by other processors.

Multiple software threads executing at different IPLs on a single processor may cause starvation or timeout of the lower IPL threads. IPL levels are inherently unfair.

Bridge implementations must guarantee forward progress on mailbox operations regardless of direct memory access or interrupt load.

8.3.2 Mailbox Pointer Register (MBPR)

The MBPR format is shown in Figure 8–2 and described in Table 8–1.

Figure 8–2: Mailbox Pointer Register Format

63 48	47 6	5 0
SBZ	Mailbox Address<47:6>	SBZ

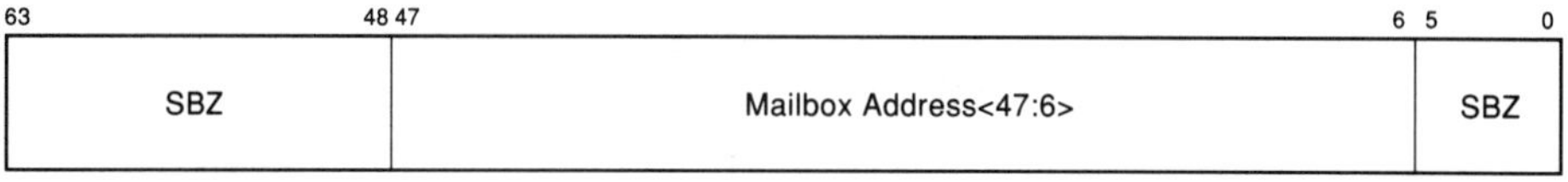

Table 8–1: Mailbox Pointer Register Format

Bit(s)	Description
<5:0>	SBZ
<47:6>	Physical address of the mailbox structure. The mailbox structure must be at least 64-byte aligned.
<63:48>	SBZ

8.3.3 Mailbox Structure

The mailbox is a 64-byte, naturally aligned, data structure. The format is shown in Figure 8–3 and described in Table 8–2.

Figure 8–3: Mailbox Data Structure Format

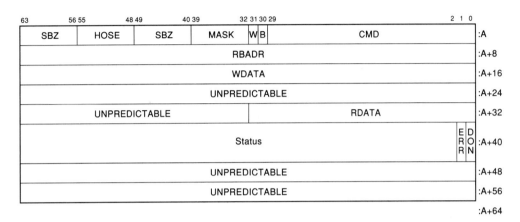

Table 8–2: Mailbox Data Structure Format

Offset	Bit(s)	Name	Description
0	<29:0>	CMD	Remote bus command. Controls the actual remote bus operation and can include fields such as address only, address width, and data width. See Section 8.6.2.
	<30>	B	Remote bridge access. If set, the command is a special or diagnostic command directed to the remote side. See Section 8.6.3.
	<31>	W	Write access. If set, the remote bus operation is a write.
	<39:32>	MASK	Disable Byte Mask. Disables bytes within the remote bus address. Mask bit <i> set causes the byte to be disabled; e.g. data byte <i> will NOT be written to the remote address. See Section 8.6.2.
	<47:40>	SBZ	
	<55:48>	HOSE	Hose. Specifies the remote bus to be accessed. Bridges may directly connect to up to 256 remote buses per hose.
	<63:56>	SBZ	
8	<63:0>	RBADR	Remote Bus Address. Contains the target address of the device on the remote bus. See Section 8.6.2.

Table 8–2 (Cont.): Mailbox Data Structure Format

Offset	Bit(s)	Name	Description
16	<63:0>	WDATA	Write Data. For write commands, contains the data to be written. For read commands, the field is not used by the bridge.
24	<63:0>		UNPREDICTABLE.
32	<31:0>	RDATA	Read Data. For read commands, contains the data returned. For write data commands, the field is UNPREDICTABLE.
	<63:32>		UNPREDICTABLE.
40	<0>	DON	Done. Indicates that the ERR, STATUS, and RDATA fields are valid; that the mailbox structure may be safely modified by host software.
	<1>	ERR	Error. If set, indicates that an error was encountered and that the STATUS field contains additional information. Valid only when DON is set. See Sections 8.3.7 and 8.3.8.
	<63:2>	STATUS	Operation completion status. Contains information specific to the bridge implementation. Valid only when DON is set. The bridge specification must include a definition of this field. See Sections 8.3.7 and 8.3.8.
48	<63:0>		UNPREDICTABLE.
56	<63:0>		UNPREDICTABLE.

8.3.4 Mailbox Access Synchronization

The ownership of the mailbox structure is exchanged between the posting software and the servicing bridge. The first 3 quadwords must be initialized by the software prior to posting the mailbox to the bridge. Once posted, the contents of the mailbox are owned by the bridge and are UNPREDICTABLE until the DON bit is set by the bridge. If the mailbox contents are altered by software prior to the DON bit becoming set, the action of the bridge and the resulting mailbox contents are UNPREDICTABLE. Once the DON bit has been set by the bridge, the mailbox contents are again owned by the software and must not be altered by the bridge.

Software use of the DON bit for synchronization is encouraged. If the DON bit is set in the mailbox at the time that the mailbox is posted, it is not possible to determine when the mailbox structure may be safely altered nor is it possible to determine when any returned information (RDATA or STATUS or ERR) becomes valid. Use of a static, not dynamically altered, mailbox structure is recommended only for true write-and-run of static data such as setting a "go" bit in a device control register.

Note that the DON bit set does NOT guarantee that a remote I/O space write has actually completed at the device. The DON bit may be set by any intervening bridge. See Section 8.3.8.

The servicing bridge ignores the contents of the DON, ERR, and STATUS fields; these fields are treated as write only.

8.3.5 Mailbox Read/Write Ordering

Mailbox accesses to a given remote bus are ordered by the MBPR and bus bridge. After posting in the MBPR, the ordering must be retained by the bridge. The bridge may reorder operations only across different hoses. Mailboxes targeted to different buses connected to the same local bridge side may occur in a sequence different from the posting order.

Mailbox operations are implicitly ordered when one and only one MBPR is used to access a given remote I/O bus. In general, there is only one path to a given remote I/O bus via a unique hose and remote side. In such configurations, the hardware must retain the ordering of mailbox accesses. In configurations in which there are multiple paths, software should order mailbox operations by using one and only one MBPR to access a given remote bus.

8.3.6 Remote I/O Space Access Granularity

The granularity of remote I/O space accesses is not symmetric:

- Mailbox reads are defined to bytes, words, and longwords.

- Mailbox writes are defined to bytes, words, longwords and quadwords.

Mailbox writes were optimized to permit efficient and atomic writes of a full 48-bit Alpha physical address.

Not all bus bridges will support all possible remote I/O space access granularities. The supported granularity will be determined by the capabilities of the remote bus and the remote bus side.

The MASK and RBADR fields are determined by the addressing and masking modes of the remote I/O bus. Invalid MASK fields, or invalid combinations of MASK and RBADR fields, will not cause ERR to be set. Error checking (if any) is done on the remote (I/O bus) side of the bridge; the local (PMI) side of the bridge employs disconnected writes. If error checking is done by the remote side of the bridge, the error is reported by an error interrupt.

On mailbox write accesses, bridges (and chains of bridges) deliver the valid WDATA, RBADR, and MASK information to the remote I/O device. The valid data may be encapsulated, along with invalid data, into larger data packets; the invalid data may simply be invalid fields from the WDATA quadword. For some remote I/O buses, the RBADR and MASK fields may be truncated or otherwise mapped.

On mailbox read accesses, bridges (and chains of bridges) deliver the valid RBADR, MASK, and command information to the remote I/O device. The bridge has no knowledge of the intended size of the read data - this is known only to the requesting software and the device, which are assumed to agree. The valid data may be encapsulated, along with invalid data, into larger data packets. Again, for some remote I/O buses, the RBADR and MASK fields may be truncated or otherwise mapped.

8.3.7 Remote I/O Space Read Accesses

The bridge must return status and data for remote I/O space reads. When the mailbox DON bit is set by the bridge, the operation has completed, and the ERR and STATUS fields may be examined. If the ERR bit is not set, the requested remote bus operation was successful and valid data was returned. If the ERR bit is set, an error was encountered and the STATUS field contains information as to the nature of the error.

Errors encountered on remote I/O space read accesses may also be reported by bridge error interrupts. The bridge side which encounters the error requests the interrupt. Thus, a non-existent hose error may be reported by the local (PMI) side of the bridge, while a non-existent remote bus address error is reported by the remote (I/O bus) side of the bridge.

Remote I/O space read accesses may be performed as follows:

```
remote_read:
        <load Rm with VA of mailbox>
        <ensure mailbox no longer in use by bridge>
        <derive and load mailbox CMD, MASK, HOSE, and RBADR fields>

        STQ     R31, 40(Rm)       ; Clear DON/ERR/STATUS fields

        MB

post_mbx:
        <derive PA of mailbox and load R1>
        <derive VA of MBPR and load R0>
        STQ_C   R1,R0
        BEQ     R1,wait_post_mbx

wait_mbxdone:
        LDQ     R0, 40(Rm)        ; Fetch STATUS/DON
        BLBS    R0, check_err     ; Branch on DON set
        <backoff delay>
        BR      wait_mbxdone

check_err:
        SRL     R0, #1, R0
        BLBS    R0, read_err

        MB

        LDQ     R0, 32(Rm)        ; Fetch RDATA
        .
        .
        .

read_err:
        <handle error>

wait_post_mbx:
        <backoff delay>
        BR      post_mbx
```

Notes:

1. The mailbox is no longer in use by a bridge whenever the DON bit has been set by the servicing bridge or is newly allocated.

2. The first barrier is required to ensure that the bridge will read the mailbox contents as updated by the processor. Any pending processor writes to the mailbox will have completed by the time that the load of the MBPR has completed.

3. The second barrier is required to ensure that the processor will read the mailbox contents as updated by the bridge. The returned data is accessed only after the DON bit is observed to be set by the servicing bridge.

4. Software need not wait for the DON bit to become set.

5. The mailbox RDATA is valid only when DON is set and ERR is clear.

8.3.8 Remote I/O Space Write Accesses

The bridge need not return status for remote I/O space writes. When the mailbox DON bit is set by the bridge, the bridge has completed access to the mailbox structure. The ERR bit and STATUS fields are testable. The actual write operation need NOT have completed at the device and the ERR bit and STATUS fields can indicate success (be cleared) even though success is not ensured. However, the ERR bit and STATUS fields, if set, do accurately report an error condition.

The actual completion of a remote I/O space write access can only be observed indirectly. Either the appropriate device state must be read back, or the device must update a memory-resident data structure and/or request an interrupt. Remote I/O space read access(es) may be posted anytime after posting the write access. Because mailbox operations to the same remote bus are guaranteed to be ordered, the read is guaranteed to occur after the write.

Errors encountered on remote I/O space write accesses are reported by bridge error interrupts. The bridge side which encounters the error requests the interrupt. Thus, a non-existent hose error may be reported by the local (PMI) side of the bridge, while a non-existent remote bus address error is reported by the remote (I/O bus) side of the bridge.

Remote I/O space write accesses may be performed as follows:

```
remote_write:

     <load Rm with VA of mailbox>
     <ensure mailbox no longer in use by bridge>
     <derive and load mailbox CMD, MASK, HOSE, and RBADR fields>
     STQ R31, 40(RM)          ; Clear DON/ERR/STATUS

     MB

post_mbx:
```

```
        <derive PA of mailbox and load R1>
        <derive VA of MBPR and load R0>
        STQ_C  R1,R0
        BEQ    R1,wait_post_mbx
          :
          :

wait_post_mbx:

        <backoff delay>
        BR     post_mbx
```

Notes:

1. The mailbox is no longer in use by a bridge whenever the DON bit has been set by the servicing bridge or is newly allocated.

2. The barrier is required to ensure that the bridge will read the mailbox contents as updated by the processor. Any pending processor writes to the mailbox will have completed by the time that the load of the MBPR has completed.

3. If the mailbox data is static, e.g. used to set a "go" bit in a device control register, the mailbox may be posted without regard to the state of the DON bit. Barriers are not required each time a static mailbox is posted, however a barrier is required after the mailbox contents are initialized and prior to its first use.

8.4 Direct Memory Accesss (DMA)

8.4.1 Access Granularity

A device or bridge side access to a memory-like region, or "DMA", is taken to be atomic when:

- It is not possible for a single device read DMA of a data structure which is updated by a single processor write to observe a partial update of that structure.

- It is not possible for a processor reading a data structure which is updated by a single device write DMA to observe a partial update of that structure.

A processor treats any memory-resident data structures which are shared with an I/O device as though the structures were shared with another processor. The processor must follow the guidelines given in *Common Architecture, Chapter 5*. Specifically, barrier instructions must be used:

1. After updating a shared memory-resident data structure and before setting an associated flag indicating that the data structure is valid.

2. After observing a newly updated flag, and prior to accessing the associated shared memory-resident data structure.

The atomic DMA size guaranteed to a local device is a function of the PMI protocol. The minimum size is an aligned hexword. Locally connected devices must obey the PMI protocol and may participate in the memory cache coherency policy. See the guidelines in *Common Architecture, Chapter 5*.

The atomic DMA size guaranteed to a remote device is a function of the remote I/O bus protocol. Remote devices are guaranteed atomic access to aligned hexwords or the remote I/O bus transfer burst size, whichever is smaller. It is the responsibility of the local bridge side to ensure the atomicity of the device DMA.

Larger atomic DMA granularity permits optimization of device control protocols. When a data structure and the associated flag are contained within a single aligned hexword, the device can update both simultaneously with a single write DMA. Similarly, the device may access both the data structure and the associated flag with a single read DMA. If the flag is valid, the data structure contains valid information; an additional read DMA is not necessary to obtain the valid data.

HARDWARE/SOFTWARE IMPLEMENTATION NOTE
The hexword write DMA size was chosen as the smallest cache block size of the first Alpha implementations.

8.4.2 Read/Write Ordering

DMAs may be divided into the "control" stream and the "data" stream. These streams differ in their ordering properties.

- Control stream accesses are guaranteed to be ordered. An implicit barrier occurs before and after each access. Control stream ordering must be preserved by all bridges between a given remote I/O device and processor memory.

- Data stream DMAs may be arbitrarily reordered if permitted by the protocol of that I/O bus. No implicit barriers are associated with this stream.

A device may use control stream DMAs to ensure ordering of the data stream DMAs and of interrupt requests as seen by a processor or other device sharing the same memory-resident structures. Data stream DMAs must not be reordered with respect to control stream DMAs. Interrupt requests must not be reordered with respect to control stream DMAs.

Control stream DMAs must be used:

- As the last DMA issued to update a memory-resident data structure before requesting a processor interrupt to notify the processor of the update. This DMA ensures that any previously issued data stream DMAs become visible to the processor prior to the interrupt.

- To update any pointer or other linkage between memory-resident data structures. Consider a status buffer which is located by a status ring pointer. The status buffer may be updated with either a control or data stream DMA. The ring pointer must be updated with a control stream DMA which is issued after the last DMA used to update the status buffer.

A bridge must preserve the ordering of control stream DMAs regardless of whether the accesses are reads or writes.

The division of direct memory accesses into the control stream and the data stream is the responsibility of the device. I/O bus protocols which do not permit the separation of control and data stream DMAs must preserve the ordering of all DMAs and interrupt requests; all DMAs are considered to be control stream DMAs. Similarly, hose protocols which do not permit the separation of control and data stream DMAs must preserve the ordering of all DMAs and interrupt requests.

Bridge implementations must guarantee forward progress on all DMA operations.

8.4.3 Device Address Translation

I/O devices use only physical addresses; devices must not access page tables for the purpose of address translation. Devices are independent of any virtual memory translation scheme and processor page size.

8.5 Interrupts

An interrupt request from an I/O device consists of an interrupt priority level and an interrupt vector. Device interrupt requests are defined to be priorities 20 to 23. The interrupt vector identifies the appropriate interrupt service routine; the starting address of the interrupt service routine is obtained by using the vector as an offset from the base of the System Control Block (SCB).

All bridge implementations must maintain both the temporal order and relative priority of device interrupts. A bridge must not expedite a lower priority request if a higher priority request has been received. With one exception, a bridge must not reorder two interrupt requests at the same priority level. A bridge is permitted to expedite delivery of a fatal bridge error interrupt; this interrupt must be at IPL 23 and may take precedence over any IPL 23 device interrupts.

A bridge may prefetch the interrupt vector from an I/O device to reduce the processor overhead associated with interrupt dispatch. Vector prefetch reduces the processor latency necessary to dispatch to the interrupt service routine by reducing the delay associated with the delivery of the interrupt vector to the processor.

When a bridge delivers an interrupt from an I/O device, any pending control stream DMA writes issued by the device must have become visible to the processors. Note that due to the ordering of control stream DMAs, any data stream DMAs writes prior to the last pending control stream DMA must also have become visible to the processors.

In multi-processor configurations, interrupts may be directed to a subset of the processors in the configuration. Such targetting is implementation specific.

8.6 I/O Bus-Specific Mailbox Usage

The following sections pertain to I/O bus-specific mailbox usage.

8.6.1 Mailbox Field Checking

Bridge sides check only implemented functions. It is the responsibility of the posting software to ensure that the mailbox data structure fields are valid and that the structure is posted correctly.

1. Local sides need not check the MASK, B, CMD, RBADR, or WDATA fields.

2. Local sides which connect to a single hose need not check the HOSE field.

3. Local sides need not pass the HOSE or W fields to the remote bridge side.

4. Remote bridge sides which do not implement masking need not check the MASK field.

5. There is no consistency checking between the W and CMD fields. If the W bit is set and the CMD field indicates a read, the result is UNPREDICTABLE. Similarly, if the W bit is clear and the CMD field indicates a write, the result is UNPREDICTABLE.

6. Remote bridge sides check only implemented CMD and RBADR bits.

8.6.2 CMD Field

The CMD field consists of two subfields:

- A remote I/O bus specific subfield.

  This subfield is common to all Alpha systems and contains the controls for a given remote bus. The common subfield must be backward compatible; all systems which connect to a given I/O bus share this subfield.

- A system-specific subfield.

  This subfield is specific to each Alpha system and contains the controls for a given bridge implementation or system-specific diagnostic functions.

The size of each is specific to the remote I/O bus. The bridge specification must include the definitions of all valid commands. This partition promotes software portability. A given device driver uses the same CMD for a given type of device access, regardless of the platform. Diagnostic software can also interpret the common field without regard to the platform on which the mailbox was posted.

8.6.3 Special Commands

The special "WHO_ARE_YOU" command (W=0, B=1, CMD=0) is common to all bridge implementations. WHO_ARE_YOU is used to determine the type of remote bridge side. In response to a mailbox operation with a WHO_ARE_YOU command and RBADR of 0, the remote bridge side returns a unique remote bus side identifier. All other commands are specific to the type of remote bus and independent of the bridge implementation.

Part II   OpenVMS Alpha Software

This section describes how the OpenVMS operating system relates to the Alpha architecture and contains the following chapters:

1. Introduction to OpenVMS Alpha

2. OpenVMS PALcode Instruction Descriptions

3. OpenVMS Memory Management

4. OpenVMS Process Structure

5. OpenVMS Internal Processor Registers

6. OpenVMS Exceptions, Interrupts, and Machine Checks

Contents

Chapter 1   Introduction to OpenVMS Alpha (II)

1.1	Register Usage	1–1
1.1.1	Processor Status	1–1
1.1.2	Stack Pointer (SP)	1–1
1.1.3	Internal Processor Registers (IPRs)	1–1

Chapter 2   OpenVMS PALcode Instruction Descriptions (II)

2.1	Unprivileged General OpenVMS PALcode Instructions	2–3
2.1.1	Breakpoint	2–4
2.1.2	Bugcheck	2–5
2.1.3	Change Mode Executive	2–6
2.1.4	Change Mode to Kernel	2–7
2.1.5	Change Mode Supervisor	2–8
2.1.6	Change Mode User	2–9
2.1.7	Generate Software Trap	2–10
2.1.8	Probe Memory Access	2–11
2.1.9	Read Processor Status	2–13
2.1.10	Return from Exception or Interrupt	2–14
2.1.11	Read System Cycle Counter	2–17
2.1.12	Swap AST Enable	2–19
2.1.13	Write Processor Status Software Field	2–20
2.2	OpenVMS Alpha Queue Data Types	2–21
2.2.1	Absolute Longword Queues	2–21
2.2.2	Self-Relative Longword Queues	2–21
2.2.3	Absolute Quadword Queues	2–25
2.2.4	Self-Relative Quadword Queues	2–26
2.3	Unprivileged OpenVMS Queue PALcode Instructions	2–30
2.3.1	Insert Entry into Longword Queue at Head Interlocked	2–31
2.3.2	Insert Entry into Longword Queue at Head Interlocked Resident	2–33
2.3.3	Insert Entry into Quadword Queue at Head Interlocked	2–35
2.3.4	Insert Entry into Quadword Queue at Head Interlocked Resident	2–37
2.3.5	Insert Entry into Longword Queue at Tail Interlocked	2–39
2.3.6	Insert Entry into Longword Queue at Tail Interlocked Resident	2–42
2.3.7	Insert Entry into Quadword Queue at Tail Interlocked	2–44
2.3.8	Insert Entry into Quadword Queue at Tail Interlocked Resident	2–46
2.3.9	Insert Entry into Longword Queue	2–48
2.3.10	Insert Entry into Quadword Queue	2–50
2.3.11	Remove Entry from Longword Queue at Head Interlocked	2–52

2.3.12   Remove Entry from Longword Queue at Head Interlocked Resident   2–55

2.3.13   Remove Entry from Quadword Queue at Head Interlocked   2–57

2.3.14   Remove Entry from Quadword Queue at Head Interlocked Resident   2–60

2.3.15   Remove Entry from Longword Queue at Tail Interlocked   2–62

2.3.16   Remove Entry from Longword Queue at Tail Interlocked Resident   2–65

2.3.17   Remove Entry from Quadword Queue at Tail Interlocked   2–67

2.3.18   Remove Entry from Quadword Queue at Tail Interlocked Resident   2–70

2.3.19   Remove Entry from Longword Queue   2–72

2.3.20   Remove Entry from Quadword Queue   2–74

2.4   Unprivileged VAX Compatibility PALcode Instructions   2–76

2.4.1   Atomic Move Operation   2–77

2.5   Unprivileged PALcode Thread Instructions   2–81

2.5.1   Read Unique Context   2–82

2.5.2   Write Unique Context   2–83

2.6   Privileged PALcode Instructions   2–84

2.6.1   Cache Flush   2–85

2.6.2   Load Quadword Physical   2–86

2.6.3   Move From Processor Register   2–87

2.6.4   Move to Processor Register   2–88

2.6.5   Store Quadword Physical   2–89

2.6.6   Swap Privileged Context   2–90

Chapter 3   OpenVMS Memory Management (II)

3.1   Introduction   3–1

3.2   Virtual Address Space   3–1

3.2.1   Virtual Address Format   3–2

3.3   Physical Address Space   3–3

3.4   Memory Management Control   3–3

3.5   Page Table Entries   3–3

3.5.1   Changes to Page Table Entries   3–6

3.6   Memory Protection   3–7

3.6.1   Processor Access Modes   3–8

3.6.2   Protection Code   3–8

3.6.3   Access Violation Fault   3–8

3.7   Address Translation   3–8

3.7.1   Physical Access for Page Table Entries   3–9

3.7.2   Virtual Access for Page Table Entries   3–10

3.8   Translation Buffer   3–11

3.9   Address Space Numbers   3–12

3.10   Memory Management Faults   3–13

Chapter 4   OpenVMS Process Structure (II)

4.1   Process Definition   4–1
4.2   Hardware Privileged Process Context   4–2
4.3   Asynchronous System Traps (AST)   4–3
4.4   Process Context Switching   4–4

Chapter 5   OpenVMS Internal Processor Registers (II)

5.1   Internal Processor Registers   5–1
5.2   Stack Pointer Internal Processor Registers   5–1
5.3   IPR Summary   5–2
5.3.1   Address Space Number (ASN)   5–4
5.3.2   AST Enable (ASTEN)   5–5
5.3.3   AST Summary Register (ASTSR)   5–7
5.3.4   Data Alignment Trap Fixup (DATFX)   5–9
5.3.5   Floating Enable (FEN)   5–10
5.3.6   Interprocessor Interrupt Request (IPIR)   5–11
5.3.7   Interrupt Priority Level (IPL)   5–12
5.3.8   Machine Check Error Summary Register (MCES)   5–13
5.3.9   Performance Monitoring Register (PERFMON)   5–15
5.3.10   Privileged Context Block Base (PCBB)   5–16
5.3.11   Processor Base Register (PRBR)   5–17
5.3.12   Page Table Base Register (PTBR)   5–18
5.3.13   System Control Block Base (SCBB)   5–19
5.3.14   Software Interrupt Request Register (SIRR)   5–20
5.3.15   Software Interrupt Summary Register (SISR)   5–21
5.3.16   Translation Buffer Check (TBCHK)   5–22
5.3.17   Translation Buffer Invalidate All (TBIA)   5–24
5.3.18   Translation Buffer Invalidate All Process (TBIAP)   5–25
5.3.19   Translation Buffer Invalidate Single (TBISx)   5–26
5.3.20   Executive Stack Pointer (ESP)   5–27
5.3.21   Supervisor Stack Pointer (SSP)   5–28
5.3.22   User Stack Pointer (USP)   5–29
5.3.23   Virtual Page Table Base (VPTB)   5–30
5.3.24   Who-Am-I (WHAMI)   5–31

Chapter 6   OpenVMS Exceptions, Interrupts, and Machine Checks (II)

6.1   Introduction   6–1
6.1.1   Contrast Between Exceptions, Interrupts, and Machine Checks   6–2
6.1.2   Exceptions, Interrupts, and Machine Checks Summary   6–2
6.2   Processor State and Exception/Interrupt/Machine Check Stack Frame   6–5
6.2.1   Processor Status   6–5
6.2.2   Program Counter   6–6
6.2.3   Processor Interrupt Priority Level (IPL)   6–7

6.2.4	Protection Modes	6–7
6.2.5	Processor Stacks	6–7
6.2.6	Stack Frames	6–7
6.3	Exceptions	6–8
6.3.1	Faults	6–9
6.3.1.1	Floating Disabled Fault	6–10
6.3.1.2	Access Control Violation (ACV) Fault.	6–10
6.3.1.3	Translation Not Valid (TNV)	6–10
6.3.1.4	Fault On Read (FOR).	6–10
6.3.1.5	Fault On Write (FOW)	6–11
6.3.1.6	Fault On Execute (FOE)	6–11
6.3.2	Arithmetic Traps	6–12
6.3.2.1	Exception Summary Parameter	6–13
6.3.2.2	Register Write Mask	6–14
6.3.2.3	Invalid Operation (INV) Trap	6–14
6.3.2.4	Division by Zero (DZE) Trap	6–14
6.3.2.5	Overflow (OVF) Trap	6–14
6.3.2.6	Underflow (UNF) Trap	6–15
6.3.2.7	Inexact Result (INE) Trap	6–15
6.3.2.8	Integer Overflow (IOV) Trap	6–15
6.3.3	Synchronous Traps.	6–15
6.3.3.1	Data Alignment Trap	6–15
6.3.3.2	Other Synchronous Traps.	6–16
6.3.3.2.1	Breakpoint Trap.	6–16
6.3.3.2.2	Bugcheck Trap	6–16
6.3.3.2.3	Illegal Instruction Trap	6–16
6.3.3.2.4	Illegal Operand Trap	6–16
6.3.3.2.5	Generate Software Trap	6–17
6.3.3.2.6	Change Mode to Kernel Trap	6–17
6.3.3.2.7	Change Mode to Executive Trap	6–17
6.3.3.2.8	Change Mode to Supervisor Trap	6–17
6.3.3.2.9	Change Mode to User Trap	6–17
6.4	Interrupts	6–17
6.4.1	Software Interrupts — IPLs 1 to 15	6–19
6.4.1.1	Software Interrupt Summary Register	6–19
6.4.1.2	Software Interrupt Request Register	6–19
6.4.2	Asynchronous System Trap — IPL 2	6–20
6.4.3	Passive Release Interrupts — IPLs 20 to 23	6–20
6.4.4	I/O Device Interrupts — IPLs 20 to 23	6–20
6.4.5	Interval Clock Interrupt — IPL 22	6–20
6.4.5.1	Interprocessor Interrupt — IPL 22	6–21
6.4.5.1.1	Interprocessor Interrupt Request Register	6–21
6.4.6	Performance Monitor Interrupts — IPL 29	6–21
6.4.7	Powerfail Interrupt — IPL 30	6–21
6.5	Machine Checks	6–22

6.5.1	Software Response	6–23
6.5.2	Logout Areas	6–24
6.6	System Control Block	6–25
6.6.1	SCB Entries for Faults	6–26
6.6.2	SCB Entries for Arithmetic Traps	6–27
6.6.3	SCB Entries for Asynchronous System Traps (ASTs)	6–27
6.6.4	SCB Entries for Data Alignment Traps	6–27
6.6.5	SCB Entries for Other Synchronous Traps	6–27
6.6.6	SCB Entries for Processor Software Interrupts	6–28
6.6.7	SCB Entries for Processor Hardware Interrupts	6–29
6.6.8	SCB Entries for I/O Device Interrupts	6–29
6.6.9	SCB Entries for Machine Checks	6–29
6.7	PALcode Support	6–31
6.7.1	Stack Writeability	6–31
6.7.2	Stack Residency	6–31
6.7.3	Stack Alignment	6–31
6.7.4	Initiate Exception or Interrupt or Machine Check	6–31
6.7.5	Initiate Exception or Interrupt or Machine Check Model	6–32
6.7.6	PALcode Interrupt Arbitration	6–34
6.7.6.1	Writing the AST Summary Register	6–34
6.7.6.2	Writing the AST Enable Register	6–35
6.7.6.3	Writing the IPL Register	6–35
6.7.6.4	Writing the Software Interrupt Request Register	6–35
6.7.6.5	Return from Exception or Interrupt	6–35
6.7.6.6	Swap AST Enable	6–36
6.7.7	Processor State Transition Table	6–36

Figures

2–1	Empty Absolute Longword Queue	2–22
2–2	Absolute Longword Queue with One Entry	2–22
2–3	Absolute Longword Queue with Two Entries	2–23
2–4	Absolute Longword Queue with Three Entries	2–23
2–5	Absolute Longword Queue with Three Entries After Removing the Second Entry	2–24
2–6	Empty Self-Relative Longword Queue	2–24
2–7	Self-Relative Longword Queue with One Entry	2–24
2–8	Self-Relative Longword Queue with Two Entries	2–25
2–9	Self-Relative Longword Queue with Three Entries	2–25
2–10	Empty Absolute Quadword Queue	2–27
2–11	Absolute Quadword Queue with One Entry	2–27
2–12	Absolute Quadword Queue with Two Entries	2–27
2–13	Absolute Quadword Queue with Three Entries	2–28
2–14	Absolute Quadword Queue with Three Entries After Removing the Second Entry	2–28
2–15	Empty Self-Relative Quadword Queue	2–28
2–16	Absolute Quadword Queue with One Entry	2–29

2–17   Self-Relative Quadword Queue with Two Entries 2–29

2–18   Self-Relative Quadword Queue with Three Entries 2–29

3–1   Virtual Address Format 3–2

3–2   Page Table Entry 3–3

4–1   Hardware Privileged Context Block 4–2

5–1   Address Space Number Register (ASN) 5–4

5–2   AST Enable Register (ASTEN) 5–5

5–3   AST Summary Register (ASTSR) 5–7

5–4   Data Alignment Trap Fixup (DATFX) 5–9

5–5   Floating Enable (FEN) Register 5–10

5–6   Interprocessor Interrupt Request Register (IPIR) 5–11

5–7   Interrupt Priority Level (IPL) 5–12

5–8   Machine Check Error Summary Register (MCES) 5–13

5–9   Performance Monitoring Register (PERFMON) 5–15

5–10   Privileged Context Block Base Register (PCBB) 5–16

5–11   Processor Base Register (PRBR) 5–17

5–12   Page Table Base Register (PTBR) 5–18

5–13   System Control Block Base Register (SCBB) 5–19

5–14   Software Interrupt Request Register (SIRR) 5–20

5–15   Software Interrupt Summary Register (SISR) 5–21

5–16   Translation Buffer Check Register (TBCHK) 5–22

5–17   Translation Buffer Invalidate All Register (TBIA) 5–24

5–18   Translation Buffer Invalidate All Process Register (TBIAP) 5–25

5–19   Translation Buffer Invalidate Single (TBIS) 5–26

5–20   Executive Stack Pointer (ESP) 5–27

5–21   Supervisor Stack Pointer (SSP) 5–28

5–22   User Stack Pointer (USP) 5–29

5–23   Virtual Page Table Base Register (VPTB) 5–30

5–24   Who-Am-I Register (WHAMI) 5–31

6–1   Current Processor Status (PS Register) 6–5

6–2   Saved Processor Status (PS on Stack) 6–5

6–3   Program Counter (PC) 6–7

6–4   Stack Frame 6–8

6–5   Exception Summary 6–13

6–6   Corrected Error and Machine Check Logout Frame 6–24

Tables

2–1   OpenVMS PALcode Instructions 2–1

2–2   Unprivileged General OpenVMS PALcode Instruction Summary 2–3

2–3   VAX Queue Palcode Instruction Summary 2–30

2–4   Unprivileged PALcode Thread Instructions 2–81

2–5   PALcode Privileged Instructions Summary 2–84

3–1   Virtual Address Options 3–3

3–2   Page Table Entry 3–4

5–1   Internal Processor Register (IPR) Summary 5–2

5–2   Internal Processor Register (IPR) Access Summary 5–3

6–1   Exceptions, Interrupts, and Machine Checks Summary 6–3

6–2   Processor Status Register Summary 6–6

6–3   Exception Summary 6–13

6–4   Corrected Error and Machine Check Logout Frame Fields 6–25

6–5   SCB Entries for Faults.. 6–26

6–6   SCB Entries for Arithmetic Traps 6–27

6–7   SCB Entries for Asynchronous System Traps 6–27

6–8   SCB Entries for Data Alignment Trap 6–27

6–9   SCB Entries for Other Synchronous Traps............................... 6–28

6–10 Entries for Processor Software Interrupts 6–28

6–11 SCB Entries for Processor Hardware Interrupts 6–29

6–12 SCB Entries for Machine Checks 6–30

6–13 Processor State Transitions 6–37

Chapter 1

Introduction to OpenVMS Alpha (II)

The goals of this design are to provide a hardware implementation independent interface between OpenVMS and the hardware. Further, the design provides the needed abstractions to minimize the impact between OpenVMS and the different hardware implementations. Finally, the design must contain only that overhead necessary to satisfy those requirements, while still supporting high-performance systems.

1.1 Register Usage

Besides those registers described in *Part I, Common Architecture*, OpenVMS defines the registers described in the following sections.

1.1.1 Processor Status

The Processor Status (PS) is a special register that contains the current status of the processor. It can be read by the CALL_PAL RD_PS instruction. The software field (PS<SW>) can be written by the CALL_PAL WR_PS_SW routine. See Chapter 6 for a description of the PS register.)

1.1.2 Stack Pointer (SP)

Integer register R30 is the Stack Pointer (SP).

The SP contains the address of the top of the stack in the current mode.

Certain PALcode instructions, such as CALL_PAL REI, use R30 as an implicit operand. During such operations, the address value in R30, interpreted as an unsigned 64-bit integer, decreases (predecrements) when items are pushed onto the stack, and increases (postincrements) when they are popped from the stack. After pushing (writing) an item to the stack, SP points to that item.

1.1.3 Internal Processor Registers (IPRs)

The IPRs provide an architected mapping to internal hardware or provide other specialized uses. They are available only to privileged software through PALcode routines and allow OpenVMS to interrogate or modify system state. The IPRs are described in Chapter 5.

Chapter 2

OpenVMS PALcode Instruction Descriptions (II)

This chapter describes the PALcode instructions that are implemented for the OpenVMS Alpha environment. The PALcode instructions are a set of unprivileged and privileged CALL_PAL instructions that are used to match specific operating system requirements to the underlying hardware implementation.

For example, privileged PALcode instructions switch the hardware context of a process structure. Unprivileged PALcode instructions implement the uninterruptable queue operations. Also, PALcode instructions provide standard interrupt and exception reporting mechanisms that are independent of the underlying hardware implementation.

Table 2–1 lists all the unprivileged and privileged OpenVMS PALcode instructions and the section in this chapter in which they are described.

Table 2–1: OpenVMS PALcode Instructions

Unprivileged OpenVMS PALcode Instructions

Mnemonic	Operation	Section
AMOVRM	Atomic move register/memory	Section 2.4
AMOVRR	Atomic move register/register	Section 2.4
BPT	Breakpoint	Section 2.1
BUGCHK	Bugcheck	Section 2.1
CHME	Change mode to executive	Section 2.1
CHMK	Change mode to kernel	Section 2.1
CHMS	Change mode to supervisor	Section 2.1
CHMU	Change mode to user	Section 2.1
GENTRAP	Generate software trap	Section 2.1
IMB	I-stream memory barrier	*Common Architecture, Chapter 6*
INSQxxx	Insert in specified queue	Section 2.3
PROBER	Probe read access	Section 2.1
PROBEW	Probe write access	Section 2.1
RD_PS	Read processor status	Section 2.1

Table 2–1 (Cont.): OpenVMS PALcode Instructions

Unprivileged OpenVMS PALcode Instructions

Mnemonic	Operation	Section
READ_UNQ	Read unique context	Section 2.5
REI	Return from exception or interrupt	Section 2.1
REMQxxx	Remove from specified queue	Section 2.3
RSCC	Read system cycle counter	Section 2.1
SWASTEN	Swap AST enable	Section 2.1
WRITE_UNQ	Write unique context	Section 2.5
WR_PS_SW	Write processor status software field	Section 2.1

Privileged OpenVMS PALcode Instructions

Mnemonic	Operation	Section
CFLUSH	Cache flush	Section 2.6
DRAINA	Drain aborts	*Common Architecture, Chapter 6*
HALT	Halt processor	*Common Architecture, Chapter 6*
LDQP	Load quadword physical	Section 2.6
MFPR	Move from processor register	Section 2.6
MTPR	Move to processor register	Section 2.6
STQP	Store quadword physical	Section 2.6
SWPCTX	Swap privileged context	Section 2.6

2.1 Unprivileged General OpenVMS PALcode Instructions

The general unprivileged instructions in this section, together with those in Sections 2.3, 2.4, and 2.5, provide support for the underlying OpenVMS Alpha model.

Table 2–2: Unprivileged General OpenVMS PALcode Instruction Summary

Mnemonic	Operation
BPT	Breakpoint
BUGCHK	Bugcheck
CHME	Change mode to executive
CHMK	Change mode to kernel
CHMS	Change mode to supervisor
CHMU	Change mode to user
GENTRAP	Generate software trap
IMB	I-stream memory barrier
	See *Common Architecture, Chapter 6*
PROBER	Probe read access
PROBEW	Probe write access
RD_PS	Read processor status
REI	Return from exception or interrupt
RSCC	Read system cycle counter
SWASTEN	Swap AST enable
WR_PS_SW	Write processor status software field

2.1.1 Breakpoint

Format:

CALL_PAL   BPT   !PALcode format

Operation:

```
{initiate BPT exception with new_mode=kernel}
```

Exceptions:

Kernel Stack Not Valid Halt

Instruction mnemonics:

CALL_PAL   BPT   Breakpoint

Description:

The BPT instruction is provided for program debugging. It switches to Kernel mode and pushes R2..R7, the updated PC, and PS on the Kernel stack. It then dispatches to the address in the Breakpoint SCB vector. See Section 6.3.3.2.1.

2.1.2 Bugcheck

Format:

CALL_PAL BUGCHK   !PALcode format

Operation:

```
{initiate BUGCHK exception with new_mode=kernel}
```

Exceptions:

Kernel Stack Not Valid Halt

Instruction mnemonics:

CALL_PAL BUGCHK Bugcheck

Description:

The BUGCHK instruction is provided for error reporting. It switches to Kernel mode and pushes R2..R7, the updated PC, and PS on the Kernel stack. It then dispatches to the address in the Bugcheck SCB vector. See Section 6.3.3.2.2.

2.1.3 Change Mode Executive

Format:

CALL_PAL   CHME   !PALcode format

Operation:

```
tmp1 ← MINU( 1, PS<CM>)
{initiate CHME exception with new_mode=tmp1}
```

Exceptions:

Kernel Stack Not Valid Halt

Instruction mnemonics:

CALL_PAL   CHME   Change Mode to Executive

Description:

The CHME instruction lets a process change its mode in a controlled manner.

A change in mode also results in a change of stack pointers: the old pointer is saved, the new pointer is loaded. R2..R7, PC and PS are pushed onto the selected stack. The saved PC addresses the instruction following the CHME instruction. Registers R22, R23, R24, and R27 are available for use by PALcode as scratch registers. The contents of these registers are not preserved across a CHME.

2.1.4 Change Mode to Kernel

Format:

CALL_PAL   CHMK   !PALcode format

Operation:

```
{initiate CHMK exception with new_mode=kernel}
```

Exceptions:

Kernel Stack Not Valid Halt

Instruction mnemonics:

CALL_PAL   CHMK   Change Mode to Kernel

Description:

The CHMK instruction lets a process change its mode to kernel in a controlled manner.

A change in mode also results in a change of stack pointers: the old pointer is saved, the new pointer is loaded. R2..R7, PC, and PS are pushed onto the kernel stack. The saved PC addresses the instruction following the CHMK instruction. Registers R22, R23, R24, and R27 are available for use by PALcode as scratch registers. The contents of these registers are not preserved across a CHMK.

2.1.5 Change Mode Supervisor

Format:

CALL_PAL   CHMS   !PALcode format

Operation:

```
tmp1 ←  MINU( 2, PS<CM>)
{initiate CHMS exception with new_mode=tmp1}
```

Exceptions:

Kernel Stack Not Valid Halt

Instruction mnemonics:

CALL_PAL   CHMS   Change Mode to Supervisor

Description:

The CHMS instruction lets a process change its mode in a controlled manner.

A change in mode also results in a change of stack pointers: the old pointer is saved, the new pointer is loaded. R2..R7, PC, and PS are pushed onto the selected stack. The saved PC addresses the instruction following the CHMS instruction.

2.1.6 Change Mode User

Format:

CALL_PAL   CHMU   !PALcode format

Operation:

```
{initiate CHMU exception with new_mode=PS<CM>}
```

Exceptions:

Kernel Stack Not Valid Halt

Instruction mnemonics:

CALL_PAL   CHMU   Change Mode to User

Description:

The CHMU instruction lets a process call a routine via the change mode mechanism.

R2..R7, PC, and PS are pushed onto the current stack. The saved PC addresses the instruction following the CHMU instruction.

The CALL_PAL CHMU instruction is provided for VAX compatibility only.

2.1.7 Generate Software Trap

Format:

CALL_PAL   GENTRAP   !PALcode format

Operation:

```
{initiate GENTRAP exception with new_mode=kernel}
! R16 contains the value encoding of the software trap
```

Exceptions:

Kernel Stack Not Valid Halt

Instruction mnemonics:

CALL_PAL   GENTRAP   Generate Software Trap

Description:

The GENTRAP instruction is provided for reporting runtime software conditions. It switches to Kernel mode, and pushes R2...R7, the updated PC and PS on the Kernel stack. It then dispatches to the address in the GENTRAP SCB Vector. See Section Section 6.6.

The value in R16 identifies the particular software condition that has occurred. The encoding for the software trap values is given in the software calling standard for the system.

2.1.8 Probe Memory Access

Format:

```
CALL_PAL   PROBE                        !PALcode format
```

Operation:

```
! R16 contains the base address
! R17 contains the signed offset
! R18 contains the access mode
! R0 receives the completion status
!      ←  1 if success
!      ←  0 if failure

first ←  R16
last  ←  {R16+R17}

IF R18<1:0> GTU PS<CM> THEN
    probe_mode ←  R18<1:0>
ELSE
    probe_mode ←  PS<CM>)

IF ACCESS(first, probe_mode) AND ACCESS(last, probe_mode) THEN
    R0 ←  1
ELSE
    R0 ←  0
```

Exceptions:

Translation Not Valid

Instruction mnemonics:

```
CALL_PAL   PROBER      Probe for Read Access
CALL_PAL   PROBEW      Probe for Write Access
```

Description:

The PROBE instruction checks the read or write accessibility of the first and last byte specified by the base address and the signed offset; the bytes in between are not checked.

System software must check all pages between the two bytes if they are to be accessed. If both bytes are accessible, PROBE returns the value 1 in R0; otherwise, PROBE returns 0. The Fault On Read and Fault On Write PTE bits are not checked. A Translation Not Valid exception is signaled only if the the mapping structures can not be accessed. A Translation Not Valid exception is signaled only if the first or second level PTE is invalid.

The protection is checked against the less privileged of the modes specified by R18<1:0> and the Current Mode (PS<CM>). See Section 6.2 for access mode encodings.

PROBE is only intended to check a single datum for accessibility. It does not check all intervening pages because this could result in excessive interrupt latency.

2.1.9 Read Processor Status

Format:

CALL_PAL   RD_PS   !PALcode format

Operation:

R0 ← PS

Exceptions:

None

Instruction mnemonics:

CALL_PAL   RD_PS   Read Processor Status

Description:

The RD_PS instruction returns the Processor Status (PS) in register R0. The Processor Status is described in Section 6.2. The PS<SP_ALIGN> field is always a zero on a RD_PS.

2.1.10 Return from Exception or Interrupt

Format:

```
CALL_PAL   REI                                    !PALcode format
```

Operation:

```
! See Chapter 6
!  for information on interrupted registers
IF SP<5:0> NE 0 THEN
     {illegal operand }
tmp1 ←  (SP)                   ! Get saved R2
tmp2 ←  (SP+8)                 ! Get saved R3
tmp3 ←  (SP+16)                ! Get saved R4
tmp4 ←  (SP+24)                ! Get saved R5
tmp5 ←  (SP+32)                ! Get saved R6
tmp6 ←  (SP+40)                ! Get saved R7
tmp7 ←  (SP+48)                ! Get new PC
tmp8 ←  (SP+56)                ! Get new PS

ps_chk ←  tmp8                 ! Copy new ps
ps_chk<cm> ←  0                ! Clear cm field
ps_chk<sp_align> ←  0          ! Clear sp_align field
ps_chk<sw> ←  0                ! Clear Software Field
intr_flag ←  0                 ! Clear except/inter/mcheck flag
{ clear lock_flag}

! If current mode is not kernel check the new ps is valid.
IF {ps<cm> NE 0} AND
    {{tmp8<cm> LT ps<cm>} OR {ps_chk NE 0}} THEN
    BEGIN
    {illegal operand}
    END

sp ←  {sp + 8*8} OR tmp8<sp_align>
IF {internal registers for stack pointers}  THEN
    CASE ps<cm>  BEGIN
     [0]: ipr_ksp ←  sp
     [1]: ipr_esp ←  sp
     [2]: ipr_ssp ←  sp
     [3]: ipr_usp ←  sp
    ENDCASE
    CASE tmp8<cm>  BEGIN
     [0]: sp ←  ipr_ksp
     [1]: sp ←  ipr_esp
     [2]: sp ←  ipr_ssp
     [3]: sp ←  ipr_usp
    ENDCASE
ELSE
   (pcbb + 8*ps<cm>) ←  sp
   sp ←  (pcbb + 8*tmp8<cm>)
ENDIF
```

```
R2  ←   tmp1
R3  ←   tmp2
R4  ←   tmp3
R5  ←   tmp4
R6  ←   tmp5
R7  ←   tmp6
PC  ←   tmp7
PS  ←   tmp8 <12:00>

{Initiate interrupts or AST interrupts that are now pending}
```

Exceptions:

Access Violation

Fault on Read

Illegal Operand

Kernel Stack Not Valid Halt

Translation Not Valid

Instruction mnemonics:

CALL_PAL   REI   Return from Exception or Interrupt

Description:

The REI instruction pops the PS, PC, and saved R2...R7 from the current stack and holds them in temporary registers.

The new PS is checked for validity and consistency. If it is invalid or inconsistent, an illegal operand exception occurs; otherwise the operation continues. A kernel to nonkernel REI with a new PS<IPL> not equal to zero may yield UNDEFINED results.

The current stack pointer is then saved and a new stack pointer is selected according to the new PS<CM> field. R2 through R7 are restored using the saved values held in the temporary registers. A check is made to determine if an AST or other interrupt is pending (see Section 6.7.6).

If the enabling conditions are present for an interrupt or AST interrupt at the completion of this instruction, the interrupt or AST interrupt occurs before the next instruction.

When an REI is issued, the current stack must be writable from the current mode or an Access Violation may occur.

IMPLEMENTATION NOTE

This is necessary so that an implementation can choose to clear the lock_flag by doing a STx_C to above the top-of-stack after popping PS, PC, and saved R2..R7 off the the current stack.

2.1.11 Read System Cycle Counter

Format:

> CALL_PAL   RSCC   !PALcode format

Operation:

> R0 ←   {System Cycle Counter}

Exceptions:

> None

Instruction mnemonics:

> CALL_PAL   RSCC   Read System Cycle Counter

Description:

The RSCC instruction writes register R0 with the value of the system cycle counter. This counter is an unsigned 64-bit integer that increments at the same rate as the process cycle counter. The cycle counter frequency, which is the number of times the system cycle counter gets incremented per second rounded to a 64-bit integer, is given in the HWRPB.

The system cycle counter is suitable for timing a general range of intervals to within 10% error and may be used for detailed performance characterization. It is required on all implementations. SCC is required for every processor, and each processor in a multiprocessor system has its own private, independent SCC.

Notes:

1. Processor initialization starts the SCC at 0.

2. SCC is required for every processor and each processor in a multiprocessor system has its own private, independent SCC.

3. SCC is monotonically increasing. On the same processor, the values returned by two successive reads of SCC must either be equal or the value of the second must be greater (unsigned) than the first.

4. SCC ticks are never lost so long as the SCC is accessed at least once per each PCC overflow period ($2^{**}32$ PCC increments) during periods when the hardware clock interrupt remains blocked. The hardware clock interrupt is blocked whenever the IPL is at or above CLOCK_IPL or whenever the processor enters console I/O mode from program I/O mode.

5. The 64-bit SCC may be constructed from the 32-bit PCC hardware counter and a 32-bit PALcode software counter. As part of the hardware clock interrupt processing, PALcode increments the software counter whenever a PCC wrap is detected. Thus, SCC ticks may be lost only when PALcode fails to detect PCC wraps. In a machine where the PCC is incremented at a 1 nsec rate, this may occur when hardware clock interrupts are blocked for greater than 4 seconds.

6. An implementation-dependent mechanism must exist to, when enabled, cause the RSCC instruction, as implemented by standard PALcode, to always return a zero in R0. This mechanism must be usable by privileged system software. A similar mechanism must exist for RPCC. Implementations are allowed to have just a single mechanism which when enabled causes both RSCC and RPCC to return zero.

2.1.12 Swap AST Enable

Format:

CALL_PAL   SWASTEN   !PALcode format

Operation:

```
R0 ← ZEXT(ASTEN<PS<CM>>)
ASTEN<PS<CM>> ← R16<0>

{check for pending ASTs}
```

Exceptions:

None

Instruction mnemonics:

CALL_PAL   SWASTEN   Swap AST Enable for Current Mode

Description:

The SWASTEN instruction swaps the AST enable bit for the current mode. The new state for the enable bit is supplied in register R16<0> and previous state of the enable bit is returned, zero extended, in R0.

A check is made to determine if an AST interrupt is pending (see Section 6.7.6.6).

If the enabling conditions are present for an AST interrupt at the completion of this instruction, the AST occurs before the next instruction.

2.1.13 Write Processor Status Software Field

Format:

CALL_PAL   WR_PS_SW   !PALcode format

Operation:

PS<SW> ← R16<1:0>

Exceptions:

None

Instruction mnemonics:

CALL_PAL   WR_PS_SW   Write Processor Status Software Field

Description:

The WR_PS_SW instruction writes the Processor Status software field (PS<SW>) with the low order two bits of R16. The Processor Status is described in Section 6.2.

2.2 OpenVMS Alpha Queue Data Types

The following sections describe the queue data types that are manipulated by the OpenVMS queue PALcode. Section 2.3 describes the PALcode instructions that perform the manipulation.

2.2.1 Absolute Longword Queues

A longword queue is a circular, doubly linked list. A longword queue entry is specified by its address. Each longword queue entry is linked to the next with a pair of longwords. A queue is classified by the type of link it uses. Absolute longword queues use absolute addresses as links.

The first (lowest addressed) longword is the forward link; it specifies the address of the succeeding longword queue entry. The second (highest addressed) longword is the backward link; it specifies the address of the preceding longword queue entry.

A longword queue is specified by a longword queue header which is identical to a pair of longword queue linkage longwords. The forward link of the header is the address of the entry termed the head of the longword queue. The backward link of the header is the address of the entry termed the tail of the longword queue. The forward link of the tail points to the header.

An empty longword queue is specified by its header at address H, as shown in Figure 2–1 If an entry at address B is inserted into an empty longword queue (at either the head or tail), the longword queue shown in Figure 2–2 results. Figures 2–3, 2–4, and 2–5, respectively, illustrate the results of subsequent insertion of an entry at address A at the head, insertion of an entry at address C at the tail, and removal of the entry at address B.

2.2.2 Self-Relative Longword Queues

Self-relative longword queues use displacements from longword queue entries as links. Longword queue entries are linked by a pair of longwords. The first longword (lowest addressed) is the forward link; it is a displacement of the succeeding longword queue entry from the present entry. The second longword (highest addressed) is the backward link; it is the displacement of the preceding longword queue entry from the present entry. A longword queue is specified by a longword queue header, which also consists of two longword links.

An empty longword queue is specified by its header at address H. Since the longword queue is empty, the self-relative links are zero, as shown in Figure 2–6.

Four types of operations can be performed on self-relative queues: insert at head, insert at tail, remove from head, and remove from tail. Furthermore, these operations are interlocked to allow cooperating processes in a multiprocessor system to access a shared list without additional synchronization. A hardware-supported, interlocked memory access mechanism is used to modify the queue header. Bit <0> of the queue header is used as a secondary interlock and is set when the queue is being accessed.

If an interlocked queue CALL_PAL instruction encounters the secondary interlock set, then, in the absence of exceptions, it terminates after setting R0 to –1 to indicate failure to gain access to the queue. If the secondary interlock bit is not set, then it is set during the interlocked queue operation and is cleared upon completion of the operation. This prevents other interlocked queue CALL_PAL instructions from operating on the same queue.

If both the secondary interlock is set and an exception condition occurs, it is UNPREDICTABLE whether the exception will be reported.

Figures 2–7, 2–8, and 2–9, respectively, illustrate the results of subsequent insertion of an entry at address B at the head, insertion of an entry at address A at the tail, and insertion of an entry at address C at the tail.

Figures 2–9, 2–8, and 2–7 (in that order) illustrate the effect of removal at the tail and removal at the head.

Figure 2–1: Empty Absolute Longword Queue

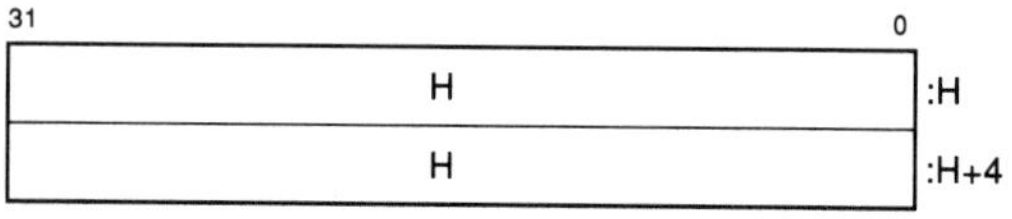

Figure 2–2: Absolute Longword Queue with One Entry

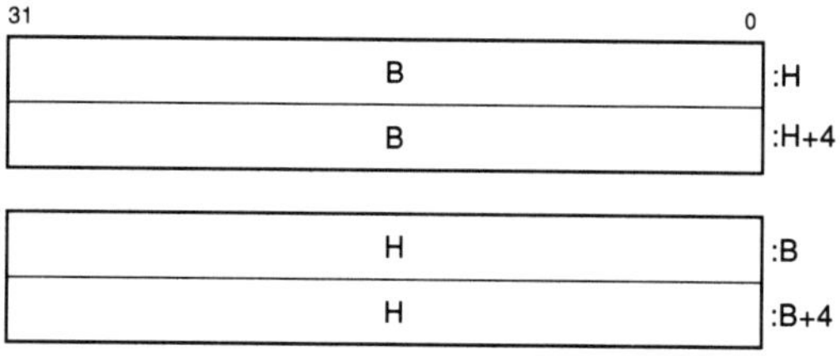

Figure 2–3: Absolute Longword Queue with Two Entries

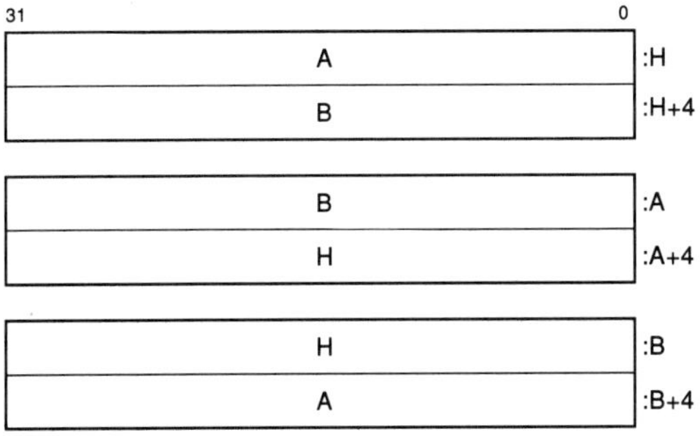

```
 31                                          0
┌─────────────────────────────────┐
│               A                 │ :H
│               B                 │ :H+4
└─────────────────────────────────┘

┌─────────────────────────────────┐
│               B                 │ :A
│               H                 │ :A+4
└─────────────────────────────────┘

┌─────────────────────────────────┐
│               H                 │ :B
│               A                 │ :B+4
└─────────────────────────────────┘
```

Figure 2–4: Absolute Longword Queue with Three Entries

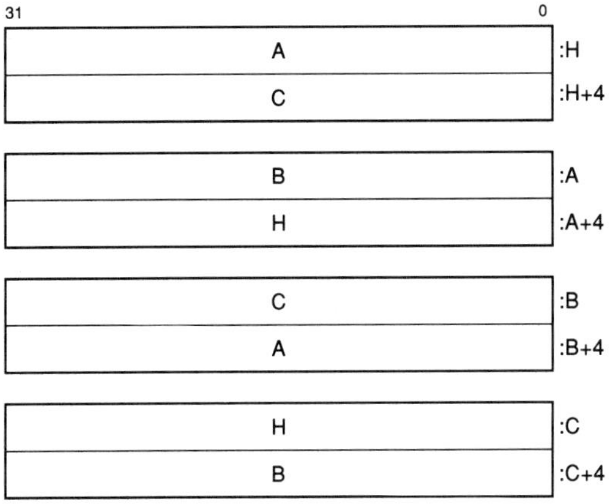

```
 31                                          0
┌─────────────────────────────────┐
│               A                 │ :H
│               C                 │ :H+4
└─────────────────────────────────┘

┌─────────────────────────────────┐
│               B                 │ :A
│               H                 │ :A+4
└─────────────────────────────────┘

┌─────────────────────────────────┐
│               C                 │ :B
│               A                 │ :B+4
└─────────────────────────────────┘

┌─────────────────────────────────┐
│               H                 │ :C
│               B                 │ :C+4
└─────────────────────────────────┘
```

Figure 2–5: Absolute Longword Queue with Three Entries After Removing the Second Entry

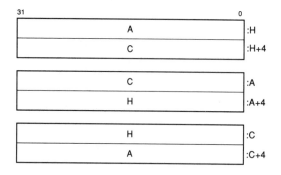

```
31                                      0
 ┌────────────────────────────────┐
 │              A                 │ :H
 ├────────────────────────────────┤
 │              C                 │ :H+4
 └────────────────────────────────┘

 ┌────────────────────────────────┐
 │              C                 │ :A
 ├────────────────────────────────┤
 │              H                 │ :A+4
 └────────────────────────────────┘

 ┌────────────────────────────────┐
 │              H                 │ :C
 ├────────────────────────────────┤
 │              A                 │ :C+4
 └────────────────────────────────┘
```

Figure 2–6: Empty Self-Relative Longword Queue

```
31                                      0
 ┌────────────────────────────────┐
 │              0                 │ :H
 ├────────────────────────────────┤
 │              0                 │ :H+4
 └────────────────────────────────┘
```

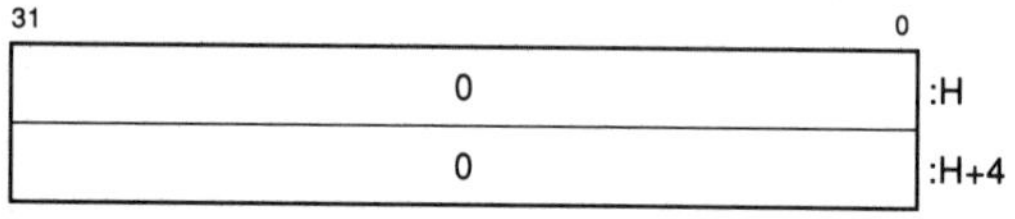

Figure 2–7: Self-Relative Longword Queue with One Entry

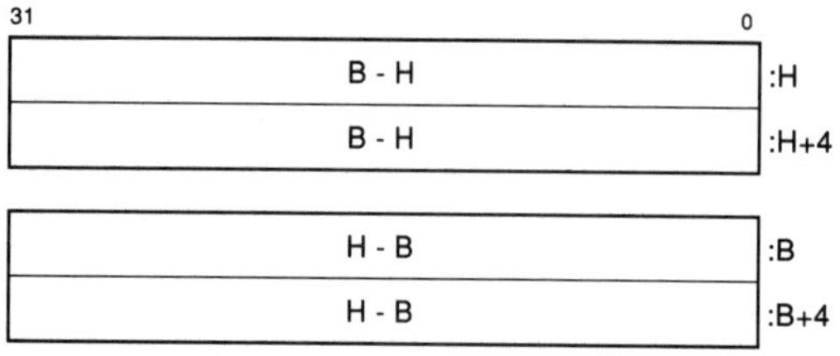

```
31                                      0
 ┌────────────────────────────────┐
 │             B - H              │ :H
 ├────────────────────────────────┤
 │             B - H              │ :H+4
 └────────────────────────────────┘

 ┌────────────────────────────────┐
 │             H - B              │ :B
 ├────────────────────────────────┤
 │             H - B              │ :B+4
 └────────────────────────────────┘
```

Figure 2–8: Self-Relative Longword Queue with Two Entries

```
31                                    0
 +-------------------------------+
 |            A - H              |  :H
 +-------------------------------+
 |            B - H              |  :H+4
 +-------------------------------+

 +-------------------------------+
 |            B - A              |  :A
 +-------------------------------+
 |            H - A              |  :A+4
 +-------------------------------+

 +-------------------------------+
 |            H - B              |  :B
 +-------------------------------+
 |            A - B              |  :B+4
 +-------------------------------+
```

Figure 2–9: Self-Relative Longword Queue with Three Entries

```
31                                    0
 +-------------------------------+
 |            A - H              |  :H
 +-------------------------------+
 |            C - H              |  :H+4
 +-------------------------------+

 +-------------------------------+
 |            B - A              |  :A
 +-------------------------------+
 |            H - A              |  :A+4
 +-------------------------------+

 +-------------------------------+
 |            C - B              |  :B
 +-------------------------------+
 |            A - B              |  :B+4
 +-------------------------------+

 +-------------------------------+
 |            H - C              |  :C
 +-------------------------------+
 |            B - C              |  :C+4
 +-------------------------------+
```

2.2.3 Absolute Quadword Queues

A quadword queue is a circular, doubly linked list. A quadword queue entry is specified by its address. Each quadword queue entry is linked to the next with a pair of quadwords. A queue is classified by the type of link it uses. Absolute quadword queues use absolute addresses as links.

The first (lowest addressed) quadword is the forward link; it specifies the address of the succeeding quadword queue entry. The second (highest addressed) quadword is the backward link; it specifies the address of the preceding quadword queue entry.

A quadword queue is specified by a quadword queue header which is identical to a pair of quadword queue linkage quadwords. The forward link of the header is the address of the entry termed the head of the quadword queue. The backward link of the header is the address of the entry termed the tail of the quadword queue. The forward link of the tail points to the header.

An empty quadword queue is specified by its header at address H, as shown in Figure 2–10. If an entry at address B is inserted into an empty quadword queue (at either the head or tail), the quadword queue shown in Figure 2–11 results. Figures 2–12, 2–13, and 2–14, respectively, illustrate the results of subsequent insertion of an entry at address A at the head, insertion of an entry at address C at the tail, and removal of the entry at address B.

2.2.4 Self-Relative Quadword Queues

Self-relative quadword queues use displacements from quadword queue entries as links. Quadword queue entries are linked by a pair of quadwords. The first quadword (lowest addressed) is the forward link; it is a displacement of the succeeding quadword queue entry from the present entry. The second quadword (highest addressed) is the backward link; it is the displacement of the preceding quadword queue entry from the present entry. A quadword queue is specified by a quadword queue header, which also consists of two quadword links.

An empty quadword queue is specified by its header at address H. Since the quadword queue is empty, the self-relative links are zero, as shown in Figure 2–15.

Four types of operations can be performed on self-relative queues: insert at head, insert at tail, remove from head, and remove from tail. Furthermore, these operations are interlocked to allow cooperating processes in a multiprocessor system to access a shared list without additional synchronization. A hardware-supported, interlocked memory access mechanism is used to modify the queue header. Bit <0> of the queue header is used as a secondary interlock and is set when the queue is being accessed.

If an interlocked queue CALL_PAL instruction encounters the secondary interlock set, then, in the absence of exceptions, it terminates after setting R0 to –1 to indicate failure to gain access to the queue. If the secondary interlock bit is not set, then it is set during the interlocked queue operation and is cleared upon completion of the operation. This prevents other interlocked queue CALL_PAL instructions from operating on the same queue.

If both the secondary interlock is set and an exception condition occurs, it is UNPREDICTABLE whether the exception will be reported.

Figures 2–16, 2–17, and 2–18, respectively, illustrate the results of subsequent insertion of an entry at address B at the head, insertion of an entry at address A at the tail, and insertion of an entry at address C at the tail.

Figures 2–18, 2–17, and 2–16, (in that order) illustrate the effect of removal at the tail and removal at the head.

Figure 2–10:   Empty Absolute Quadword Queue

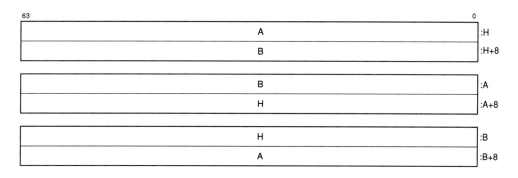

63	0	
H		:H
H		:H+8

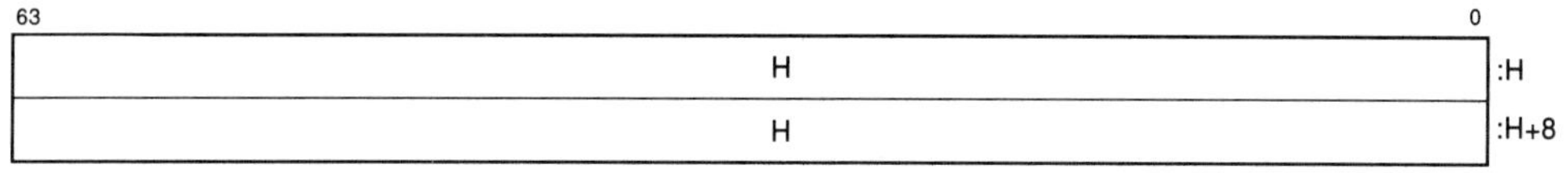

Figure 2–11:   Absolute Quadword Queue with One Entry

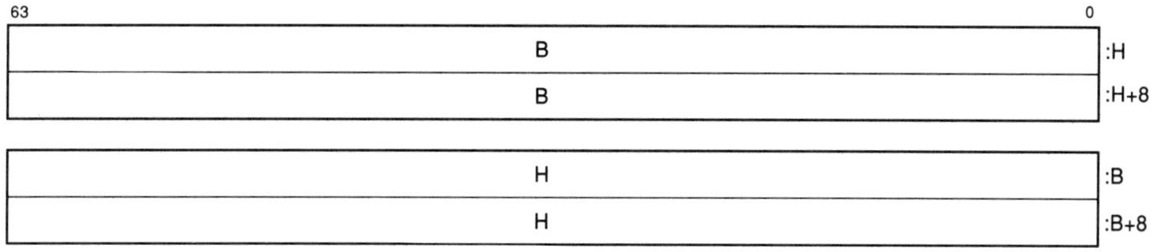

63	0	
B		:H
B		:H+8

H		:B
H		:B+8

Figure 2–12:   Absolute Quadword Queue with Two Entries

63	0	
A		:H
B		:H+8

B		:A
H		:A+8

H		:B
A		:B+8

Figure 2–13: Absolute Quadword Queue with Three Entries

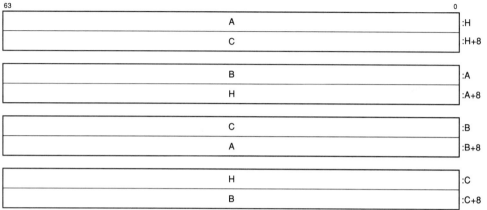

63		0	
	A		:H
	C		:H+8
	B		:A
	H		:A+8
	C		:B
	A		:B+8
	H		:C
	B		:C+8

Figure 2–14: Absolute Quadword Queue with Three Entries After Removing the Second Entry

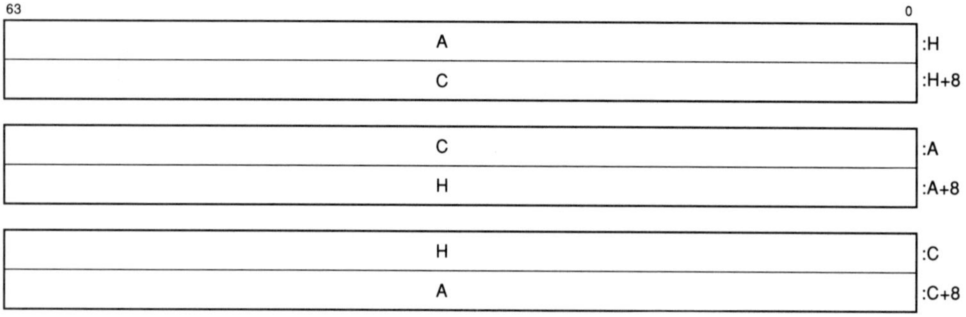

63		0	
	A		:H
	C		:H+8
	C		:A
	H		:A+8
	H		:C
	A		:C+8

Figure 2–15: Empty Self-Relative Quadword Queue

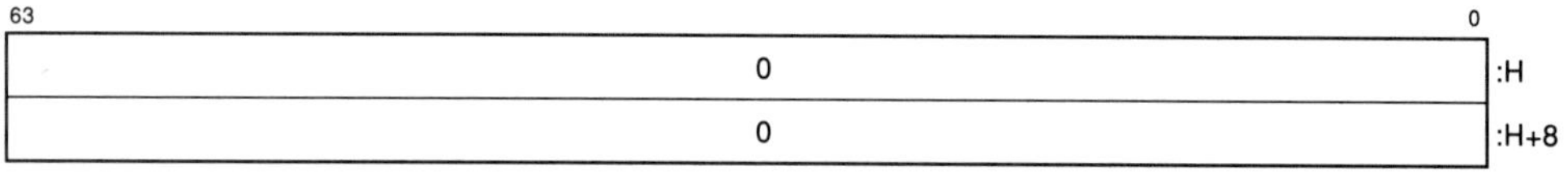

63		0	
	0		:H
	0		:H+8

Figure 2–16: Absolute Quadword Queue with One Entry

63		0	
B - H			:H
B - H			:H+8

63		0	
H - B			:B
H - B			:B+8

Figure 2–17: Self-Relative Quadword Queue with Two Entries

63		0	
A - H			:H
B - H			:H+8

63		0	
B - A			:A
H - A			:A+8

63		0	
H - B			:B
A - B			:B+8

Figure 2–18: Self-Relative Quadword Queue with Three Entries

63		0	
A - H			:H
C - H			:H+8

63		0	
B - A			:A
H - A			:A+8

63		0	
C - B			:B
A - B			:B+8

63		0	
H - C			:C
B - C			:C+8

2.3 Unprivileged OpenVMS Queue PALcode Instructions

The following unprivileged PALcode instructions perform atomic modification of the queue data types that are described in Section 2.2.

Table 2–3: VAX Queue Palcode Instruction Summary

Mnemonic	Operation
INSQHIL	Insert into longword queue at head, interlocked
INSQHILR	Insert into longword queue at head, interlocked, resident
INSQHIQ	Insert into quadword queue at head, interlocked
INSQHIQR	Insert into quadword queue at head, interlocked, resident
INSQTIL	Insert into longword queue at tail, interlocked
INSQTILR	Insert into longword queue at tail, interlocked, resident
INSQTIQ	Insert into quadword queue at tail, interlocked
INSQTIQR	Insert into quadword queue at tail, interlocked, resident
INSQUEL	Insert into longword queue
INSQUEQ	Insert into quadword queue
REMQHIL	Remove from longword queue at head, interlocked
REMQHILR	Remove from longword queue at head, interlocked, resident
REMQHIQ	Remove from quadword queue at head, interlocked
REMQHIQR	Remove from quadword queue at head, interlocked, resident
REMQTIL	Remove from longword queue at tail, interlocked
REMQTILR	Remove from longword queue at tail, interlocked, resident
REMQTIQ	Remove from quadword queue at tail, interlocked
REMQTIQR	Remove from quadword queue at tail, interlocked, resident
REMQUEL	Remove from longword queue
REMQUEQ	Remove from quadword queue

2.3.1 Insert Entry into Longword Queue at Head Interlocked

Format:

```
CALL_PAL    INSQHIL                          !PALcode format
```

Operation:

```
! R16 contains the address of the queue header
! R17 contains the address of the new entry
! R0 receives status:
!    -1 if the secondary interlock was set
!     0 if the queue was not empty before adding this entry
!     1 if the queue was empty before adding this entry
!
! Must have write access to header and queue entries
! Header and entries must be quadword aligned.
! Header cannot be equal to entry.
!
! check entry and header alignment and
! that the header and entry not same location and
! that the header and entry are valid 32 bit addresses

IF {R16<2:0> NE 0} OR {R17<2:0> NE 0} OR {R16 EQ R17} OR
   {SEXT(R16<31:0>) NE R16} OR {SEXT(R17<31:0>) NE R17} THEN
   BEGIN
      {illegal operand exception}
   END

N <- {retry_amount}                 ! Implementation-specific
REPEAT
   LOAD_LOCKED (tmp0 ←  (R16))    ! Acquire hardware interlock.
   IF tmp0<0> EQ 1 THEN           ! Try to set secondary interlock.
      R0 ←  -1, {return}          ! Already set
   done ← STORE_CONDITIONAL ((R16) ← {TMP0 OR R1} )
   N ←  N - 1
UNTIL {done EQ 1} OR {N EQ 0}
IF done NEQ 1, R0 ←  -1, {return} ! Retry exceeded

MB
tmp1 ←  SEXT(tmp0<31:0>)
IF {tmp1<2:1> NE 0} THEN BEGIN    ! Check alignment
   BEGIN                          ! Release secondary interlock.
     (R16) ←  tmp0
     {illegal operand exception}
   END

! Check if following addresses can be written
! without causing a memory management exception:
!             entry
!             header + tmp1
IF {all memory accesses can NOT be completed} THEN
   BEGIN                          ! Release secondary interlock.
     (R16) ←  tmp0
     {initiate memory management fault}
   END
```

```
                 ! All accesses can be done so enqueue the entry

tmp2 ←  SEXT({R16 - R17}<31:0>)
(R17)<31:0> ←  tmp1 + tmp2                  ! Forward link
(R17 + 4)<31:0> ←  tmp2                     ! Backward link
(R16 + tmp1 + 4)<31:0> ←  -tmp1 - tmp2 ! Successor back link

MB

(R16)<31:0> ←  -tmp2                        ! Forward link of header
                                           ! Release lock
IF tmp1 EQ 0 THEN
  R0 ←  1                                   ! Queue was empty
ELSE
  R0 ←  0                                   ! Queue was not empty
END
```

Exceptions:

Access Violation

Fault on Read

Fault on Write

Illegal Operand

Translation Not Valid

Instruction mnemonics:

CALL_PAL   INSQHIL   Insert into Longword Queue at Head Interlocked

Description:

If the secondary interlock is clear, INSQHIL inserts the entry specified in R17 into the self-relative queue following the header specified in R16.

If the entry inserted was the first one in the queue, R0 is set to a 1; else it is set to a 0. The insertion is a non-interruptible operation. The insertion is interlocked to prevent concurrent interlocked insertions or removals at the head or tail of the same queue by another process, in a multiprocessor environment. Before the insertion, the processor validates that the entire operation can be completed. This ensures that if a memory management exception occurs, the queue is left in a consistent state (see Chapters 3 and 6). If the instruction fails to acquire the secondary interlock after "N" retry attempts, then (in the absence of exceptions) R< 0> is set to a –1. The value "N" is implementation dependent.

2.3.2 Insert Entry into Longword Queue at Head Interlocked Resident

Format:

```
CALL_PAL   INSQHILR                        !PALcode format
```

Operation:

```
! R16 contains the address of the queue header
! R17 contains the address of the new entry
! R0 receives status:
!    -1 if the secondary interlock was set
!     0 if the queue was not empty before adding this entry
!     1 if the queue was empty before adding this entry
!
! Must have write access to header and queue entries
! Header and entries must be quadword aligned.
! Header cannot be equal to entry.
! All parts of the Queue must be memory resident

N <- {retry_amount}                     ! Implementation-specific
REPEAT
    LOAD_LOCKED (tmp0 ←  (R16))    ! Acquire hardware interlock.
    IF tmp0<0> EQ 1 THEN           ! Try to set secondary interlock.
        R0 ←  -1, {return}         ! Already set
    done ← STORE_CONDITIONAL ((R16) ← {TMP0 OR R1} )
    N ←  N - 1
UNTIL {done EQ 1} OR {N EQ 0}
IF done NEQ 1, R0 ←  -1, {return} ! Retry exceeded

MB

tmp1 ←  SEXT(tmp0<31:0>)
tmp2 ←  SEXT({R16 - R17}<31:0>)           ! Enqueue the entry
(R17)<31:0> ←  tmp1 + tmp2                 ! Forward link of entry.
(R17 + 4)<31:0> ←  tmp2                    ! Backward link of entry.
(R16 + tmp1 + 4)<31:0> ←  -tmp1 - tmp2 ! Successor back link

MB
(R16)<31:0> ←  -tmp2                       ! Forward link of header
                                          ! Release the lock

IF tmp1 EQ 0 THEN
    R0 ←  1                                ! Queue was empty
ELSE
    R0 ←  0                                ! Queue was not empty
END
```

Exceptions:

Illegal Operand

Instruction mnemonics:

CALL_PAL   INSQHILR   Insert Entry into Longword Queue
at Head Interlocked Resident

Description:

If the secondary interlock is clear, INSQHILR inserts the entry specified in R17 into the self-relative queue following the header specified in R16.

If the entry inserted was the first one in the queue, R0 is set to a 1; else it is set to a 0. The insertion is a non-interruptible operation. The insertion is interlocked to prevent concurrent interlocked insertions or removals at the head or tail of the same queue by another process, in a multiprocessor environment. If the instruction fails to acquire the secondary interlock after "N" retry attempts, then (in the absence of exceptions) R< 0> is set to a –1. The value "N" is implementation dependent.

This instruction requires that the queue be memory resident and that the queue header and elements are quadword aligned. No alignment or memory management checks are made before starting queue modifications to verify these requirements. Therefore, should any of these requirements not be met, the queue may be left in an unpredictable state and an illegal operand fault may be reported.

2.3.3 Insert Entry into Quadword Queue at Head Interlocked

Format:

```
CALL_PAL    INSQHIQ                     !PALcode format
```

Operation:

```
! R16 contains the address of the queue header
! R17 contains the address of the new entry
! R0 receives status:
!         -1 if the secondary interlock was set
!          0 if the entry was not empty before adding this entry
!          1 if the entry was empty before adding this entry
!
! Must have write access to header and queue entries
! Header and entries must be octaword aligned.
! Header cannot be equal to entry.
!
! check entry and header alignment and
! that the header and entry not same location
IF {R16<3:0> NE 0} OR {R17<3:0> NE 0} OR {R16 EQ R17} THEN
    BEGIN
     {illegal operand exception}
    END

N <- {retry_amount}                 ! Implementation-specific
REPEAT
    LOAD_LOCKED (tmp0 ←   (R16))    ! Acquire hardware interlock.
    IF tmp0<0> EQ 1 THEN            ! Try to set secondary interlock.
        R0 ←   -1, {return}        ! Already set
    done ← STORE_CONDITIONAL ((R16) ← {TMP0 OR R1} )
    N ←   N - 1
UNTIL {done EQ 1} OR {N EQ 0}
IF done NEQ 1, R0 ←   -1, {return} ! Retry exceeded

MB

IF {tmp1<3:1> NE 0} THEN BEGIN  ! Check Alignment
  BEGIN                         ! Release secondary interlock
    (R16) ←   tmp1
    {illegal operand exception}
  END

! Check if following addresses can be written
!  without causing a memory management exception:
!          entry
!          header + tmp1
IF {all memory accesses can NOT be completed} THEN
  BEGIN                         ! Release secondary interlock
    (R16) ←   tmp1
    {initiate memory management fault}
  END
```

```
! All accesses can be done so enqueue the entry
tmp2 ← R16 - R17
(R17) ← tmp1 + tmp2                   ! Forward link
(R17 + 8) ← tmp2                      ! Backward link
(R16 + tmp1 + 8) ← -tmp1 - tmp2       ! Successor back link

MB

(R16) ← -tmp2                         ! Forward link of header
                                     ! Release the lock.
IF tmp1 EQ 0 THEN
    R0 ← 1                           ! Queue was empty
ELSE
    R0 ← 0                           ! Queue was not empty
END
```

Exceptions:

Access Violation

Fault on Read

Fault on Write

Illegal Operand

Translation Not Valid

Instruction mnemonics:

CALL_PAL   INSQHIQ   Insert into Quadword Queue at Head Interlocked

Description:

If the secondary interlock is clear, INSQHIQ inserts the entry specified in R17 into the self-relative queue following the header specified in R16.

If the entry inserted was the first one in the queue, R0 is set to a 1; else it is set to a 0. The insertion is a non-interruptible operation. The insertion is interlocked to prevent concurrent interlocked insertions or removals at the head or tail of the same queue by another process, in a multiprocessor environment. Before the insertion, the processor validates that the entire operation can be completed. This ensures that if a memory management exception occurs, the queue is left in a consistent state (see Chapters 3 and 6). If the instruction fails to acquire the secondary interlock after "N" retry attempts, then (in the absence of exceptions) R< 0> is set to a –1. The value "N" is implementation dependent.

2.3.4 Insert Entry into Quadword Queue at Head Interlocked Resident

Format:

```
CALL_PAL   INSQHIQR                        !PALcode format
```

Operation:

```
! R16 contains the address of the queue header
! R17 contains the address of the new entry
! R0 receives status:
!        -1 if the secondary interlock was set
!         0 if the entry was not empty before adding this entry
!         1 if the entry was empty before adding this entry
!
! Must have write access to header and queue entries
! Header and entries must be octaword aligned.
! Header cannot be equal to entry.
! All parts of the Queue must be memory resident

N <- {retry_amount}               ! Implementation-specific
REPEAT
   LOAD_LOCKED (tmp0 ←  (R16))    ! Acquire hardware interlock.
   IF tmp0<0> EQ 1 THEN           ! Try to set secondary interlock.
      R0 ←  -1, {return}          ! Already set
   done ← STORE_CONDITIONAL ((R16) ← {TMP0 OR R1} )
   N ←  N - 1
UNTIL {done EQ 1} OR {N EQ 0}
IF done NEQ 1, R0 ←  -1, {return} ! Retry exceeded

MB

tmp2 ←  R16 - R17                 ! Enqueue the entry
(R17) ←  tmp1 + tmp2             ! Forward link of entry.
(R17 + 8) ←  tmp2               ! Backward link of entry.
(R16 + tmp1 + 8) ←  -tmp1 - tmp2 ! Successor back link

MB
(R16) ←  -tmp2                   ! Forward link of header,
                                  ! Release the lock

IF tmp1 EQ 0 THEN
   R0 ←  1                       ! Queue was empty
ELSE
   R0 ←  0                       ! Queue was not empty
END
```

Exceptions:

Illegal Operand

Instruction mnemonics:

CALL_PAL   INSQHIQR   Insert Entry into Quadword Queue
at Head Interlocked Resident

Description:

If the secondary interlock is clear, INSQHIQR inserts the entry specified in R17 into the self_relative queue following the header specified in R16.

If the entry inserted was the first one in the queue, R0 is set to a 1; else it is set to a 0. The insertion is a non-interruptible operation. The insertion is interlocked to prevent concurrent interlocked insertions or removals at the head or tail of the same queue by another process, in a multiprocessor environment. If the instruction fails to acquire the secondary interlock after "N" retry attempts, then (in the absence of exceptions) R< 0> is set to a –1. The value "N" is implementation dependent.

This instruction requires that the queue be memory resident and that the queue header and elements are octaword aligned. No alignment or memory management checks are made before starting queue modifications to verify these requirements. Therefore, should any of these requirements not be met, the queue may be left in an unpredictable state and an illegal operand fault may be reported.

2.3.5 Insert Entry into Longword Queue at Tail Interlocked

Format:

```
CALL_PAL    INSQTIL                          !PALcode format
```

Operation:

```
! R16 contains the address of the queue header
! R17 contains the address of the new entry
! R0 receives status:
!     -1 if the secondary interlock was set
!      0 if the entry was not empty before adding this entry
!      1 if the entry was empty before adding this entry
!
! Must have write access to header and queue entries
! Header and entries must be quadword aligned.
! Header cannot be equal to entry.
!
! check entry and header alignment and
! that the header and entry not same location and
! that the header and entry are valid 32 bit addresses
IF {R16<2:0> NE 0} OR {R17<2:0> NE 0} OR {R16 EQ R17} OR
   {SEXT(R16<31:0>) NE R16} OR {SEXT(R17<31:0>) NE R16} THEN
   BEGIN
    {illegal operand exception}
   END

N <- {retry_amount}                 ! Implementation-specific
REPEAT
   LOAD_LOCKED (tmp0 ←  (R16))      ! Acquire hardware interlock.
   IF tmp0<0> EQ 1 THEN             ! Try to set secondary interlock.
      R0 ←  -1, {return}           ! Already set
   done ← STORE_CONDITIONAL ((R16) ← {TMP0 OR R1} )
   N ←  N - 1
UNTIL {done EQ 1} OR {N EQ 0}
IF done NEQ 1, R0 ←  -1, {return} ! Retry exceeded

MB

tmp1 ←  SEXT(tmp0<31:0>)
tmp2 ←  SEXT(tmp0<63:32>)

IF {tmp1<2:1> NE 0} OR {tmp2<2:0> NE 0} THEN    ! Check Alignment
   BEGIN                                ! Release secondary interlock
    (R16) ←  tmp0
    {illegal operand exception}
   END
```

```
! Check if following addresses can be written
!   without causing a memory management exception:
!           entry
!           header + (header + 4)
IF {all memory accesses can NOT be completed} THEN
   BEGIN                           ! Release secondary interlock
   (R16) ← tmp0
   {initiate memory management fault}
   END

! All Accesses can be done so enqueue entry
tmp3 ← SEXT( {R16 - R17}<31:0>)
(R17)<31:0> ← tmp3                 ! Forward link
(R17 + 4)<31:0> ← tmp2 + tmp3      ! Backward link
IF {tmp2 NE 0} THEN                ! Forward link of predecessor
   (R16+tmp2)<31:0> ← -tmp3 - tmp2
ELSE
   tmp1 ← SEXT({-tmp3 - tmp2}<31:0>)
   (R16+4)<31:0> ← -tmp3           ! Backward link of header

MB

(R16)<31:0> ← tmp1                 ! Forward link, release lock
IF tmp1 EQ -tmp3 THEN
   R0 ← 1                          ! Queue was empty
ELSE
   R0 ← 0                          ! Queue was not empty
END
```

Exceptions:

Access Violation

Fault on Read

Fault on Write

Illegal Operand

Translation Not Valid

Instruction mnemonics:

CALL_PAL   INSQTIL   Insert into Longword Queue at Tail Interlocked

Description:

If the secondary interlock is clear, INSQTIL inserts the entry specified in R17 into the self-relative queue preceding the header specified in R16.

If the entry inserted was the first one in the queue, R0 is set to a 1; else it is set to a 0. The insertion is a non-interruptible operation. The insertion is interlocked to prevent concurrent interlocked insertions or removals at the head or tail of the same queue by another process, in a multiprocessor environment. Before performing any part of the operation, the processor validates that the insertion can be completed.

This ensures that if a memory management exception occurs, the queue is left in a consistent state (see Chapters 3 and 6). If the instruction fails to acquire the secondary interlock after "N" retry attempts, then (in the absence of exceptions) R< 0> is set to a –1. The value "N" is implementation dependent.

2.3.6 Insert Entry into Longword Queue at Tail Interlocked Resident

Format:

```
CALL_PAL    INSQTILR                          !PALcode format
```

Operation:

```
! R16 contains the address of the queue header
! R17 contains the address of the new entry
! R0 receives status:
!    -1 if the secondary interlock was set
!     0 if the entry was not empty before adding this entry
!     1 if the entry was empty before adding this entry
!
! Must have write access to header and queue entries
! Header and entries must be quadword aligned.
! Header cannot be equal to entry.
! All parts of the Queue must be memory resident

N <- {retry_amount}                ! Implementation-specific
REPEAT
   LOAD_LOCKED (tmp0 ←  (R16))   ! Acquire hardware interlock.
   IF tmp0<0> EQ 1 THEN          ! Try to set secondary interlock.
      R0 ←  -1, {return}         ! Already set
   done ← STORE_CONDITIONAL ((R16) ← {TMP0 OR R1} )
   N ←  N - 1
UNTIL {done EQ 1} OR {N EQ 0}
IF done NEQ 1, R0 ←  -1, {return} ! Retry exceeded

MB

tmp1 ←  SEXT(tmp0<31:0>)
tmp2 ←  SEXT(tmp0<63:32>)
tmp3 ←  SEXT( {R16 - R17}<31:0>)
(R17)<31:0> ←  tmp3                ! Forward link
(R17 + 4)<31:0> ←  tmp2 + tmp3     ! Backward link
IF {tmp2 NE 0} THEN                ! Forward link of predecessor
   (R16+tmp2)<31:0> ←  -tmp3 - tmp2
ELSE
   tmp1 ←  <- SEXT({-tmp3 - tmp2}<31:0>)

(R16+4)<31:0> ←  -tmp3             ! Backward link of header

MB

(R16)<31:0> ←  tmp1                ! Forward link
                                   ! Release the lock
IF tmp1 EQ -tmp3 THEN
   R0 ←  1                         ! Queue was empty
ELSE
   R0 ←  0                         ! Queue was not empty
END
```

Exceptions:

Illegal Operand

Instruction mnemonics:

CALL_PAL   INSQTILR   Insert Entry into Longword Queue
at Tail Interlocked Resident

Description:

If the secondary interlock is clear, INSQTILR inserts the entry specified in R17 into the self-relative queue preceding the header specified in R16.

If the entry inserted was the first one in the queue, R0 is set to a 1; else it is set to a 0. The insertion is a non-interruptible operation. The insertion is interlocked to prevent concurrent interlocked insertions or removals at the head or tail of the same queue by another process, in a multiprocessor environment. If the instruction fails to acquire the secondary interlock after "N" retry attempts, then (in the absence of exceptions) R< 0> is set to a –1. The value "N" is implementation dependent.

This instruction requires that the queue be memory resident and that the queue header and elements are quadword aligned. No alignment or memory management checks are made before starting queue modifications to verify these requirements. Therefore, should any of these requirements not be met, the queue may be left in an unpredictable state and an illegal operand fault may be reported.

2.3.7 Insert Entry into Quadword Queue at Tail Interlocked

Format:

> CALL_PAL   INSQTIQ   !PALcode format

Operation:

```
! R16 contains the address of the queue header
! R17 contains the address of the new entry
! R0 receives status:
!     -1 if the secondary interlock was set
!      0 if the entry was not empty before adding this entry
!      1 if the entry was empty before adding this entry
!
! Must have write access to header and queue entries
! Header and entries must be octaword aligned.
! Header cannot be equal to entry.
!
! check entry and header alignment and
! that the header and entry not same location
IF {R16<3:0> NE 0} OR {R17<3:0> NE 0} OR {R16 EQ R17} THEN
    BEGIN
     {illegal operand exception}
    END

N <- {retry_amount}                  ! Implementation-specific
REPEAT
    LOAD_LOCKED (tmp0 ←  (R16))   ! Acquire hardware interlock.
    IF tmp0<0> EQ 1 THEN              ! Try to set secondary interlock.
        R0 ←  -1, {return}           ! Already set
    done ← STORE_CONDITIONAL ((R16) ← {TMP0 OR R1} )
    N ←  N - 1
UNTIL {done EQ 1} OR {N EQ 0}
IF done NEQ 1, R0 ←  -1, {return} ! Retry exceeded

MB

tmp2 ←  (R16+8)
IF {tmp1<3:1> NE 0} OR {tmp2<3:0> NE 0} THEN   ! Check Alignment.
    BEGIN                                  ! Release secondary interlock.
     (R16) ←  tmp1
     {illegal operand exception}
    END

! Check if following addresses can be written
!  without causing a memory management exception:
!            entry
!            header + (header + 8)
IF {all memory accesses can NOT be completed} THEN
    BEGIN                               ! Release secondary interlock.
     (R16) ←  tmp1
     {initiate memory management fault}
    END
```

```
! All accesses can be done so enqueue the entry
tmp3 ←  R16 - R17
(R17) ←  tmp3                          ! Forward link
(R17 + 8) ←  tmp2 + tmp3               ! Backward link
IF {tmp2 NE 0} THEN                    ! Forward link of predecessor
    (R16+tmp2) ←  -tmp3 - tmp2
ELSE
    tmp1 ←  {-tmp3 - tmp2}
(R16+8) ←  -tmp3                       ! Backward link of header

MB

(R16) ←  tmp1                          ! Forward link
                                       ! Release the lock

IF tmp1 EQ -tmp3  THEN
  R0 ←  1                              ! Queue was empty
ELSE
  R0 ←  0                              ! Queue was not empty
END
```

Exceptions:

Access Violation

Fault on Read

Fault on Write

Illegal Operand

Translation Not Valid

Instruction mnemonics:

CALL_PAL INSQTIQ   Insert into Quadword Queue at Tail Interlocked

Description:

If the secondary interlock is clear, INSQTIQ inserts the entry specified in R17 into the self-relative queue preceding the header specified in R16.

If the entry inserted was the first one in the queue, R0 is set to a 1 else it is set to a 0. The insertion is a non-interruptible operation. The insertion is interlocked to prevent concurrent interlocked insertions or removals at the head or tail of the same queue by another process, in a multiprocessor environment. Before performing any part of the operation, the processor validates that the insertion can be completed. This ensures that if a memory management exception occurs, the queue is left in a consistent state (see Chapters 3 and 6). If the instruction fails to acquire the secondary interlock after "N" retry attempts, then (in the absence of exceptions) R< 0> is set to a –1. The value "N" is implementation dependent.

2.3.8 Insert Entry into Quadword Queue at Tail Interlocked Resident

Format:

```
CALL_PAL    INSQTIQR                        !PALcode format
```

Operation:

```
! R16 contains the address of the queue header
! R17 contains the address of the new entry
! R0 receives status:
!     -1 if the secondary interlock was set
!      0 if the entry was not empty before adding this entry
!      1 if the entry was empty before adding this entry
!
! Must have write access to header and queue entries
! Header and entries must be octaword aligned.
! Header cannot be equal to entry.
! All parts of the Queue must be memory resident

N <- {retry_amount}                 ! Implementation-specific
REPEAT
    LOAD_LOCKED (tmp0 ←  (R16))     ! Acquire hardware interlock.
    IF tmp0<0> EQ 1 THEN             ! Try to set secondary interlock.
       R0 ←  -1, {return}           ! Already set
       done ← STORE_CONDITIONAL ((R16) ← {TMP0 OR R1} )
       N ←  N - 1
UNTIL {done EQ 1} OR {N EQ 0}
IF done NEQ 1, R0 ←  -1, {return} ! Retry exceeded

MB

tmp2 ←  (R16+8)
tmp3 ←  R16 - R17
(R17) ←  tmp3                       ! Forward link
(R17 + 8) ←  tmp2 + tmp3            ! Backward link
IF {tmp2 NE 0} THEN                 ! Forward link of predecessor
    (R16+tmp2) ←  -tmp3 - tmp2
ELSE
    tmp1 ←  {-tmp3 - tmp2}
(R16+8) ←  -tmp3                    ! Backward link of header

MB

(R16) ←  tmp1                       ! Forward link and release the lock
IF tmp1 EQ -tmp3 THEN
    R0 ←  1                         ! Queue was empty
ELSE
    R0 ←  0                         ! Queue was not empty
END
```

Exceptions:

Illegal Operand

Instruction mnemonics:

CALL_PAL   INSQTIQR   Insert Entry into Quadword Queue
at Tail Interlocked Resident

Description:

If the secondary interlock is clear, INSQTIQR inserts the entry specified in R17 into the self_relative queue preceding the header specified in R16.

If the entry inserted was the first one in the queue, R0 is set to a 1 else it is set to a 0. The insertion is a non-interruptible operation. The insertion is interlocked to prevent concurrent interlocked insertions or removals at the head or tail of the same queue by another process, in a multiprocessor environment. If the instruction fails to acquire the secondary interlock after "N" retry attempts, then (in the absence of exceptions) R< 0> is set to a –1. The value "N" is implementation dependent.

This instruction requires that the queue be memory resident and that the queue header and elements are octaword aligned. No alignment or memory management checks are made before starting queue modifications to verify these requirements. Therefore, should any of these requirements not be met, the queue may be left in an unpredictable state and an illegal operand fault may be reported.

2.3.9 Insert Entry into Longword Queue

Format:

```
CALL_PAL   INSQUEL                            !PALcode format
```

Operation:

```
! R16 contains the address of the predecessor entry
!     or the 32 bit address of the 32 bit address of the
!     predecessor entry for INSQUEL/D
! R17 contains the address of the new entry
! R0 receives status:
!          0 if the queue was not empty before adding this entry
!          1 if the queue was empty before adding this entry
!
! Must have write access to header and queue entries
IF opcode EQ INSQUEL/D THEN
    tmp2 ←  SEXT((R16)<31:0>)            ! Address of predecessor
ELSE
    tmp2 ←  R16

IF {all memory accesses can be completed} THEN
    BEGIN
    tmp<31:0> ←  SEXT((tmp2)<31:0>)   ! Get Forward Link
    (R17)<31:0> ←  tmp                ! Set forward link
    (R17 + 4)<31:0> ←  tmp2           ! Backward link
    (SEXT((tmp2)<31:0>) + 4)<31:0> ←  R17
                                      ! Backward link of Successor
    (tmp2)<31:0> ←  R17               ! Forward link of Predecessor
    IF tmp EQ tmp2 THEN
        R0 ←  1
    ELSE
        R0 ←  0
    END
ELSE
  BEGIN
    {initiate fault}
  END
END
```

Exceptions:

Access Violation

Fault on Read

Fault on Write

Translation Not Valid

Instruction mnemonics:

CALL_PAL   INSQUEL   Insert Entry into Longword Queue

CALL_PAL   INSQUEL/D   Insert Entry into Longword Queue Deferred

Description:

INSQUEL inserts the entry specified in R17 into the absolute queue following the entry specified by the predecessor addressed by R16. INSQUEL/D performs the same operation on the entry specified by the contents of the longword addressed by R16.

In either case, if the entry inserted was the first one in the queue, a 1 is returned in R0; otherwise a 0 is returned in R0. The insertion is a non-interruptible operation. Before performing any part of the insertion, the processor validates that the entire operation can be completed. This ensures that if a memory management exception occurs, the queue is left in a consistent state (see Chapters 3 and 6).

2.3.10 Insert Entry into Quadword Queue

Format:

CALL_PAL   INSQUEQ   !PALcode format

Operation:

```
! R16 contains the address of the predecessor entry
!     or the address of the address of the
!     predecessor entry for INSQUEQ/D
! R17 contains the address of the new entry
! R0 receives status:
!        0 if the queue was not empty before adding this entry
!        1 if the queue was empty before adding this entry
!
! Must have write access to header and queue entries
! Header and entries must be octaword aligned
IF opcode EQ INSQUEQ/D THEN
   IF {r16<3:0> NE 0} THEN
     BEGIN
      {illegal operand exception}
     END
    tmp2 ←  (R16)         ! Address of predecessor
ELSE
    tmp2 ←  R16
END
IF {tmp2<3:0> NE 0} OR {R17<3:0> NE 0} THEN
   BEGIN
    {illegal operand exception}
    END
IF {all memory accesses can be completed} THEN
   BEGIN
    tmp ←  (tmp2)          ! Get forward link of entry
    IF {tmp<3:0> NE 0} THEN
     BEGIN                 ! Check alignment
      {illegal operand exception}
     END
    (R17) ←  tmp           ! Set forward link of entry
    (R17 + 8) ←  tmp2      ! Backward link of entry
    (tmp + 8) ←  R17       ! Backward link of successor
    (tmp2) ←  R17          ! Forward link of predecessor
    IF tmp EQ tmp2 THEN
     R0 ←   1
    ELSE
     R0 ←   0
   END
ELSE
  BEGIN
   {initiate fault}
   END
END
```

Exceptions:

Access Violation

Fault on Read

Fault on Write

Translation Not Valid

Illegal Operand

Instruction mnemonics:

CALL_PAL   INSQUEQ   Insert Entry into Quadword Queue

CALL_PAL   INSQUEQ/D Insert Entry into Quadword Queue Deferred

Description:

INSQUEQ inserts the entry specified in R17 into the absolute queue following the entry specified by the predecessor addressed by R16. INSQUEQ/D performs the same operation on the entry specified by the contents of the quadword addressed by R16.

In either case, if the entry inserted was the first one in the queue, a 1 is returned in R0; otherwise a 0 is returned in R0. The insertion is a non-interruptible operation. Before performing any part of the insertion, the processor validates that the entire operation can be completed. This ensures that if a memory management exception occurs, the queue is left in a consistent state (see Chapters 3 and 6). R0 is unpredictable if an exception occurs. The relative order of reporting memory management and illegal operand exceptions is unpredictable.

2.3.11 Remove Entry from Longword Queue at Head Interlocked

Format:

```
CALL_PAL    REMQHIL                        !PALcode format
```

Operation:

```
! R16 contains the address of the queue header
! R0 receives status:
!       -1 if the secondary interlock was set
!        0 if the queue was empty
!        1 if entry removed and queue still not empty
!        2 if entry removed and queue empty
! R1 receives the address of the removed entry
!
! Must have write access to header and queue entries
! Header and entries must be quadword aligned.
!
! Check header alignment and
! that the header is a valid 32 bit address
IF {R16<2:0> NE 0} OR {SEXT(R16<31:0>) NE R16} THEN
   BEGIN
     {illegal operand exception}
   END

N <- {retry_amount}                ! Implementation-specific
REPEAT
   LOAD_LOCKED (tmp0 ←   (R16))    ! Acquire hardware interlock.
   IF tmp0<0> EQ 1 THEN            ! Try to set secondary interlock.
      R0 ←   -1, {return}          ! Already set
   done ← STORE_CONDITIONAL ((R16) ← {TMP0 OR R1} )
   N ←   N - 1
UNTIL {done EQ 1} OR {N EQ 0}
IF done NEQ 1, R0 ←   -1, {return} ! Retry exceeded

MB

tmp1 ←   SEXT(tmp0<31:0>)
IF tmp1<2:0> NE 0 THEN           ! Check Alignment
  BEGIN                          ! Release secondary interlock
    (R16) ←   tmp0
    {illegal operand exception}
  END
! Check if the following can be done without
! causing a memory management exception:
!   read contents of header + tmp1 {if tmp1 NE 0}
!   write into header + tmp1 + (header + tmp1) {if tmp1 NE 0}
IF {all memory accesses can NOT be completed} THEN
  BEGIN                          ! Release secondary interlock
    (R16) ←   tmp0
    {initiate memory management fault}
  END
```

```
tmp2 ← SEXT({R16 + tmp1}<31:0>)
IF {tmp1 EQL 0} THEN
  tmp3 ← R16
ELSE
  tmp3 ← SEXT({tmp2 + SEXT((tmp2)<31:0>)})

IF tmp3<2:0> NE 0 THEN          ! Check Alignment
  BEGIN                          ! Release secondary interlock
   (R16) ← tmp0
   {illegal operand exception}
  END

(tmp3 + 4)<31:0> ← R16 - tmp3 ! Backward link of successor

MB

(R16)<31:0> ← tmp3 - R16        ! Forward link of header
                                ! Release lock
IF tmp1 EQ 0 THEN
  R0 ← 0                        ! Queue was empty
ELSE
  BEGIN
   IF {tmp3 - R16} EQ 0 THEN
     R0 ← 2                     ! Queue now empty
   ELSE
     R0 ← 1                     ! Queue not empty
  END
END
R1 ← tmp2                       ! Address of removed entry
```

Exceptions:

Access Violation

Fault on Read

Fault on Write

Illegal Operand

Translation Not Valid

Instruction mnemonics:

CALL_PAL   REMQHIL   Remove from Longword Queue at Head Interlocked

Description:

If the secondary interlock is clear, REMQHIL removes from the self-relative queue the entry following the header, pointed to by R16, and the address of the removed entry is returned in R1.

If the queue was empty prior to this instruction and secondary interlock succeeded, a 0 is returned in R0. If the interlock succeeded and the queue was not empty at the start of the removal and the queue is empty after the removal, a 2 is returned in R0. If the instruction fails to acquire the secondary interlock after "N" retry attempts, then (in the absence of exceptions) R< 0> is set to a –1. The value "N" is implementation dependent.

The removal is interlocked to prevent concurrent interlocked insertions or removals at the head or tail of the same queue by another process, in a multiprocessor environment. The removal is a non-interruptible operation. Before performing any part of the removal, the processor validates that the entire operation can be completed. This ensures that if a memory management exception occurs, the queue is left in a consistent state (see Chapters 3 and 6).

2.3.12 Remove Entry from Longword Queue at Head Interlocked Resident

Format:

```
CALL_PAL    REMQHILR                          !PALcode format
```

Operation:

```
! R16 contains the address of the queue header
! R0 receives status:
!          -1 if the secondary interlock was set
!           0 if the queue was empty
!           1 if entry removed and queue still not empty
!           2 if entry removed and queue empty
! R1 receives the address of the removed entry
!
! Must have write access to header and queue entries
! Header and entries must be quadword aligned.
! All parts of the Queue must be memory resident
N <- {retry_amount}                 ! Implementation-specific
REPEAT
   LOAD_LOCKED (tmp0 ←   (R16))    ! Acquire hardware interlock.
   IF tmp0<0> EQ 1 THEN             ! Try to set secondary interlock.
     R0 ←  -1, {return}            ! Already set
   done ← STORE_CONDITIONAL ((R16) ← {TMP0 OR R1} )
   N ←  N - 1
UNTIL {done EQ 1} OR {N EQ 0}
IF done NEQ 1, R0 ←  -1, {return} ! Retry exceeded

MB

tmp1 ←   SEXT(tmp0<31:0>)
tmp2 ←   SEXT({R16 + tmp1}<31:0>)
IF {tmp1 EQL 0} THEN
   tmp3 ←   R16
ELSE
   tmp3 ←   SEXT({tmp2 + SEXT((tmp2)<31:0>)})
END

(tmp3 + 4)<31:0> ←   R16 - tmp3        ! Backward link of successor

MB
(R16)<31:0> ←   tmp3 - R16             ! Forward link of header
                                       ! Release lock
IF tmp1 EQ 0 THEN
   R0 ←   0                            ! Queue was empty
ELSE
  BEGIN
   IF {tmp3 - R16} EQ 0 THEN
     R0 ←   2                          ! Queue now empty
   ELSE
     R0 ←   1                          ! Queue not empty
  END
END
R1 ←   tmp2                            ! Address of removed entry
```

Exceptions:

Illegal Operand

Instruction mnemonics:

CALL_PAL   REMQHILR   Remove Entry from Longword Queue
at Head Interlocked Resident

Description:

If the secondary interlock is clear, REMQHILR removes from the self-relative queue the entry following the header, pointed to by R16, and the address of the removed entry is returned in R1.

If the queue was empty prior to this instruction and secondary interlock succeeded, a 0 is returned in R0. If the interlock succeeded and the queue was not empty at the start of the removal and the queue is empty after the removal, a 2 is returned in R0. If the instruction fails to acquire the secondary interlock after "N" retry attempts, then (in the absence of exceptions) R< 0> is set to a –1. The value "N" is implementation dependent.

The removal is interlocked to prevent concurrent interlocked insertions or removals at the head or tail of the same queue by another process, in a multiprocessor environment. The removal is a non-interruptible operation.

This instruction requires that the queue be memory resident and that the queue header and elements are quadword aligned. No alignment or memory management checks are made before starting queue modifications to verify these requirements. Therefore, should any of these requirements not be met, the queue may be left in an unpredictable state and an illegal operand fault may be reported.

2.3.13 Remove Entry from Quadword Queue at Head Interlocked

Format:

CALL_PAL   REMQHIQ   !PALcode format

Operation:

```
! R16 contains the address of the queue header
! R0 receives status:
!        -1 if the secondary interlock was set
!         0 if the queue was empty
!         1 if entry removed and queue still not empty
!         2 if entry removed and queue empty
! R1 receives the address of the removed entry
!
! Must have write access to header and queue entries
! Header and entries must be octaword aligned.
!
! Check header alignment
IF {R16<3:0> NE 0} THEN
   BEGIN
    {illegal operand exception}
   END

N <- {retry_amount}              ! Implementation-specific
REPEAT
   LOAD_LOCKED (tmp0 ←  (R16))   ! Acquire hardware interlock.
   IF tmp0<0> EQ 1 THEN          ! Try to set secondary interlock.
     R0 ←  -1, {return}          ! Already set
   done ← STORE_CONDITIONAL ((R16) ← {TMP0 OR R1} )
   N ←  N - 1
UNTIL {done EQ 1} OR {N EQ 0}
IF done NEQ 1, R0 ←  -1, {return} ! Retry exceeded

MB

IF tmp1<3:0> NE 0 THEN    ! Check Alignment
   BEGIN                  ! Release secondary interlock
    (R16) ←  tmp1
    {illegal operand exception}
   END

! Check if the following can be done without
!  causing a memory management exception:
!  read contents of header + tmp1 {if tmp1 NE 0}
!  write into header + tmp1 + (header + tmp1) {if tmp1 NE 0}
IF {all memory accesses can NOT be completed} THEN
   BEGIN                  ! Release secondary interlock
    (R16) ←  tmp0
    {initiate memory management fault}
   END
```

```
tmp2 ←  R16 + tmp1
IF {tmp1 EQL 0} THEN
    tmp3 ←  R16
ELSE
    tmp3 ←  tmp2 + (tmp2)

IF tmp3<3:0> NE 0 THEN         ! Check Alignment
    BEGIN                      ! Release secondary interlock
     (R16) ←  tmp1
     {illegal operand exception}
    END

(tmp3 + 8) ←  R16 - tmp3      ! Backward link of successor
MB

(R16) ←  tmp3 - R16           ! Forward link of header
                              ! Release lock
IF tmp1 EQ 0 THEN
    R0 ←  0                   ! Queue was empty
ELSE
  BEGIN
    IF {tmp3 - R16} EQ 0 THEN
       R0 ←  2                ! Queue now empty
    ELSE
       R0 ←  1                ! Queue not empty
  END
END
R1 ←  tmp2                    ! Address of removed entry
```

Exceptions:

Access Violation

Fault on Read

Fault on Write

Illegal Operand

Translation Not Valid

Instruction mnemonics:

CALL_PAL   REMQHIQ   Remove from Quadword Queue at Head
                       Interlocked

Description:

If the secondary interlock is clear, REMQHIQ removes from the self-relative queue the entry following the header, pointed to by R16, and the address of the removed entry is returned in R1.

If the queue was empty prior to this instruction and secondary interlock succeeded, a 0 is returned in R0. If the interlock succeeded and the queue was not empty at the start of the removal, and the queue is empty after the removal a 2 is returned in R0. If the instruction fails to acquire the secondary interlock after "N" retry attempts, then (in the absence of exceptions) R< 0> is set to a –1. The value "N" is implementation dependent.

The removal is interlocked to prevent concurrent interlocked insertions or removals at the head or tail of the same queue by another process, in a multiprocessor environment. The removal is a non-interruptible operation. Before performing any part of the removal, the processor validates that the entire operation can be completed. This ensures that if a memory management exception occurs, the queue is left in a consistent state (see Chapters 3 and 6).

2.3.14 Remove Entry from Quadword Queue at Head Interlocked Resident

Format:

```
CALL_PAL    REMQHIQR                          !PALcode format
```

Operation:

```
! R16 contains the address of the queue header
! R0 receives status:
!          -1 if the secondary interlock was set
!           0 if the queue was empty
!           1 if entry removed and queue still not empty
!           2 if entry removed and queue empty
! R1 receives the address of the removed entry
!
! Must have write access to header and queue entries
! Header and entries must be octaword aligned.
! All parts of the Queue must be memory resident
N <- {retry_amount}                  ! Implementation-specific
REPEAT
   LOAD_LOCKED (tmp0 ←  (R16))     ! Acquire hardware interlock.
   IF tmp0<0> EQ 1 THEN              ! Try to set secondary interlock.
      R0 ←  -1, {return}            ! Already set
   done ← STORE_CONDITIONAL ((R16) ← {TMP0 OR R1} )
      N ←  N - 1
UNTIL {done EQ 1} OR {N EQ 0}
IF done NEQ 1, R0 ←  -1, {return} ! Retry exceeded

MB

tmp2 ←  R16 + tmp1
IF {tmp1 EQL 0} THEN
   tmp3 ←  R16
ELSE
   tmp3 ←  tmp2 + (tmp2)
END
(tmp3 + 8) ←  R16 - tmp3               ! Backward link of successor

MB

(R16) ←  tmp3 - R16                    ! Forward link of header
                                       ! Release lock
IF tmp1 EQ 0 THEN
   R0 ←  0                            ! Queue was empty
ELSE
  IF {tmp3 - R16} EQ 0 THEN
     R0 ←  2                          ! Queue now empty
  ELSE
     R0 ←  1                          ! Queue not empty
END
R1 ←  tmp2                             ! Address of removed entry
```

Exceptions:

Illegal Operand

Instruction mnemonics:

CALL_PAL   REMQHIQR   Remove Entry from Quadword Queue
at Head Interlocked Resident

Description:

If the secondary interlock is clear, REMQHIQR removes from the self-relative queue the entry following the header, pointed to by R16, and the address of the removed entry is returned in R1.

If the queue was empty prior to this instruction and secondary interlock succeeded, a 0 is returned in R0. If the interlock succeeded and the queue was not empty at the start of the removal, and the queue is empty after the removal a 2 is returned in R0. If the instruction fails to acquire the secondary interlock after "N" retry attempts, then (in the absence of exceptions) R< 0> is set to a –1. The value "N" is implementation dependent.

The removal is interlocked to prevent concurrent interlocked insertions or removals at the head or tail of the same queue by another process, in a multiprocessor environment. The removal is a non-interruptible operation.

This instruction requires that the queue be memory resident and that the queue header and elements are octaword aligned. No alignment or memory management checks are made before starting queue modifications to verify these requirements. Therefore, should any of these requirements not be met, the queue may be left in an unpredictable state and an illegal operand fault may be reported.

2.3.15 Remove Entry from Longword Queue at Tail Interlocked

Format:

```
CALL_PAL    REMQTIL                          !PALcode format
```

Operation:

```
! R16 contains the address of the queue header
! R0 receives status:
!         -1 if the secondary interlock was set
!          0 if the queue was empty
!          1 if entry removed and queue still not empty
!          2 if entry removed and queue empty
! R1 receives the address of the removed entry
!
! Must have write access to header and queue entries
! Header and entries must be quadword aligned.
!
! Check header alignment and
! that the header is a valid 32 bit address
IF {R16<2:0> NE 0} OR {SEXT(R16<31:0>) NE R16} THEN
   BEGIN
     {illegal operand exception}
   END

N <- {retry_amount}                  ! Implementation-specific
REPEAT
   LOAD_LOCKED (tmp0 ←   (R16))   ! Acquire hardware interlock.
   IF tmp0<0> EQ 1 THEN              ! Try to set secondary interlock.
      R0 ←  -1, {return}            ! Already set
   done ← STORE_CONDITIONAL ((R16) ← {TMP0 OR R1} )
   N ←  N - 1
UNTIL {done EQ 1} OR {N EQ 0}
IF done NEQ 1, R0 ←  -1, {return} ! Retry exceeded

MB

tmp1 ←   SEXT(tmp0<31:0>)
tmp5 ←   SEXT(tmp0<63:32>)
IF tmp5<2:0> NE 0 THEN      ! Check alignment
  BEGIN                            ! Release secondary interlock
    (R16) ←   tmp0
    {illegal operand exception}
  END

!Check if the following can be done without
! causing a memory management exception:
!   read contents of header + (header + 4) {if tmp1 NE 0}
!   write into header + (header + 4)
!    + (header + 4 + (header + 4)){if tmp1 NE 0}
IF {all memory accesses can NOT be completed} THEN
  BEGIN                            ! Release secondary interlock
    (R16) ←   tmp0
    {initiate memory management fault}
  END
```

```
addr ←   SEXT( {R16 + tmp5}<31:0> )
tmp2 ←   SEXT( {addr + SEXT( (addr+4)<31:0>)}<31:0> )
IF tmp2<2:0> NE 0 THEN          ! Check alignment
  BEGIN                         ! Release secondary interlock
    (R16) ←   tmp0
    {illegal operand exception}
  END

(R16 + 4)<31:0> ←   tmp2 - R16  ! Backward link of header
IF {tmp2 EQL R16} THEN
    (R16)<31:0> ←   0           ! Forward link, release lock
ELSE
  BEGIN
    (tmp2)<31:0> ←   R16 - tmp2 ! Forward link of predecessor
  MB
    (R16)<31:0> ←   tmp1        ! Release lock
  END
IF tmp1 EQ 0 THEN
  R0 ←   0                      ! Queue was empty
ELSE
  BEGIN
    IF {tmp2 - R16} EQ 0 THEN
      R0 ←   2                  ! Queue now empty
    ELSE
      R0 ←   1                  ! Queue not empty
  END
R1 ←   addr                     ! Address of removed entry
```

Exceptions:

Access Violation

Fault on Read

Fault on Write

Illegal Operand

Translation Not Valid

Instruction mnemonics:

CALL_PAL   REMQTIL   Remove from Longword Queue at Tail Interlocked

Description:

If the secondary interlock is clear, REMQTIL removes from the self-relative queue
the entry preceding the header, pointed to by R16, and the address of the removed
entry is returned in R1.

If the queue was empty prior to this instruction and secondary interlock succeeded,
a 0 is returned in R0. If the interlock succeeded and the queue was not empty at
the start of the removal, and the queue is empty after the removal a 2 is returned
in R0. If the instruction fails to acquire the secondary interlock after "N" retry

attempts, then (in the absence of exceptions) R< 0> is set to a –1. The value "N" is implementation dependent.

The removal is interlocked to prevent concurrent interlocked insertions or removals at the head or tail of the same queue by another process, in a multiprocessor environment. The removal is a non-interruptible operation. Before performing any part of the removal, the processor validates that the entire operation can be completed. This ensures that if a memory management exception occurs, the queue is left in a consistent state (see Chapters 3 and 6).

2.3.16 Remove Entry from Longword Queue at Tail Interlocked Resident

Format:

CALL_PAL   REMQTILR   !PALcode format

Operation:

```
! R16 contains the address of the queue header
! R0 receives status:
!        -1 if the secondary interlock was set
!         0 if the queue was empty
!         1 if entry removed and queue still not empty
!         2 if entry removed and queue empty
! R1 receives the address of the removed entry
!
! Must have write access to header and queue entries
! Header and entries must be quadword aligned.
! All parts of the Queue must be memory resident

N <- {retry_amount}                 ! Implementation-specific
REPEAT
   LOAD_LOCKED (tmp0 ←  (R16))    ! Acquire hardware interlock.
   IF tmp0<0> EQ 1 THEN           ! Try to set secondary interlock.
      R0 ←  -1, {return}          ! Already set
   done ← STORE_CONDITIONAL ((R16) ← {TMP0 OR R1} )
   N ←  N - 1
UNTIL {done EQ 1} OR {N EQ 0}
IF done NEQ 1, R0 ←  -1, {return} ! Retry exceeded

MB

tmp1 ←   SEXT(tmp0<31:0>)
tmp5 ←   SEXT(tmp0<63:32>)
addr ←   SEXT( {R16 + tmp5}<31:0> )
tmp2 ←   SEXT( {addr + SEXT( (addr+4)<31:0>)}<31:0> )
(R16 + 4)<31:0> ←  tmp2 - R16       ! Backward link of header
IF {tmp2 EQL R16} THEN
   (R16)<31:0> ←  0                 ! Forward link, release lock
ELSE
  BEGIN
   (tmp2)<31:0> ←  R16 - tmp2       ! Forward link of predecessor
   MB
   (R16)<31:0> ←  tmp1              ! Release lock
  END
  IF tmp1 EQ 0 THEN
    R0 ←  0                         ! Queue was empty
  ELSE
    IF {tmp2 - R16} EQ 0 THEN
       R0 ←  2                      ! Queue now empty
    ELSE
       R0 ←  1                      ! Queue not empty
  END
END
R1 ←  addr                          ! Address of removed entry
```

Exceptions:

Illegal Operand

Instruction mnemonics:

CALL_PAL   REMQTILR   Remove Entry from Longword Queue
at Tail Interlocked Resident

Description:

If the secondary interlock is clear, REMQTILR removes from the self-relative queue the entry preceding the header, pointed to by R16, and the address of the removed entry is returned in R1.

If the queue was empty prior to this instruction and secondary interlock succeeded, a 0 is returned in R0. If the interlock succeeded and the queue was not empty at the start of the removal, and the queue is empty after the removal a 2 is returned in R0. If the instruction fails to acquire the secondary interlock after "N" retry attempts, then (in the absence of exceptions) R< 0> is set to a –1. The value "N" is implementation dependent.

The removal is interlocked to prevent concurrent interlocked insertions or removals at the head or tail of the same queue by another process, in a multiprocessor environment. The removal is a non-interruptible operation.

This instruction requires that the queue be memory resident and that the queue header and elements are quadword aligned. No alignment or memory management checks are made before starting queue modifications to verify these requirements. Therefore, should any of these requirements not be met, the queue may be left in an unpredictable state and an illegal operand fault may be reported.

2.3.17 Remove Entry from Quadword Queue at Tail Interlocked

Format:

```
CALL_PAL    REMQTIQ                        !PALcode format
```

Operation:

```
! R16 contains the address of the queue header
! R0 receives status:
!         -1 if the secondary interlock was set
!          0 if the queue was empty
!          1 if entry removed and queue still not empty
!          2 if entry removed and queue empty
! R1 receives the address of the removed entry
!
! Must have write access to header and queue entries
! Header and entries must be octaword aligned.
!
! Check header alignment
IF {R16<3:0> NE 0} THEN
  BEGIN
   {illegal operand exception}
  END

N <- {retry_amount}                 ! Implementation-specific
REPEAT
   LOAD_LOCKED (tmp0 ←  (R16))      ! Acquire hardware interlock.
   IF tmp0<0> EQ 1 THEN             ! Try to set secondary interlock.
      R0 ←  -1, {return}            ! Already set
   done ← STORE_CONDITIONAL ((R16) ← {TMP0 OR R1} )
   N ←  N - 1
UNTIL {done EQ 1} OR {N EQ 0}
IF done NEQ 1, R0 ←  -1, {return} ! Retry exceeded

MB

tmp5 ←  (R16+8)
IF tmp5<3:0> NE 0 THEN     ! Check Alignment
   BEGIN                   ! Release secondary interlock
    (R16) ←  tmp1
    {illegal operand exception}
   END
! Check if the following can be done without
!  causing a memory management exception:
!   read contents of header + (header + 8) {if tmp1 NE 0}
!   write into header + (header + 8)
!   + (header + 8 + (header + 8)){if tmp1 NE 0}
IF {all memory accesses can NOT be completed} THEN
   BEGIN                   ! Release secondary interlock
    (R16) ←  tmp1
    {initiate memory management fault}
   END
```

```
                   addr ←  R16 + tmp5
                   tmp2 ←  addr + (addr + 8)
                   IF tmp2<3:0> NE 0 THEN      ! Check alignment
                      BEGIN                    ! Release secondary interlock
                       (R16) ←  tmp1
                       {illegal operand exception}
                      END

                   (R16 + 8) ←  tmp2 - R16     ! Backward link of header
                   IF {tmp2 EQL R16} THEN
                       (R16) ←  0              ! Forward link, release lock
                   ELSE
                      BEGIN
                       (tmp2) ←  R16 - tmp2     ! Forward link of predecessor
                       MB
                       (R16) ←  tmp1            ! Release lock
                      END
                   END
                   IF tmp1 EQ 0 THEN
                     R0 ←  0                    ! Queue was empty
                   ELSE
                     BEGIN
                      IF {tmp2 - R16} EQ 0 THEN
                        R0 ←  2                 ! Queue now empty
                      ELSE
                        R0 ←  1                 ! Queue not empty
                     END
                   END
                   R1 ←  addr                   ! Address of removed entry
```

Exceptions:

Access Violation

Fault on Read

Fault on Write

Illegal Operand

Translation Not Valid

Instruction mnemonics:

CALL_PAL   REMQTIQ   Remove from Quadword Queue at Tail Interlocked

Description:

If the secondary interlock is clear, REMQTIQ removes from the self-relative queue the entry preceding the header, pointed to by R16, and the address of the removed entry is returned in R1.

If the queue was empty prior to this instruction and secondary interlock succeeded, a 0 is returned in R0. If the interlock succeeded and the queue was not empty at the start of the removal, and the queue is empty after the removal a 2 is returned in R0. If the instruction fails to acquire the secondary interlock after "N" retry attempts, then (in the absence of exceptions) R< 0> is set to a –1. The value "N" is implementation dependent.

The removal is interlocked to prevent concurrent interlocked insertions or removals at the head or tail of the same queue by another process, in a multiprocessor environment. The removal is a non-interruptible operation. Before performing any part of the removal, the processor validates that the entire operation can be completed. This ensures that if a memory management exception occurs, the queue is left in a consistent state (see Chapters 3 and 6).

2.3.18 Remove Entry from Quadword Queue at Tail Interlocked Resident

Format:

CALL_PAL   REMQTIQR   !PALcode format

Operation:

```
! R16 contains the address of the queue header
! R0 receives status:
!          -1 if the secondary interlock was set
!           0 if the queue was empty
!           1 if entry removed and queue still not empty
!           2 if entry removed and queue empty
! R1 receives the address of the removed entry
!
! Must have write access to header and queue entries
! Header and entries must be octaword aligned.
! All parts of the Queue must be memory resident
N <- {retry_amount}                  ! Implementation-specific
REPEAT
    LOAD_LOCKED (tmp0 ←  (R16))   ! Acquire hardware interlock.
    IF tmp0<0> EQ 1 THEN              ! Try to set secondary interlock.
        R0 ←  -1, {return}           ! Already set
    done ← STORE_CONDITIONAL ((R16) ← {TMP0 OR R1} )
    N ←  N - 1
UNTIL {done EQ 1} OR {N EQ 0}
IF done NEQ 1, R0 ←  -1, {return} ! Retry exceeded

MB

tmp5 ←  (R16+8)
addr ←  R16 + tmp5
tmp2 ←  addr + (addr + 8)
(R16 + 8) ←  tmp2 - R16                  ! Backward link of header
IF {tmp2 EQL R16} THEN
    (R16) ←  0                           ! Forward link, release lock
ELSE
  BEGIN
    (tmp2) ←  R16 - tmp2                 ! Forward link of predecessor
    MB
    (R16) ←  tmp1                        ! Release lock
  END
END
IF tmp1 EQ 0 THEN
    R0 ←  0                              ! Queue was empty
ELSE
    IF {tmp2 - R16} EQ 0 THEN
        R0 ←  2                          ! Queue now empty
    ELSE
        R0 ←  1                          ! Queue not empty
END
R1 ←  addr                               ! Address of removed entry
```

Exceptions:

Illegal Operand

Instruction mnemonics:

CALL_PAL   REMQTIQR   Remove Entry from Quadword Queue
at Tail Interlocked Resident

Description:

If the secondary interlock is clear, REMQTIQR removes from the self-relative queue the entry preceding the header, pointed to by R16, and the address of the removed entry is returned in R1.

If the queue was empty prior to this instruction and secondary interlock succeeded, a 0 is returned in R0. If the interlock succeeded and the queue was not empty at the start of the removal, and the queue is empty after the removal a 2 is returned in R0. If the instruction fails to acquire the secondary interlock after "N" retry attempts, then (in the absence of exceptions) R< 0> is set to a –1. The value "N" is implementation dependent.

The removal is interlocked to prevent concurrent interlocked insertions or removals at the head or tail of the same queue by another process, in a multiprocessor environment. The removal is a non-interruptible operation.

This instruction requires that the queue be memory resident and that the queue header and elements are octaword aligned. No alignment or memory management checks are made before starting queue modifications to verify these requirements. Therefore, should any of these requirements not be met, the queue may be left in an unpredictable state and an illegal operand fault may be reported.

2.3.19 Remove Entry from Longword Queue

Format:

```
CALL_PAL    REMQUEL                         !PALcode format
```

Operation:

```
! R16 contains the address of the entry to remove
!     or the address of the 32 bit address of the
!     entry for REMQUEL/D
! R0 receives status:
!        -1 if the queue was empty
!         0 if the queue is empty after removing an entry
!         1 if the queue is not empty after removing an entry
! R1 receives the address of the removed entry
!
! Must have write access to header and queue entries
IF opcode EQ REMQUEL/D THEN
    R1 ←  SEXT((R16)<31:0>)
ELSE
    R1 ←  SEXT(R16<31:0>)

IF {all memory accesses can be completed} THEN
    BEGIN
    tmp1 ←  (R1)<31:0>                 ! Forward Link of Predecessor
    ((R1+4)<31:0>)<31:0> ←  tmp1
    tmp2 ←  (R1+4)<31:0>               ! Backward Link of Successor
    ((R1)<31:0>+4)<31:0> ←  tmp2
    R0 ←  1                            ! Queue not empty
    IF {tmp1 EQ tmp2} THEN
      R0 ←  0                          ! Queue now empty
    IF {R1 EQ tmp2} THEN
      R0 ←  -1                         ! Queue was empty
    END
ELSE
  BEGIN
  {initiate fault}
  END
END
```

Exceptions:

Access Violation

Fault on Read

Fault on Write

Translation Not Valid

Instruction mnemonics:

CALL_PAL	REMQUEL	Remove Entry from Longword Queue
CALL_PAL	REMQUEL/D	Remove Entry from Longword Queue Deferred

Description:

REMQUEL removes the entry addressed by R16 from the longword absolute queue. The address of the removed entry is returned in R1. REMQUEL/D performs the same operation on the queue entry addressed by the longword addressed by R16.

In either case, if there was no entry in the queue to be removed, R0 is set to –1. If there was an entry to remove and the queue is empty at the end of this instruction, R0 is set to 0. If there was an entry to remove and the queue is not empty at the end of this instruction, R0 is set to 1. The removal is a non-interruptible operation. Before performing any part of the removal, the processor validates that the entire operation can be completed. This ensures that if a memory management exception occurs, the queue is left in a consistent state (see Chapters 3 and 6).

2.3.20 Remove Entry from Quadword Queue

Format:

```
CALL_PAL    REMQUEQ                              !PALcode format
```

Operation:

```
! R16 contains the address of the entry to remove
!     or address of address of entry for REMQUEQ/D
! R0 receives status:
!       -1 if the queue was empty
!        0 if the queue is empty after removing an entry
!        1 if the queue is not empty after removing an entry
! R1 receives the address of the removed entry
! Must have write access to header and queue entries
! Header and entries must be octaword aligned
IF opcode EQ REMQUEQ/D THEN
   IF {r16<3:0> NE 0} THEN
     BEGIN
     {illegal operand exception}
     END
   R1 ←  (R16)
ELSE
   R1 ←  R16
IF {R1<3:0> NE 0} THEN    ! Check alignment
   BEGIN
   {illegal operand exception}
   END
 IF {all memory accesses can be completed} THEN
   BEGIN
   tmp1 ←  (R1)          ! Forward link of Predecessor
   IF {tmp1<3:0> NE 0} THEN
    BEGIN                ! Check alignment
     {illegal operand exception}
    END
   tmp2 ←  (R1+8)        ! Find predecessor
   IF {tmp2<3:0> NE 0} THEN
    BEGIN                ! Check alignment
     {illegal operand exception}
    END
   (tmp2) ←  tmp1        ! Update Forward link of predecessor
   ((R1)+8) ←  tmp2
   R0 ←  1               ! Queue not empty
   IF {tmp1 EQ tmp2} THEN
    R0 ←  0              ! Queue now empty
   IF {R1 EQ tmp2} THEN
    R0 ←  -1             ! Queue was empty
   END
ELSE
   BEGIN
   {initiate fault}
   END
END
```

Exceptions:

Access Violation

Fault on Read

Fault on Write

Translation Not Valid

Illegal Operand

Instruction mnemonics:

CALL_PAL	REMQUEQ	Remove Entry from Quadword Queue
CALL_PAL	REMQUEQ/D	Remove Entry from Quadword Queue Deferred

Description:

REMQUEQ removes the queue entry addressed by R16 from the quadword absolute queue. The address of the removed entry is returned in R1. REMQUEL/D performs the same operation on the queue entry addressed by the quadword addressed by R16.

In either case, if there was no entry in the queue to be removed, R0 is set to –1. If there was an entry to remove and the queue is empty at the end of this instruction, R0 is set to 0. If there was an entry to remove and the queue is not empty at the end of this instruction, R0 is set to 1. The removal is a non-interruptible operation. Before performing any part of the removal, the processor validates that the entire operation can be completed. This ensures that if a memory management exception occurs, the queue is left in a consistent state (see Chapters 3 and 6). R0 and R1 are unpredictable if an exception occurs. The relative order of reporting memory management and illegal operand exceptions is unpredictable.

2.4 Unprivileged VAX Compatibility PALcode Instructions

The Alpha architecture provides the following PALcode instructions for use in translated VAX code. These instructions are not a permanent part of the architecture and will not be available in some future implementations. They are provided to help customers preserve VAX instruction atomicity assumptions in porting code from VAX to Alpha. These calls should be user mode. They must not be used by any code other than that generated by the VEST software translator and its supporting runtime code (TIE).

2.4.1 Atomic Move Operation

Format:

AMOVRR   !PALcode format

AMOVRM   !PALcode format

Operation:

```
! R16 contains the first source
! R17 contains the first destination address
! R18 contains the first length
! R19 contains the second source
! R20 contains the second destination address
! R21 contains the second length
CASE
  AMOVRR:
        IF intr_flag EQ 0 THEN
            R18 ←  0
            {return}
        END

        intr_flag ←  0
        (R17) ←  R16  ! length specified by R18<1:0>
        (R20) ←  R19  ! length specified by R21<1:0>
        IF {both moves successful} THEN
            R18 ←  1
        ELSE
            R18 ←  0
        END

     AMOVRM:
        IF intr_flag EQ 0 THEN
            R18 ←  0
            {return}
        END

        intr_flag ←  0
        (R17) ←  R16  ! length specified by R18<1:0>
        IF R21<5:0> NE 0 THEN
            BEGIN
                IF R19<1:0> NE 00 OR R20<1:0> NE 00
                    {Illegal operand exception}
                ELSE
                    (R20) ←  (R19) ! length specified by R21<5:0>
                END
        IF {both moves successful} THEN
            R18 ←  1
        ELSE
            R18 ←  0
        END
ENDCASE
```

Exceptions:

AMOVRR: Access Violation

              Fault On Write

              Translation Not Valid

AMOVRM: Access Violation

              Fault On Read

              Fault On Write

              Illegal Operand

              Translation Not Valid

Instruction mnemonics:

CALL_PAL   AMOVRR   Atomic Move Register/Register

CALL_PAL   AMOVRM   Atomic Move Register/Memory

Description:

NOTE

The CALL_PAL AMOVxx instructions are *only* for the support of translated VAX code. They will disappear from the architecture at some time in the future. They must be used *only* in translated VAX code and its support routines (TIE).

CALL_PAL AMOVRR

The CALL_PAL AMOVRR instruction specifies two multiprocessor safe register stores to arbitrary byte addresses. Either both stores are done or neither store is done. R18 is set to one if both stores are done, and zero otherwise. The two source registers are R16 and R19. The two destination byte addresses are in R17 and R20. The two lengths are specified in R18<1:0> and R21<1:0>. The length encoding is: 00 - store byte, 01 - store word, 10 - store longword, 11 - store quadword. The low 1, 2, 4, or 8 bytes of the source register are used, respectively. The unused bytes of the source registers are ignored. The unused bits of the length registers (R18<63:2> and R21<63:2>) should be zero (SBZ).

If, upon entry to the PALcode routine, the intr_flag is clear then the instruction sets R18 to zero and exits, doing no stores. Otherwise, intr_flag is cleared and the PALcode routine proceeds. This is the same per-processor intr_flag used by the RS and RC instructions.

The AMOVRR memory addresses may be unaligned. If either store would result in a Translation Not Valid fault, Fault on Write, or Access Violation fault, neither store is done and the corresponding fault is taken. If both stores would result in faults, it is UNPREDICTABLE which one is taken.

NOTE

A fault does not set R18, since the instruction has not been completed.

If both stores can be completed without faulting, they are both attempted using multiprocessor-safe LDQ_L..STQ_C sequences. If all the sequences store successfully with no interruption, the PALcode routine completes with R18 set to one. Otherwise, the PALcode routine completes with R18 set to zero. In addition, R16, R17, R19, R20 and R21 are UNPREDICTABLE upon return from the PALcode routine, even if an exception has occurred.

If the destinations overlap, the stores must appear be done in the order specified.

CALL_PAL AMOVRM

The CALL_PAL AMOVRM instruction specifies one multiprocessor safe register store to an arbitrary byte address, plus an atomic memory-to-memory move of 0 to 63 aligned longwords. Either the store and the move are both done in their entirety or neither is done. R18 is set to one if both are done, and zero otherwise.

The first source register is R16, the first destination address is in R17, and the first length is in R18. These three are specified exactly as in AMOVRR.

The second source address is in R19, the second destination address is in R20, and the second length is in R21<5:0>. The length is a longword length, in the range 0 to 63 longwords (0 to 252 bytes). The unused bytes of the source register R16 are ignored. The unused bits of the length registers registers (R18<63:2> and R21<63:6>) should be zero (SBZ).

If, upon entry to the PALcode routine, the intr_flag is clear then the instruction sets R18 to zero and exits, doing no stores. Otherwise, intr_flag is cleared and the PALcode routine proceeds. This is the same per-processor intr_flag used by the RS and RC instructions.

The memory address in R17 may be unaligned.

If the length for the move is zero, no move is done, no memory accesses are made via R19 and R20, and no fault checking of these addresses is done. In this case, the move is always considered to have succeeded in determining the setting of R18.

If the length in R21 is non-zero, the two addresses in R19 and R20 must be aligned longword addresses, otherwise an Illegal Operand exception is taken.

If either the store or the move would result in a Translation Not Valid, Fault on Read, Fault on Write, or Access Violation fault, neither is done and the corresponding fault is taken. If both would result in faults, it is UNPREDICTABLE which one is taken.

NOTE

A fault does not set R18, since the instruction has not been completed.

If both the store and the move can be completed without faulting, they are both attempted, using multiprocessor-safe LDQ_L..STQ_C sequences for the store. If all the operations store successfully with no interruption, the PALcode routine completes with R18 set to one. Otherwise, the PALcode routine completes with R18 set to zero. In addition, R16, R17, R19, R20 and R21 are UNPREDICTABLE upon return from the PALcode routine, even if an exception has occurred.

If the memory fields overlap, the store must appear be done first, followed by the move. The ordering of the reads and writes of the move is unspecified. Thus, if the move destination overlaps the move source, the move results are UNPREDICTABLE.

These instructions contain no implicit MB.

Notes:

- Typical use of these instructions would be a sequence starting with CALL_PAL RS and ending with CALL_PAL AMOVxx, Bxx R18,label. The failure path from the conditional branch would eventually go back to the RS instruction. When such a sequence succeeds, it has done everything from the RS up to and including the CALL_PAL AMOVxx completely with no interrupts or exceptions.

- The CALL_PAL AMOVxx instruction is typically be followed by a conditional branch on R18. If the CALL_PAL AMOVxx is likely to succeed, the conditional branch should be a FORWARD branch on failure (BEQ R18,forward_label) or backward branch on success (BNE R18, backward_label), to match the architected branch-prediction rule.

2.5 Unprivileged PALcode Thread Instructions

The PALcode thread instructions provide support for multithread implementations, which require that a given thread be able to generate a reproducable unique value in a "timely" fashion. This value can then be used to index into a structure or otherwise generate further thread unique data.

The two instructions in Table 2–4 are provided to read and write a process unique value from the process's hardware context.

Table 2–4: Unprivileged PALcode Thread Instructions

Mnemonic	Operation
READ_UNQ	Read unique context
WRITE_UNQ	Write unique Context

The process unique value is stored in the HWPCB at [HWPCB+72] when the process is not active. When the process is active, the process unique value can be cached in hardware internal storage or resident in the HWPCB only.

2.5.1 Read Unique Context

Format:

CALL_PAL   READ_UNQ   !PALcode format

Operation:

```
IF {internal storage for process unique context} THEN
   R0 ←  {process unique context}
ELSE
   R0 ←  (HWPCB+72)
```

Exceptions:

None

Instruction mnemonics:

CALL_PAL   READ_UNQ   Read Unique Context

Description:

The READ_UNQ instruction causes the hardware process (thread) unique context value to be placed in R0. If this value has not previously been written using a CALL_PAL WRITE_UNQ or stored into the quadword in the HWPCB at [HWPCB+72] while the thread was inactive then the result returned in R0 is UNPREDICTABLE. Implementations can cache this unique context value while the hardware process is active. The unique context may be thought of as a "slow register". Typically, this value will be used by software to establish a unique context for a given thread of execution.

2.5.2 Write Unique Context

Format:

CALL_PAL   WRITE_UNQ   !PALcode format

Operation:

```
!R16 contains value to be written to the hardware process
!              unique context

IF {internal storage for process unique context} THEN
    {process unique context} ← R16
ELSE
    (HWPCB+72) ← R16
```

Exceptions:

None

Instruction mnemonics:

CALL_PAL   WRITE_UNQ   Write Unique Context

Description:

The WRITE_UNQ instruction causes the value of R16 to be stored in internal storage for hardware process (thread) unique context, if implemented, or in the HWPCB at [HWPCB+72], if the internal storage is not implemented. When the process is context switched, SWPCTX ensures this value is stored in the HWPCB at [HWPCB+72]. Implementations can cache this unique context value in internal storage while the hardware process is active. The unique context may be thought of as a "slow register". Typically, this value will be used by software to establish a unique context for a given thread of execution.

2.6 Privileged PALcode Instructions

Privileged instructions can be called in Kernel mode only; otherwise, a privileged instruction exception occurs. The following privileged instructions are provided:

Table 2–5: PALcode Privileged Instructions Summary

Mnemonic	Operation
CFLUSH	Cache flush
DRAINA	Drain aborts
	See *Common Architecture, Chapter 6*
HALT	Halt processor
	See *Common Architecture, Chapter 6*
LDQP	Load quadword physical
MFPR	Move from processor register
MTPR	Move to processor register
STQP	Store quadword physical
SWPCTX	Swap privileged context

2.6.1 Cache Flush

Format:

CALL_PAL   CFLUSH   !PALcode format

Operation:

```
! R16 contains the Page Frame Number (PFN)
!      of the page to be flushed

IF  PS<CM> NE 0  THEN
   {privileged instruction exception}

{Flush page out of cache(s)}
```

Exceptions:

Privileged Instruction

Instruction mnemonics:

CALL_PAL   CFLUSH   Cache Flush

Description:

The CFLUSH instruction may be used to flush an entire physical page specified by the PFN in R16 from any data caches associated with the current processor. All processors must implement this instruction.

On processors which implement a backup power option which maintains only the contents of memory in the event of a powerfail, this instruction is used by the powerfail interrupt handler to force data written by the handler to the battery backed up main memory. After a CFLUSH, the first subsequent load (on the same processor) to an arbitrary address in the target page is either fetched from physical memory or from the data cache of another processor.

Note that in some multiprocessor systems, CFLUSH is not sufficient to ensure that the data are actually written to memory and not exchanged between processor caches. Additional platform-specific cooperation between the powerfail interrupt handlers executing on each processor may be required.

On systems which implement other backup power options (including none), CFLUSH may return without affecting the data cache contents.

To order CFLUSH properly with respect to preceding writes, an MB instruction is needed before the CFLUSH; to order CFLUSH properly with respect to subsequent reads, an MB instruction is needed after the CFLUSH.

2.6.2 Load Quadword Physical

Format:

CALL_PAL   LDQP   !PALcode format

Operation:

```
! R16 contains the quadword aligned physical address
! R0 receives the data from memory

IF PS<CM> NE 0 THEN
  {Privileged Instruction exception}

R0 ← (R16) {physical access}
```

Exceptions:

Privileged Instruction

Instruction mnemonics:

CALL_PAL   LDQP   Load Quadword Physical

Description:

The LDQP instruction fetches and writes to R0 the quadword aligned memory operand, whose physical address is in R16.

If the operand address in R16 is not quadword aligned, the result is UNPREDICTABLE.

2.6.3 Move From Processor Register

Format:

CALL_PAL   MFPR_IPR_Name   !PALcode format

Operation:

```
IF  PS<CM> NE 0  THEN
    {privileged instruction exception}

! R16 may contain an IPR specific source operand
{R0 ←  result of IPR specific function}
```

Exceptions:

Privileged Instruction

Instruction mnemonics:

CALL_PAL   MFPR_xxx   Move from Processor Register xxx

Description:

The MFPR_xxx instruction reads the internal processor register specified by the PALcode function field and writes it to R0.

Registers R1, R16, and R17 contain unpredictable results after an MFPR.

See Chapter 5 for a description of each IPR.

2.6.4 Move to Processor Register

Format:

CALL_PAL   MTPR_IPR_Name   !PALcode format

Operation:

```
IF  PS<CM> NE 0  THEN
   {privileged instruction exception}
! R16 may contain an IPR specific source operand

{R0 ←  result of IPR specific function}
{IPR ←  result of IPR specific function}
```

Exceptions:

Privileged Instruction

Instruction mnemonics:

CALL_PAL   MTPR_xxx   Move to Processor Register xxx

Description:

The MTPR_xxx instruction writes the IPR-specific source operands in integer registers R16 and R17 (R17 reserved for future use) to the internal processor register specified by the PALcode function field. The effect of loading a processor register is guaranteed to be active on the next instruction.

Registers R1, R16, and R17 contain unpredictable results after an MTPR. The MTPR may return results in R0. If the specific IPR being accessed does not return results in R0, then R0 contains an unpredictable result after an MTPR.

See Chapter 5 for a description of each IPR.

2.6.5 Store Quadword Physical

Format:

    CALL_PAL   STQP   !PALcode format

Operation:

```
! R16 contains the quadword aligned physical address
! R17 contains the data to be written

IF PS<CM> NE 0 then
  {Privileged Instruction exception}

(R16) ←  R17 {physical access}
```

Exceptions:

Privileged Instruction

Instruction mnemonics:

    CALL_PAL   STQP   Store Quadword Physical

Description:

The STQP instruction writes the quadword contents of R17 to the memory location whose physical address is in R16.

If the operand address in R16 is not quadword aligned, the result is UNPREDICTABLE.

2.6.6 Swap Privileged Context

Format:

CALL_PAL   SWPCTX   !PALcode format

Operation:

```
! R16 contains the physical address of the new HWPCB.

! check HWPCB alignment

IF R16<6:0> NE 0 THEN
  {reserved operand exception}
IF {PS<CM> NE 0} THEN
  {privileged instruction exception}

! Store old HWPCB contents

(IPR_PCBB + HWPCB_KSP) ←  SP
IF {internal registers for stack pointers}  THEN
  BEGIN
    (IPR_PCBB + HWPCB_ESP) ←  IPR_ESP
    (IPR_PCBB + HWPCB_SSP) ←  IPR_SSP
    (IPR_PCBB + HWPCB_USP) ←  IPR_USP
  END

IF {internal registers for ASTxx}  THEN
  BEGIN
    (IPR_PCBB + HWPCB_ASTSR) ←  IPR_ASTSR
    (IPR_PCBB + HWPCB_ASTEN) ←  IPR_ASTEN
  END
tmp1 ←  PCC
tmp2 ←  ZEXT(tmp1<31:0>)
tmp3 ←  ZEXT(tmp1<63:32>)
(IPR_PCBB + HWPCB_PCC) ←  {tmp2 + tmp3}<31:0>
IF {internal storage for process unique value} THEN
  BEGIN
    (IPR_PCBB + HWPCB_UNQ) ←  process unique value
  END

! Load new HWPCB contents

IPR_PCBB ←  R16

IF {ASNs not implemented in virtual instruction cache} THEN
    {flush instruction cache}

IF {ASNs not implemented in TB} THEN
    IF {IPR_PTBR NE (IPR_PCBB + HWPCB_PTBR)} THEN
      {invalidate trans. buffer entries with PTE<ASM> EQ 0}
ELSE
    IPR_ASN ←  (IPR_PCBB + HWPCB_ASN)
```

```
SP  ←  (IPR_PCBB + HWPCB_KSP)
IF {internal registers for stack pointers} THEN
  BEGIN
    IPR_ESP  ←  (IPR_PCBB + HWPCB_ESP)
    IPR_SSP  ←  (IPR_PCBB + HWPCB_SSP)
    IPR_USP  ←  (IPR_PCBB + HWPCB_USP)
  END

IPR_PTBR  ←  (IPR_PCBB + HWPCB_PTBR)

IF {internal registers for ASTxx}  THEN
  BEGIN
    IPR_ASTSR  ←  (IPR_PCBB + HWPCB_ASTSR)
    IPR_ASTEN  ←  (IPR_PCBB + HWPCB_ASTEN)
  END

IPR_FEN  ←  (IPR_PCBB + HWPCB_FEN)
  tmp4  ←  ZEXT((IPR_PCBB + HWPCB_PCC)<31:0>)
  tmp4  ←  tmp4 - tmp2
  PCC<63:32>  ←  tmp4<31:0>
IF {internal storage for process unique value} THEN
  BEGIN
    process unique value  ←  (IPR_PCBB + HWPCB_UNQ)
  END
IF {internal storage for Data Alignment trap setting} THEN
  BEGIN
    DAT  ←  (IPR_PCBB + HWPCB_DAT)
  END
```

Exceptions:

Reserved Operand

Privileged Instruction

Instruction mnemonics:

CALL_PAL   SWPCTX   Swap Privileged Context

Description:

The SWPCTX instruction returns ownership of the current Hardware Privileged
Context Block (HWPCB) to the operating system and passes ownership of the new
HWPCB to the processor. The HWPCB is described in Chapter 4.

SWPCTX saves the privileged context from the internal processor registers into the
HWPCB specified by the physical address in the PCBB internal processor register.
It then loads the privileged context from the new HWPCB specified by the physical
address in R16. Note that the actual sequence of the save and restore operation is
not specified so any overlap of the current and new HWPCB storage areas produces
UNDEFINED results.

The privileged context includes the four stack pointers, the Page Table Base Register
(PTBR), the Address Space Number (ASN), the AST enable and summary registers,

the Floating-point enable register (FEN), the Performance monitor (PME) register, the Data alignment trap (DAT) register, and the process cycle counter (PCC). However, PTBR is never saved in the HWPCB and it is UNPREDICTABLE whether or not ASN is saved. These values cannot be changed for a running process. The process integer and floating registers are saved and restored by the operating system. See Figure 4–1 for the HWPCB format.

Any change to the current HWPCB while the processor has ownership results in UNDEFINED operation. All the values in the current HWPCB can be read through IPRs.

If the HWPCB is read while ownership resides with the processor, it is UNPREDICTABLE whether the original or an updated value of a field is read. The processor is free to update an HWPCB field at any time. The decision as to whether or not a field is updated is made individually for each field.

If the enabling conditions are present for an interrupt at the completion of this instruction, the interrupt occurs before the next instruction.

PALcode sets up the PCBB at boot time to point to the HWPCB storage area in the Hardware Restart Parameter Block (HWRPB).

The operation is UNDEFINED if SWPCTX accesses a non-memory region.

A reference to non-existent memory causes a machine check. Unimplemented physical address bits are SBZ. The operation is UNDEFINED if any of these bits are set.

NOTE

Processors may keep a copy of each of the per-process stack pointers in internal registers. In those processors, SWPCTX stores the internal registers into the HWPCB. Processors that do not keep a copy of the stack pointers in internal registers, keep only the stack pointer for the current access mode in SP and switch this with the HWPCB contents whenever the current access mode changes.

Chapter 3
OpenVMS Memory Management (II)

3.1 Introduction

Memory management consists of the hardware and software which control the allocation and use of physical memory. Typically, in a multiprogramming system, several processes may reside in physical memory at the same time; see Chapter 4. OpenVMS Alpha uses memory protection and multiple address spaces to ensure that one process will not affect either other processes or the operating system.

To improve further software reliability, four hierarchical access modes provide memory access control. They are, from most to least privileged: kernel, executive, supervisor, and user. Protection is specified at the individual page level, where a page may be inaccessible, read-only, or read/write for each of the four access modes. Accessible pages can be restricted to have only data or instruction access.

A program uses virtual addresses to access its data and instructions. However, before these virtual addresses can be used to access memory, they must be translated into physical addresses. Memory management software maintains tables of mapping information (page tables) that keep track of where each virtual page is located in physical memory. The processor utilizes this mapping information when it translates virtual addresses to physical addresses.

Therefore, memory management provides both memory protection and memory mapping mechanisms. The OpenVMS Alpha memory management architecture is designed to meet several goals:

- Provide a large address space for instructions and data.

- Allow programs to run on hardware with physical memory smaller than the virtual memory used.

- Provide convenient and efficient sharing of instructions and data.

- Allow sparse use of a large address space without excessive page table overhead.

- Contribute to software reliability.

- Provide independent read and write access protection.

3.2 Virtual Address Space

A virtual address is a 64-bit unsigned integer specifying a byte location within the virtual address space. Implementations subset the address space supported to one of four sizes (43, 47, 51, or 55 bits) as a function of page size. The minimal virtual address size supported is 43 bits. If an implementation supports less than 64-bit virtual addresses it must check that all the VA<63:VA_SIZE> bits are equal to VA<VA_SIZE-1>. This gives two disjoint ranges for valid virtual addresses. For example, for a 43-bit virtual address space valid virtual addresses ranges are $0..3FF\ FFFF\ FFFF_{16}$ and $FFFF\ FC00\ 0000\ 0000_{16}..FFFF\ FFFF\ FFFF\ FFFF_{16}$. Accesses to virtual addresses outside of the valid virtual address ranges for an implementation cause an access violation exception.

The virtual address space is broken into pages, which are the units of relocation, sharing, and protection. The page size ranges from 8K bytes to 64K bytes. System software should, therefore, allocate regions with differing protection on 64-Kbyte virtual address boundaries to ensure image compatibility across all Alpha implementations.

Memory management provides the mechanism to map the active part of the virtual address space to the available physical address space. The operating system controls the virtual-to-physical address mapping tables, and saves the inactive parts of the virtual address space on external storage media.

3.2.1 Virtual Address Format

The processor generates a 64-bit virtual address for each instruction and operand in memory. The virtual address consists of three level-number fields, and a byte_within_page field.

Figure 3–1: Virtual Address Format

The byte_within_page field can be either 13, 14, 15, or 16 bits depending on a particular implementation. Thus, the allowable page sizes are 8K bytes, 16K bytes, 32K bytes, and 64K bytes. Each level-number field contains 0-n bits, where n is, for example, 9 with an 8K-byte page size. The level-number fields are the same size for a given implementation.

The level number fields are a function of the page size; all page table entries at any given level do not exceed one page. The PFN field in the PTE is always 32 bits wide. Thus, as the page size grows the virtual and physical address size also grows.

Table 3–1: Virtual Address Options

Page Size (bytes)	Byte Offset (bits)	Level Size (bits)	Virtual Address (bits)	Physical Address (bits)
8 K	13	10	43	45
16 K	14	11	47	46
32 K	15	12	51	47
64 K	16	13	55	48

3.3 Physical Address Space

Physical addresses are at most 48 bits. A processor may choose to implement a smaller physical address space by not implementing some number of high order bits. The two most significant implemented physical address bits select a caching policy or implementation dependent type of address space. Implementations will use these bits as appropriate for their systems. For example, in a workstation with a 30-bit physical address space, bit <29> might select between memory and non-memory like regions, and bit <28> could enable or disable caching; see *Common Architecture, Chapter 5.*

3.4 Memory Management Control

Memory management is always enabled. Implementations must provide an environment for PALcode to service exceptions and to initialize and boot the processor. For example PALcode might run with I-stream mapping disabled and use the privileged CALL_PAL LDQP and STQP instructions to access data stored in physical addresses.

3.5 Page Table Entries

The processor uses a quadword Page Table Entry (PTE) to translate virtual addresses to physical addresses. A PTE contains hardware and software control information and the physical Page Frame Number.

Figure 3–2: Page Table Entry

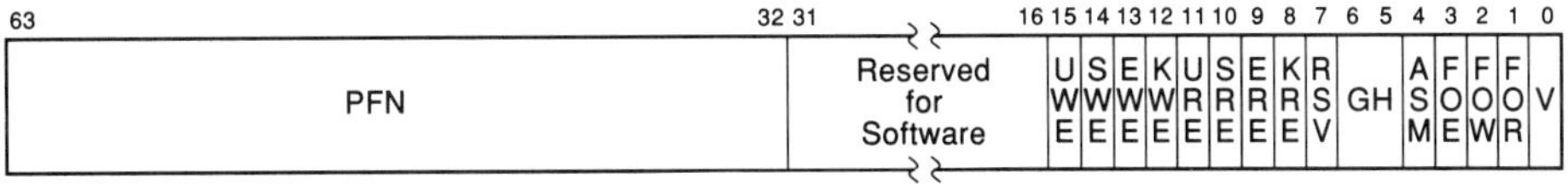

Fields in the page table entry are interpreted as shown in Table 3–2.

Table 3–2: Page Table Entry

Bits	Description
0	Valid (V)
	Indicates the validity of the the PFN field. When V is set the PFN field is valid for use by hardware. When V is clear, the PFN field is reserved for use by software. The V bit does not affect the validity of PTE<15:1> bits.
1	Fault On Read (FOR)
	When set, a Fault On Read exception occurs on an attempt to read any location in the page.
2	Fault On Write (FOW)
	When set, a Fault On Write exception occurs on an attempt to write any location in the page.
3	Fault On Execute (FOE)
	When set, a Fault On Execute exception occurs on an attempt to execute an instruction in the page.
4	Address Space Match (ASM)
	When set, this PTE matches all Address Space Numbers. For a given VA, ASM must be set consistently in all processes, otherwise the address mapping is UNPREDICTABLE.

Table 3–2 (Cont.): Page Table Entry

Bits	Description

6:5   Granularity hint (GH)

Software may set these bits to a non-zero value to supply a hint to translation buffer implementations that a block of pages can be treated as a single larger page:

1. The block is an aligned group of $8^{**}N$ pages, where N is the value of PTE<6:5>, e.g. a group of 1, 8, 64, or 512 pages starting at a virtual address with page_size + 3*N low-order zeros.

2. The block is a group of physically contiguous pages that are aligned both virtually and physically. Within the block, the low 3*N bits of the PFNs describe the identity mapping and the high 32-3*N PFN bits are all equal.

3. Within the block, all PTEs have the same values for bits <15:0>, i.e. protection, fault, granularity, and valid bits.

Hardware may use this hint to map the entire block with a single TB entry, instead of 8, 64, or 512 separate TB entries.

Note that it is UNPREDICTABLE which PTE values within the block are used if the granularity bits are set inconsistently.

> **PROGRAMMING NOTE**
> A granularity hint might be appropriate for a large memory structure such as a frame buffer or nonpaged pool that in fact is mapped into contiguous virtual pages with identical protection, fault, and valid bits.

7   Reserved for future use by Digital.

> **PROGRAMMING NOTE**
> The reserved bit will be used by future hardware systems and should not be used by software even if PTE<V> is clear.

8   Kernel Read Enable (KRE)

This bit enables reads from kernel mode. If this bit is a 0 and a LOAD or instruction fetch is attempted while in kernel mode, an Access Violation occurs. This bit is valid even when V=0.

9   Executive Read Enable (ERE)

This bit enables reads from executive mode. If this bit is a 0 and a LOAD or instruction fetch is attempted while in executive mode, an Access Violation occurs. This bit is valid even when V=0.

Table 3–2 (Cont.): Page Table Entry

Bits	Description
10	Supervisor Read Enable (SRE)
	This bit enables reads from supervisor mode. If this bit is a 0 and a LOAD or instruction fetch is attempted while in supervisor mode, an Access Violation occurs. This bit is valid even when V=0.
11	User Read Enable (URE)
	This bit enables reads from user mode. If this bit is a 0 and a LOAD or instruction fetch is attempted while in user mode, an Access Violation occurs. This bit is valid even when V=0.
12	Kernel Write Enable (KWE)
	This bit enables writes from kernel mode. If this bit is a 0 and a STORE is attempted while in kernel mode, an Access Violation occurs. This bit is valid even when V=0.
13	Executive Write Enable (EWE)
	This bit enables writes from executive mode. If this bit is a 0 and a STORE is attempted while in executive mode, an Access Violation occurs. This bit is valid even when V=0.
14	Supervisor Write Enable (SWE)
	This bit enables writes from supervisor mode. If this bit is a 0 and a STORE is attempted while in supervisor mode, an Access Violation occurs. This bit is valid even when V=0.
15	User Write Enable (UWE)
	This bit enables writes from user mode. If this bit is a 0 and a STORE is attempted while in user mode, an Access Violation occurs. This bit is valid even when V=0.

NOTE

If a write enable bit is set and the corresponding read enable bit is not, the operation of the processor is UNDEFINED.

Bits	Description
31:16	Reserved for software.
63:32	Page Frame Number (PFN)
	The PFN field always points to a page boundary. If V is set, the PFN is concatenated with the byte_within_page bits of the virtual address to obtain the physical address; see Section 3.7. If V is clear, this field may be used by software.

3.5.1 Changes to Page Table Entries

The operating system changes PTEs as part of its memory management functions. For example, the operating system may set or clear the valid bit, change the PFN field as pages are moved to and from external storage media, or modify the software bits. The processor hardware never changes PTEs.

Software must guarantee that each PTE is always consistent within itself. Changing a PTE one field at a time may give incorrect system operation, e.g., setting PTE<V> with one instruction before establishing PTE<PFN> with another. Execution of an interrupt service routine between the two instructions could use an address that would map using the inconsistent PTE. Software can solve this problem by building a complete new PTE in a register and then moving the new PTE to the page table using a Store Quadword instruction (STQ).

Multiprocessing makes the problem more complicated. Another processor could be reading (or even changing) the same PTE that the first processor is changing. Such concurrent access must produce consistent results. Software must use some form of software synchronization to modify PTEs that are already valid. Once a processor has modified a valid PTE, it is possible that other processors in a multiprocessor system may have old copies of that PTE in their Translation Buffer. Software must inform other processors of changes to PTEs.

Software may write new values into invalid PTEs using quadword store instructions (i.e., STQ). Hardware must ensure that aligned quadword reads and writes are atomic operations. The following procedure must be used to change any of the PTE bits <15:0> of a shared valid PTE (PTE<0>=1) such that an access that was allowed before the change is not allowed after the change.

1. The PTE<0> is cleared without changing any of the PTE bits <63:32> and <15:1>.

2. All processors do a TBIS for the VA mapped by the PTE that changed. The VA used in the TBIS must assume that the PTE Granularity hint bits are zero.

3. After all processors have done the TBIS, the new PTE may be written changing any or all fields.

PROGRAMMING NOTE
The procedure above allows the QUEUE instructions that have probed to check that all can complete, to service a TB miss. The QUEUE instruction will use the PTE even though the V bit is clear, if during its initial probe flow the V bit was set.

3.6 Memory Protection

Memory protection is the function of validating whether a particular type of access is allowed to a specific page from a particular access mode. Access to each page is controlled by a protection code that specifies, for each access mode, whether read or write references are allowed.

The processor uses the following to determine whether an intended access is allowed:

• The virtual address, which is used to index page tables.

• The intended access type (read data, write data, or instruction fetch).

• The current access mode from the Processor Status.

If the access is allowed and the address can be mapped (the Page Table Entry is valid), the result is the physical address corresponding to the specified virtual address.

For protection checks, the intended access is read for data loads and instruction fetch, and write for data stores.

If an operand is an address operand, then no reference is made to memory. Hence, the page need not be accessible nor map to a physical page.

3.6.1 Processor Access Modes

There are four processor modes:

- Kernel

- Executive

- Supervisor

- User

The access mode of a running process is stored in the Current Mode bits of the Processor Status (PS); see Section 6.2.

3.6.2 Protection Code

Every page in the virtual address space is protected according to its use. A program may be prevented from reading or writing portions of its address space. Associated with each page is a protection code that describes the accessibility of the page for each processor mode. The code allows a choice of read or write protection for each processor mode.

- Each mode's access can be read/write, read-only, or no-access.

- Read and write accessibility are specified independently.

- The protection of each mode can be specified independently.

The protection code is specified by 8 bits in the PTE; see Table 3–2.

The OpenVMS Alpha architecture allows a page to be designated as execute only by setting the read enable bit for the access mode and by setting the fault on read and write bits in the PTE.

3.6.3 Access Violation Fault

An Access Violation fault occurs if an illegal access is attempted, as determined by the current processor mode and the page's protection field.

3.7 Address Translation

The page tables can be accessed from physical memory, or (to reduce overhead) through a mapping to a linear region of the virtual address space. All implementations must support the virtual access method and are expected to use it as the primary access method to enhance performance.

The following sections describe both access methods.

3.7.1 Physical Access for Page Table Entries

Physical address translation is performed by accessing entries in a three-level page table structure. The Page Table Base Register (PTBR) contains the physical Page Frame Number of the highest level (Level 1) page table. Bits <level1> of the virtual address are used to index into the first level page table to obtain the physical page frame number of the base of the second level (Level 2) page table. Bits <level2> of the virtual address are used to index into the second level page table to obtain the physical page frame number of the base of the third level (Level 3) page table. Bits <level3> of the virtual address are used to index the third level page table to obtain the physical Page Frame Number (PFN) of the page being referenced. The PFN is concatenated with virtual address bits <byte_within_page> to obtain the physical address of the location being accessed.

If part of any page table resides in I/O space, or in nonexistent memory, the operation of the processor is UNDEFINED.

If the first-level or second-level PTE is valid, the protection bits are ignored; the protection code in the third-level PTE is used to determine accessibility. If a first-level or second-level PTE is invalid, an Access Violation occurs if the PTE<KRE> equals zero. An Access Violation on a first-level or second-level PTE implies that all lower-level page tables mapped by that PTE do not exist.

PROGRAMMING NOTE
This mapping scheme does not require multiple contiguous physical pages. There are no length registers. With a page size of 8K bytes, 3 pages (24K bytes) map 8M bytes of virtual address space; 1026 pages (approximately 8M bytes) map an 8-Gbyte address space; and 1,049,601 pages (approximately 8G bytes) map the entire 8T byte $2**43$ byte address space.

The algorithm to generate a physical address from a virtual address follows:

```
IF {SEXT(VA<63:VA_SIZE>) NEQ SEXT(VA<VA_SIZE-1>} THEN
   {initiate Access Violation fault}

! Read Physical

level1_pte ← ({PTBR * page_size} + {8 * VA<level1_number>})

IF level1_pte<V> EQ 0 THEN
   IF level1_pte<KRE> EQ 0 THEN
      {initiate Access Violation fault}
   ELSE
      {initiate Translation Not Valid fault}

! Read Physical

level2_pte ←
   ({level1_pte<PFN> * page_size} + {8 * VA<level2_number>})
```

```
IF level2_pte<V> EQ 0 THEN
    IF level2_pte<KRE> EQ 0 THEN
        {initiate Access Violation fault}
    ELSE
        {initiate Translation Not Valid fault}

! Read Physical

level3_pte ←
    ({level2_pte<PFN> * page_size} + {8 * VA<level3_number>})

IF {{{level3_pte<UWE> EQ 0} AND {write access} AND {PS<CM> EQ 3}} OR
    {{level3_pte<URE> EQ 0} AND {read  access} AND {PS<CM> EQ 3}} OR
    {{level3_pte<SWE> EQ 0} AND {write access} AND {PS<CM> EQ 2}} OR
    {{level3_pte<SRE> EQ 0} AND {read  access} AND {PS<CM> EQ 2}} OR
    {{level3_pte<EWE> EQ 0} AND {write access} AND {PS<CM> EQ 1}} OR
    {{level3_pte<ERE> EQ 0} AND {read  access} AND {PS<CM> EQ 1}} OR
    {{level3_pte<KWE> EQ 0} AND {write access} AND {PS<CM> EQ 0}} OR
    {{level3_pte<KRE> EQ 0} AND {read  access} AND {PS<CM> EQ 0}}}
THEN
    {initiate Access Violation fault}
ELSE
    IF level3_pte<V> EQ 0 THEN
        {initiate Translation Not Valid fault}

IF {level3_pte<FOW> EQ 1} AND { write   access} THEN
    {initiate Fault On Write fault}
IF {level3_pte<FOR> EQ 1} AND { read    access} THEN
    {initiate Fault On Read fault}
IF {level3_pte<FOE> EQ 1} AND { execute access} THEN
    {initiate Fault On Execute fault}

Physical_Address ←
    {level3_pte<PFN> * page_size} OR VA<byte_within_page>
```

3.7.2 Virtual Access for Page Table Entries

To reduce the overhead associated with the address translation in a three-level page table structure, the page tables are mapped into a linear region of the virtual address space. The virtual address of the base of the page table structure is set on a system wide basis and is contained in the VPTB IPR.

When a native mode DTB or ITB Miss occurs, the TBMISS flows attempt to load the level three page table entry using a single virtual mode load instruction.

The algorithm involving the manipulation of the missing VA is:

```
tmp ←   left_shift(VA, {64 - {{lg(PageSize) *4} -9 }} )
tmp ←
    right_shift(tmp,{64 - {{lg(PageSize)*4} -9} + lg(PageSize) -3})
tmp ←   VPTB OR tmp
tmp<2:0> ←    0
```

At this point, tmp contains the VA of the level 3 page table entry. A LDQ from that VA will result in the acquistion of the PTE needed to satisfy the initial TBMISS condition.

However, in the PALcode environment, if a TBMISS occurs during an attempt to fetch the level3 PTE, then it is necessary to use the longer sequence of three dependent loads described in Section 3.7.

Chapter 5 contains the description of the VPTB IPR used to contain the virtual address of the base of the page table structure.

The mapping of the page tables necessary for the correct function of the algorithm is done as follows:

1. Select a $2^{(3*\lg(\text{page\_size}/8))+3}$) byte-aligned region (an address with 3*lg(page_size /8)+3 low order zeros) in the virtual address space. This value will be written into the VPTB register.

2. Create a level1 PTE to map the page tables as follows:

```
Level1_PTE            ←   0      ! Init all fields to 0
Level1_PTE<63:32> ←   PFN of Level1 Pagetable
                              ! Set PFN to PFN of level1 pagetable
Level1_PTE<8>      ←   1      ! Kernel Read Enable  (KRE)
Level1_PTE<0>      ←   1      ! Valid bit
```

3. Write the created level1 PTE into the Level1 page table entry that corresponds to the VPTB value.

4. Set all Level1 and Level2 Valid PTEs to allow kernel read access.

5. Write the VPTB register with the selected base value.

> **NOTE**
> No validity checks need be made on the value stored in the VPTB in a running system. Therefore, if the VPTB contains an invalid address, the operation is UNDEFINED.

3.8 Translation Buffer

In order to save actual memory references when repeatedly referencing the same pages, hardware implementations include a translation buffer to remember successful virtual address translations and page states.

When the process context is changed, a new value is loaded into the Address Space Number (ASN) internal processor register with a Swap Privileged Context instruction (CALL_PAL SWPCTX); see Section 2.6 and Chapter 4. This causes address translations for pages with PTE<ASM> clear to be invalidated on a processor that does not implement address space numbers. Additionally, when the software changes any part (except for the Software field) of a valid Page Table Entry, it must also move a virtual address within the corresponding page to the Translation Buffer Invalidate Single (TBIS) internal processor register with the MTPR instruction; see Chapter 5.

Some implementations may invalidate the entire Translation Buffer on an MTPR to TBIS. In general, implementations may invalidate more than the required translations in the TB.

The entire Translation Buffer can be invalidated by doing a write to Translation Buffer Invalidate All register (CALL_PAL MTPR_TBIA), and all ASM=0 entries can be invalidated by doing a write to Translation Buffer Invalidate All Process register (CALL_PAL MTPR_TBIAP); see Chapter 5.

The Translation Buffer must not store invalid PTEs. Therefore, the software is not required to invalidate Translation Buffer entries when making changes for PTEs that are already invalid.

The TBCHK internal processor register is available for interrogating the presence of a valid translation in the Translation Buffer; see Chapter 5.

IMPLEMENTATION NOTE

Hardware implementors should be aware that a single, direct mapped TB has a potential problem when a load /store instruction and its data map to the same TB location. If TB misses are handled in PALcode, there could be an endless loop unless the instruction is held in an instruction buffer or a translated physical PC is maintained by the hardware.

3.9 Address Space Numbers

The Alpha architecture allows a processor to optionally implement address space numbers (process tags) to reduce the need for invalidation of cached address translations for process specific addresses when a context switch occurs. The supported ASN range is 0..MAX_ASN.

NOTE

If an ASN outside of the range 0..MAX_ASN is assigned to a process, the operation of the processor is UNDEFINED.

The address space number for the current process is loaded by software in the Address Space Number (ASN) internal processor register with a Swap Privileged Context instruction. ASNs are processor specific and the hardware makes no attempt to maintain coherency across multiple processors. In a multiprocessor system, software is responsible for ensuring the consistency of TB entries for processes that might be rescheduled on different processors.

PROGRAMMING NOTE

System software should not assume that the number of ASNs is a power of two. This allows, for example, hardware to use N TB tag bits to encode $(2**N)-3$ ASN values, one value for ASM=1 PTEs, and one for invalid.

There are several possible ways of using ASNs. There are several complications in a multiprocessor system. Consider the case where a process that executed on processor–1 is rescheduled on processor–2. If a page is deleted or its protection is changed, the TB in processor–1 has stale data. One solution would be to send an interprocessor interrupt to all the processors on which this process could have run and cause them to invalidate the changed PTE. This results in significant overhead in a system with several processors. Another solution would be to have software invalidate all TB entries for a process on a new processor before it can begin execution, if the process executed on another processor during its previous execution. This ensures the deletion of possibly stale TB entries on the new processor. A third solution would assign a new ASN whenever a process is run on a processor that is not the same as the last processor on which it ran.

3.10 Memory Management Faults

Five types of faults are associated with memory access and protection:

- Access Control Violation (ACV)

  Taken when the protection field of the third-level PTE that maps the data indicates that the intended page reference would be illegal in the specified access mode. An Access Control Violation fault is also taken if the KRE bit is zero in an invalid first or second level PTE.

- Fault On Read (FOR)

  Occurs when a read is attempted with PTE<FOR> set.

- Fault On Write (FOW)

  Occurs when a write is attempted with PTE<FOW> set.

- Fault On Execute (FOE)

  Occurs when instruction execution is attempted with PTE<FOE> set.

- Translation Not Valid (TNV)

  Taken when a read or write reference is attempted through an invalid PTE in a first-, second-, or third-level page table.

See Chapter 6 for a detailed description of these faults.

Note that these five faults have distinct vectors in the System Control Block. The Access Violation (ACV) fault takes precedence over the faults TNV, FOR, FOW, and

FOE. The Translation Not Valid (TNV) fault takes precedence over the faults FOR, FOW, and FOE.

The faults FOR and FOW can occur simultaneously in the CALL_PAL queue instructions, in which case the order that the exceptions are taken is UNPREDICTABLE; see Section 2.1.

Chapter 4

OpenVMS Process Structure (II)

4.1 Process Definition

A process is the basic entity that is scheduled for execution by the processor. A process represents a single thread of execution and consists of an address space and both hardware and software context.

The hardware context of a process is defined by:

- 31 Integer registers and 31 Floating-point registers

- Processor Status (PS)

- Program Counter (PC)

- 4 stack pointers

- Asynchronous System Trap Enable and summary registers (ASTEN, ASTSR)

- Process Page Table Base Register (PTBR)

- Address Space Number (ASN)

- Floating Enable Register (FEN)

- Process Cycle counter (PCC)

- Process Unique value

- Data Alignment Trap (DAT)

- Performance Monitoring Enable Register (PME)

The software context of a process is defined by operating system software and is system dependent.

A process may share the same address space with other processes or have an address space of its own. There is, however, no separate address space for system software, and therefore, the operating system must be mapped into the address space of each process; see Chapter 3.

In order for a process to execute, its hardware context must be loaded into the integer registers, Floating-point registers, and internal processor registers. While a process is executing, its hardware context is continuously updated. When a process is not being executed, its hardware context is stored in memory.

Saving the hardware context of the current process in memory, followed by loading the hardware context for a new process, is termed context switching. Context switching occurs as one process after another is scheduled by the operating system for execution.

4.2 Hardware Privileged Process Context

The hardware context of a process is defined by a privileged part which is context switched with the Swap Privileged Context instruction (SWPCTX) (see Section 2.6), and a non-privileged part which is context switched by operating system software.

When a process is not executing, its privileged context is stored in a 128 byte naturally aligned memory structure called the Hardware Privileged Context Block (HWPCB).

Figure 4–1: Hardware Privileged Context Block

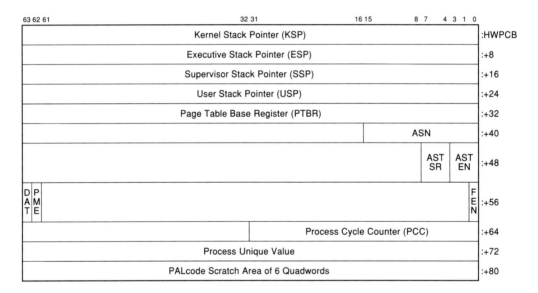

The Hardware Privileged Context Block (HWPCB) for the current process is specified by the Privileged Context Block Base register (PCBB); see Chapter 5.

The Swap Privileged Context instruction (SWPCTX) saves the privileged context of the current process into the HWPCB specified by PCBB, loads a new value into PCBB, and then loads the privileged context of the new process into the appropriate hardware registers.

The new value loaded into PCBB, as well as the contents of the Privileged Context Block, must satisfy certain constraints or an UNDEFINED operation results:

1. The physical address loaded into PCBB must be 128 byte aligned and describes sixteen contiguous quadwords that are in a memory-like region; see *Common Architecture, Chapter 5*.

2. The value of PTBR must be the Page Frame Number of an existent page that is in a memory-like region.

It is the responsibility of the operating system to save and load the non-privileged part of the hardware context.

The SWPCTX instruction returns ownership of the current HWPCB to operating system software and passes ownership of the new HWPCB from the operating system to the processor. Any attempt to write a HWPCB while ownership resides with the processor has UNDEFINED results. If the HWPCB is read while ownership resides with the processor, it is UNPREDICTABLE whether the original or an updated value of a field is read. The processor is free to update an HWPCB field at any time. The decision as to whether or not a field is updated is made individually for each field.

If ASNs are not implemented, the ASN field is not read or written by PALcode.

The FEN bit reflects the setting of the FEN IPR.

The DAT bit controls whether data alignment traps that are fixed up in PALcode are reported to the operating system. If the bit is clear, the trap is reported. If the bit is set, after the fixup, return is to the user. See Section 6.6.

Setting the PME bit alerts any performance hardware or software in the system to monitor the performance of this process.

The Process Unique value is that value used in support of multithread implementations. The value is stored in the HWPCB when the process is not active. When the process is active, the value may be cached in hardware internal storage or kept in the HWPCB only.

4.3 Asynchronous System Traps (AST)

Asynchronous System Traps (ASTs) are a means of notifying a process of events that are not synchronized with its execution but which must be dealt with in the context of the process with minimum delay.

Asynchronous System Traps (ASTs) interrupt process execution and are controlled by the AST Enable (ASTEN) and AST Summary (ASTSR) internal processor registers; see Chapter 5.

The AST Enable register (ASTEN) contains an enable bit for each of the four processor access modes. When the bit corresponding to an access mode is set, ASTs for that mode are enabled. The AST enable bit for an access mode may be changed by executing a Swap AST Enable instruction (SWASTEN; see Section 2.6), or by executing a Move To Processor Register instruction specifying ASTEN (MTPR ASTEN; see Chapter 5).

The AST Summary Register (ASTSR) contains a pending bit for each of the four processor access modes. When the bit corresponding to an access mode is set, an AST is pending for that mode.

Kernel mode software may request an AST for a particular access mode by executing a Move To Processor Register instruction specifying ASTSR (MTPR ASTSR); see Chapter 5).

Hardware or PALcode monitors the state of ASTEN, ASTSR, PS<CM>, and PS<IPL>. If PS<IPL> is less than 2, and there is an AST pending and enabled for an access mode that is less than or equal to PS<CM> (i.e. an equal or more privileged access mode), an AST is initiated at IPL 2.

ASTs that are pending and enabled for a less privileged access mode are not allowed to interrupt execution in a more privileged access mode.

4.4 Process Context Switching

Process context switching occurs as one process after another is scheduled for execution by operating system software. Context switching requires the hardware context of one process to be saved in memory followed by the loading of the hardware context for another process into the hardware registers.

The privileged hardware context is swapped with the CALL_PAL Swap Privileged Context instruction (SWPCTX). Other hardware context must be saved and restored by operating system software.

The sequence in which process context is changed is important since the SWPCTX instruction changes the environment in which the context switching software itself is executing. Also, although not enforced by hardware, it is advisable to execute the actual context switching software in an environment which cannot be context switched (i.e. at an IPL high enough that rescheduling cannot occur).

The SWPCTX instruction is the only method provided for loading certain internal processor registers. The SWPCTX instruction always saves the privileged context of the old process and loads the privileged context of a new process. Therefore, a valid HWPCB must be available to save the privileged context of the old process as well as load the privileged context of the new process.

Chapter 5

OpenVMS Internal Processor Registers (II)

5.1 Internal Processor Registers

This chapter describes the OpenVMS Alpha Internal Processor Registers (IPRs). These registers are read and written with Move From Processor Register (MFPR) and Move To Processor Register (MTPR) instructions; see Section 2.6.

These instructions accept an input operand in R16 and return a result, if any, in R0. Registers R1, R16, and R17 are UNPREDICTABLE after a CALL_PAL MxPR routines. If a CALL_PAL MxPR routine does not return a result in R0, then R0 is also UNPREDICTABLE on return.

Some IPRs (for example, ASTSR, ASTEN, IPL) may be both read and written in a combined operation by performing an MTPR instruction.

Internal Processor Registers may or may not be implemented as actual hardware registers. An implementation may choose any combination of PALcode and hardware to produce the architecturally specified function.

Internal Processor Registers are only accessible from Kernel mode.

5.2 Stack Pointer Internal Processor Registers

The stack pointers for User, Supervisor, and Executive stacks are accessible as IPRs through the CALL_PAL MTPR and MFPR instructions. An implementation may retain some or all of these stack pointers only in the HWPCB. In this case, MTPR and MFPR for these registers must access the corresponding PCB locations. However, implementations that have these stack pointers in internal hardware registers are not required to access the corresponding HWPCB locations for MTPR and MFPR. The HWPCB locations get updated when a SWPCTX instruction is executed.

An implementation may also choose to keep the Kernel Stack Pointer (KSP) in an internal hardware register (labelled IPR_KSP); however, this register is not directly accessible through MTPR and MFPR instructions. Because access to the KSP requires Kernel mode, the actual KSP is the current mode stack pointer (R30); thus access to KSP is provided through R30 and no MTPR or MFPR access is required. PALcode routines can directly access IPR_KSP as needed.

At system initialization, the value of the KSP is taken from the initial HWPCB (see Chapter 4).

5.3 IPR Summary

Table 5–1: Internal Processor Register (IPR) Summary

Register Name	Mnemonic	Access[1]	Input R16	Output R0	Context Switched
Address Space Number	ASN	R	—	number	Yes
AST Enable	ASTEN	R/W*	mask	mask	Yes
AST Summary Register	ASTSR	R/W*	mask	mask	Yes
Data Align Trap Fixup	DATFX	W	value	—	Yes
Floating-point Enable	FEN	R/W	value	value	Yes
Interprocessor Int. Request	IPIR	W	number	—	No
Interrupt Priority Level	IPL	R/W*	value	value	No
Machine Check Error Summary	MCES	R/W	value	value	No
Performance Monitor	PERFMON	W*	IMP	IMP	No
Privileged Context Block Base	PCBB	R	—	address	No
Processor Base Register	PRBR	R/W	value	value	No
Page Table Base Register	PTBR	R	—	frame	Yes
System Control Block Base	SCBB	R/W	frame	frame	No
Software Int. Request Register	SIRR	W	level	—	No
Software Int. Summary Register	SISR	R	—	mask	No
TB Check	TBCHK	R	number	status	No
TB Invalid. All	TBIA	W	—	—	No
TB Invalid. All Process	TBIAP	W	—	—	No
TB Invalid. Single	TBIS	W	address	—	No
TB Invalid. Single Data	TBISD	W	address	—	No
TB Invalid. Single Instruct.	TBISI	W	address	—	No
Kernel Stack Pointer	KSP	None	—	—	Yes
Exec Stack Pointer	ESP	R/W	address	address	Yes
Supervisor Stack Pointer	SSP	R/W	address	address	Yes
User Stack Pointer	USP	R/W	address	address	Yes
Virtual Page Table Base	VPTB	R/W	address	address	No
Who-Am-I	WHAMI	R	—	number	No

[1] Access symbols are defined in Table 5–2.

Table 5–2: Internal Processor Register (IPR) Access Summary

Access Type	Meaning
R	Access by MFPR only.
W	Access by MTPR only.
R/W	Access by MFPR or MTPR.
W*	Read and Write access accomplished by MTPR; see Section 5.1 for details.
R/W*	Access by MFPR or MTPR. Read and Write access accomplished by MTPR; see Section 5.1 for details.
None	Not accessible by MTPR or MFPR; accessed by PALcode routines as needed.

5.3.1 Address Space Number (ASN)

Access:

Read

Operation:

```
IF {ASN are implemented} THEN
   R0 ←  ZEXT(ASN)
ELSE
   R0 ←  0
```

Value at System Initialization:

Zero

Format:

Figure 5–1: Address Space Number Register (ASN)

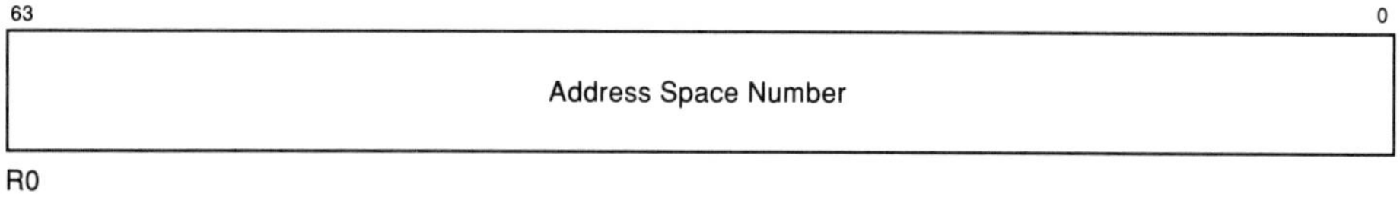

63	0
Address Space Number	

R0

Description:

Address Space Numbers (ASNs) are used to further qualify Translation Buffer references; see Chapter 3. If ASNs are implemented, the current ASN may be read by executing an MFPR instruction specifying ASN.

As processes are scheduled for execution, the ASN for the next process to execute is loaded using the Swap Privileged Context (SWPCTX) instruction; see Chapters 2 and 4.

The ASN register is an implicit operand to the CALL_PAL MFPR_IPR, TBCHK, and TBISx PALcode instructions, in which it is used to qualify the virtual address supplied in R16.

5.3.2 AST Enable (ASTEN)

Access:

Read

Write*

Operation:

```
R0 ←  ZEXT (ASTEN<3:0>)            ! Read (MFPR)
R0 ←  ZEXT(ASTEN<3:0>)             ! Write* (MTPR)
ASTEN<3:0> ←  {{ASTEN<3:0> AND R16<3:0>} OR R16<7:4>}
{check for pending ASTs}
```

Value at System Initialization:

Zero

Format:

Figure 5–2: AST Enable Register (ASTEN)

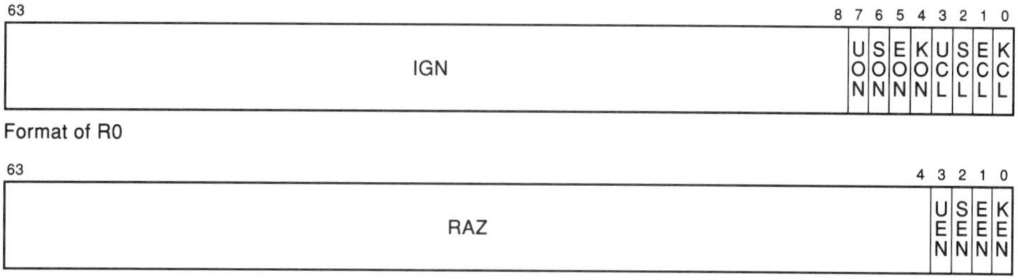

Format of R0

Description:

The AST Enable Register records the AST enable state for each of the modes: Kernel (KEN), Executive (EEN), Supervisor (SEN) and User (UEN). By writing R16 appropriately and then executing an MTPR instruction specifying ASTEN, the value of ASTEN may be simultaneously read and modified. R16 contains bit masks used to determine the new value of ASTEN:

- Bits R16<0> and R16<4> control the new state of Kernel enable.

- Bits R16<1> and R16<5> control the new state of Executive enable.

- Bits R16<2> and R16<6> control the new state of Supervisor enable.

- Bits R16<3> and R16<7> control the new state of User enable.

An MFPR to ASTEN reads the current value of the ASTEN and returns this value in R0.

An MTPR to ASTEN begins by reading the current value of ASTEN and returning this value in R0. The current value of ASTEN is then ANDed with bits R16<3:0>; these bits preserve (if set to '1') or clear (if equal to '0') the current state of their corresponding enable modes. The value produced by this operation is then ORed with bits R16<7:4>; these bits turn on (if set to '1') or do not affect (if equal to '0') their corresponding enable modes. The resulting value is then written to the ASTEN.

NOTE

All AST enables can be cleared by loading a zero into R16 and executing an MTPR instruction specifying ASTEN. To enable an AST for a given mode, load R16 with a mask that has bits <3:0> set and one of the bits <7:4> corresponding to the AST mode to be set. Then execute an MTPR instruction specifying ASTEN.

As processes are scheduled for execution, the state of the AST enables for the next process to execute is loaded using the Swap Privileged Context (SWPCTX) instruction. The Swap AST Enable (SWASTEN) instruction can be used to change the enable state for the current access mode; See Chapters 2 and 4.

5.3.3 AST Summary Register (ASTSR)

Access:

Read

Write*

Operation:

```
R0 ←   ZEXT(ASTSR<3:0>)       ! Read (MFPR)
R0 ←   ZEXT(ASTSR<3:0>)       ! Write* (MTPR)
ASTSR<3:0> ←   {{ASTSR<3:0> AND R16<3:0>} OR R16<7:4>}
{check for pending ASTs}
```

Value at System Initialization:

Zero

Format:

Figure 5–3: AST Summary Register (ASTSR)

	8	7	6	5	4	3	2	1	0
63 IGN		UON	SON	EON	KON	UCL	SCL	ECL	KCL

R16

	4	3	2	1	0
63 RAZ		UPD	SPD	EPD	KPD

R0

Description:

The AST Summary Register records the AST pending state for each of the modes: Kernel (KPD), Executive (EPD), Supervisor (SPD), and User (UPD).

By writing R16 appropriately and then executing an MTPR instruction specifying ASTSR, the value of ASTSR may be simultaneously read and modified. R16 contains bit masks used to determine the new value of ASTSR:

- Bits R16<0> and R16<4> control the new state of Kernel pending.

- Bits R16<1> and R16<5> control the new state of Executive pending.

- Bits R16<2> and R16<6> control the new state of Supervisor pending.

- Bits R16<3> and R16<7> control the new state of User pending.

An MFPR reads the current value of ASTSR and returns this value in R0.

An MTPR to ASTSR begins by reading the current value of ASTSR and returning this value in R0. The current value of ASTSR is then ANDed with bits R16<3:0>; these bits preserve (if set to '1') or clear (if equal to '0') the current state of their corresponding pending modes. The value produced by this operation is then ORed with bits R16<7:4>; these bits turn on (if set to '1') or do not affect (if equal to '0') their corresponding pending modes. The resulting value is then written to the ASTSR.

NOTE

All AST requests can be cleared by loading a zero in R16 and executing an MTPR instruction specifying ASTSR. To request an AST for a given mode, load R16 with a mask that has bits <3:0> set and one of the bits <7:4> corresponding to the AST mode to be set. Then execute an MTPR instruction specifying ASTSR.

As processes are scheduled for execution, the pending AST state for the next process to execute is loaded using the Swap Privileged Context (SWPCTX) instruction; see Chapters 2 and 4.

When the processor IPL is less than 2, and proper enabling conditions are present, an AST interrupt is initiated at IPL 2 and the corresponding access mode bit in ASTSR is cleared; see Section 6.7.6.

5.3.4 Data Alignment Trap Fixup (DATFX)

Access:

Write

Operation:

```
DATFX  ←   R16<0>
(HWPCB+56)<63> ←   DATFX
```

Value at System Initialization:

Zero

Format:

Figure 5–4:   Data Alignment Trap Fixup (DATFX)

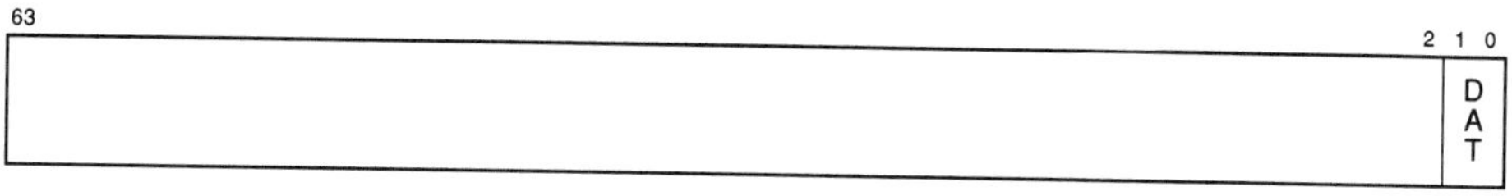

Description:

Data Alignment traps are fixed up in PALcode and are reported to the operating system under the control of the DAT bit. If the bit is zero, the trap is reported. For the LDx_L and STx_C instructions, no fixup is possible and an illegal operand exception is generated. For the description of the data alignment traps, see Section 6.6.

5.3.5 Floating Enable (FEN)

Access:

Read/Write

Operation:

```
R0 ←   ZEXT(FEN)              ! Read
FEN ←   R16<0>                ! Write
(HWPCB+56)<0> ←   FEN         ! Update PCB on Write
```

Value at System Initialization:

Zero

Format:

Figure 5–5: Floating Enable (FEN) Register

Description:

The Floating-point unit can be disabled. If the Floating Enable Register (FEN) is zero, all instructions that have floating registers as operands cause a Floating-point disabled fault; see Section 6.3.1.1.

5.3.6 Interprocessor Interrupt Request (IPIR)

Access:

Write

Operation:

```
IPIR ←   R16
```

Value at System Initialization:

Not applicable

Format:

Figure 5–6: Interprocessor Interrupt Request Register (IPIR)

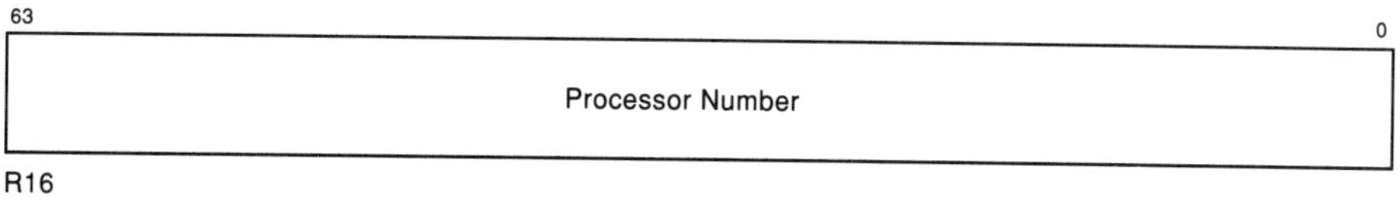

```
63                                                                              0
┌──────────────────────────────────────────────────────────────────────────────┐
│                              Processor Number                                  │
└──────────────────────────────────────────────────────────────────────────────┘
R16
```

Description:

An interprocessor interrupt can be requested on a specified processor by writing that processor's number into the IPIR register through an MTPR instruction. The interrupt request is recorded on the target processor and is initiated when proper enabling conditions are present.

> **PROGRAMMING NOTE**
> The interrupt need not be initiated before the next instruction is executed on the requesting processor, even if the requesting processor is also the target processor for the request.

For additional information on interprocessor interrupts, see Section 6.4.5.1.

5.3.7 Interrupt Priority Level (IPL)

Access:

Read/Write*

Operation:

```
R0 ←   ZEXT(PS<IPL>)     ! Read
R0 ←   ZEXT(PS<IPL>)     ! Write*
PS<IPL> ←   R16<4:0>     ! Write
{check for pending ASTs or interrupts}
```

Value at System Initialization:

31

Format:

Figure 5–7: Interrupt Priority Level (IPL)

63	5 4	0
SBZ		IPL

Description:

An MFPR IPL returns the current interrupt priority level in R0. An MTPR IPL returns the current interrupt priority level in R0 and sets the interrupt priority level to the value in R16. If proper enabling conditions are present, an interrupt or AST is initiated prior to issuing the next instruction; see Sections 6.4.1 and 6.7.6. R16<63:5> are defined as RAZ/SBZ. Therefore, the presence of non-zero bits upon write in R16<63:5> may cause UNDEFINED results.

5.3.8 Machine Check Error Summary Register (MCES)

Access:

Read/Write

Operation:

```
R0 ←  ZEXT(MCES)                      ! Read
IF {R16<0> EQ 1} THEN MCES<0> ←  0   ! Write
IF {R16<1> EQ 1} THEN MCES<1> ←  0
IF {R16<2> EQ 1} THEN MCES<2> ←  0
MCES<3> ←  R16<3>
MCES<4> ←  R16<4>
```

Value at System Initialization:

Zero

Format:

Figure 5–8:   Machine Check Error Summary Register (MCES)

63	32	31				5 4 3 2 1 0
IMP			Reserved			DSC DPC PCE SCC MCK

Description:

The use of the MCES IPR is described in Section 6.5.

MCES<0> is set by the hardware or PALcode when a processor or system machine check occurs.   MCES<1> is set by the hardware or PALcode when a system correctable error occurs.   MCES<2> is set by the hardware or PALcode when a processor correctable error occurs. Writing a 1 to any of these three bits clears that bit.

MCES<0> is cleared by the operating system machine check error handler and used by the hardware or PALcode to detect double machine checks.   MCES<1> and MCES<2> are cleared by the operating system system or processor system correctable error handlers; these bits are used to indicate that the associated correctable error logout area may be reused by hardware or PALcode. In the event of double correctable errors, PALcode does not overwrite the logout area and does not force the processor to enter console I/O mode; see Section 6.5.1.

MCES<4:3> are used to disable reporting of correctable errors. When set, the error is corrected, but no system correctable error interrupt or processor correctable machine check is generated.

Implementation dependent (IMP) bits may be used to report implementation specific errors.

5.3.9 Performance Monitoring Register (PERFMON)

Access:

Write*

Operation:

```
! R<16> contains implementation specific input values
! R<0>  may return implementation specific values
! Operations and actions taken are implementation specific
```

Value at System Initialization:

Implementation Dependent

Format:

Figure 5–9: Performance Monitoring Register (PERFMON)

63	0
IMP	

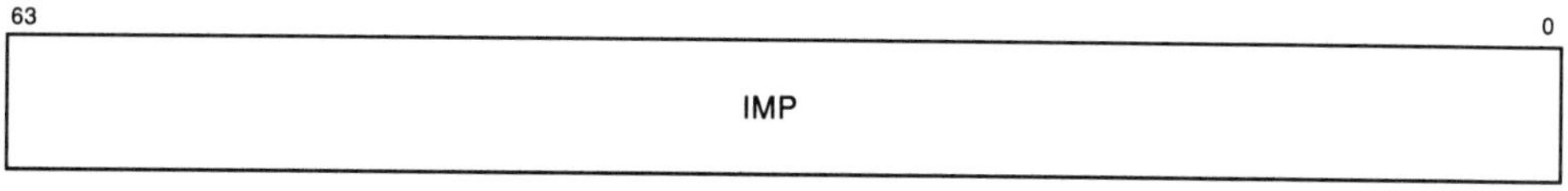

Description:

The arguments and actions of this performance monitoring function are platform and chip dependent.

R<16> contains implementation dependent input values. Implementation specific values may be returned in R<0>.

5.3.10 Privileged Context Block Base (PCBB)

Access:

Read

Operation:

```
R0  ←   ZEXT(PCBB)
```

Value at System Initialization:

Address of processor's bootstrap HWPCB

Format:

Figure 5–10: Privileged Context Block Base Register (PCBB)

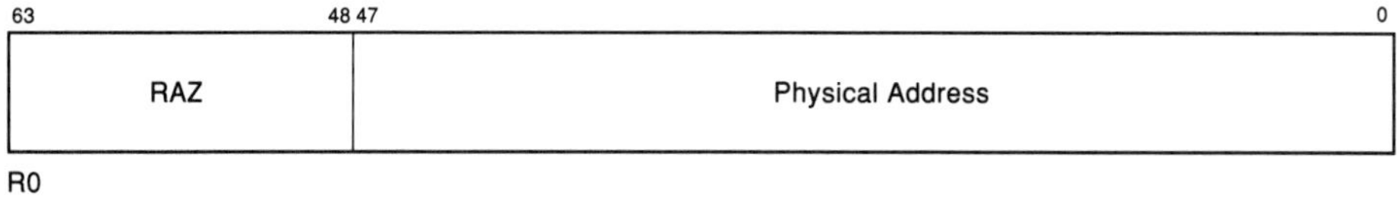

63	48 47	Physical Address	0
RAZ		Physical Address	

R0

Description:

The Privileged Context Block Base Register contains the physical address of the privileged context block for the current process. It may be read by executing an MFPR instruction specifying PCBB.

PCBB is written by the Swap Privileged Context (SWPCTX) instruction; see Chapters 2 and 4.

5.3.11 Processor Base Register (PRBR)

Access:

Read/Write

Operation:

```
R0  ←   PRBR            ! Read
PRBR ←   R16            ! Write
```

Value at System Initialization:

UNPREDICTABLE

Format:

Figure 5–11: Processor Base Register (PRBR)

```
63                                                                    0
┌──────────────────────────────────────────────────────────────────┐
│                  Operating System-Dependent Value                  │
└──────────────────────────────────────────────────────────────────┘
```

Description:

In a multiprocessor system, it is desirable for the operating system to be able to locate a processor-specific data structure in a simple and straightforward manner. The Processor Base Register provides a quadword of operating system-dependent state that can be read and written via MFPR and MTPR instructions that specify PRBR.

5.3.12 Page Table Base Register (PTBR)

Access:

Read

Operation:

R0 ← PTBR

Value at System Initialization:

Value in the bootstrap HWPCB

Format:

Figure 5–12:   Page Table Base Register (PTBR)

63	32 31	0
RAZ		Page Frame Number

R0

Description:

The Page Table Base Register contains the page frame number of the first-level page table for the current process. It may be read by executing an MFPR instruction specifying PTBR; see Chapter 3.

As processes are scheduled for execution, the PTBR for the next process to execute is loaded using the Swap Privileged Context (SWPCTX) instruction; see Chapters 2 and 4.

5.3.13 System Control Block Base (SCBB)

Access:

Read/Write

Operation:

```
R0 ←  ZEXT(SCBB)            ! Read
SCBB ←  R16                 ! Write
```

Value at System Initialization:

UNPREDICTABLE

Format:

Figure 5–13: System Control Block Base Register (SCBB)

63	32 31	0
IGN/RAZ		Page Frame Number

Description:

The System Control Block Base Register holds the Page Frame Number (PFN) of the System Control Block, which is used to dispatch exceptions and interrupts, and may be read and written by executing MFPR and MTPR instructions that specify SCBB; see Section 6.6.

When SCBB is written, the specified physical address must be the PFN of a page which is neither in I/O space nor non-existent memory, or UNDEFINED operation will result.

5.3.14 Software Interrupt Request Register (SIRR)

Access:

Write

Operation:

```
IF R16<3:0> NE 0 THEN
    SISR<R16<3:0>> ←  1
```

Value at System Initialization:

Not applicable

Format:

Figure 5–14: Software Interrupt Request Register (SIRR)

```
63                                                    4 3    0
┌──────────────────────────────────────────────────┬───────┐
│                                                    │       │
│                        IGN                         │  LVL  │
│                                                    │       │
└──────────────────────────────────────────────────┴───────┘
R16
```

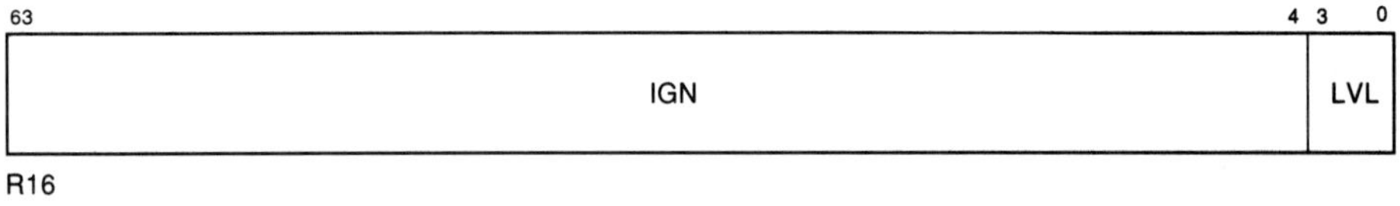

Description:

A software interrupt may be requested for a particular Interrupt Priority Level (IPL) by executing an MTPR instruction specifying SIRR. Software interrupts may be requested at levels 0 through 15 (requests at level 0 are ignored).

An MTPR SIRR sets the bit corresponding to the specified interrupt level in the Software Interrupt Summary Register (SISR).

If proper enabling conditions are present, a software interrupt is initiated prior to issuing the next instruction; see Sections 6.4.1 and 6.7.6.

5.3.15 Software Interrupt Summary Register (SISR)

Access:

Read

Operation:

```
R0 ←  ZEXT(SISR<15:0>)
```

Value at System Initialization:

Zero

Format:

Figure 5–15: Software Interrupt Summary Register (SISR)

```
63                                                     16 15 14 13 12 11 10 9  8  7  6  5  4  3  2  1  0
┌──────────────────────────────────────────────────────┬──┬──┬──┬──┬──┬──┬──┬──┬──┬──┬──┬──┬──┬──┬──┬──┐
│                                                       │I │I │I │I │I │I │I │I │I │I │I │I │I │I │I │R │
│                      RAZ                              │R │R │R │R │R │R │R │R │R │R │R │R │R │R │R │A │
│                                                       │F │E │D │C │B │A │9 │8 │7 │6 │5 │4 │3 │2 │1 │Z │
└──────────────────────────────────────────────────────┴──┴──┴──┴──┴──┴──┴──┴──┴──┴──┴──┴──┴──┴──┴──┴──┘
R0
```

Description:

The Software Interrupt Summary Register records the interrupt pending state for each of the interrupt levels 1 through 15. The current interrupt pending state may be read by executing an MFPR instruction specifying SISR.

MTPR SIRR (see SIRR) requests an interrupt at a particular interrupt level and sets the corresponding pending bit in SISR.

When the processor IPL falls below the level of a pending request, an interrupt is initiated and the corresponding bit in SISR is cleared; see Sections 6.4.1 and 6.7.6.

5.3.16 Translation Buffer Check (TBCHK)

Access:

Read

Operation:

```
R0 ←  0
IF {implemented} THEN
    R0<0> ←  {entry in TB for VA in R16}
ELSE
    R0<63> ←  1
```

Value at System Initialization:

Correct results are always returned

Format:

Figure 5–16:   Translation Buffer Check Register (TBCHK)

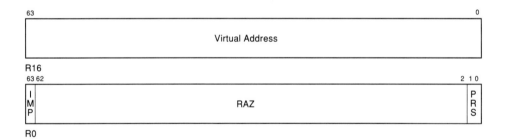

Description:

The Translation Buffer Check Register provides the capability to determine if a virtual address is present in the Translation Buffer by executing an MFPR instruction specifying TBCHK; see Chapter 3.

The virtual address to be checked is specified in R16 and may be any address within the desired page. If ASNs are implemented, only those Translation Buffer entries which are associated with the current value of the ASN IPR will be checked for the virtual address. The value read contains an indication of whether the function is implemented and whether the virtual address is present in the Translation Buffer.

If the function is not implemented, a value is returned with bit <63> set and bit <0> clear. Otherwise, a value is returned with bit <63> clear, and with bit <0> indicating whether the virtual address is present in (1) or absent from (0) the Translation Buffer.

The TBCHK Register can be used by system software for working set management.

5.3.17 Translation Buffer Invalidate All (TBIA)

Access:

Write

Operation:

{Invalidate all TB entries}

Value at System Initialization:

Not applicable

Format:

Figure 5–17: Translation Buffer Invalidate All Register (TBIA)

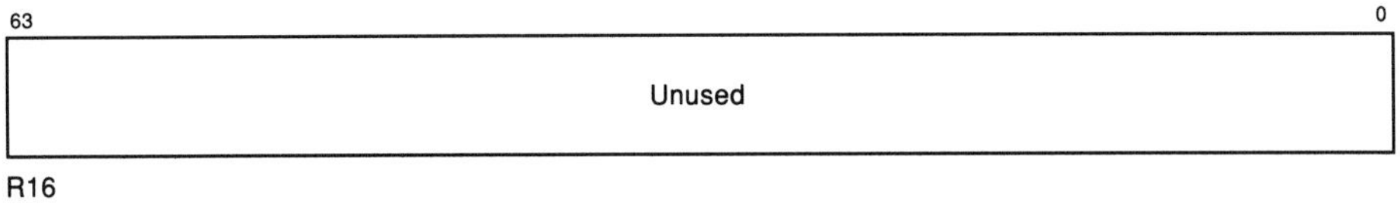

```
63                                                                    0
┌──────────────────────────────────────────────────────────────────┐
│                                                                    │
│                              Unused                                │
│                                                                    │
└──────────────────────────────────────────────────────────────────┘
R16
```

Description:

The Translation Buffer Invalidate All Register provides the capability to invalidate all entries in the Translation Buffer by executing an MTPR instruction specifying TBIA; see Chapter 3.

5.3.18 Translation Buffer Invalidate All Process (TBIAP)

Access:

Write

Operation:

```
{Invalidate all TB entries with PTE<ASM> clear}
```

Value at System Initialization:

Not applicable

Format:

Figure 5–18:   Translation Buffer Invalidate All Process Register (TBIAP)

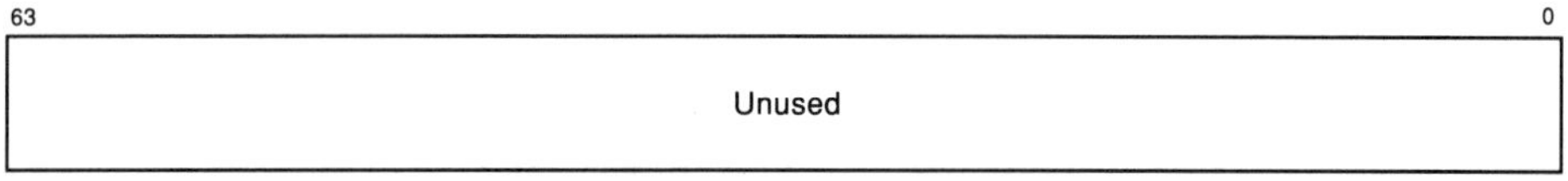

63	0
Unused	

R16

Description:

The Translation Buffer Invalidate All Process Register provides the capability to invalidate all entries in the Translation Buffer that do not have the ASM bit set by executing an MTPR instruction specifying TBIAP; see Chapter 3.

Notes:

More entries may be invalidated by this operation.   For example, some implementations may flush the entire TB on a TBIAP.

5.3.19 Translation Buffer Invalidate Single (TBISx)

Access:

Write

Operation:

```
TBIS:
    {Invalidate single Data TB entry using R16}
    {Invalidate single Instruction TB entry using R16}
TBISD:
    {Invalidate single Data TB entry using R16}
TBISI:
    {Invalidate single Instruction TB entry using R16}
```

Value at System Initialization:

Not applicable

Format:

Figure 5–19: Translation Buffer Invalidate Single (TBIS)

63	0
Virtual Address	

R16

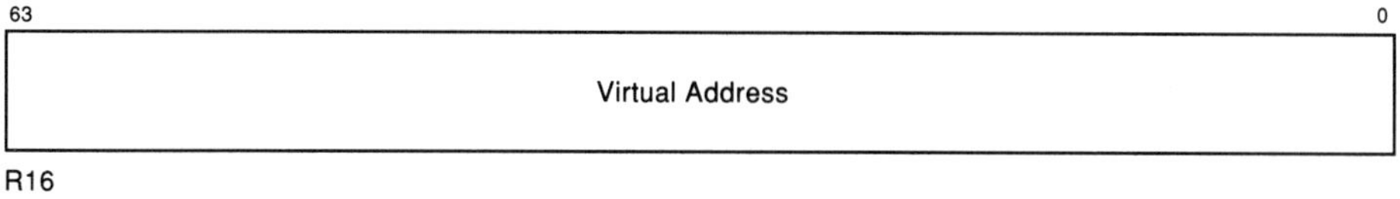

Description:

The Translation Buffer Invalidate Single Registers provide the capability to invalidate a single entry in the Instruction Translation Buffer (TBISI), the Data Translation Buffer (TBISD), or both translation buffers (TBIS). The virtual address to be invalidated is passed in R16 and may be any address within the desired page.

Notes:
More than the single entry may be invalidated by this operation. For example some implementations may flush the entire TB on a TBIS. As a result, if the specified address does not match any entry in the Translation Buffer, then it is implementation-dependent whether the state of the Translation Buffer is affected by the operation.

5.3.20 Executive Stack Pointer (ESP)

Access:

Read/Write

Operation:

```
IF {internal registers for stack pointers}  THEN      ! Read
    R0 ←  ESP
ELSE
    R0 ←  (IPR_PCBB + HWPCB_ESP)

IF {internal registers for stack pointers}  THEN      ! Write
    ESP ←  R16
ELSE
    (IPR_PCBB + HWPCB_ESP) ←  R16
```

Value at System Initialization:

Value in the initial HWPCB

Format:

Figure 5–20: Executive Stack Pointer (ESP)

63	0
Stack Address	

Description:

This register allows the stack pointer for Executive mode (ESP) to be read and written via MFPR and MTPR instructions that specify ESP.

The current stack pointer may be read and written directly by specifying scalar register SP (R30).

As processes are scheduled for execution, the stack pointers for the next process to execute are loaded using the Swap Privileged Context (SWPCTX) instruction; see Section 2.6 and Chapter 4.

5.3.21 Supervisor Stack Pointer (SSP)

Access:

Read/Write

Operation:

```
IF {internal registers for stack pointers}  THEN      ! Read
    R0 ←  SSP
ELSE
    R0 ←  (IPR_PCBB + HWPCB_SSP)
IF {internal registers for stack pointers}  THEN      ! Write
    SSP ←  R16
ELSE
    (IPR_PCBB + HWPCB_SSP) ←  R16
```

Value at System Initialization:

Value in the initial HWPCB

Format:

Figure 5–21: Supervisor Stack Pointer (SSP)

63	0
Stack Address	

Description:

This register allows the stack pointer for Supervisor mode (SSP) to be read and written via MFPR and MTPR instructions that specify SSP.

The current stack pointer may be read and written directly by specifying scalar register SP (R30).

As processes are scheduled for execution, the stack pointers for the next process to execute are loaded using the Swap Privileged Context (SWPCTX) instruction; see Section 2.6 and Chapter 4.

5.3.22 User Stack Pointer (USP)

Access:

Read/Write

Operation:

```
IF {internal registers for stack pointers}  THEN      ! Read
    R0 ←  USP
ELSE
    R0 ←  (IPR_PCBB + HWPCB_USP)
IF {internal registers for stack pointers}  THEN      ! Write
    USP ←  R16
ELSE
    (IPR_PCBB + HWPCB_USP) ←  R16
```

Value at System Initialization:

Value in the initial HWPCB

Format:

Figure 5–22: User Stack Pointer (USP)

63	0
Stack Address	

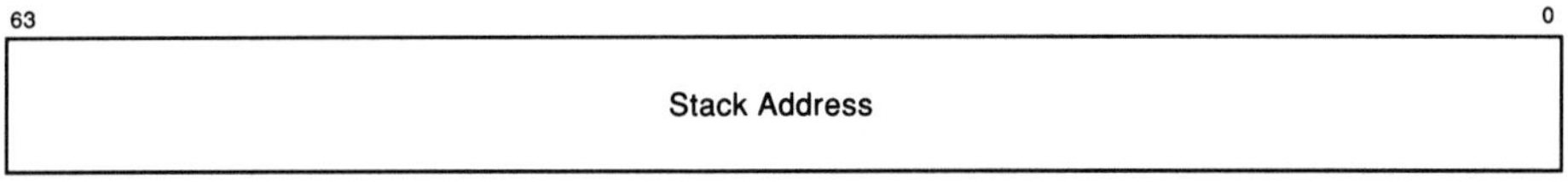

Description:

This register allows the stack pointer for User mode (USP) to be read and written via MFPR and MTPR instructions that specify USP.

The current stack pointer may be read and written directly by specifying scalar register SP (R30).

As processes are scheduled for execution, the two stack pointers for the next process to execute are loaded using the Swap Privileged Context (SWPCTX) instruction; see Section 2.6 and Chapter 4.

5.3.23 Virtual Page Table Base (VPTB)

Access:

Read/Write

Operation:

```
R0  ←  VPTB                ! Read
VPTB  ←  R16               ! Write
```

Value at System Initialization:

Initialized by the console in the bootstrap address space.

Format:

Figure 5–23: Virtual Page Table Base Register (VPTB)

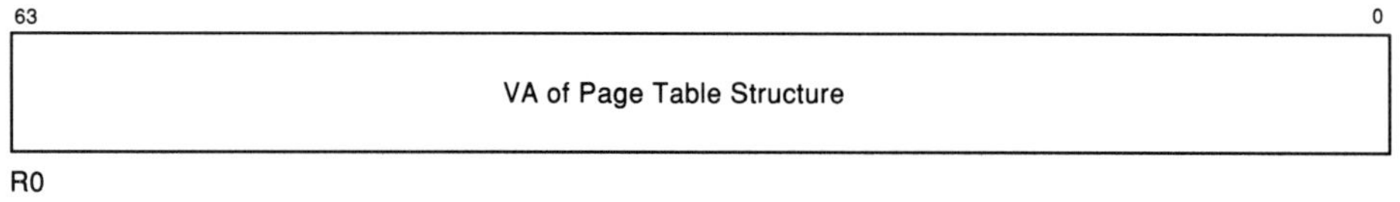

```
63                                                                    0
+---------------------------------------------------------------------+
|                      VA of Page Table Structure                     |
+---------------------------------------------------------------------+
R0
```

Description:

The Virtual Page Table Base Register contains the virtual address of the base of the entire three-level Page table structure. It may be read by executing an MFPR instruction specifying VPTB. It is written at system initialization using an MTPR instruction specifying VPTB. See Section 3.7.2 for initialization considerations.

5.3.24 Who-Am-I (WHAMI)

Access:

Read

Operation:

```
R0 ←  WHAMI
```

Value at System Initialization:

Processor number

Format:

Figure 5–24: Who-Am-I Register (WHAMI)

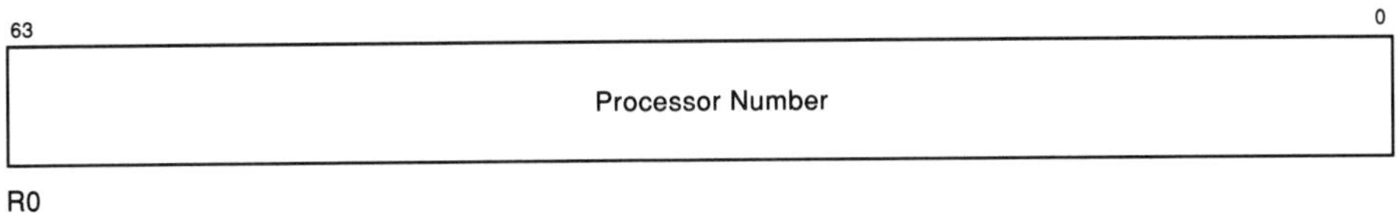

```
63                                                                              0
┌───────────────────────────────────────────────────────────────────────────────┐
│                                                                                 │
│                              Processor Number                                   │
│                                                                                 │
└───────────────────────────────────────────────────────────────────────────────┘
R0
```

Description:

The Who-Am-I Register provides the capability to read the current processor number by executing an MFPR instruction specifying WHAMI. The processor number returned is in the range 0 to the number of processors minus one that can be configured in the system. Processor number FFFF FFFF FFFF $FFFF_{16}$ is reserved.

The current processor number is useful in a multiprocessing system to index arrays that store per processor information. Such information is operating system dependent.

Chapter 6

OpenVMS Exceptions, Interrupts, and Machine Checks (II)

6.1 Introduction

At certain times during the operation of a system, events within the system require the execution of software outside the explicit flow of control. When such an exceptional event occurs, an Alpha processor forces a change in control flow from that indicated by the current instruction stream. The notification process for such events is of one of three types:

- Exceptions

  These events are relevant primarily to the currently executing process and normally invoke software in the context of the current process. The three types of exceptions are faults, arithmetic traps, and synchronous traps. Exceptions are described in Section 6.3.

- Interrupts

  These events are primarily relevant to other processes, or to the system as a whole, and are typically serviced in a system-wide context.

  Some interrupts are of such urgency that they require high-priority service, while others must be synchronized with independent events. To meet these needs, each processor has priority logic that grants interrupt service to the highest priority event at any point in time. Interrupts are described in Section 6.4.

- Machine Checks

  These events are generally the result of serious hardware failure. The registers and memory are potentially in an indeterminate state such that the instruction execution cannot necessarily be correctly restarted, completed, simulated, or undone. Machine checks are described in Section 6.5.

For all such events, the change in flow of control involves changing the Program Counter (PC), possibly changing the execution mode (current mode) and/or interrupt priority level (IPL) in the Processor Status (PS), and saving the old values of the PC and PS. The old values are saved on the target stack as part of an Exception, Interrupt, or Machine Check Stack Frame. Collectively, those elements are described in Section 6.2.

The service routines that handle exceptions, interrupts, and machine checks are specified by entry points in the System Control Block (SCB), described in Section 6.6.

Return from an exception, interrupt, or machine check, is done via the CALL_PAL REI instruction. As part of its work, CALL_PAL REI restores the saved values of PC and PS and pops them off the stack.

6.1.1 Contrast Between Exceptions, Interrupts, and Machine Checks

Generally, exceptions, interrupts, and machine checks are similar. However, there are four important differences:

1. An exception condition is caused by the execution of an instruction. An interrupt is caused by some activity in the system that may be independent of any instruction. A machine check is associated with a hardware error condition.

2. The IPL of the processor is not changed when the processor initiates an exception. The IPL is always raised when an interrupt is initiated. The IPL is always raised when a machine check is initiated, and for all machine checks other than system correctable, is raised to 31 (highest priority level). (For system correctable machine checks, the IPL is raised to 20.)

3. Exceptions are always initiated immediately, no matter what the processor IPL is. Interrupts are deferred until the processor IPL drops below the IPL of the requesting source. Machine checks can be initiated immediately or deferred, depending on error conditions.

4. Some exceptions can be selectively disabled by selecting instructions that do not check for exception conditions. If an exception condition occurs in such an instruction, the condition is totally ignored and no state is saved to signal that condition at a later time.

   If an interrupt request occurs while the processor IPL is equal to or greater than that of the interrupting source, the condition will eventually initiate an interrupt if the interrupt request is still present and the processor IPL is lowered below that of the interrupting source.

   Machine checks cannot be disabled. Machine checks can be initiated immediately or deferred, depending on the error condition. Also, they can be deliberately generated by software.

6.1.2 Exceptions, Interrupts, and Machine Checks Summary

The table below summarizes the actions taken on an exception, interrupt, or machine check. The remaining sections in this chapter describe these in greater detail.

- The "SavedPC" column describes what is saved in the "PC" field of the exception or interrupt or machine check stack frame. Here,

  1. "Current" indicates the PC of the instruction at which the exception or interrupt or machine check was taken, while

  2. "Next" indicates the PC of the successor instruction.

- The "NewMode" column specifies the mode and stack that the exception or interrupt or machine check routine will start with. For change mode traps, "MostPrv" indicates the more privileged of the current and new modes.

- The "R2" column specifies the value with which R2 is loaded, after its original value has been saved in the exception or interrupt or machine check stack frame. The SCB vector quadword, "SCBv", is loaded into R2 for all interrupts and exceptions and machine checks.

- The "R3" column specifies the value with which R3 is loaded, after its original value has been saved in the exception or interrupt or machine check stack frame. The SCB parameter quadword, "SCBp", is loaded into R3 for all interrupts and exceptions and machine checks.

- The "R4" column specifies the value with which R4 is loaded, after its original value has been saved in the exception or interrupt or machine check stack frame. If the "R4" column is blank the value in R4 is UNPREDICTABLE on entry to an interrupt or exception. Here,

    1. "VA" indicates the exact virtual address which triggered a memory management fault or data alignment trap.

    2. "Mask" indicates the Register Write Mask.

    3. "LAOff" indicates the offset from the base of the logout area in the HWRPB; see Section 6.5.2.

- The "R5" column specifies the value with which R5 is loaded, after its original value has been saved in the exception or interrupt or machine check stack frame. If the "R5" column is blank the value in R5 is UNPREDICTABLE on entry to an interrupt or exception or machine check. Here,

    1. "MMF" indicates the Memory Management Flags.

    2. "Exc" indicates the Exception Summary parameter.

    3. "RW" indicates Read/Load =0 Write/Store =1 for data align traps

Table 6–1: Exceptions, Interrupts, and Machine Checks Summary

	SavedPC	NewMode	R2	R3	R4	R5
Exceptions - Faults						
Floating Disabled Fault	Current	Kernel	SCBv	SCBp		
Memory Management Faults						
Access Control Violation	Current	Kernel	SCBv	SCBp	VA	MMF
Translation Not Valid	Current	Kernel	SCBv	SCBp	VA	MMF
Fault on Read	Current	Kernel	SCBv	SCBp	VA	MMF
Fault on Write	Current	Kernel	SCBv	SCBp	VA	MMF
Fault on Execute	Current	Kernel	SCBv	SCBp	VA	MMF

Table 6–1 (Cont.): Exceptions, Interrupts, and Machine Checks Summary

	SavedPC	NewMode	R2	R3	R4	R5
Exceptions - Arithmetic Traps						
Arithmetic Traps	Next	Kernel	SCBv	SCBp	Mask	Exc
Exceptions - Synchronous Traps						
Breakpoint Trap	Next	Kernel	SCBv	SCBp		
Bugcheck Trap	Next	Kernel	SCBv	SCBp		
Change Mode to K/E/S/U	Next	MostPrv	SCBv	SCBp		
Illegal Instruction	Next	Kernel	SCBv	SCBp		
Illegal Operand	Next	Kernel	SCBv	SCBp		
Data Alignment Trap	Next	Kernel	SCBv	SCBp	VA	RW
Interrupts						
Asynch System Trap (4)	Current	Kernel	SCBv	SCBp		
Interval Clock	Current	Kernel	SCBv	SCBp		
Interprocessor Interrupt	Current	Kernel	SCBv	SCBp		
Software Interrupts	Current	Kernel	SCBv	SCBp		
Performance monitor	Current	Kernel	SCBv	SCBp	IMP	IMP
Passive Release	Current	Kernel	SCBv	SCBp		
Powerfail	Current	Kernel	SCBv	SCBp		
I/O Device	Current	Kernel	SCBv	SCBp		
Machine Checks						
Processor Correctable	Current	Kernel	SCBv	SCBp	LAOff	
System Correctable	Current	Kernel	SCBv	SCBp	LAOff	
System	Current	Kernel	SCBv	SCBp	LAOff	
Processor	Current	Kernel	SCBv	SCBp	LAOff	

6.2 Processor State and Exception/Interrupt/Machine Check Stack Frame

Processor state consists of a quadword of privileged information called the Processor Status (PS) and a quadword containing the Program Counter (PC), which is the virtual address of the next instruction.

When an exception, interrupt, or machine check is initiated, the current processor state during the exception, interrupt, or machine check must be preserved. This is accomplished by automatically pushing the PS and the PC on the target stack.

Subsequently, instruction execution can be continued at the point of the exception, interrupt, or machine check by executing a CALL_PAL REI instruction; see Chapter 2.

Process context such as memory mapping information is not saved or restored on each exception, interrupt, or machine check. Instead, it is saved and restored when process context switching is performed. Other processor status is changed even less frequently; see Chapter 4.

6.2.1 Processor Status

The PS can be explicitly read with the CALL_PAL RD_PS instruction. The PS<SW> field can be explicitly written with the CALL_PAL WR_PS_SW instruction. See Section 2.1.

The terms current PS and saved PS are used to distinguish between this status information when it is stored internal to the processor and when copies of it are materialized in memory.

Figure 6–1: Current Processor Status (PS Register)

63		13 12	8	7	6 5	4 3	2 1	0
MBZ		IPL	VMM	MBZ	CM	IP	SW

Figure 6–2: Saved Processor Status (PS on Stack)

63 62	56 55		13 12	8	7	6 5	4 3	2 1	0
MBZ	SP_ALIGN	MBZ	IPL	VMM	MBZ	CM	IP	SW

Table 6–2: Processor Status Register Summary

Bits	Description
1:0	Reserved for Software (SW). These bits are reserved for software use and can be read and written at any time by the software, regardless of the current mode. The value of these bits is ignored by the hardware. The software field is set to zero at the initiation of either an exception or an interrupt.
2	Interrupt pending (IP). Set when an interrupt (software or hardware but NOT AST) is initiated; indicates an interrupt is in progress.
4:3	Current mode (CM). The access mode of the currently executing process as follows: 0 - Kernel 1 - Executive 2 - Supervisor 3 - User
6:5	Reserved to Digital, MBZ.
7	Virtual machine monitor (VMM) - When set, the processor is executing in a virtual machine monitor. When clear, the processor is running in either real or virtual machine mode. **PROGRAMMING NOTE** This bit is only meaningful when running with PALcode that implements virtual machine capabilities.
12:8	Interrupt priority level (IPL) - The current processor priority, in the range 0 to 31.
55:13	Reserved to Digital, MBZ.
61:56	Stack alignment (SP_ALIGN) - The previous stack byte alignment within a 64 byte aligned area, in the range 0 to 63. This field is set in the saved PS during the act of taking an exception or interrupt; it is used by the CALL_PAL REI instruction to restore the previous stack byte alignment.
63:62	Reserved to Digitial, MBZ.

At bootstrap, the initial value of PS is set to $1F00_{16}$. Previous stack alignment is zero, IPL is 31, VMM is clear, CM is Kernel, and the SW and IP fields are zero.

6.2.2 Program Counter

The PC is a 64-bit virtual address. All instructions are aligned on longword boundaries and, therefore, hardware can assume zero for the two low-order PC bits.

The PC can be explicitly read with the Unconditional Branch (BR) instruction. All branching instructions also load a new value into the PC.

Figure 6–3: Program Counter (PC)

63	2 1 0
Instruction Virtual Address <63:2>	I G N

6.2.3 Processor Interrupt Priority Level (IPL)

Each processor has 32 interrupt priority levels (IPLs) divided into 16 software levels (numbered 0 to 15), and 16 hardware levels (numbered 16 to 31). User applications and most operating system software run at IPL 0, which may be thought of as process level. Higher numbered interrupt levels have higher priority; i.e., any request at an interrupt level higher than the processor's current IPL will interrupt immediately, but requests at lower or equal levels are deferred.

Interrupt levels 0 to 15 exist solely for use by software. No hardware event can request an interrupt on these levels. Conversely, interrupt levels 16 to 31 exist solely for use by hardware. Serious system failures, such as a machine check abort, however, raise the IPL to the highest level (31), to minimize processor interruption until the problem is corrected, and execute in Kernel mode on the Kernel stack.

6.2.4 Protection Modes

Each processor has four protection modes. The modes are Kernel, Executive, Supervisor, and User. Per-page memory protection varies as a function of mode (for example, a page can be made read-only in User mode, but read-write in Supervisor, Executive, or Kernel mode).

For each process, there is a separate stack associated with each mode. Corruption of one stack does not affect use of the other stacks.

Some instructions, termed privileged instructions, may only be executed in Kernel mode.

6.2.5 Processor Stacks

Each processor has four stacks. There are four process-specific stacks associated with the four modes of the current process. At any given time, only one of these stacks is actively used as the current stack.

6.2.6 Stack Frames

When an exception, interrupt, or machine check occurs, a stack frame is pushed on the target stack. Regardless of the type of event notification, this stack frame consists of a 64 byte-aligned structure containing the saved contents of registers R2..R7, the Program Counter (PC), and the Processor Status (PS). Registers R2 and R3 are then loaded with vector and parameter from the SCB for the exception, interrupt, or machine check. Registers R4 and R5 may be loaded with data pertaining to the exception, interrupt, or machine check. The specific data loaded is described below in conjunction with each exception, interrupt, or machine check; if no specific data is specified, the contents of R4 and R5 are UNPREDICTABLE. After the stack is built, the contents of registers R6 and R7 are UNPREDICTABLE.

The Program Counter value saved is that of the instruction encountering the exception in the case of faults, that of the next instruction in the case of traps and interrupts, and, on a best-effort basis, and that of the next instruction in the case of machine checks. Return from an exception, interrupt, or machine check is done via the CALL_PAL REI instruction, which restores the saved values of PC, PS, and R2..R7, thus re-executing the instruction in the case of faults, and proceeding to the next instruction in the case of traps, interrupts, and machine checks.

Figure 6–4: Stack Frame

63	0	
R2	:SP
R3	:+08
R4	:+16
R5	:+24
R6	:+32
R7	:+40
Program Counter (PC)	:+48
Processor Status (PS)	:+56

6.3 Exceptions

Exception service routines execute in response to exception conditions caused by software. Most exception service routines execute in Kernel mode, on the Kernel stack; all exception service routines execute at the current processor IPL. Change Mode exception routines for CHMU/CHMS/CHME execute in the more privileged of the current mode or the target mode (U/S/E), on the matching stack. Exception service routines are usually coded to avoid exceptions; however, nested exceptions can occur.

There are three types of exceptions:

- A fault is an exception condition that occurs during an instruction and leaves the registers and memory in a consistent state such that elimination of the fault condition and subsequent re-execution of the instruction will give correct results. Faults are not guaranteed to leave the machine in exactly the same state it was in immediately prior to the fault, but rather in a state such that the instruction can be correctly executed if the fault condition is removed. The PC saved in the exception stack frame is the address of the faulting instruction. A CALL_PAL REI instruction to this PC will reexecute the faulting instruction.

- An arithmetic trap is an exception condition that occurs at the completion of the operation that caused the exception. Since several instructions may be in various stages of execution at any point in time, it is possible for multiple arithmetic traps to occur simultaneously. The PC that is saved in the exception frame on traps is that of the next instruction that would have been issued if the trapping condition(s) had not occurred. This is not necessarily the address of the instruction immediately following the one(s) encountering the trap condition, and intervening instructions may have changed operands or other state used by the instruction(s) encountering the trap condition(s). A CALL_PAL REI instruction to this PC will not reexecute the trapping instruction(s), nor will it reexecute any intervening instructions; it will simply continue execution from the point at which the trap was taken.

   In general, it is difficult to fixup results and continue program execution at the point of an arithmetic trap. Software can force a trap to be continued more easily without the need for complicated fixup code. This is accomplished by following a set of code-generation restrictions in code that could cause arithmetic traps which are to be completed by a software trap handler (see *Common Architecture, Chapter 4*), including specifying the /S software completion modifier in each such instruction.

   The AND of all the software completion modifiers for trapping instructions is provided to the arithmetic trap handler in the exception summary SWC bit. If SWC is set, a trap handler may find the trigger instruction by scanning backward from the trap PC until each register in the register write mask has been an instruction destination. The trigger instruction is the first instruction in I-stream order to get a trap within a trap shadow (see *Common Architecture, Chapter 4* for definition of trap shadow). If the SWC bit is clear, no fixup is possible (the trigger instruction may have been followed by a taken branch, so the trap PC cannot be used to find it).

- A synchronous trap is an exception condition that occurs at the completion of the operation that caused the exception (or, if the operation can only be partially carried out, at the completion of that part of the operation), and no subsequent instruction is issued before the trap occurs.

   Synchronous traps are divided into data alignment traps and all other synchronous traps.

6.3.1 Faults

The six types of faults signal that an instruction or its operands are in some way illegal. These faults are all initiated in Kernel mode and push an exception stack frame onto the stack. Upon entry to the exception routine, the saved PC (in the exception stack frame) is the virtual address of the faulting instruction.

The six faults include the Floating Disable Fault described in the next subsection and five memory management faults.

Memory management faults occur when a virtual address translation encounters an exception condition. This can occur as the result of instruction fetch or during a load or store operation.

Immediately following a memory management fault, register R4 contains the exact virtual address encountering the fault condition.

The register R5 contains the "MM Flag" quadword.

"MM Flag" is set as follows:

$0000\ 0000\ 0000\ 0000_{16}$ for a faulting data read

$0000\ 0000\ 0000\ 0001_{16}$ for a faulting I-fetch operation

$8000\ 0000\ 0000\ 0000_{16}$ for a faulting write operation

The faulting instruction is the instruction whose fetch faulted, or the load, store, or PALcode instruction that encountered the fault condition.

Chapter 3 describes the memory management architecture of Alpha in more detail.

6.3.1.1 Floating Disabled Fault

A Floating Disabled Fault is an exception that occurs when an attempt is made to execute a floating-point instruction and the floating enable (FEN) bit in the HWPCB is not set.

6.3.1.2 Access Control Violation (ACV) Fault

An ACV fault is a memory management fault indicating that an attempted access to a virtual address was not allowed in the current mode.

ACV faults usually indicate program errors, but in some cases, such as automatic stack expansion, can mean implicit operating system functions.

ACV faults take precedence over Translation Not Valid, Fault on Read, Fault on Write, and Fault on Execute faults.

ACV faults take precedence over Translation Not Valid faults so that a malicious user could not degrade system performance by causing spurious page faults to pages for which no access is allowed.

6.3.1.3 Translation Not Valid (TNV)

A TNV fault is a memory management fault that indicates that an attempted access was made to a virtual address whose Page Table Entry (PTE) was not valid.

Software may use TNV faults to implement virtual memory capabilities.

6.3.1.4 Fault On Read (FOR)

An FOR fault is a memory management fault that indicates that an attempted data read access was made to a virtual address whose Page Table Entry (PTE) had the Fault on Read bit set.

As a part of initiating the FOR fault, the processor invalidates the Translation Buffer entry that caused the fault to be generated.

This allows an implementation only to invalidate entries from the Data-stream Translation Buffer on Fault On Read faults.

Note that the Translation Buffer may reload and cache the old PTE value between the time when the FOR fault invalidates the old value from the Translation Buffer and the time when software updates the PTE in memory. Software that depends on the processor-provided invalidate must thus be prepared to take another FOR fault on a page after clearing the page's PTE<FOR> bit. The second fault will invalidate the stale PTE from the Translation Buffer, and the processor cannot load another stale copy. Thus in the worst case, a multiprocessor system will take an initial FOR fault and then an additional FOR fault on each processor. In practice, even a single repetition is unlikely.

Software may use FOR faults to implement watchpoints, to collect page usage statistics, and to implement execute-only pages.

6.3.1.5 Fault On Write (FOW)

A FOW fault is a memory management fault that indicates that an attempted data write access was made to a virtual address whose Page Table Entry (PTE) had the Fault On Write bit set.

As a part of initiating the FOW fault, the processor invalidates the Translation Buffer entry that caused the fault to be generated.

IMPLEMENTATION NOTE

This allows an implementation only to invalidate entries from the Data-stream Translation Buffer on Fault On Write faults.

Note that the Translation Buffer may reload and cache the old PTE value between the time when the FOW fault invalidates the old value from the Translation Buffer and the time when software updates the PTE in memory. Software that depends on the processor-provided invalidate must thus be prepared to take another FOW fault on a page after clearing the page's PTE<FOW> bit. The second fault will invalidate the stale PTE from the Translation Buffer, and the processor cannot load another stale copy. Thus in the worst case, a multiprocessor system will take an initial FOW fault and then an additional FOW fault on each processor. In practice, even a single repetition is unlikely.

Software may use FOW faults to maintain modified page information, to implement copy on write and watchpoint capabilities, and to collect page usage statistics.

6.3.1.6 Fault On Execute (FOE)

An FOE fault is a memory management fault indicating that an attempted instruction stream access was made to a virtual address whose Page Table Entry (PTE) had the Fault On Execute bit set.

As a part of initiating the FOE fault, the processor invalidates the Translation Buffer entry that caused the fault to be generated.

IMPLEMENTATION NOTE

This allows an implementation only to invalidate entries from the Instruction-stream Translation Buffer on Fault On Execute faults.

Note that the Translation Buffer may reload and cache the old PTE value between the time when the FOE fault invalidates the old value from the Translation Buffer and the time when software updates the PTE in memory. Software that depends on the processor-provided invalidate must thus be prepared to take another FOE fault on a page after clearing the page's PTE<FOE> bit. The second fault will invalidate the stale PTE from the Translation Buffer, and the processor cannot load another stale copy. Thus in the worst case, a multiprocessor system will take an initial FOE fault and then an additional FOE fault on each processor. In practice, even a single repetition is unlikely.

Software may use FOE faults to implement access mode changes and protected entry to Kernel mode, to collect page usage statistics, and to detect programming errors that try to execute data.

6.3.2 Arithmetic Traps

An arithmetic trap is an exception that occurs as the result of performing an arithmetic or conversion operation.

If integer register R31 or floating register F31 is specified as the destination of an operation that can cause an arithmetic trap, it is UNPREDICTABLE whether the trap will actually occur, even if the operation would definitely produce an exceptional result.

Arithmetic traps are initiated in Kernel mode and push the exception stack frame on the Kernel stack. The Register Write Mask is saved in R4, and the Exception Summary parameter is saved in R5. These are described below.

When an arithmetic exception condition is detected, several instructions may be in various stages of execution. These instructions are allowed to complete before the arithmetic trap can be initiated. Some of these instructions may themselves cause further arithmetic traps. Thus it is possible for several arithmetic traps to be reported simultaneously.

It is also possible for the result of an instruction that causes an arithmetic trap to be used as an operand in a subsequent instruction before the trap is taken. If this would produce undesired behavior, software is responsible for inserting appropriate TRAPB instructions to cause the trap to be recognized before the result is used.

Integer exceptional results (integer overflow) can be forwarded to the address calculation for load and store instructions, to the address calculation for jump instructions, as the source data for a store instruction, or as the source data for a conditional branch instruction. This can result in the generation of an inappropriate address, the storing of exceptional results in memory, or an unintended branch.

If this would produce undesired behavior, software is responsible for inserting appropriate TRAPB instructions to cause the trap to be recognized before the result is used.

6.3.2.1 Exception Summary Parameter

The Exception Summary parameter records the various types of arithmetic traps that can occur together. These types of traps are described in subsections below.

Figure 6–5: Exception Summary

63		7 6 5 4 3 2 1 0
	Zero	I I U O D I S / O N N V Z N W / V E F F E V C

Table 6–3: Exception Summary

Bit	Description
0	Software Completion (SWC)
	Is set when all of the other arithmetic exception bits were set by floating-operate instructions with the /S software completion trap modifier set. See *Common Architecture, Chapter 4* for rules about setting the /S modifier in code that may cause an arithmetic trap, and Section 6.3 for rules about using the SWC bit in a trap handler.
1	Invalid Operation (INV)
	An attempt was made to perform a floating arithmetic, conversion, or comparison operation, and one or more of the operand values were illegal.
2	Division by Zero (DZE)
	An attempt was made to perform a floating divide operation with a divisor of zero.
3	Overflow (OVF)
	A floating arithmetic or conversion operation overflowed the destination exponent.
4	Underflow (UNF)
	A floating arithmetic or conversion operation underflowed the destination exponent.
5	Inexact Result (INE)
	A floating arithmetic or conversion operation gave a result that differed from the mathematically exact result.
6	Integer Overflow (IOV)
	An integer arithmetic operation or a conversion from floating to integer overflowed the destination precision.

6.3.2.2 Register Write Mask

The Register Write Mask parameter records all registers that were targets of instructions that set the bits in the exception summary register. There is a one-to-one correspondence between bits in the Register Write Mask quadword and the register numbers. The quadword records, starting at bit 0 and proceeding right to left, which of the registers R0 through R31, then F0 through F31, received an exceptional result.

NOTE

For a sequence such as:

```
ADDF    F1,F2,F3
MULF    F4,F5,F3
```

if the add overflows and the multiply does not, the OVF bit is set in the exception summary, and the F3 bit is set in the register mask, even though the overflowed sum in F3 can be overwritten with an in-range product by the time the trap is taken. (This code violates the destination reuse rule for software completion. See *Common Architecture, Chapter 4* for the destination reuse rules.)

The PC value saved in the exception stack frame is the virtual address of the next instruction. This is defined as the virtual address of the first instruction not executed after the trap condition was recognized.

6.3.2.3 Invalid Operation (INV) Trap

An INV trap is reported for most floating-point operate instructions with an input operand that is a VAX reserved operand, VAX dirty zero, IEEE NaN, IEEE infinity, or IEEE denormal.

Floating INV traps are always enabled. If this trap occurs, the result register is written with an UNPREDICTABLE value.

6.3.2.4 Division by Zero (DZE) Trap

A DZE trap is reported when a finite number is divided by zero. Floating DZE traps are always enabled. If this trap occurs, the result register is written with an UNPREDICTABLE value.

6.3.2.5 Overflow (OVF) Trap

An OVF trap is reported when the destination's largest finite number is exceeded in magnitude by the rounded true result. Floating OVF traps are always enabled. If this trap occurs, the result register is written with an UNPREDICTABLE value.

6.3.2.6 Underflow (UNF) Trap

A UNF trap is reported when the destination's smallest finite number exceeds in magnitude the non-zero rounded true result. Floating UNF trap enable can be specified in each floating-point operate instruction. If underflow occurs, the result register is written with a true zero.

6.3.2.7 Inexact Result (INE) Trap

An INE trap is reported if the rounded result of an IEEE operation is not exact. INE trap enable can be specified in each IEEE floating-point operate instruction. The unchanged result value is stored in all cases.

6.3.2.8 Integer Overflow (IOV) Trap

An IOV trap is reported for any integer operation whose true result exceeds the destination register size. IOV trap enable can be specified in each arithmetic integer operate instruction and each floating-point convert-to-integer instruction. If integer overflow occurs, the result register is written with the truncated true result.

6.3.3 Synchronous Traps

A synchronous trap is an exception condition that occurs at the completion of the operation that caused the exception (or, if the operation can only be partially carried out, at the completion of that part of the operation), but no successor instruction is allowed to start. All traps that are not arithmetic traps are synchronous traps.

Some synchronous traps are caused by PALcode instructions: BPT, BUGCHK, CHMU, CHMS, CHME, and CHMK. For synchronous traps, the PC saved in the exception stack frame is the address of the instruction immediately following the one causing the trap condition. A CALL_PAL REI instruction to this PC will continue without reexecuting the trapping instruction. The following subsections describe the synchronous traps in detail.

6.3.3.1 Data Alignment Trap

All data must be naturally aligned or an alignment trap may be generated. Natural alignment means that data bytes are on byte boundaries, data words are on word boundaries, data longwords are on longword boundaries, and data quadwords are on quadword boundaries.

A Data Alignment trap is generated by the hardware when an attempt is made to load or store a longword or quadword to/from a register using an address that does not have the natural alignment of the particular data reference.

Data alignment traps are fixed up by the PALcode and are optionally reported to the operating system under the control of the DAT bit. If the bit is zero, the trap will be reported. If the bit is set, after the alignment is corrected, control is returned to the user. In either case, if the PALcode detects a LDx_L or STx_C instruction, no correction is possible and an illegal operand exception is generated.

The system software is notified via the generation of a Kernel mode exception through the Unaligned_Access SCB vector (280_{16}) The virtual address of the unaligned data being accessed is stored in R4. R5 indicates whether the operation was a read or a write (0 = read/load 1 = write/store).

PALcode may write partial results to memory without probing to make sure all writes will succeed when dealing with unaligned store operations.

If a memory management exception condition occurs while reading or writing part of the unaligned data, the appropriate memory management fault is generated.

Software should avoid data misalignment whenever possible since the emulation performance penalty may be as large as 100 to 1.

The Data Alignment trap control bit is included in the HWPCB at offset +56 bit 63. In order to change this bit for the currently executing process, the DATFX IPR may be written via a CALL_PAL MTPR_DATFX instruction. This operation will also update the value in the HWPCB.

6.3.3.2 Other Synchronous Traps

With the traps described in this subsection, the SCB vector quadword is saved in R2 and the SCB parameter quadword is saved in R3. The change mode traps are initiated in the more privileged of the current mode and the target mode, while the other traps are initiated in Kernel mode.

6.3.3.2.1 Breakpoint Trap

A Breakpoint trap is an exception that occurs when a CALL_PAL BPT instruction is executed; see Chapter 2. Breakpoint traps are intended for use by debuggers and can be used to place breakpoints in a program.

Breakpoint traps are initiated in Kernel mode so that system debuggers can capture breakpoint traps that occur while the user is executing system code.

6.3.3.2.2 Bugcheck Trap

A Bugcheck trap is an exception that occurs when a CALL_PAL BUGCHK instruction is executed; see Chapter 2. Bugchecks are used to log errors detected by software.

6.3.3.2.3 Illegal Instruction Trap

An Illegal instruction Trap is an exception that occurs when an attempt is made to execute an instruction whose opcode is reserved to Digital, is a subsetted opcode that requires emulation on the host implementation, or is a privileged instruction and the current mode is not Kernel.

6.3.3.2.4 Illegal Operand Trap

An Illegal Operand Trap occurs when an attempt is made to execute PALcode with operand values that are illegal or reserved for future use by Digital.

Illegal operands include:

- An invalid combination of bits in the PS restored by the CALL_PAL REI instruction.

- An unaligned operand passed to PALcode.

6.3.3.2.5 Generate Software Trap

A Generate Software Trap is an exception that occurs when a CALL_PAL GENTRAP instruction is executed; see Chapter 2. The intended use is for low-level compiler-generated code that detects conditions such as divide-by-zero, range errors, subscript bounds and negative string lengths.

6.3.3.2.6 Change Mode to Kernel Trap

A Change Mode to Kernel trap is an exception that occurs when a CALL_PAL CHMK instruction is executed; see Chapter 2. Change Mode to Kernel traps are initiated in Kernel mode and push the exception frame on the Kernel stack.

6.3.3.2.7 Change Mode to Executive Trap

A Change Mode to Executive trap is an exception that occurs when a CALL_PAL CHME instruction is executed; see Chapter 2. Change Mode to Executive traps are initiated in the more privileged of the current mode and Executive mode, and push the exception frame on the target stack.

6.3.3.2.8 Change Mode to Supervisor Trap

A Change Mode to Supervisor trap is an exception that occurs when a CALL_PAL CHMS instruction is executed; see Chapter 2. Change Mode to Supervisor traps are initiated in the more privileged of the current mode and Supervisor mode, and push the exception frame on the target stack.

6.3.3.2.9 Change Mode to User Trap

A Change Mode to User trap is an exception that occurs when a CALL_PAL CHMU instruction is executed; see Chapter 2. Change Mode to User traps are initiated in the more privileged of the current mode and User mode, and push the exception frame on the target stack.

6.4 Interrupts

The processor arbitrates interrupt requests according to priority. When the priority of an interrupt request is higher than the current processor IPL, the processor will raise the IPL and service the interrupt request. The interrupt service routine is entered at the IPL of the interrupting source, in Kernel mode, and on the Kernel stack. Interrupt requests can come from I/O devices, memory controllers, other processors, or the processor itself.

The priority level of one processor does not affect the priority level of other processors. Thus, in a multiprocessor system, interrupt levels alone cannot be used to synchronize access to shared resources.

Synchronization with other processors in a multiprocessor system involves a combination of raising the IPL and executing an interlocking instruction sequence. Raising the IPL prevents the synchronization sequence itself from being interrupted on a single processor while the interlock sequence guarantees mutual exclusion with other processors. Alternately, one processor can issue explicit interprocessor interrupts (and wait for acknowledgment) to put other processors in a known software state, thus achieving mutual exclusion.

In some implementations, several instructions may be in various stages of execution simultaneously. Before the processor can service an interrupt request, all active instructions must be allowed to complete without exception. Thus, when an exception occurs in a currently active instruction, the exception is initiated and the exception stack frame built immediately before the interrupt is initiated and its stack frame built.

The following events will cause an interrupt:

- Software interrupts — IPL 1 to 15
- Asynchronous System Traps — IPL 2
- Passive Release interrupts — IPL 20 to 23
- I/O Device interrupts — IPL 20 to 23
- Interval Clock interrupt — IPL 22
- Interprocessor interrupt — IPL 22
- Performance Monitor interrupt — IPL 29
- Powerfail interrupt — IPL 30

Interrupts are initiated in Kernel mode and push the interrupt stack frame of eight quadwords onto the Kernel stack. The PC saved in the interrupt stack frame is the virtual address of the first instruction not executed after the interrupt condition was recognized. A CALL_PAL REI instruction to the saved PC/PS will continue execution at the point of interrupt.

Each interrupt source has a separate vector location (offset) within the System Control Block (SCB); see Section 6.6. With the exception of I/O device interrupts, each of the above events has a unique fixed vector. I/O device interrupts occupy a range of vectors that can be both statically and dynamically assigned. Upon entry to the interrupt service routine, R2 contains the SCB vector quadword and R3 contains the SCB parameter quadword. For Corrected Error interrupts, R4 optionally locates additional information; see Section 6.5.2.

In order to reduce interrupt overhead, no memory mapping information is changed when an interrupt occurs. Therefore, the instructions, data, and the contents of the interrupt vector for the interrupt service routine must be present in every process at the same virtual address.

Interrupt service routines should follow the discipline of not lowering IPL below their initial level. Lowering IPL in this way could result in an interrupt at an intermediate level which would cause the stack nesting to be incorrect.

Kernel mode software may need to raise and lower IPL during certain instruction sequences that must synchronize with possible interrupt conditions (such as powerfail). This can be accomplished by specifying the desired IPL and executing a CALL_PAL MTPR_IPL instruction or by executing a CALL_PAL REI instruction that restores a PS that contains the desired IPL; see Chapter 2.

6.4.1 Software Interrupts — IPLs 1 to 15

6.4.1.1 Software Interrupt Summary Register

The architecture provides fifteen priority interrupt levels for use by software (level 0 is also available for use by software but interrupts can never occur at this level). The Software Interrupt Summary Register (SISR) stores a mask of pending software interrupts. Bit positions in this mask which contain a 1 correspond to the levels on which software interrupts are pending.

When the processor IPL drops below that of the highest requested software interrupt, a software interrupt is initiated and the corresponding bit in the SISR is cleared.

The SISR is a read-only internal processor register which may be read by Kernel mode software by executing a CALL_PAL MFPR_SISR instruction; see Section 5.3.

6.4.1.2 Software Interrupt Request Register

The Software Interrupt Request Register (SIRR) is a write-only internal processor register used for making software interrupt requests.

Kernel mode software may request a software interrupt at a particular level by executing a CALL_PAL MTPR_SIRR instruction; see Section 5.3.

If the requested interrupt level is greater than the current IPL, the interrupt will occur before the execution of the next instruction. If, however, the requested level is equal to or less than the current processor IPL, the interrupt request will be recorded in the Software Interrupt Summary Register (SISR) and deferred until the processor IPL drops to the appropriate level.

Note that no indication is given if there is already a request at the specified level. Therefore, the respective interrupt service routine must not assume that there is a one-to-one correspondence between interrupts requested and interrupts generated. A valid protocol for generating this correspondence is:

1. The requester places information in a control block and then inserts the control block in a queue associated with the respective software interrupt level.

2. The requester uses CALL_PAL MTPR_SIRR to request an interrupt at the appropriate level.

3. When enabling conditions arise, processor HW clears the appropriate SISR bit as part of initiating the software interrupt.

4. The interrupt service routine attempts to remove a control block from the request queue. If there are no control blocks in the queue, the interrupt is dismissed with a CALL_PAL REI instruction.

5. If a valid control block is removed from the queue, the requested service is performed and Step 3 is repeated.

6.4.2 Asynchronous System Trap — IPL 2

Asynchronous System Traps (ASTs) are a means of notifying a process of events that are not synchronized with its execution, but which must be dealt with in the context of the process. An AST is initiated in Kernel mode at IPL 2 when the current mode is less privileged than or equal to a mode for which an AST is pending and not disabled, with PS<IPL> less than 2; see Sections 6.7.6 and 4.3.

There are four separate per-mode SCB vectors, one for each of Kernel, Executive, Supervisor, and User modes.

On encountering an AST, the interrupt stack frame is pushed on the Kernel stack; the value of the PC saved in this stack frame is the address of the next instruction to have been executed if the interrupt had not occurred. The SCB vector quadword is saved in R2 and the SCB parameter quadword in R3.

6.4.3 Passive Release Interrupts — IPLs 20 to 23

Passive releases occur when the source of an interrupt granted by a processor cannot be determined. This can happen when the requesting I/O device determines that it no longer requires an interrupt after requesting one, or when a previously requested interrupt has already been serviced by another processor in some multiprocessor configurations. The interrupt handler for passive releases executes at the priority level of the interrupt request.

6.4.4 I/O Device Interrupts — IPLs 20 to 23

The architecture provides four priority levels for use by I/O devices. I/O device interrupts are requested when the device encounters a completion, attention, or error condition and the respective interrupt is enabled.

6.4.5 Interval Clock Interrupt — IPL 22

The Interval Clock requests an interrupt periodically.

At least 1000 interval clock interrupts occur per second. An entry in the HWRPB contains the number of interval clock interrupts per second that occur in an actual Alpha implementation, scaled up by 4096, and rounded to a 64-bit integer.

The accuracy of the interval clock must be at least 50 parts per million (ppm).

HARDWARE/SOFTWARE NOTE

For example, an interval of 819.2 usec derived from a 10 MHz Ethernet clock and a 13-bit counter is acceptable.

To guarantee software progress, the interval clock interrupt should be no more frequent than the time it takes to do 500 main memory accesses. Over the life of the architecture, this interval may well decrease much more slowly than CPU cycle time decreases.

Other constraints may apply to Secure Kernel systems.

6.4.5.1 Interprocessor Interrupt — IPL 22

Interprocessor interrupts are provided to enable operating system software running on one processor to interrupt activity on another processor and cause operating system dependent actions to be performed.

6.4.5.1.1 Interprocessor Interrupt Request Register

The Interprocessor Interrupt Request Register (IPIR) is a write-only internal processor register used for making a request to interrupt a specific processor.

Kernel mode software may request to interrupt a particular processor by executing a CALL_PAL MTPR_IPIR instruction; see Section 5.3.

If the specified processor is the same as the current processor and the current IPL is less than 22, then the interrupt may be delayed and not initiated before the execution of the next instruction.

Note that, like software interrupts, no indication is given as to whether there is already an interprocessor interrupt pending when one is requested. Therefore, the interprocessor interrupt service routine must not assume there is a one-to-one correspondence between interrupts requested and interrupts generated. A valid protocol similar to the one for software interrupts for generating this correspondence is:

1. The requester places information in a control block and then inserts the control block in a queue associated with the target processor.

2. The requester uses CALL_PAL MTPR_IPIR to request an interprocessor interrupt on the target processor.

3. The interprocessor interrupt service routine on the target processor attempts to remove a control block from its request queue. If there are no control blocks remaining, the interrupt is dismissed with a CALL_PAL REI instruction.

4. If a valid control block is removed from the queue, the specified action is performed and Step 3 is repeated.

6.4.6 Performance Monitor Interrupts — IPL 29

These interrupts provide some of the support for processor or system performance measurements. The implementation is processor or system specific.

6.4.7 Powerfail Interrupt — IPL 30

If the system power supply backup option permits powerfail recovery, a Powerfail interrupt is generated to each processor when power is about to fail.

In systems in which the backup option maintains only the contents of memory and keeps system time with the BB_WATCH, the power supply requests a powerfail interrupt to permit volatile system state to be saved. Prior to dispatching to the powerfail interrupt service routine, PALcode is responsible for saving all system state which is not visible to system software. Such state includes, but is not limited to, processor internal registers and PALcode temporary variables.

PALcode is also responsible for saving the contents of any writeback caches or buffers, including the powerfail interrupt stack frame. System software is responsible for saving all other system state. Such state includes, but is not limited to, processor registers and writeback cache contents. State can be saved by forcing all written data to a backed-up part of the memory subsystem; software may use the CALL_PAL CFLUSH instruction.

The Powerfail interrupt will not be initiated until the processor IPL drops below 30. Thus, critical code sequences can block the power-down sequence by raising the IPL to 31. Software, however, must take extra care not to lock out the power-down sequence for an extended period of time.

Explicit state is not provided by the architecture for software to directly determine whether there were outstanding interrupts when powerfail occurred. It is the responsibility of software to leave sufficient information in memory so that it may determine the proper action on power-up.

6.5 Machine Checks

A Machine Check, or mcheck, indicates that a hardware error condition was detected and may or may not be successfully corrected by hardware or PALcode. Such error conditions can occur either synchronously or asynchronously with respect to instruction execution. There are four types:

1. System Machine Check (IPL 31)

    These machine checks are generated by error conditions which are detected asynchronously to processor execution but are not successfully corrected by hardware or PALcode. Examples of system machine check conditions include protocol errors on the processor-memory-interconnect and unrecoverable memory errors.

    System machine checks are always maskable and deferred until processor IPL drops below IPL 31.

2. Processor Machine Check (IPL 31)

    These machine checks indicate that a processor internal error was detected and not successfully corrected by hardware or PALcode. Examples of processor machine check conditions include processor internal cache errors, translation buffer parity errors, or read access to a non-existent local I/O space location (NXM).

    Processor machine checks may be nonmaskable or maskable. If nonmaskable, they are initiated immediately, even if the processor IPL is 31. If maskable, they are deferred until processor IPL drops below IPL 31.

3. System Correctable Machine Check (IPL 20)

    These machine checks are generated by error conditions that are detected asynchronously to processor execution and are successfully corrected by hardware or PALcode. Examples of system correctable machine check conditions include single bit errors within the memory subsystem.

System correctable machine checks are always maskable and deferred until processor IPL drops below IPL 20.

4. Processor Correctable Machine Check (IPL 31)

These machine checks indicate that a processor internal error was detected and successfully corrected by hardware or PALcode. Examples of processor correctable machine check conditions include corrected processor internal cache errors and corrected translation buffer tab errors.

Processor correctable machine checks may be nonmaskable or maskable. If nonmaskable, they are initiated immediately, even if the processor IPL is 31. If maskable, they are deferred until processor IPL drops below IPL 31.

Machine Checks are initiated in Kernel mode, on the Kernel stack, and cannot be disabled.

Correctable machine checks permit the pattern and frequency of certain errors to be captured. The delivery of these machine checks to system software can be disabled by setting IPR MCES<4:3>, as described in Chapter 5. Note that setting IPR MCES<4:3> does not disable the generation of the machine check or the correction of the error, but rather suppresses the reporting of that correction to system software.

The PC in the machine check stack frame is that of the next instruction that would have issued if the machine check condition had not occurred. This is not necessarily the address of the instruction immediately following the one encountering the error, and intervening instructions may have changed operands or other state used by the instruction encountering the error condition. A CALL_PAL REI instruction to this PC will simply continue execution from the point at which the machine check was taken.

NOTE

On machine checks, a meaningful PC is delivered on a best-effort basis. The machine state, processor registers, memory, and I/O devices may be indeterminate.

Machine checks may be deliberately generated by software, such as by probing non-existent-memory during memory sizing or searching for local I/O devices. In such a case, the DRAINA PALcode instruction can be called to force any outstanding machine checks to be taken before continuing.

6.5.1 Software Response

The reaction of system software to machine checks is specific to the characteristics of the processor, platform, and system software. System software must determine if operation should be discontinued on an implementation-specific basis.

To assist system software, PALcode provides a retry flag in the machine check logout frame (see Figure 6–6. If set, the state of the processor and platform hardware has not been compromised; system software operation should be able to continue.

If the retry flag is clear, the state of the processor is either unknown or is known to have been updated during partial execution of one or more instructions. System software operation can continue only after system software determines that the hardware state change permits and/or takes corrective action.

PALcode should take appropriate implementation-specific actions prior to setting the retry flag. PALcode should also attempt to ensure that each encountered error condition generates only one machine check.

IMPLEMENTATION NOTE

An important example of using the retry flag is read NXM.

Also, a read NXM should not generate both a Processor Machine Check and a System Machine Check.

PALcode sets an internal Machine-Check-In-Progress flag in the Machine Check Error Summary (MCES) register prior to initiating a system or processor machine check. System software must clear that flag to dismiss the machine check If a second uncorrectable machine check hardware error condition is detected while the flag is set, or if PALcode cannot deliver the machine check, PALcode forces the processor to enter console I/O mode, and subsequent actions, such as processor restart, are taken by the console. The REASON FOR HALT code is "double error abort encountered".

Similiarly, PALcode sets an internal correctable Machine-Check-In-Progress flag in the Machine Check Error Summary (MCES) register prior to initiating a system correctable error interrupt or processor correctable machine check. System software must clear that flag to dismiss the condition and permit the reuse of the logout area. If a second correctable hardware error condition is detected while the flag is set, the error is corrected, but not reported. PALcode does not overwrite the logout area and the processor remains in program I/O mode.

6.5.2 Logout Areas

When a hardware error condition is encountered, PALcode optionally builds a logout frame prior to passing control to the machine check service routine.

Figure 6–6: Corrected Error and Machine Check Logout Frame

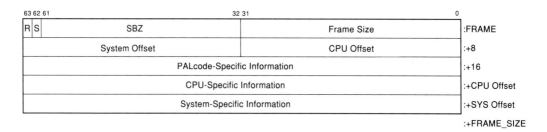

Table 6–4: Corrected Error and Machine Check Logout Frame Fields

Offset	Description
FRAME	FRAME SIZE - Size in bytes of the logout frame including the FRAME SIZE longword.
+04	FRAME FLAGS - Informational flags.

Bit	Description
31	RETRY FLAG - Indicates whether execution can be resumed after dismissing this machine check. Set on Corrected Error interrupts; may be set on Machine Checks.
30	SECOND ERROR FLAG - Indicates that a second correctable error was encountered. Set on Corrected Error interrupts when a correctable error was encountered while the relevant correctable error bit (PCE or SCE) is set in the MCES register. Clear on Machine Checks.
29–0	SBZ.

Offset	Description
+08	CPU OFFSET - Offset in bytes from the base of the logout frame to the cpu-specific information. If 16 the frame contains no PALcode-specific information. If CPU OFFSET is equal to SYS OFFSET, the frame contains no cpu-specific information.
+12	SYS OFFSET - Offset in bytes from the base of the logout frame to the system-specific information. If SYS OFFSET is equal to FRAME SIZE, the frame contains no system-specific information.
+16	PALCODE INFORMATION - PALcode-specific logout information.
+CPU OFFSET	CPU INFORMATION - Cpu-specific logout information.
+SYS OFFSET	SYS INFORMATION - System platform-specific logout information.

The logout frame is optional; the service routine uses R4 to locate the frame, if any. Upon entry to the service routine, R4 contains the byte offset of the logout frame from the base of the logout area. If no frame was built, R4 contains −1 (FFFF FFFF FFFF FFFF$_{16}$).

6.6 System Control Block

The System Control Block (SCB) specifies the entry points for exception, interrupt, and machine check service routines. The block is from 8K to 32K bytes long, must be page aligned, and must be physically contiguous. The PFN is specified by the value of the System Control Block Base (SCBB) internal register.

The SCB consists of from 512 to 2048 entries, each 16 bytes long. The first 8 bytes of an entry, the vector, specify the virtual address of the service routine associated with that entry. The second 8 bytes, the parameter, are an arbitrary quadword value to be passed to the service routine.

The SCB entries are grouped into those for:

1. Faults

2. Arithmetic traps

3. Asynchronous system traps

4. Data alignment trap

5. Other synchronous traps

6. Processor software interrupts

7. Processor hardware interrupts

8. I/O device interrupts

9. Machine checks

The first 512 entries (offsets 0000 through $1FF0_{16}$) contain all architecturally defined and any statically allocated entries. All remaining SCB entries, if any, are used only for those I/O device interrupt vectors that are assigned dynamically by system software. It is the responsibility of that software to ensure the consistency of the assigned vector and the SCB entry.

6.6.1 SCB Entries for Faults

The exception handler for a fault executes with the IPL unchanged, in Kernel mode, on the Kernel stack.

Table 6–5: SCB Entries for Faults

Byte offset$_{16}$	Entry name
000	Unused
010	Floating disabled fault
020-070	Unused
080	Access Control Violation fault
090	Translation Not Valid fault
0A0	Fault on Read fault
0B0	Fault on Write fault
0C0	Fault on Execute fault
0A0-0F0	Unused

6.6.2 SCB Entries for Arithmetic Traps

The exception handler for an arithmetic trap executes with the IPL unchanged, in Kernel mode, on the Kernel stack.

Table 6–6:   SCB Entries for Arithmetic Traps

Byte offset$_{16}$	Entry name
200	Arithmetic Trap
210-230	Unused

6.6.3 SCB Entries for Asynchronous System Traps (ASTs)

The interrupt handler for an asynchronous system trap executes at IPL 2, in Kernel mode, on the Kernel stack.

Table 6–7:   SCB Entries for Asynchronous System Traps

Byte offset$_{16}$	Entry name
240	Kernel Mode AST
250	Executive Mode AST
260	Supervisor Mode AST
270	User Mode AST

6.6.4 SCB Entries for Data Alignment Traps

The exception handler for a data alignment trap executes with the IPL unchanged in Kernel mode, on the Kernel Stack.

Table 6–8:   SCB Entries for Data Alignment Trap

Byte offset$_{16}$	Entry name
280	Unaligned_Access
290-3F0	Unused

6.6.5 SCB Entries for Other Synchronous Traps

The exception handler for a synchronous trap, other than those described above, executes with the IPL unchanged, in the mode and on the stack indicated below. "MostPriv" indicates that the handler executes in either the original mode or the new mode, whichever is the most privileged.

Table 6–9: SCB Entries for Other Synchronous Traps

Byte Offset$_{16}$	Entry Name	Mode
400	Breakpoint Trap	Kernel
410	Bug Check Trap	Kernel
420	Illegal Instruction Trap	Kernel
430	Illegal Operand Trap	Kernel
440	Generate Software Trap	Kernel
450	Unused	
460	Unused	
470	Unused	
480	Change Mode to Kernel	Kernel
490	Change Mode to Executive	MostPriv
4A0	Change Mode to Supervisor	MostPriv
4B0	Change Mode to User	Current
4C0-4F0	Reserved for Digital	

6.6.6 SCB Entries for Processor Software Interrupts

The exception handler for a processor software interrupt executes at the target IPL, in Kernel mode, on the Kernel stack.

Table 6–10: Entries for Processor Software Interrupts

Byte Offset$_{16}$	Entry Name	Target IPL$_{10}$
500	Unused	
510	Software interrupt level 1	1
520	Software interrupt level 2	2
530	Software interrupt level 3	3
540	Software interrupt level 4	4
550	Software interrupt level 5	5
560	Software interrupt level 6	6
570	Software interrupt level 7	7
580	Software interrupt level 8	8
590	Software interrupt level 9	9
5A0	Software interrupt level 10	10

Table 6–10 (Cont.): Entries for Processor Software Interrupts

Byte Offset$_{16}$	Entry Name	Target IPL$_{10}$
5B0	Software interrupt level 11	11
5C0	Software interrupt level 12	12
5D0	Software interrupt level 13	13
5E0	Software interrupt level 14	14
5F0	Software interrupt level 15	15

6.6.7 SCB Entries for Processor Hardware Interrupts

The interrupt handler for a processor hardware interrupt executes at the target IPL, in Kernel mode, on the Kernel stack.

Table 6–11: SCB Entries for Processor Hardware Interrupts

Byte Offset$_{16}$	Entry name	Target IPL$_{10}$
600	Interval clock interrupt	22
610	Interprocessor interrupt	22
640	Powerfail interrupt	30
650	Performance monitor	29
680-6E0	Reserved — processor specific	
6F0	Passive Release	20-23

Processor-specific SCB entries include those used by console devices (if any) or other peripherals dedicated to system support functions.

6.6.8 SCB Entries for I/O Device Interrupts

The interrupt handler for an I/O device interrupt executes at the target IPL, in Kernel mode, on the Kernel stack. SCB entries for offsets of 800_{16} through $7FF0_{16}$ are reserved for I/O device interrupts.

6.6.9 SCB Entries for Machine Checks

The handler for machine checks executes in Kernel mode, on the Kernel stack. The handler for system correctable machine checks executes at IPL 20; the handler for all other machine checks executes at IPL 31.

Table 6–12: SCB Entries for Machine Checks

Byte Offset$_{16}$	Entry Name	Target IPL$_{10}$
620	System correct. machine check	20
630	Processor correct. machine check	31
660	System machine check	31
670	Processor machine check	31

6.7 PALcode Support

6.7.1 Stack Writeability

In response to various exceptions, interrupts, and machine checks, PALcode pushes information on the Kernel stack. PALcode may write this information without first probing to ensure that all such writes to the Kernel stack will succeed. If a memory management exception occurs while pushing information, PALcode forces the processor to enter console I/O mode, and subsequent actions, such as processor restart, are taken by the console. The REASON FOR HALT code is "processor halted due to kernel-stack-not-valid".

6.7.2 Stack Residency

The User, Supervisor, and Executive stacks for the current process do not need to be resident. Software running in Kernel mode can bring in or allocate stack pages as TNV faults occur. However, since this activity is taking place in Kernel mode, the Kernel stack must be fully resident.

The faults TNV, ACV, FOR, and FOW, occurring on Kernel mode references to the Kernel stack, are considered serious system failures from which recovery is not possible. If any of these faults occur, PALcode forces the processor to enter console I/O mode, and subsequent actions, such as processor restart, are taken by the console. The REASON FOR HALT code is "processor halted due to kernel-stack-not-valid".

6.7.3 Stack Alignment

Stacks may have arbitrary byte alignment, but performance may suffer if at least octaword alignment is not maintained by software.

PALcode creates stack frames in response to exceptions and interrupts. Before doing so, the target stack is aligned to a 64-byte boundary by setting the six low bits of the target SP to 000000_2. The previous value of these bits is stored in the SP_ALIGN field of the saved PS in memory, for use by a CALL_PAL REI instruction.

Software-constructed stack frames must be 64 byte aligned and have SP_ALIGN properly set; otherwise, a CALL_PAL REI instruction will take an illegal operand trap.

6.7.4 Initiate Exception or Interrupt or Machine Check

Exceptions and interrupts and machine checks are initiated by PALcode with interrupts disabled. When an exception, interrupt, or machine check, is initiated, the associated SCB vector is read to determine the address of the service routine. PALcode then attempts to push the PC, PS, and R2..R7 onto the target stack. When an interrupt (software or hardware but not AST) is initiated, PS<IP> is set to 1 to indicate an interrupt is in progress. Additional parameters may be passed in R4 and R5 on exceptions and machine checks.

During the attempt to push this information, the exceptions (faults) TNV, ACV, and FOW can occur:

- If any of those faults occur when the target stack is User, Supervisor, or Executive, then the fault is taken on the Kernel stack.

- If any of those faults occur when the target stack is the Kernel stack, PALcode forces the processor to enter console I/O mode, and subsequent actions, such as processor restart, are taken by the console. The REASON FOR HALT code is "processor halted due to kernel-stack-not-valid".

6.7.5 Initiate Exception or Interrupt or Machine Check Model

```
check_for_exception_or_interrupt_or_mcheck:
  IF NOT {ready_to_initiate_exception OR
          ready_to_initiate_interrupt OR
          ready_to_initiate_mcheck} THEN
    BEGIN
      {fetch next instruction}
      {decode and execute instruction}
    END
  ELSE
    BEGIN
      {wait for instructions in progress to complete}
                    ! clear interrupt pending
      tmp ← 0

      IF {unmaskable mcheck pending} THEN
        BEGIN
          {back up implementation specific state if necessary}
          {attempt correction if appropriate}
          IF {uncorrectable AND MCES<0> = 1} THEN
            {enter console}
          ELSE IF {uncorrectable} THEN
            new_mode ← Kernel
            new_ipl ← 31
                              ! set mcheck error flag
            MCES<0> ← 1
          ELSE IF {reporting enabled} THEN
            new_mode ← Kernel
            new_ipl ← 31
            MCES<2> ← 1
        END
      END

    ELSE IF {data alignment trap} THEN
        new_mode ← Kernel

    ELSE IF {synchronous trap} THEN
      CASE {opcode} OF
        {back up implementation specific state if necessary}
        CHME: new_mode ← min(PS<CM>,Executive)
        CHMS: new_mode ← min(PS<CM>,Supervisor)
        CHMU: new_mode ← min(PS<CM>,User)
        otherwise: new_mode ← Kernel
      ENDCASE
```

```
ELSE IF {maskable uncorrectable mcheck pending and IPL < 31} THEN
  BEGIN
    {back up implementation specific state if necessary}
    IF {MCES<0> = 1} THEN
        {enter console}
    ELSE
        new_mode ← Kernel
        new_ipl ← 31
        MCES<0> ← 1 ! set mcheck error flag
    END
  END

ELSE
    new_mode ← Kernel

END

IPR_SP[PS<CM>] ← SP
new_sp ← IPR_SP[new_mode]

IF {exception pending} THEN
  BEGIN
    {back up implementation specific state if necessary}
    new_ipl ← PS<IPL>
  END
ELSE IF {interrupt pending} THEN
    new_ipl ← {interrupt source IPL}
    tmp ← 1 ! set interrupt pending

ELSE IF {maskable correctable mcheck pending AND
        reporting enabled} THEN
    new_ipl ← 20
    MCES<1> ← 1
END

save_align ← new_sp<5:0>
new_sp<5:0> ← 0

PUSH(PS OR LEFT_SHIFT(save_align,56), old_pc, new_mode)
PUSH(R7, R6, new_mode)
PUSH(R5, R4, new_mode)
PUSH(R3, R2, new_mode)

PS<SW> ← 0
PS<CM> ← new_mode
PS<IP> ← tmp
PS<IPL> ← new_ipl
SP ← new_sp

IF {memory management fault} THEN
    R4 ← VA
    R5 ← MMF
END

IF {data alignment trap} THEN
    R4 ← VA
    R5 ← { 0 if read/load  1 if write/store }
END
```

```
                 IF {mcheck or correctable error interrupt} THEN
                     IF {logout frame built}
                         R4 ←  logout_area_offset
                     ELSE
                         R4 ←  -1
                     END
                 END

                 IF {arithmetic Trap} THEN
                     R4 ←  register write mask
                     R5 ←  exception summary
                 END

                 IF {software interrupt} THEN
                     SISR ←  SISR AND NOT{ 2**{ PRIORITY_ENCODE(SISR) } }
                 END

                 vector ←  {exception or interrupt or mcheck SCB offset}

                 R2 ←  (SCBB + vector)
                 R3 ←  (SCBB + vector + 8)
                 PC ←  R2

             END

             GOTO check_for_exception_or_interrupt_or_mcheck
         PROCEDURE PUSH(first, last, mode)
             BEGIN
                 IF ACCESS(new_sp - 16, mode) THEN
                     BEGIN
                         (new_sp - 8) ←  first
                         (new_sp - 16) ←  last
                         new_sp ←  new_sp - 16
                         RETURN
                     END
                 ELSE
                     {initiate ACV, TNV, or FOW fault, or
                      Kernel Stack Not Valid restart sequence}
                 END
             END
```

6.7.6 PALcode Interrupt Arbitration

The following sections describe the logic for the interrupt conditions produced by the specified operation.

6.7.6.1 Writing the AST Summary Register

Writing the ASTSR internal processor register (see Section 5.3) requests an AST for any of the four processor modes. This may request an AST on a formerly inactive level and thus cause an AST interrupt.

The logic required to check for this condition is:

```
ASTSR<3:0> ←  {ASTSR<3:0> AND R16<3:0>} OR R16<7:4>
IF ASTEN<0> AND ASTSR<0> AND {PS<IPL> LT 2} THEN
    {initiate AST interrupt at IPL 2}
```

6.7.6.2 Writing the AST Enable Register

Writing the ASTEN internal processor register (see Section 5.3) enables ASTs for any of the four processor modes. This may enable an AST on a formerly inactive level and thus cause an AST interrupt.

The logic required to check for this condition is:

```
ASTEN<3:0> ←  {ASTEN<3:0> AND R16<3:0>} OR R16<7:4>
IF ASTEN<0> AND ASTSR<0> AND {PS<IPL> LT 2} THEN
    {initiate AST interrupt at IPL 2}
```

6.7.6.3 Writing the IPL Register

Writing the IPL internal processor register (see Section 5.3) changes the current IPL. This may enable an AST or software interrupt on a formerly inactive level and thus cause an AST or software interrupt.

The logic required to check for this condition is:

```
PS<IPL> ←  R16<4:0>

! check for software interrupt at level 2..15

IF {RIGHT_SHIFT({SISR AND FFFC16 }, PS<IPL> + 1) NE 0} THEN
    {initiate software interrupt at IPL of high bit set in SISR}

! check for AST

IF ASTEN<0> AND ASTSR<0> AND {PS<IPL> LT 2} THEN
    {initiate AST interrupt at IPL 2}

! check for software interrupt at level 1

IF SISR<1> AND {PS<IPL> EQ 0} THEN
    {initiate software interrupt at IPL 1}
```

6.7.6.4 Writing the Software Interrupt Request Register

Writing the SIRR internal processor register (see Section 5.3) requests a software interrupt at one of the fifteen software interrupt levels. This may cause a formerly inactive level to cause a software interrupt.

The logic required to check for this condition is:

```
SISR<level> ←  1
IF level GT PS<IPL> THEN
    {initiate software interrupt at IPL level}
```

6.7.6.5 Return from Exception or Interrupt

The CALL_PAL REI instruction (see Chapter 2) writes both the Current Mode and IPL fields of the PS; see Section 6.2. This may enable a formerly disabled AST or software interrupt to occur.

The logic required to check for this condition is:

```
PS ←  New PS

! check for software interrupt at level 2..15
```

```
IF {RIGHT_SHIFT({SISR AND FFFC_16 }, PS<IPL> + 1) NE 0} THEN
    {initiate software interrupt at IPL of high bit set in SISR}

! check for AST

tmp ← NOT LEFT_SHIFT(1110(bin), PS<CM>)
IF {{tmp AND ASTEN AND ASTSR}<3:0> NE 0} AND {PS<IPL> LT 2} THEN
    {initiate AST interrupt at IPL 2}

! check for software interrupt at level 1

IF SISR<1> AND {PS<IPL> EQ 0} THEN
    {initiate software interrupt at IPL 1}
```

6.7.6.6 Swap AST Enable

Swapping the AST enable state for the Current Mode results in writing the ASTEN internal processor register (see Section 5.3). This may enable a formerly disabled AST to cause an AST interrupt.

The logic required to check for this condition is:

```
R0 ← ZEXT(ASTEN<PS<CM>>)
ASTEN<PS<CM>> ← R16<0>

IF ASTEN<PS<CM>> AND ASTSR<PS<CM>> AND {PS<IPL> LT 2} THEN
    {initiate AST interrupt at IPL 2}
```

6.7.7 Processor State Transition Table

Table 6–13 shows the operations that can produce a state transition and the specific transition produced. For example, if a processor's initial state is Supervisor mode, it is not possible for the processor to transition to a program halt condition. A processor can only transition to program halt from Kernel mode.

In Table 6–13:

- *REI* increases mode or lowers IPL.

- *MTPR* changes IPL, or is a CALL_PAL MTPR_ASTSR or CALL_PAL MTPR_ASTEN instruction that causes an interrupt request.

- *Exc* is a state change caused by an exception.

- *Int* is a state change caused by an interrupt.

- *Mcheck* is a state change caused by a machine check.

Table 6–13: Processor State Transitions

Initial State:	Final State:				
	User	Super.	Exec.	Kernel	Program Halt
User	CHMU REI	CHMS	CHME	CHMK Exc Int Mcheck SWASTEN	Not Possible
Supervisor	REI	CHMS REI	CHME	CHMK Exc Int Mcheck SWASTEN	Not Possible
Executive	REI	REI	CHME REI	CHMK Exc Int Mcheck SWASTEN	Not Possible
Kernel	REI	REI	REI	CHMK REI Int Exc Mcheck MTPR SWASTEN	HALT

Part III   DEC OSF/1 Alpha Software

This section describes how DEC OSF/1 operating system relates to the Alpha architecture and includes the following chapters:

1. Introduction to DEC OSF/1 Alpha
2. OSF/1 PALcode Instruction Descriptions
3. OSF/1 Memory Management
4. OSF/1 Process Structure
5. OSF/1 Exceptions and Interrupts

Contents

Chapter 1 Introduction to DEC OSF/1 Alpha (III)

1.1	Programming Model	1–2
1.1.1	Code Flow Constants	1–2
1.1.2	Machine State Terms	1–2
1.1.3	Code Flow Terms	1–4

Chapter 2 OSF/1 PALcode Instruction Descriptions (III)

2.1	Unprivileged PALcode Instructions	2–1
2.1.1	Breakpoint Trap	2–2
2.1.2	Bugcheck Trap	2–3
2.1.3	System Call	2–4
2.1.4	Generate Trap	2–5
2.1.5	Read Unique Value	2–6
2.1.6	Write Unique Value	2–7
2.2	Privileged OSF/1 PALcode Instructions	2–8
2.2.1	Read Processor Status	2–9
2.2.2	Read User Stack Pointer	2–10
2.2.3	Read System Value	2–11
2.2.4	Return From System Call	2–12
2.2.5	Return From Trap, Fault or Interrupt	2–13
2.2.6	Swap Process Context	2–14
2.2.7	Swap IPL	2–16
2.2.8	TB Invalidate	2–17
2.2.9	Who Am I	2–18
2.2.10	Write System Entry Address	2–19
2.2.11	Write Floating-Point Enable	2–21
2.2.12	Write Kernel Global Pointer	2–22
2.2.13	Write User Stack Pointer	2–23
2.2.14	Write System Value	2–24
2.2.15	Write Virtual Page Table Pointer	2–25

Chapter 3 OSF/1 Memory Management (III)

3.1	Virtual Address Spaces	3–1
3.1.1	Segment Seg0 and Seg1 Virtual Address Format	3–1
3.1.2	Kseg Virtual Address Format	3–2
3.2	Physical Address Space	3–3
3.3	Memory Management Control	3–3

3.4	Page Table Entries	3–3
3.4.1	Changes to Page Table Entries	3–5
3.5	Memory Protection	3–5
3.5.1	Processor Access Modes	3–6
3.5.2	Protection Code	3–6
3.5.3	Access-Violation Faults	3–6
3.6	Address Translation for Seg0 and Seg1	3–6
3.6.1	Physical Access for Seg0 and Seg1 PTEs	3–6
3.6.2	Virtual Access for Seg0 or Seg1 PTEs	3–7
3.7	Translation Buffer	3–8
3.8	Address Space Numbers	3–8
3.9	Memory-Management Faults	3–9

Chapter 4   OSF/1 Process Structure (III)

4.1	Process Definition	4–1
4.2	Process Control Block (PCB)	4–1

Chapter 5   OSF/1 Exceptions and Interrupts (III)

5.1	Introduction	5–1
5.1.1	Exceptions	5–1
5.1.2	Interrupts	5–2
5.2	Processor Status	5–2
5.3	Stack Frames	5–3
5.4	System Entry Addresses	5–3
5.4.1	System Entry Arithmetic Trap (entArith)	5–4
5.4.1.1	Exception Summary Register	5–4
5.4.1.2	Exception Register Write Mask	5–6
5.4.2	System Entry Instruction Fault (entIF)	5–6
5.4.3	System Entry Hardware Interrupts (entInt)	5–6
5.4.4	System Entry MM Fault (entMM)	5–7
5.4.5	System Entry Call System (entSys)	5–8
5.4.6	System Entry Unaligned Access (entUna)	5–8
5.5	PALcode Support	5–8
5.5.1	Stack Writeability and Alignment	5–8

Figures

3–1	Virtual Address Format	3–2
3–2	Kseg Virtual Address Format	3–2
3–3	Page Table Entry (PTE)	3–3
4–1	Process Control Block (PCB)	4–2
5–1	Stack Frame Layout	5–3
5–2	Exception Summary Register	5–4
5–3	Logout Area	5–7

Tables

1–1	DEC OSF/1 Alpha Register Usage	1–1
1–2	Code Flow Constants	1–2
1–3	Machine State Terms	1–2
1–4	Code Flow Terms	1–4
2–1	Unprivileged OSF/1 PALcode Instructions	2–1
2–2	Privileged OSF/1 PALcode Instructions	2–8
3–1	Virtual Address Space Segments	3–1
3–2	Virtual Address Options	3–2
3–3	Page Table Entry (PTE) Bit Summary	3–3
3–4	Memory-Management Fault Type Codes	3–9
5–1	Processor Status Summary	5–2
5–2	Entry Point Address Registers	5–3
5–3	Exception Summary Register Bit Definitions	5–4
5–4	System Entry Hardware Interrupts	5–7

Chapter 1

Introduction to DEC OSF/1 Alpha (III)

The goals of this design are to provide a hardware implementation independent interface between the hardware and DEC OSF/1 Alpha. The interface needs to provide the needed abstractions to minimize the impact of different hardware implementations on the operating system. The interface also needs to be low in overhead to support high-performance systems. Lastly the interface needs to only support the features used by DEC OSF/1 Alpha.

The register usage in this interface is based on the current calling standard used by DEC OSF/1 Alpha. If the calling standard changes, this interface will be changed to reflect that. The current calling standard register usage is shown in Table 1–1.

Table 1–1: DEC OSF/1 Alpha Register Usage

Register Name	Software Name	Use and linkage
r0	v0	Used for expression evaluations and to hold integer function results.
r1..r8	t0..t7	Temporary registers; not preserved across procedure calls.
r9..r14	s0..s5	Saved registers; their values must be preserved across procedure calls.
r15	FP or s6	Frame pointer or a saved register.
r16..r21	a0..a5	Argument registers; used to pass the first 6 integer type arguments; their values are not preserved across procedure calls.
r22..r25	t8..t11	Temporary registers; not preserved across procedure calls.
r26	ra	Contains the return address; used for expression evaluation.
r27	pv or t12	Procedure value or a temporary register.
r28	at	Assembler temporary register; not preserved across procedure calls.
r29	GP	Global pointer.
r30	SP	Stack pointer.
r31	zero	Always has the value 0.

1.1 Programming Model

The programming model of the machine is the combination of the state visible either directly via instructions, or indirectly via actions of the machine. The following four tables define constants, state variables, terms, and subroutines used in the rest of the document.

1.1.1 Code Flow Constants

Table 1-2: Code Flow Constants

Term	Meaning and value
IPL = 2:0	The range 2:0 used in the PS to access the IPL field of the PS (PS<IPL>).
maxCPU	The maximum number of processors in a given system.
mode = 3	Used as a subscript in PS to select current mode (PS<mode>).
pageSize	Size of a page in an implementation in bytes.
vaSize	Size of virtual address in bits in a given implementation.

1.1.2 Machine State Terms

Table 1-3: Machine State Terms

Term	Meaning
ASN	An implementation-dependent size register to hold the current address space number (ASN). The size and existence of ASN is an implementation choice.
entArith<63:0>	The arithmetic trap entry address register. The entArith is an internal processor register that holds the dispatch address on an arithmetic trap. There can be a hardware register for the entArith or the PALcode can use private scratch memory.
entIF<63:0>	The instruction fault entry address register. The entIF is an internal processor register that holds the dispatch address on an instruction fault. There can be a hardware register for the entIF or the PALcode can use private scratch memory.
entInt<63:0>	The interrupt entry address register. The entInt is an internal processor register that holds the dispatch address on an interrupt. There can be a hardware register for the entInt or the PALcode can use private scratch memory.
entMM<63:0>	The memory-management fault entry address register. The entMM is an internal processor register that holds the dispatch address on a memory-management fault. There can be a hardware register for the entMM or the PALcode can use private scratch memory.

Table 1–3 (Cont.): Machine State Terms

Term	Meaning
entSys<63:0>	The system call entry address register. The entSys is an internal processor register that holds the dispatch address on an callsys instruction. There can be a hardware register for the entSys or the PALcode can use private scratch memory.
entUna<63:0>	The unaligned fault entry address register. The entUna is an internal processor register that holds the dispatch address on an unaligned fault. There can be a hardware register for the entUna or the PALcode can use private scratch memory.
FEN<0>	The floating-point enable register. The FEN is a one-bit register that is used to enable or disable floating-point instructions. If a floating-point instruction is executed with FEN equal to zero, a FEN fault is initiated.
instruction<31:0>	The current instruction being executed. This is a fake register used in the flows to CASE on different instructions.
intr_flag	A per-processor state bit. The intr_flag bit is cleared if that processor executes an rti or retsys instruction.
KGP<63:0>	The kernel global pointer. The KGP is an internal processor register that holds the kernel global pointer that is loaded into R15, the GP, when an exception is initiated. There can be a hardware register for the KGP or the PALcode can use private scratch memory.
KSP<63:0>	The kernel stack pointer. The KSP is an internal processor register that holds the kernel stack pointer while in user mode. There can be a hardware register for the KSP or the storage space in the PCB can be used.
lock_flag<0>	A one-bit register that is used by the load locked and store conditional instructions.
PC<63:0>	The program counter. The PC is a pointer to the next instruction in the flows. The low-order two bits of the PC always read as zero and writes to them are ignored.
PCB	The process control block. The PCB holds the state of the process.
PCBB<63:0>	The process control block base address register. The PCBB holds the address of the PCB for the current process.
PS<3:0>	The processor status. The PS is a four-bit register that stores the current mode in bit <3> and stores the three-bit IPL in bits <2:0>. The mode is 0 for kernel and 1 for user.
PTBR<63:0>	The page table base register. The PTBR contains the physical page frame number (PFN) of the highest level (level 1) page table.

Table 1–3 (Cont.): Machine State Terms

Term	Meaning
SP<63:0>	Another name for R30. The SP points to the top of the current stack.
	PALcode only accesses the kernel stack. The kernel stack must be quadword aligned whenever PALcode reads or writes it. If the PALcode accesses the kernel stack and the stack is not aligned, a kernel-stack-not-valid halt is initiated. Although PALcode does not access the user stack, that stack should also be at least quadword aligned for best performance.
sysvalue<63:0>	The system value register. The sysvalue holds the per-processor unique value. There can be a hardware register for the sysvalue register or the storage space in the PALcode scratch memory can be used.
	The sysvalue register can only be accessed by kernel mode code and there is one sysvalue register per CPU.
unique<63:0>	The process unique value register. The unique register holds the per-process unique value. There can be a hardware register for the unique register or the storage space in the PCB can be used.
	The unique register can be accessed by both user and kernel code and there is one unique register per process.
USP<63:0>	The user stack pointer. The USP is an internal processor register that holds the user stack pointer while in kernel mode. There can be a hardware register for the USP or the storage space in the PCB can be used.
VPTPTR<63:0>	The virtual page table pointer. The VPTPTR holds the virtual address of the first level page table.
whami<63:0>	The processor number of the current processor. This number is in the range 0..maxCPU−1.

1.1.3 Code Flow Terms

Table 1–4: Code Flow Terms

Term	Meaning
opDec	An attempt was made to execute a reserved instruction or execute a privileged instruction in user mode.

Chapter 2

OSF/1 PALcode Instruction Descriptions (III)

2.1 Unprivileged PALcode Instructions

Table 2–1 lists the OSF/1 PALcode unprivileged instruction mnemonics, names, and the environment from which they can be called:

Table 2–1: Unprivileged OSF/1 PALcode Instructions

Mnemonic	Name	Calling environment
bpt	Breakpoint trap	Kernel and user modes
bugchk	Bugcheck trap	Kernel and user modes
callsys	System call	User mode
gentrap	Generate trap	Kernel and user modes
imb	I-Stream memory barrier	Kernel and user modes Described in *Common Architecture, Chapter 6*
rdunique	Read unique	Kernel and user modes
wrunique	Write unique	Kernel and user modes

2.1.1 Breakpoint Trap

Format:

```
bpt                                  ! PALcode format
```

Operation:

```
temp ←  PS
if (ps<mode> NE 0)  then
         USP ←  SP                  !  Mode is user so switch to kernel
         SP  ←  KSP
         PS  ←  0
endif
SP ←  SP - {6 * 8}
(SP+00) ←  temp
(SP+08) ←  PC
(SP+16) ←  GP
(SP+24) ←  a0
(SP+32) ←  a1
(SP+40) ←  a2
a0 ←  0
GP ←  KGP
PC ←  entIF
```

Exceptions:

Kernel stack not valid

Instruction mnemonics:

```
bpt            Breakpoint trap
```

Description:

The breakpoint trap (bpt) instruction switches mode to kernel, builds a stackframe on the kernel stack, loads the GP with the KGP, loads a value of 0 into a0, and dispatches to the breakpoint code pointed to by the entIF register. The registers a1..a2 are UNPREDICTABLE on entry to the trap handler. The saved PC at (SP+08) is the address of the instruction following the trap instruction that caused the trap.

Notes:

- The opcode and function code for the bpt instruction are the same in the OpenVMS and the OSF/1 PALcode.

2.1.2 Bugcheck Trap

Format:

```
bugchk                              ! PALcode format
```

Operation:

```
temp ←  PS
if (PS<mode> NE 0)  then
        USP ←  SP                   !  Mode is user so switch to kernel
        SP  ←  KSP
        PS  ←  0
endif
SP ←  SP - {6 * 8}
(SP+00) ←  temp
(SP+08) ←  PC
(SP+16) ←  GP
(SP+24) ←  a0
(SP+32) ←  a1
(SP+40) ←  a2
a0 ←  1
GP ←  KGP
PC ←  entIF
```

Exceptions:

Kernel stack not valid

Instruction mnemonics:

bugchk   Bugcheck trap

Description:

The bugcheck trap (bugchk) instruction switches mode to kernel, builds a stackframe on the kernel stack, loads the GP with the KGP, loads a value of 1 into a0, and dispatches to the breakpoint code pointed to by the entIF register. The registers a1..a2 are UNPREDICTABLE on entry to the trap handler. The saved PC at (SP+08) is the address of the instruction following the trap instruction that caused the trap.

Notes:

• The opcode and function code for the bugchk instruction are the same in the OpenVMS and the OSF/1 PALcode.

2.1.3 System Call

Format:

```
callsys                              ! PALcode format
```

Operation:

```
if (PS<mode> EQ 0)  then
        machineCheck
endif
USP ←  SP
SP  ←  KSP
PS  ←  0                     ! Mode=kernel
SP  ←  SP - {6*8}
(SP+00) ←   8                ! PS of mode=user, IPL=0
(SP+08) ←   PC
(SP+08) ←   GP
GP ←  KGP
PC ←  entSys
```

Exceptions:

Machine check—invalid kernel mode callsys

Kernel stack not valid

Instruction mnemonics:

callsys   System call

Description:

The system call (callsys) instruction is supported only from user mode. (Issuing a callsys from kernel mode causes a machine check exception).

The callsys instruction switches mode to kernel and builds a callsys stack frame. The GP is loaded with the KGP. The exception then dispatches to the system call code pointed to by the entsys register. On entry to the callsys code, the scratch registers t8..t11 are UNPREDICTABLE.

2.1.4 Generate Trap

Format:

gentrap   ! PALcode format

Operation:

```
temp ←  PS
if (PS<mode> NE 0)  then
        USP ←  SP                ! Mode is user so switch to kernel
        SP  ←  KSP
        PS  ←  0
endif
SP  ←  SP - {6 * 8}
(SP+00) ←  temp
(SP+08) ←  PC
(SP+16) ←  GP
(SP+24) ←  a0
(SP+32) ←  a1
(SP+40) ←  a2
a0 ←  2
GP ←  KGP
PC ←  entIF
```

Exceptions:

Kernel stack not valid

Instruction mnemonics:

gentrap   Generate trap

Description:

The generate trap (gentrap) instruction switches mode to kernel, builds a stackframe on the kernel stack, loads the GP with the KGP, loads a value of 2 into a0, and dispatches to the breakpoint code pointed to by the entIF register. The registers a1..a2 are UNPREDICTABLE on entry to the trap handler. The saved PC at (SP+08) is the address of the instruction following the trap instruction that caused the trap.

Notes:

• The opcode and function code for the gentrap instruction are the same in the OpenVMS and the OSF/1 PALcode.

2.1.5 Read Unique Value

Format:

rdunique   ! PALcode format

Operation:

v0 ← unique

Exceptions:

None

Instruction mnemonics:

rdunique   Read unique value

Description:

The read unique value (rdunique) instruction returns the process unique value in
v0. The write unique value (wrunique) instruction, described in Section 2.1.6, sets
the process unique value register.

Notes:

- The opcode and function code for the rdunique instruction are the same in the
  OpenVMS and the OSF/1 PALcode.

2.1.6 Write Unique Value

Format:

wrunique   ! PALcode format

Operation:

unique ← a0

Exceptions:

None

Instruction mnemonics:

wrunique   Write unique value

Description:

The write unique value (wrunique) instruction sets the process unique register to
the value passed in a0. The read unique value (rdunique) instruction, described in
Section 2.1.5, returns the process unique value.

Notes:

• The opcode and function code for the wrunique instruction are the same in the
OpenVMS and the OSF/1 PALcode.

2.2 Privileged OSF/1 PALcode Instructions

The Privileged OSF/1 PALcode instructions provide an abstracted interface to control the privileged state of the machine.

Table 2–2: Privileged OSF/1 PALcode Instructions

Mnemonic	Name
halt	Halt the processor Described in *Common Architecture, Chapter 6*
rdps	Read processor status
rdusp	Read user stack pointer
rdval	Read system value
retsys	Return from system call
rti	Return from trap, fault, or interrupt
swpctx	Swap process context
swpipl	Swap IPL
tbi	TB (translation buffer) invalidate
whami	Who am I
wrent	Write system entry address
wrfen	Write floating-point enable
wrkgp	Write kernal global pointer
wrvptptr	Write virtual page table pointer

2.2.1 Read Processor Status

Format:

rdps   ! PALcode format

Operation:

```
if (PS<mode> EQ 1) then
        {Initiate opDec fault}
endif
v0 ←  PS
```

Exceptions:

Opcode reserved to Digital

Instruction mnemonics:

rdps   Read processor status

Description:

The read processor status (rdps) instruction returns the PS in v0. On return from the rdps instruction, registers t0 and t8..t11 are UNPREDICTABLE.

2.2.2 Read User Stack Pointer

Format:

```
rdusp                                  ! PALcode format
```

Operation:

```
if (PS<mode> EQ 1) then
        {Initiate opDec fault}
endif
v0 ←  USP
```

Exceptions:

Opcode reserved to Digital

Instruction mnemonics:

```
rdusp         Read user stack pointer
```

Description:

The read user stack pointer (rdusp) instruction returns the user stack pointer in v0. The user stack pointer is written by the wrusp instruction, described in Section 2.2.13. On return from the rdusp instruction, registers t0 and t8..t11 are UNPREDICTABLE.

2.2.3 Read System Value

Format:

rdval   !PALcode format

Operation:

```
if (PS<mode> EQ 1) then
        {Initiate opDec fault}
endif
v0 ←  sysvalue
```

Exceptions:

Opcode reserved to Digital

Instruction mnemonics:

rdval   Read system value

Description:

The read system value (rdval) instruction returns the sysvalue in v0, allowing access to a 64-bit per-processor value for use by the operating system. On return from the rdval instruction, registers t0 and t8..t11 are UNPREDICTABLE.

2.2.4 Return From System Call

Format:

retsys   ! PALcode format

Operation:

```
if {PS<mode> EQ 1} then
        {Initiate opDec fault}
endif
tmp ←  (SP+08)
GP  ←  (SP+16)
KSP ←  SP + {6*8}
SP  ←  USP
intr_flag = 0                    ! Clear the interrupt flag
lock_flag = 0                    ! Clear the load lock flag
PS  ←  8                         ! Mode=user
PC  ←  tmp
```

Exceptions:

Opcode reserved to Digital

Kernel stack not valid (halt)

Instruction mnemonics:

retsys   Return from system call

Description:

The return from system call (retsys) instruction pops the return address and the user mode global pointer from the kernel stack. It then saves the kernel stack pointer, sets the mode to user, sets the IPL to zero, and enters the user mode code at the address popped off the stack.

2.2.5 Return From Trap, Fault or Interrupt

Format:

```
rti                                    ! PALcode format
```

Operation:

```
if (PS<mode> EQ 1) then
        {Initiate opDec fault}
endif
tempps  ←  (SP+0)
temppc  ←  (SP+8)
GP  ←  (SP+16)
a0  ←  (SP+24)
a1  ←  (SP+32)
a2  ←  (SP+40)
SP  ←  SP + {6 * 8}
if { tempps<3> EQ 1} then
        KSP  ←  SP              !  New mode is user
        SP  ←  USP
        tempps  ←  8
endif
intr_flag = 0                      ! Clear the interrupt flag
lock_flag = 0                      ! Clear the load lock flag
PS  ←  tempps<3:0>                 ! Set new PS
PC  ←  temppc
```

Exceptions:

Opcode reserved to Digital

Kernel stack not valid (halt)

Instruction mnemonics:

rti   Return from trap, fault, or interrupt

Description:

The return from fault, trap, or interrupt (rti) instruction pops registers (a0..a3, and GP), the PC, and the PS, from the kernel stack. If the new mode is user, the kernel stack is saved and the user stack is restored.

2.2.6 Swap Process Context

Format:

```
swpctx                                        ! PALcode format
```

Operation:

```
if (PS<mode> EQ 1)
        {Initiate opDec fault}
endif
(PCBB)   ←   SP                        ! Save current state
(PCBB+8) ←   USP
tmp ←   PCC
tmp1 ←   tmp<31:0> + tmp<63:32>
(PCBB+24)<31:0> ←   tmp1<31:0>
v0 ←   PCBB                            ! Return old PCBB
PCBB ←   a0                            ! Switch PCBB
SP ←   (PCBB)                          ! Restore new state
USP ←   (PCBB+8)
oldPTBR ←   PTBR
PTBR ←   (PCBB+16)
tmp1 ←   (PCBB+24)
PCC<63:32> ←   {tmp1 - tmp}<31:0>
FEN ←   (PCBB+40)
if {process unique register implemented} then
        (v0+32) ←   unique
        unique ←   (PCBB+32)
endif
if {ASN implemented}
        ASN ←   tmp1<63:32>
else
        if (oldPTBR  NE PTBR)
                {Invalidate all TB entries with ASM=0}
        endif
endif
```

Exceptions:

Opcode reserved to Digital

Instruction mnemonics:

swpctx   Swap process context

Description:

The swap process context (swpctx) instruction saves the current process data in the current PCB. Then swpctx switches to the PCB passed in a0 and loads the new process context. The old PCBB is returned in v0. On return from the swpctx instruction, registers t0, t8..t11, and a0 are UNPREDICTABLE.

2.2.7 Swap IPL

Format:

swpipl   ! PALcode format

Operation:

```
if (PS<mode> EQ 1) then
        {Initiate opDec fault}
endif
v0 ←  PS<IPL>
PS<IPL> ←  a0<2:0>
```

Exceptions:

Opcode reserved to Digital

Instruction mnemonics:

swpipl   Swap IPL

Description:

The swap IPL (swpipl) instruction returns the current value of the PS<IPL> bits in
v0 and sets the IPL to the value passed in a0. On return from the spwipl instruction,
registers t0, t8..t11, and a0 are UNPREDICTABLE.

2.2.8 TB Invalidate

Format:

    tbi   ! PALcode format

Operation:

```
if (PS<mode> EQ 1) then
      {Initiate opDec fault}
endif
case a0 begin
      1: ! tbisi
               {Invalidate ITB entry for va=a1}
               break;
      2: ! tbisd
               {Invalidate DTB entry for va=a1}
               break;
      3: ! tbis
               {Invalidate both ITB and DTB entry for va=a1}
               break;
      -1: ! tbiap
               {Invalidate all TB entries with ASM=0}
               break;
      -2: ! tbia
               {Flush all TBs}
               break;
      otherwise:
               break;
endcase
```

Exceptions:

Opcode reserved to Digital

Instruction mnemonics:

    tbi   TB (translation buffer) invalidate

Description:

The TB invalidate (tbi) instruction removes specified entries from the I and D translation buffers (TBs) when the mapping changes. The tbi instruction removes specific entry types based on a CASE selection of the value passed in register a0. On return from the tbi instruction, registers t0, t8..t11, a0, and a1 are UNPREDICTABLE.

2.2.9 Who Am I

Format:

```
whami                               ! PALcode format
```

Operation:

```
if (PS<mode> EQ 1) then
        {Initiate opDec fault}
endif
v0 ←  whami
```

Exceptions:

Opcode reserved to Digital

Instruction mnemonics:

```
whami        Who am I
```

Description:

The who am I (whami) instruction returns the processor number for the current processor in v0. The processor number is in the range 0 to the number of processors minus one (0..maxCPU−1) that can be configued in the system. On return from the whami instruction, registers t0 and t8..t11 are UNPREDICTABLE.

2.2.10 Write System Entry Address

Format:

wrent   ! PALcode format

Operation:

```
if (PS<mode> EQ 1) then
        {Initiate opDec fault}
endif
case al begin
        0:  ! Write the EntInt:
                entInt ← a0
                break;
        1:  ! Write the EntArith:
                entArith ← a0
                break;
        2:  ! Write the EntMM:
                entMM ← a0
                break;
        3:  ! Write the EntIF:
                entIF ← a0
                break;
        4:  ! Write the EntUna:
                entUna ← a0
                break;
        5:  ! Write the EntSys:
                entSys ← a0
                break;
        otherwise:
                break;
endcase;
```

Exceptions:

Opcode reserved to Digital

Instruction mnemonics:

wrent   Write system entry address

Description:

The write system entry address (wrent) instruction determines the specific system
entry point based on a CASE selection of the value passed in register al. The wrent
instruction then sets the virtual address of the specified system entry point to the
value passed in a0.

For best performance all the addresses should be kseg addresses. (See Chapter 3 for a definition of kseg addresses).

On return from the wrent instruction, registers t0, t8..t11, a0, and a1 are UNPREDICTABLE.

2.2.11 Write Floating-Point Enable

Format:

```
wrfen                                ! PALcode format
```

Operation:

```
if (PS<mode> EQ 1) then
        {Initiate opDec fault}
endif
FEN ←  a0<0>
(PCBB+40) ←  a0 AND 1
```

Exceptions:

Opcode reserved to Digital

Instruction mnemonics:

```
wrfen          Write floating-point enable
```

Description:

The write floating-point enable (wrfen) instruction writes bit zero of the value passed in a0 to the floating-point enable register. The wrfen instruction also writes the value for FEN to the PCB at offset (PCBB+40). On return from the wrfen instruction, registers t0, t8..t11, and a0 are UNPREDICTABLE.

2.2.12 Write Kernel Global Pointer

Format:

wrkgp   ! PALcode format

Operation:

```
if (PS<mode> EQ 1) then
        {Initiate opDec fault}
endif
KGP ←   a0
```

Exceptions:

Opcode reserved to Digital

Instruction mnemonics:

wrkgp   Write kernal global pointer

Description:

The write kernel global pointer (wrkgp) instruction writes the value passed in a0 to the kernel global pointer (KGP) internal register. The KGP is used to load the GP on exceptions. On return from the wrkgp instruction, registers t0, t8..t11, and a0 are UNPREDICTABLE.

2.2.13 Write User Stack Pointer

Format:

wrusp   ! PALcode format

Operation:

```
if (PS<mode> EQ 1) then
        {Initiate opDec fault}
endif
USP ←  a0
```

Exceptions:

Opcode reserved to Digital

Instruction mnemonics:

wrusp   Write user stack pointer

Description:

The write user stack pointer (wrusp) instruction writes the value passed in a0 to the user stack pointer. On return from the wrusp instruction, registers t0, t8..t11, and a0 are UNPREDICTABLE.

2.2.14 Write System Value

Format:

wrval   !PALcode format

Operation:

```
if (PS<mode> EQ 1) then
        {Initiate opDec fault}
endif
sysvalue ←  a0
```

Exceptions:

Opcode reserved to Digital

Instruction mnemonics:

wrval   Write system value

Description:

The write system value (wrval) instruction writes the value passed in a0 to a 64-bit system value register. The combination of wrval with the rdval instruction, described in Section 2.2.3, allows access by the operating system to a 64-bit per-processor value. On return from the wrval instruction, registers t0, t8..t11, and a0 are UNPREDICTABLE.

2.2.15 Write Virtual Page Table Pointer

Format:

```
wrvptptr                          ! PALcode format
```

Operation:

```
if (PS<mode> EQ 1) then
        {Initiate opDec fault}
endif
VPTPTR ←  a0
```

Exceptions:

Opcode reserved to Digital

Instruction mnemonics:

wrvptptr   Write virtual page table pointer

Description:

The write virtual page table pointer (wrvptptr) instruction writes the pointer passed in a0 to the virtual page table pointer register (VPTPTR). The VPTPTR is described in Chapter 3. On return from the wrvptptr instruction, registers t0, t8..t11, and a0 are UNPREDICTABLE.

Chapter 3

OSF/1 Memory Management (III)

3.1 Virtual Address Spaces

A virtual address is a 64-bit unsigned integer that specifies a byte location within the virtual address space. Implementations subset the supported address space to one of four sizes (43, 47, 51, or 55 bits) as a function of page size. The minimal supported virtual address size is 43 bits. If an implementation supports less than 64-bit virtual addresses, it must check that all the VA<63:vaSize> bits are equal to VA<vaSize−1>. This gives two disjoint ranges for valid virtual addresses. For example, for a 43-bit virtual address space, valid virtual address ranges are $0..3FFFFFFFFFF_{16}$ and $FFFFFC0000000000_{16}..FFFFFFFFFFFFFFFF_{16}$. Access to virtual addresses outside of an implementation's valid virtual address range cause an access-violation fault.

The virtual address space is divided into 3 segments. The two bits va<vaSize−1:vaSize−2> select a segment as shown in Table 3–1.

Table 3–1: Virtual Address Space Segments

VA<vaSize−1:vaSize−2>	Name	Mapping	Access Control
0x	seg0	Mapped via TB	Programmed in PTE
10	kseg	PA ← sext(VA<vaSize−3:0>)	Kernel Read/Write
11	seg1	Mapped via TB	Programmed in PTE

For kseg, the relocation, sharing, and protection are fixed. For seg0 and seg1, the virtual address space is broken into pages, which are the units of relocation, sharing, and protection. The page size ranges from 8 Kbytes to 64 Kbytes. Therefore, system software should allocate regions with differing protection on 64 Kbyte virtual address boundaries to ensure image compatibility across all Alpha implementations.

Memory management provides the mechanism to map the active part of the virtual address space to the available physical address space. The operating system controls the virtual-to-physical address mapping tables and saves the inactive (but used) parts of the virtual address space on external storage media.

3.1.1 Segment Seg0 and Seg1 Virtual Address Format

The processor generates a 64-bit virtual address for each instruction and operand in memory. A seg0 or seg1 virtual address consists of three level-number fields and a byte_within_page field, as shown in Figure 3–1.

Figure 3–1: Virtual Address Format

63				0
SEXT (level1 <level size-3>)	level1	level2	level3	byte_within_page

Figure 3–2: Kseg Virtual Address Format

63		0
SEXT (segment_select<1>)	Segment Select=10_2	Physical Address

The byte_within_page field can be either 13, 14, 15, or 16 bits depending on a particular implementation. Thus, the allowable page sizes are 8 Kbytes, 16 Kbytes, 32 Kbytes, and 64 Kbytes. Each level-number field is 0-n bits long, where, for example, n is 9 for an 8K page size. Level-number fields are the same size for a given implementation.

The level-number fields are a function of the page size; all page table entries at any given level do not exceed one page. The PFN field in the PTE is always 32 bits wide. Thus as the page size grows the virtual and physical address size also grows.

In Table 3–2, the physical address column is the maximum physical address supported by the smaller of seg0/seg1 or kseg, as indicated.

Table 3–2: Virtual Address Options

Page Size (bytes)	Byte Offset (bits)	Level Size (bits)	Virtual Address (bits)	Physical Address (bits)	Physical Address Limited by
8K	13	10	43	41	kseg
16K	14	11	47	45	kseg
32K	15	12	51	47	seg0/seg1
64K	16	13	55	48	seg0/seg1

3.1.2 Kseg Virtual Address Format

The processor generates a 64-bit virtual address for each instruction and operand in memory. A kseg virtual address consists of segment select field with a value of 10_2 and a physical address field. The segment select field is the two bits va<vaSize–1:vaSize–2>. The physical address field is va<vaSize–3:0>.

3.2 Physical Address Space

Physical addresses are at most vaSize–2 bits. This allows all of physical memory to be accessed via kseg. A processor may choose to implement a smaller physical address space by not implementing some number of high order bits. The two most significant implemented physical address bits select a caching policy or implementation dependent type of address space. Implementations will use these bits as appropriate for their systems. For example, in a workstation with a 30-bit physical address space, bit<29> might select between memory and non-memory like regions, and bit <28> could enable or disable caching; see *Common Architecture, Chapter 5.*

3.3 Memory Management Control

Memory management is always enabled. Implementations must provide an environment for PALcode to service exceptions and to initialize and boot the processor. For example PALcode might run with I-stream mapping disabled.

3.4 Page Table Entries

The processor uses a quadword page table entry (PTE) to translate seg0 and seg1 virtual addresses to physical addresses. A PTE contains hardware and software control information and the physical page frame number (PFN). A PTE is a quadword with the following fields:

Figure 3–3: Page Table Entry (PTE)

```
63                              32 31        16 15 14 13 12 11 10 9  8  7  6  5  4  3  2  1  0
                                            R  U  K  R  U  K  R           A  F  F  F
          PFN                     SW        S  W  W  S  R  R  S  GH       S  O  O  O  V
                                            V  E  E  V  E  E  V           M  E  W  R
                                            0           1           2
```

Table 3–3: Page Table Entry (PTE) Bit Summary

Bits	Name	Meaning
63:32	PFN	Page frame number
		The PFN field always points to a page boundary. If V is set, the PFN is concatenated with the byte_within_page bits of the virtual address to obtain the physical address.
31:16	SW	Reserved for software.
15:14	RSV0	Reserved for hardware; SBZ.

Table 3–3 (Cont.): Page Table Entry (PTE) Bit Summary

Bits	Name	Meaning
13	UWE	User write enable.
		This bit enables writes from user mode. If this bit is 0 and a store is attempted while in user mode, an access-violation fault occurs. This bit is valid even when V=0.
12	KWE	Kernel write enable.
		This bit enables writes from kernel mode. If this bit is 0 and a store is attempted while in kernel mode, an access-violation fault occurs. This bit is valid even when V=0.
11:10	RSV1	Reserved for hardware; SBZ.
9	URE	User read enable.
		This bit enables reads from user mode. If this bit is 0 and a load or instruction fetch is attempted while in user mode, an Access Violation occurs. This bit is valid even when V=0.
8	KRE	Kernel read enable.
		This bit enables reads from kernel mode. If this bit is 0 and a load or instruction fetch is attempted while in kernel mode, an access-violation fault occurs. This bit is valid even when V=0.
7	RSV2	Reserved for hardware; SBZ.
6:5	GH	Granularity hint.

Software may set these bits to a non-zero value to supply a hint to translation buffer implementations that a block of pages can be treated as a single larger page:

1. A block is an aligned group of $8^{**}N$ pages where N is the value of PTE<6:5>, e.f. a group of 1, 8, 64, or 512 pages starting at a virtual address with page_size + 3*N low-order zeros.

2. The block is a group of physically contiguous pages that are aligned both virtually and physically. Within the block, the low 3*N bits of the PFNs describe the identity mapping and the high 32−3*N PFN bits are all equal.

3. Within the block, all PTEs have the same values for bits <15:0>. Hardware may use this hint to map the entire block with a single TB entry, instead of 8, 64, or 512 separare TB entries.

Bits	Name	Meaning
4	ASM	Address space match.
		When set, this PTE matches all address space numbers. For a given VA, ASM must he set consistently in all processes, otherwise the address mapping is UNPREDICTABLE.
3	FOE	Fault on execute.
		When set, a Fault on Execute exception occurs on an attempt to execute any location in the page.

Table 3–3 (Cont.): Page Table Entry (PTE) Bit Summary

Bits	Name	Meaning
2	FOW	Fault on write.
		When set, a Fault on Write exception occurs on an attempt to write any location in the page.
1	FOR	Fault on read.
		When set, a Fault on Read exception occurs on an attempt to read any location in the page.
0	V	Valid.
		Indicates the validity of the PFN field. When V is set the PFN field is valid for use by hardware. When V is clear, the PFN field is reserved for use by software. The V bit does not affect the validity of PTE<15:1> bits.

3.4.1 Changes to Page Table Entries

The operating system changes PTEs as part of its memory management functions. For example, the operating system may set or clear the V bit, change the PFN field as pages are moved to and from external storage media, or modify the software bits. The processor hardware never changes PTEs.

Software must guarantee that each PTE is always consistent within itself. Changing a PTE one field at a time can cause incorrect system operation, such as setting PTE<V> with one instruction before establishing PTE<PFN> with another. Execution of an interrupt service routine between the two instructions could use an address that would map using the inconsistent PTE. Software can solve this problem by building a complete new PTE in a register and then moving the new PTE to the page table by using an STQ instruction.

Multiprocessing makes the problem more complicated. Another processor could be reading (or even changing) the same PTE that the first processor is changing. Such concurrent access must produce consistent results. Software must use some form of software synchronization to modify PTEs that are already valid. Whenever a processor modifies a valid PTE, it is possible that other processors in a multiprocessor system may have old copies of that PTE in their translation buffer. Software must inform other processors of changes to PTEs. Hardware must ensure that aligned quadword reads and writes are atomic operations. Hardware must not cache invalid PTEs (PTEs with the V bit equal to 0) in translation buffers. See Section 3.7 for more information.

3.5 Memory Protection

Memory protection is the function of validating whether a particular type of access is allowed to a specific page from a particular access mode. Access to each page is controlled by a protection code that specifies, for each access mode, whether read or write references are allowed. The processor uses the following to determine whether an intended access is allowed:

- The virtual address, which is used to either select kseg mapping or provide the index into the page tables.
- The intended access type (read or write).
- The current access mode base on Processor Mode.

For protection checks, the intended access is read for data loads and instruction fetches, and write for data stores.

3.5.1 Processor Access Modes

There are two processor modes, user and kernel. The access mode of a running process is stored in the processor status mode bit (PS<mode>).

3.5.2 Protection Code

Every page in the virtual address space is protected according to its use. A program may be prevented from reading or writing portions of its address space. Associated with each page is a protection code that describes the accessibility of the page for each processor mode.

For seg0 and seg1, the code allows a choice of read or write protection for each processor mode. For each mode, access can be read/write, read-only, or no-access. Read and write accessibility and the protection for each mode are specified independently.

For kseg, the protection code is kernel read/write, user no-access.

3.5.3 Access-Violation Faults

An access-violation memory-management fault occurs if an illegal access is attempted, as determined by the current processor mode and the page's protection.

3.6 Address Translation for Seg0 and Seg1

The page tables can be accessed from physical memory, or (to reduce overhead) can be mapped to a linear region of the virtual address space. The following sections describe both access methods.

3.6.1 Physical Access for Seg0 and Seg1 PTEs

Seg0 and seg1 address translation can be performed by accessing entries in a three-level page table structure. The page table base register (PTBR) contains the physical page frame number (PFN) of the highest level (level 1) page table. Bits <level1> of the virtual address are used to index into the first level page table to obtain the physical PFN of the base of the second level (level 2) page table. Bits <level2> of the virtual address are used to index into the second level page table to obtain the physical PFN of the base of the third level (level 3) page table. Bits <level3> of the virtual address are used to index the third level page table to obtain the physical PFN of the page being referenced. The PFN is concatenated with virtual address bits <byte_within_page> to obtain the physical address of the location being accessed.

If part of any page table does not reside in a memory-like region, or does reside in nonexistent memory, the operation of the processor is UNDEFINED.

If the first-level or second-level PTE is valid, the protection bits are ignored; the protection code in the third-level PTE is used to determine accessibility. If a first level or second level PTE is invalid, an access-violation fault occurs if the PTE<KRE> equals zero. An access-violation fault on a first-level or second-level PTE implies that all lower-level page tables mapped by that PTE do not exist.

The algorithm to generate a physical address from a seg0 or seg1 virtual address follows:

```
IF {SEXT(VA<vaSize-1:0>) neq VA} THEN
      { initiate access-violation fault}

level1_PTE ←  ({PTBR * page_size} + {8 * VA<level1>} )          ! Read physical
IF level1_PTE<v> EQ 0 THEN
         IF level1_PTE<KRE> eq 0 THEN
                  { initiate access-violation fault}
         ELSE
                  { initiate translation-not-valid fault}

level2_PTE ←  ({level1_PTE<PFN> * page_size} + {8 * VA<level2>} )   ! Read physical
IF level2_PTE<v> EQ 0 THEN
         IF level2_PTE<KRE> eq 0 THEN
                  { initiate access-violation fault}
         ELSE
                  { initiate translation-not-valid fault}

level3_PTE ←  ({level2_PTE<PFN> * page_size} + {8 * VA<level3>} )   ! Read physical

IF {{{level3_PTE<UWE> eq 0} AND {write access} AND {ps<mode> EQ 1} } OR
    {{level3_PTE<URE> eq 0} AND {read access}  AND {ps<mode> EQ 1} } OR
    {{level3_PTE<KWE> eq 0} AND {write access} AND {ps<mode> EQ 0} } OR
    {{level3_PTE<KRE> eq 0} AND {read access}  AND {ps<mode> EQ 0} } }
       THEN
                 {initiate memory-management fault}
       ELSE
                 IF level3_PTE<v> EQ 0 THEN
                         {initiate memory-management fault}

IF { level3_PTE<FOW> eq 1} AND {write access} THEN
       {initiate memory-management fault}
IF { level3_PTE<FOR> eq 1} AND {read access} THEN
       {initiate memory-management fault}
IF { level3_PTE<FOE> eq 1} AND {execute access} THEN
       {initiate memory-management fault}

Physical_address ←  {level3_PTE<PFN> * page_size} OR VA<byte_within_page>
```

3.6.2 Virtual Access for Seg0 or Seg1 PTEs

The page tables can be mapped into a linear region of the virtual address space, reducing the overhead for seg0 and seg1 PTE accesses. The mapping is done as follows:

1. Select a $2^{(3*\lg(pageSize/8))+3}$ byte-aligned region (an address with $3*\lg(pageSize/8)+3$ low-order zeros) in the seg0 or seg1 address space. Set the virtual page table pointer (VPTPTR) with a write virtual page table pointer instruction (wrvptptr) to the selected value.

2. Create a level1 PTE to map the page tables as follows.

```
level1_PTE = 0              ! Initialize all fields to 0
level1_PTE<63:32> = pfn_of_Level_1_pagetable
                           ! Set the PFN to the PFN of the level one pagetable
level1_PTE<8>  = 1         ! Set the kernel read enable bit
level1_PTE<0>  = 1         ! Set the valid bit
```

3. Set the level1 page table entry that corresponds to the VPTB to the created level1_PTE.

4. Set all level1 and level 2 valid PTEs to allow kernel read access. With this setup in place the algorithm to fetch a seg0 or seg1 PTE is:

```
tmp  ←  left_shift (va, {64 - {{lg(pageSize) *4} - 9}} )
tmp  ←  right_shift (tmp, {64 - {{lg(pageSize) *4} - 9} + lg(pageSize) - 3} )
tmp  ←  VPTB OR tmp
tmp<2:0> ←  0
level3_PTE  ←  (tmp)        ! Load PTE using it's virtual address
```

The virtual access method is used by PALcode for most TB fills.

3.7 Translation Buffer

In order to save actual memory references when repeatedly referencing the same pages, hardware implementations include a translation buffer to remember successful virtual address translations and page states. When the process context is changed, a new value is loaded into the address space number (ASN) internal processor register with a swap process context (swpctx) instruction. This causes address translations for pages with PTE<ASM> clear to be invalidated on a processor that does not implement address space numbers.

Additionally, when the software changes any part (except the software field) of a valid PTE, it must also execute a CALL_PAL tbi instruction. The entire translation buffer can be invalidated by tbia, and all ASM=0 entries can be invalidated by tbiap. The translation buffer must not store invalid PTEs. Therefore, the software is not required to invalidate translation buffer entries when making changes for PTEs that are already invalid.

3.8 Address Space Numbers

The Alpha architecture allows a processor to optionally implement address space numbers (process tags) to reduce the need for invalidation of cached address translations for process specific addresses when a context switch occurs.

The address space number for the current process is loaded by software in the address space number (ASN) with a swpctx instruction. ASNs are processor specific and the hardware makes no attempt to maintain coherency across multiple processors. In a multiprocessor system, software is responsible for ensuring the consistency of TB entries for processes that might be rescheduled on different processors.

System software should not assume that the number of ASNs is a power of two. This allows, for example, hardware to use N TB tag bits to encode (2**N)–3 ASN values, one value for ASM=1 PTEs, and one for invalid.

There are several possible ways of using ASNs. There are several complications in a multiprocessor system. Consider the case where a process that executed on processor–1 is rescheduled on processor–2. If a page is deleted or its protection is changed, the TB in processor–1 has stale data. One solution would be to send an interprocessor interrupt to all the processors on which this process could have run and cause them to invalidate the changed PTE. This results in significant overhead in a system with several processors. Another solution would be to have software invalidate all TB entries for a process on a new processor before it can begin execution, if the process executed on another processor during its previous execution. This ensures the deletion of possibly stale TB entries on the new processor. A third solution would assign a new ASN whenever a process is run on a processor that is not the same as the last processor on which it ran.

3.9 Memory-Management Faults

On a memory-management fault, the fault code (MMCSR) is passed in a1 to specify the type of fault encountered, as shown in Table 3–4.

Table 3–4: Memory-Management Fault Type Codes

Fault	MMCSR value
Translation not valid	0
Access violation	1
Fault on read	2
Fault on execute	3
Fault on write	4

- A translation-not-valid fault is taken when a read or write reference is attempted through an invalid PTE in a first, second, or third-level page table.

- An access-violation fault is taken on a reference to a seg0 or seg1 address when the protection field of the third-level PTE that maps the data indicates that the intended page reference would be illegal in the specified access mode. An access-violation fault is also taken if the KRE bit is a zero in an invalid first or second level PTE. An access-violation fault is generated for any access to a kseg address when the mode is user (PS<mode> EQ 1).

- A fault-on-read (FOR) fault occurs when a read is attempted with PTE<FOR> set.

- A fault-on-execute (FOE) fault occurs when an instruction fetch is attempted with PTE<FOE> set.

- A fault-on-write (FOW) fault occurs when a write is attempted with PTE<FOW> set.

Chapter 4

OSF/1 Process Structure (III)

4.1 Process Definition

A process is a single thread of execution. It is the basic entity that can be scheduled and is executed by the processor. A process consists of an address space and both software and hardware context. The hardware context of a process is defined by the the following:

- 30 integer registers (excluding R31 and SP)

- 31 floating-point registers (excluding F31)

- The program counter (PC)

- The two per-process stack pointers (USP/KSP)

- The processor status (PS)

- The address space number (ASN)

- The process cycle counter (PCC)

- The page table base register (PTBR)

- The process unique value (unique)

This information must be loaded if a process is to execute.

While a process is executing, some of its hardware context is being updated in the internal registers. When a process is not being executed, its hardware context is stored in memory in a software structure termed the process control block (PCB). Saving the process context in the PCB and loading new values from another PCB for a new context is termed context switching. Context switching occurs as one process after another is scheduled for execution.

4.2 Process Control Block (PCB)

As shown in Figure 4–1, the PCB holds the state of a process.

The contents of the PCB are loaded and saved by the swpctx instruction. The PCB must be quadword aligned and should be 64 byte aligned for best performance. Kernel mode code can read the PTBR, the ASN, and the FEN for the current process from the PCB. Kernel mode code must use the rdusp/wrusp instructions to access the USP. The PCC must be read with the rpcc instruction. The unique value can be accessed with the rdunique and wrunique instructions.

Figure 4–1: Process Control Block (PCB)

63	32	31	1	0	
Kernel Stack Pointer (KSP)					:00
User Stack Pointer (USP)					:08
Page Table Base Register (PTBR)					:16
Address Space Number (ASN)		Cycle Counter (PCC)			:24
Process Unique Value (unique)					:32
				F E N	:40
Reserved to Digital					:48
Reserved to Digital					:56

Chapter 5
OSF/1 Exceptions and Interrupts (III)

5.1 Introduction

At certain times during the operation of a system, events within the system require the execution of software outside the explicit flow of control. When such an event occurs, an Alpha processor forces a change in control flow from that indicated by the current instruction stream. The notification process for such an event is either an exception or an interrupt.

5.1.1 Exceptions

Exceptions are relevant primarily to the currently executing process. Exception service routines execute in response to exception conditions caused by software. All exception service routines execute in kernel mode on the kernel stack. Exception conditions consist of faults, arithmetic traps, and synchronous traps:

- A fault occurs during an instruction and leaves the registers and memory in a consistent state such that elimination of the fault condition and subsequent reexecution of the instruction gives correct results. Faults are not guaranteed to leave the machine in exactly the same state it was in immediately prior to the fault, but rather in a state such that the instruction can be correctly executed if the fault condition is removed. The PC saved in the exception stack frame is the address of the faulting instruction. An rti instruction to that PC reexecutes the faulting instruction.

- An arithmetic trap occurs at the completion of the operation that caused the exception. Since several instructions may be in various stages of execution at any point in time, it is possible for multiple arithmetic traps to occur simultaneously.

  The PC that is saved in the exception frame on traps is that of the next instruction that would have been issued if the trapping conditions had not occurred. However, that PC is *not* necessarily the address of the instruction immediately following the instructions that encountered the trap condition. Further, intervening instructions may have changed operands or other state used by the instructions encountering the trap conditions.

  An rti instruction to that PC does not reexecute the trapping instructions, nor does it reexecute any intervening instructions; it simply continues execution from the point at which the trap was taken.

  In general, it is difficult to fix up results and continue program execution at the point of an arithmetic trap. Software can force a trap to be continued more easily without the need for complicated fixup code. This is accomplished by following a set of code generation restrictions in the code that could cause arithmetic traps which are to be completed by a software trap handler (see *Common Architecture, Chapter 4*), including specifying the /S software completion modifier in each such instruction.

The AND of all the software completion modifiers for trapping instructions is provided to the arithmetic trap handler in the exception summary SWC bit. If the SWC is set, a trap handler may find the trigger instruction by scanning backward from the trap PC until each register in the register write mask has been an instruction destination. The trigger instruction is the first instruction in the I-stream order to get a trap within a trap shadow. (See *Common Architecture, Chapter 4* for a definition of trap shadow.) If the SWC bit is clear, no fixup is possible.

- A synchronous trap occurs at the completion of the operation that caused the exception. No instructions can be issued between the completion of the operation that caused the exception and the trap.

5.1.2 Interrupts

The processor arbitrates interrupt requests. When the interrupt priority level (IPL) of an outstanding interrupt is greater than the current IPL, the processor raises IPL to the level of the interrupt and dispatches to entInt, the interrupt entry to the OS. Interrupts are serviced in kernel mode on the kernel stack. Interrupts can come from one of four sources: I/O devices, the clock, performance counters, or machine checks.

5.2 Processor Status

The processor status (PS) is a four-bit register that contains the current mode (PS<mode>) in bit <3> and a three-bit interrupt priority level (PS<IPL>) in bits <2..0>. The PS<mode> bit is zero for kernel mode and one for user mode. The PS<IPL> bits are always zero if the mode is user and can be 0 to 7 if the mode is kernel. The PS is changed when an interrupt or exception is initiated and by the rti, retsys, and swpipl instructions.

The uses of the PS values are shown in Table 5–1.

Table 5–1: Processor Status Summary

PS<mode>	PS<IPL>	Mode	Use
1	0	User	User software
0	0	Kernel	System software
0	1	Kernel	System software
0	2	Kernel	System software
0	3	Kernel	Low priority device interrupts
0	4	Kernel	High priority device interrupts

Table 5–1 (Cont.): Processor Status Summary

PS<mode>	PS<IPL>	Mode	Use
0	5	Kernel	Clock, and interprocessor interrupts
0	6	Kernel	Real time devices
0	7	Kernel	Machine checks

5.3 Stack Frames

There are two types of system entries—those for the callsys instruction and those for exceptions and interrupts. Both types use the same stack frame layout, as shown in Figure 5–1. The stack frame contains space for the PC, the PS, the saved GP, and the saved registers a0, a1, a2. On entry, the SP points to the saved PS.

The callsys entry saves the PC, the PS, and the GP. The exception and interrupt entries save the PC, the PS, the GP, and also save the registers a0..a2.

Figure 5–1: Stack Frame Layout

63	0	
PS		:00
PC		:08
GP		:16
a0		:24
a1		:32
a2		:40

5.4 System Entry Addresses

All system entries are in kernel mode. The interrupt priority PS bits (PS<IPL>) are set as shown in the following table. The system entry point address is set by the CALL_PAL wrent instruction, as described in Section 2.2.10.

Table 5–2: Entry Point Address Registers

Entry Point	Value in a0	Value in a1	Value in a2	PS<IPL>
entArith	Exception summary	Register mask	UNPREDICT-ABLE	Unchanged
entIF	Fault Type code	UNPREDICT-ABLE	UNPREDICT-ABLE	Unchanged

Table 5–2 (Cont.): Entry Point Address Registers

Entry Point	Value in a0	Value in a1	Value in a2	PS<IPL>
entInt	Interrupt type	Vector	UNPREDICT-ABLE	Priority of interrupt
entMM	VA	MMCSR	Cause	Unchanged
entSys	p0	p1	p2	Unchanged
entUna	VA	Opcode	Src/Dst	Unchanged

5.4.1 System Entry Arithmetic Trap (entArith)

The arithmetic trap entry, entArith, is called when an arithmetic trap occurs. On entry, a0 contains the exception summary register and a1 contains the exception register write mask. Section 5.4.1.1 describes the exception summary register and Section 5.4.1.2 describes the register write mask.

5.4.1.1 Exception Summary Register

The exception summary register, shown in Figure 5–2 and described in Table 5–3, records the various types of arithmetic exceptions that can occur together. Those types of exceptions are listed and described in Table 5–3.

Figure 5–2: Exception Summary Register

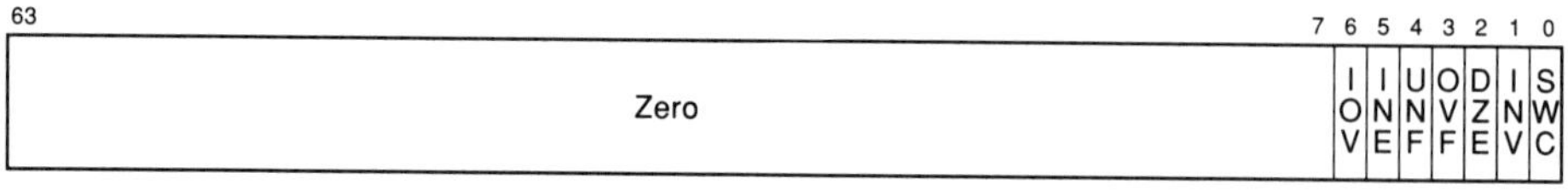

Table 5–3: Exception Summary Register Bit Definitions

Bit	Description
0	Software completion (SWC)

Is set when all of the other arithmetic exception bits were set by floating-operate instructions with the /S software completion trap modifier set. See *Common Architecture, Chapter 4* for rules about setting the /S modifier in code that may cause an arithmetic trap, and Section 5.1.1 for rules about using the SWC bit in a trap handler.

Table 5–3 (Cont.): Exception Summary Register Bit Definitions

Bit	Description

1   Invalid operation (INV)

An attempt was made to perform a floating arithmetic, conversion, or comparison operation, and one or more of the operand values were illegal.

An INV trap is reported for most floating-point operate instructions with an input operand that is an IEEE NaN, IEEE infinity, or IEEE denormal.

Floating invalid operation traps are always enabled. If this trap occurs, the result register is written with an UNPREDICTABLE value.

2   Division by zero (DZE)

An attempt was made to perform a floating divide operation with a divisor of zero.

A DZE trap is reported when a finite number is divided by zero. Floating divide by zero traps are always enabled. If this trap occurs, the result register is written with an UNPREDICTABLE value.

3   Overflow (OVF)

A floating arithmetic or conversion operation overflowed the destination exponent.

An OVF trap is reported when the destination's largest finite number is exceeded in magnitude by the rounded true result. Floating overflow traps are always enabled. If this trap occurs, the result register is written with an UNPREDICTABLE value.

4   Underflow (UNF)

A floating arithmetic or conversion operation underflowed the destination exponent.

An UNF trap is reported when the destination's smallest finite number exceeds in magnitude the non-zero rounded true result. Floating underflow trap enable can be specified in each floating-point operate instruction. If underflow occurs, the result register is written with a true zero.

5   Inexact result (INE)

A floating arithmetic or conversion operation gave a result that differed from the mathematically exact result.

An INE trap is reported if the rounded result of an IEEE operation is not exact. Inexact result trap enable can be specified in each IEEE floating-point operate instruction. The rounded result value is stored in all cases.

6   Integer overflow (IOV)

An integer arithmetic operation or a conversion from floating to integer overflowed the destination precision.

An IOV trap is reported for any integer operation whose true result exceeds the destination register size. Integer overflow trap enable can be specified in each arithmetic integer operate instruction and each floating-point convert-to-integer instruction. If integer overflow occurs, the result register is written with the truncated true result.

5.4.1.2 Exception Register Write Mask

The exception register write mask parameter records all registers that were targets of instructions that set the bits in the exception summary register. There is a one-to-one correspondence between bits in the register write mask quadword and the register numbers. The quadword records, starting at bit 0 and proceeding right to left, which of the registers r0 through r31, then f0 through f31, received an exceptional result.

NOTE

For a sequence such as:

```
ADDF F1,F2,F3
MULF F4,F5,F3
```

if the add overflows and the multiply does not, the OVF bit is set in the exception summary, and the F3 bit is set in the register mask, even though the overflowed sum in F3 can be overwritten with an in-range product by the time the trap is taken. (This code violates the destination reuse rule for software completion. See *Common Architecture, Chapter 4* for the destination reuse rules.)

The PC value saved in the exception stack frame is the virtual address of the next instruction. This is defined as the virtual address of the first instruction not executed after the trap condition was recognized.

5.4.2 System Entry Instruction Fault (entIF)

The instruction fault entry is called for bpt, bugchk, gentrap, opDec, and for a FEN fault (floating-point instruction when the floating-point unit is disabled, FEN EQ 0). On entry, a0 contains a 0 for a bpt, a 1 for bugchk, a 2 for gentrap, a 3 for FEN fault, and a 4 for opDec. No additional data is passed in a1..a2. The saved PC at (SP+00) is the address of the instruction that caused the fault for FEN faults. The saved PC at (SP+00) is the address of the instruction after the instruction that caused the fault bpt, bugchk, gentrap, and opDec faults.

5.4.3 System Entry Hardware Interrupts (entInt)

The interrupt entry is called to service a hardware interrupt, or a machine check. Table 5–4 shows what is passed in a0..a2 and the PS<IPL> setting for various interrupts.

Table 5–4: System Entry Hardware Interrupts

Entry Type	Value in a0	Value in a1	Value in a2	PS<IPL>
Interprocessor interrupt	0	UNPREDICT-ABLE	UNPREDICT-ABLE	5
Clock	1	UNPREDICT-ABLE	UNPREDICT-ABLE	5
Machine check	2	Interrupt vector	Pointer to Logout Area	7
I/O device interrupt	3	Interrupt vector	UNPREDICT-ABLE	Level of device
Performance counter	4	Interrupt vector	UNPREDICT-ABLE	6

On entry to the hardware interrupt routine, the IPL has been set to the level of the interrupt. For hardware interrupts, register a1 contains a platform-specific interrupt vector. That platform-specific interrupt vector is typically the same value as the SCB offset value that would be returned if the platform was running OpenVMS PALcode.

For a machine check, a2 contains kseg address of the logout area. The first 4 longwords of the logout area are implementation-independent. The rest of the logout area is system specific. The first longword of the logout area is a machine check in progress flag. If the flag is non zero when a machine check is being initiated, a double machine check halt is initiated instead. The machine check handler needs to clear the machine check in progress flag when it can handle a new machine check. Figure 5–3 describes the logout area.

Figure 5–3: Logout Area

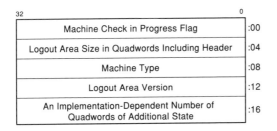

32	0	
Machine Check in Progress Flag		:00
Logout Area Size in Quadwords Including Header		:04
Machine Type		:08
Logout Area Version		:12
An Implementation-Dependent Number of Quadwords of Additional State		:16

5.4.4 System Entry MM Fault (entMM)

The memory-management fault entry is called when a memory management exception occurs. On entry, a0 contains the faulting virtual address and a1 contains the MMCSR (See Section 3.9). On entry, a2 is set to a minus one (–1) for an instruction fetch fault, to a plus one (+1) for a fault caused by a store instruction, or to a 0 for a fault caused by a load instruction.

5.4.5 System Entry Call System (entSys)

The system call entry is called when a callsys instruction is executed in user mode. On entry, only registers (t8..t11) have been modified. The PC+4 of the callsys instruction, the user global pointer, and the current PS are saved on the kernel stack. Additional space for a0..a2 is allocated. After completion of the system service routine, the kernel code executes a CALL_PAL retsys instruction.

5.4.6 System Entry Unaligned Access (entUna)

The unaligned access entry is called when a load or store access is not aligned. On entry, a0 contains the faulting virtual address, a1 contains the zero extended six-bit opcode (bits <31:26>) of the faulting instruction, and a2 contains the zero extended data source or destination register number (bits<25:21> of the faulting instruction)

5.5 PALcode Support

5.5.1 Stack Writeability and Alignment

PALcode only accesses the kernel stack. Any PALcode accesses to the kernel stack that would produce a memory-management fault will result in a kernel-stack-not-valid halt. The stack pointer must always point to a quadword-aligned address. If the kernel stack is not quadword aligned on a PALcode access, a kernel-stack-not-valid halt is initiated.

Appendixes

This section contains the following appendixes:

A. Software Considerations

B. IEEE Floating-Point Conformance

C. Instruction Encodings

Contents

Part I   Appendixes

Appendix A   Software Considerations

A.1	Hardware-Software Compact	A–1
A.2	Instruction-Stream Considerations	A–2
A.2.1	Instruction Alignment	A–2
A.2.2	Multiple Instruction Issue — Factor of 3	A–2
A.2.3	Branch Prediction and Minimizing Branch-Taken — Factor of 3	A–3
A.2.4	Improving I-Stream Density — Factor of 3	A–5
A.2.5	Instruction Scheduling — Factor of 3	A–5
A.3	Data-Stream Considerations	A–6
A.3.1	Data Alignment — Factor of 10	A–6
A.3.2	Shared Data in Multiple Processors — Factor of 3	A–7
A.3.3	Avoiding Cache/TB Conflicts — Factor of 1	A–8
A.3.4	Sequential Read/Write — Factor of 1	A–10
A.3.5	Prefetching — Factor of 3	A–10
A.4	Code Sequences	A–11
A.4.1	Aligned Byte/Word Memory Accesses	A–11
A.4.2	Division	A–12
A.4.3	Stylized Code Forms	A–12
A.4.3.1	NOP	A–13
A.4.3.2	Clear a Register	A–13
A.4.3.3	Load Literal	A–13
A.4.3.4	Register-to-Register Move	A–14
A.4.3.5	Negate	A–14
A.4.3.6	NOT	A–14
A.4.3.7	Booleans	A–14
A.4.4	Trap Barrier	A–14
A.4.5	Pseudo-Operations (Stylized Code Forms)	A–14
A.5	Timing Considerations: Atomic Sequences	A–17

Appendix B   IEEE Floating-Point Conformance

B.1	Alpha Choices for IEEE Options	B–1
B.2	Alpha Hardware Support of Software Exception Handlers	B–2
B.3	Mapping to IEEE Standard	B–3

Appendix C   Instruction Encodings

C.1	Memory Format Instructions	C–1
C.2	Branch Format Instructions	C–2
C.3	Operate Format Instructions	C–2
C.4	Floating-Point Operate Format	C–3
C.4.1	IEEE Floating-Point Instructions	C–4
C.4.2	VAX Floating-Point Instructions	C–5
C.5	Opcode Summary	C–6
C.6	OpenVMS PALcode Format Instructions	C–8
C.6.1	Unprivileged OpenVMS PALcode Function Codes	C–8
C.6.2	Privileged OpenVMS PALcode Function Codes	C–8
C.7	Unprivileged OSF/1 PALcode Function Codes	C–9
C.8	Privileged OSF/1 PALcode function codes	C–9
C.9	Required PALcode Function Codes	C–10
C.10	Opcodes Reserved to PALcode	C–10
C.11	Opcodes Reserved to Digital	C–10

Figures

B–1	IEEE Trap Handling Behavior	B–4

Tables

A–1	Decodable Pseudo-Operations (Stylized Code Forms)	A–15
B–1	IEEE Floating-Point Trap Handling	B–5
B–2	IEEE Standard Charts	B–10
C–1	Memory Format Instruction Opcodes	C–1
C–2	Memory Format Instructions with a Function Code	C–1
C–3	Memory Format Branch Instruction Opcodes	C–2
C–4	Branch Format instruction Opcodes	C–2
C–5	Operate Format Instruction Opcodes and Function Codes	C–2
C–6	Function Codes for Floating Data Type Independent Operations	C–3
C–7	IEEE Floating-Point Instruction Function Codes	C–4
C–8	VAX Floating-Point Instruction Function Codes	C–5
C–9	Opcode Summary	C–7
C–10	Key to Opcode Summary (Table C–9)	C–7
C–11	Unprivileged OpenVMS PALcode Function codes	C–8
C–12	Privileged OpenVMS PALcode Function Codes	C–8
C–13	Unprivileged OSF/1 PALcode Function Codes	C–9
C–14	Privileged OSF/1 PALcode Function Codes	C–9

C–15 Required PALcode Function Codes C–10
C–16 Opcodes Reserved for PALcode C–10
C–17 Opcodes Reserved for Digital C–10

Software Considerations

A.1 Hardware-Software Compact

The Alpha architecture, like all RISC architectures, depends on careful attention to data alignment and instruction scheduling to achieve high performance.

Since there will be various implementations of the Alpha architecture, it is not obvious how compilers can generate high-performance code for all implementations. This chapter gives some scheduling guidelines that, if followed by all compilers and respected by all implementations, will result in good performance. As such, this section represents a good-faith compact between hardware designers and software writers. It represents a set of common goals, not a set of architectural requirements. Thus, an Appendix, not a Chapter.

Many of the performance optimizations discussed below are advantageous only for frequently executed code. For rarely executed code, they may produce a bigger program that is not any faster. Some of the branching optimizations also depend on good prediction of which path from a conditional branch is more frequently executed. These optimizations are best done by using an execution profile, either an estimate generated by compiler heuristics, or a real profile of a previous run, such as that gathered by PC-sampling in PCA.

Each computer architecture has a "natural word size." For the PDP–11, it is 16 bits; for VAX, 32 bits; and for Alpha, 64 bits. Other architectures also have a natural word size that varies between 16 and 64 bits. Except for very low-end implementations, ALU data paths, cache access paths, chip pin buses, and main memory data paths are all usually the natural word size.

As an architecture becomes commercially successful, high-end implementations inevitably move to double-width data paths that can transfer an *aligned* (at an even natural word address) pair of natural words in one cycle. For Alpha, this means eventual 128-bit wide data paths. It is hard to get much speed advantage from paired transfers unless the code being executed has instructions and data appropriately aligned on aligned octaword boundaries. Since this is hard to retrofit to old code, the following sections sometimes encourage "over-aligning" to octaword boundaries in anticipation of high-speed Alpha implementations.

In some cases, there are performance advantages in aligning instructions or data to cache-block boundaries, or putting data whose use is correlated into the same cache block, or trying to avoid cache conflicts by not having data whose use is correlated placed at addresses that are equal modulo the cache size. Since the Alpha architecture will have many implementations, an exact cache design cannot be outlined here. Nonetheless, some expected bounds can be stated.

1. Small (first-level) cache sizes will likely be in the range 2 KB to 64 KB

2. Small cache block sizes will likely be 16, 32, 64, or 128 bytes

3. Large (second- or third-level) cache sizes will likely be in the range 128 KB to 8 MB

4. Large cache block sizes will likely be 32, 64, 128, or 256 bytes

5. TB sizes will likely be in the range 16 to 1024 entries

Thus, if two data items need to go in different cache blocks, it is desirable to make them at least 128 bytes apart (modulo 2 KB). Doing that creates a high probability of allowing both items to be in a small cache simultaneously, for all Alpha implementations.

In each case below, the performance implication is given by an order-of-magnitude number: 1, 3, 10, 30, or 100. A factor of 10 means that the performance difference being discussed will likely range from 3 to 30 across all Alpha implementations.

A.2 Instruction-Stream Considerations

The following sections describe considerations for the instruction stream.

A.2.1 Instruction Alignment

Code PSECTs should be octaword-aligned. Targets of frequently taken branches should be at least quadword-aligned, and octaword-aligned for very frequent loops. Compilers could use execution profiles to identify frequently taken branches.

Most Alpha implementations will fetch aligned quadwords of instruction stream (two instructions), and many will waste an instruction-issue cycle on a branch to an odd longword. High-end implementations may eventually fetch aligned octawords, and waste up to 3 issue cycles on a branch to an odd longword. Some implementations may only be able to fetch wide chunks of instructions every other CPU cycle. Fetching four instructions from an aligned octaword can get at most one cache miss, while fetching them from an odd longword address can get 2 or even 3 cache misses.

Quadword I-fetch implementors should give first priority to executing aligned quadwords quickly. Octaword-fetch implementors should give first priority to executing aligned octawords quickly, and second priority to executing aligned quadwords quickly. Dual-issue implementations should give first priority to issuing both halves of an aligned quadword in one cycle, and second priority to buffering and issuing other combinations.

A.2.2 Multiple Instruction Issue — Factor of 3

Some Alpha implementations will issue multiple instructions in a single cycle. To improve the odds of multiple-issue, compilers should choose pairs of instructions to put in aligned quadwords. Pick one from column A and one from column B (but only a total of one load/store/branch per pair).

Column A	Column B
Integer Operate	Floating Operate
Floating Load/Store	Integer Load/Store
Floating Branch	Integer Branch
	BR/BSR/JSR

Implementors of multiple-issue machines should give first priority to dual-issuing at least the above pairs, and second priority to multiple-issue of other combinations.

In general, the above rules will give a good hardware-software match, but compilers may want to implement model-specific switches to generate code tuned more exactly to a specific implementation.

A.2.3 Branch Prediction and Minimizing Branch-Taken — Factor of 3

In many Alpha implementations, an unexpected change in I-stream address will result in about 10 lost instruction times. "Unexpected" may mean any branch-taken or may mean a mispredicted branch. In many implementations, even a correctly predicted branch to a quadword target address will be slower than straight-line code.

Compilers should follow these rules to minimize unexpected branches:

1. Implementations will predict all forward conditional branches as not-taken, and all backward conditional branches as taken. Based on execution profiles, compilers should physically rearrange code so that it has matching behavior.

2. Make basic blocks as big as possible. A good goal is 20 instructions on average between branch-taken. This means unrolling loops so that they contain at least 20 instructions, and putting subroutines of less than 20 instructions directly in line. It also means using execution profiles to rearrange code so that the frequent case of a conditional branch falls through. For very high-performance loops, it will be profitable to move instructions across conditional branches to fill otherwise wasted instruction issue slots, even if the instructions moved will not always do useful work. Note that the Conditional Move instructions can sometimes be used to avoid breaking up basic blocks.

3. In an if-then-else construct whose execution profile is skewed even slightly away from 50%-50% (51-49 is enough), put the infrequent case completely out of line, so that the frequent case encounters *zero* branch-takens, and the infrequent case encounters *two* branch-takens. If the infrequent case is rare (5%), put it far enough away that it never comes into the I-cache. If the infrequent case is extremely rare (error message code), put it on a page of rarely executed code and expect that page *never* to be paged in.

4. There are two functionally identical branch-format opcodes, BSR and BR.

Compilers should use the first one for subroutine calls, and the second for GOTOs. Some implementations may push a stack of predicted return addresses for BSR and not push the stack for BR. Failure to compile the correct opcode will result in mispredicted return addresses, and hence make subroutine returns slow.

5. The memory-format JSR instruction has 16 unused bits. These should be used by the compilers to communicate a hint about expected branch-target behavior (see *Common Architecture, Chapter 4*):

If the JSR is used for a computed GOTO or a CASE statement, compile bits <15:14> as 00, and bits <13:0> such that (updated PC+Instr<13:0>*4) <15:0> equals (likely_target_addr) <15:0>. In other words, pick the low 14 bits so that a normal PC+displacement*4 calculation will match the low 16 bits of the most likely target longword address. (Implementations will likely prefetch from the matching cache block.)

If the JSR is used for a computed subroutine call, compile bits <15:14> as 01, and bits <13:0> as above. Some implementations will prefetch the call target using the prediction and also push updated PC on a return-prediction stack.

If the JSR is used as a subroutine return, compile bits <15:14> as 10. Some implementations will pop an address off a return-prediction stack.

If the JSR is used as a coroutine linkage, compile bits <15:14> as 11. Some implementations will pop an address off a return-prediction stack and also push updated PC on the return-prediction stack.

Implementors should give first priority to executing straight-line code with no branch-takens as quickly as possible, second priority to predicting conditional branches based on the sign of the displacement field (backward taken, forward not-taken), and third priority to predicting subroutine return addresses by running a small prediction stack. (VAX traces show a stack of 2 to 4 entries correctly predicts most branches.)

A.2.4 Improving I-Stream Density — Factor of 3

Compilers should try to use profiles to make sure almost 100 percent of the bytes brought into an I-cache are actually executed. This means aligning branch targets and putting rarely executed code out of line. Doing so would consistently make an I-cache appear about two times larger, compared to current VAX practice.

The example below shows the bytes actually brought into a VAX cache (from part of an address trace of a DLINPAC). The dots represent bytes brought into the cache but never executed. They occupy about half of the cache.

Each line shows the use of an aligned 64-byte I-cache block. A portion of DLINPAC and a portion of OpenVMS 4.x are shown. Uppercase I is the first byte of an instruction, and lowercase i marks subsequent bytes. Period (.) shows a byte brought into the cache but never executed.

```
I-fetch   Byte 0                                                    Byte 63

--------  ----------------------------------------------------------------
000268C0  .......................IiiiIiiIiiIiiiiiiiiiIiii...............
00026900  ...........................................IiiiiIiiiiiiiiiii
00026940  IiIiiIiIiiIiIiiIiIiIiIiiiIiIiiIiIiiiiiiiiIiiIiii................
00026980  .........................................IiiiIiiIiiIiiIiiiIiIiiIii
000269C0  I.............IiiiiIiiIiiiiIiIiiiiIiiiITiIiIiiIiIiiiIiIiii.....
00026A00  ..........................IiIiiiiiiiiiiiIiIiiiIiii.........
00026A40  ............................IiiiiiiiiiIiiiiiiiiiIiIiiiIiiIii
00026A80  IiIiiiiiIiIiIiiiIiIiIiIiiiiiiiiiIiiIiiiIiii...............IiiIii
00026AC0  IiiIiii.........................................................

80004440  ...........................................IiiiIiIiii.........
80004680  ....IiiiiiIiii..................................................
80004900  ..............IiiIiiIiiIiiiiIiIiiIiiIiiIiiiIiIiiiiIiIiiiIiiiiI
80004940  IiiiiIiiiIiiIiIiii...........IiiiiIiii.........................
80004A00  ........................................................IiiiiIiiIiiiii
80004A40  IiIiiIiiiiIiiiIiiiIiiiIiiiIiii...........IiiiiiIIiiiiiIiiiiIiiIiiiiI
80004A80  IiiiiIiiiIiiIiiIiii....IiiIiiIiii...........................
80004F40  ...........................IiiiiiIiiiiiiiIiiiIiiiiiiiIiii.......
80004F80  ....................IiiiIiiiiiiiiIiiIiIiiiIiiiiiiiiiiiiiiiIiiiI
80004FC0  IIiiiiiIiiiiIiIiiiIiii....IiiiiIiIiii..........................
80008A40  ...................................................IiiiIiii
80008A80  IIiiIiiiIiiIiIiiiIiIiIiiiIiIiiIiiiIiIiiIiiiiiIiiIiiIiiIiiiiiiiiIiIiiiIiii.
```

A.2.5 Instruction Scheduling — Factor of 3

The performance of Alpha programs will be sensitive to how carefully the code is scheduled to minimize instruction-issue delays.

"Result latency" is defined as the number of CPU cycles that must elapse between an instruction that writes a result register and one that uses that register, if execution-time stalls are to be avoided. Thus, a latency of zero means that the instruction writes a result register and the instruction that uses that register can be multiple-issued in the *same* cycle. A latency of 2 means that if the writing instruction is issued at cycle N, the reading instruction can issue no earlier than cycle N+2. Latency is implementation-specific.

Most Alpha instructions have a non-zero result latency. Compilers should schedule code so that a result is not used too soon, at least in frequently executed code (inner loops, as identified by execution profiles). In general, this will require loop unrolling and short procedure inlining.

"Too soon" is currently ill-defined, since no implementations have been designed yet. For starters, assume that implementations can dual-issue instructions. Assume that Load and JSR instructions have a latency of 3, shifts and byte manipulation a latency of 2, integer multiply a latency of 10, and other integer operates a latency of 1. Assume floating multiply has a latency of 5, floating divide a latency of 10, and other floating operates a latency of 4. Scheduling to these latencies will give at least reasonable performance on currently anticipated implementations.

Compilers should try to schedule code to match the above latency rules and also to match the multiple-issue rules. If doing both is impractical for a particular sequence of code, the latency rules are more important (since they apply even in single-issue implementations).

Implementors should give first priority to minimizing the latency of back-to-back integer operations, of address calculations immediately followed by load/store, of load immediately followed by branch, and of compare immediately followed by branch. Second priority should be given to minimizing latencies in general.

A.3 Data-Stream Considerations

The following sections describe considerations for the data stream.

A.3.1 Data Alignment — Factor of 10

Data PSECTs should be at least octaword-aligned, so that aggregates (arrays, some records, subroutine stack frames) can be allocated on aligned octaword boundaries to take advantage of any implementations with aligned octaword data paths, and to decrease the number of cache fills in almost all implementations.

Aggregates (arrays, records, common blocks, and so forth) should be allocated on at least aligned octaword boundaries whenever language rules allow this. In some implementations, a series of writes that completely fill a cache block may be a factor of 10 faster than a series of writes that partially fill a cache block, when that cache block would give a read miss. This is true of writeback caches that read a partially filled cache block from memory, but optimize away the read for completely filled blocks.

For such implementations, long strings of sequential writes will be faster if they start on a cache-block boundary (a multiple of 128 bytes will do well for most, if not all, Alpha implementations). This applies to array results that sweep through large portions of memory, and also to register-save areas for context switching, graphics frame buffer accesses, and other places where exactly 8, 16, 32, or more quadwords are stored sequentially. Allocating the targets at multiples of 8, 16, 32, or more quadwords, respectively, and doing the writes in order of increasing address will maximize the write speed.

Items within aggregates that are forced to be unaligned (records, common blocks) should generate compile-time warning messages and inline byte extract/insert code.

Users must be educated that the warning message means that they are taking a factor of 30 performance hit.

Compilers should consider supplying a switch that allows the compiler to pad aggregates to avoid unaligned data.

Compiled code for parameters should assume that the parameters are aligned. Unaligned actuals will therefore cause runtime alignment traps and very slow fixups. The fixup routine, if invoked, should generate warning messages to the user, preferably giving the first few statement numbers that are doing unaligned parameter access, and at the end of a run the total number of alignment traps (and perhaps an estimate of the performance improvement if the data were aligned). Again, users must be educated that the trap routine warning message means they are taking a factor of 30 performance hit.

Frequently used scalars should reside in registers. Each scalar datum allocated in memory should normally be allocated an aligned quadword to itself, even if the datum is only a byte wide. This allows aligned quadword loads and stores and avoids partial-quadword writes (which may be half as fast as full-quadword writes, due to such factors as read-modify-write a quadword to do quadword ECC calculation).

Implementors should give first priority to fast reads of aligned octawords and second priority to fast writes of full cache blocks. Partial-quadword writes need not have a fast repetition rate.

A.3.2 Shared Data in Multiple Processors — Factor of 3

Software locks are aligned quadwords and should be allocated to large cache blocks that either contain no other data, or read-mostly data whose usage is correlated with the lock.

Whenever there is high contention for a lock, one processor will have the lock and be using the guarded data, while other processors will be in a read-only spin loop on the lock bit. Under these circumstances, *any* write to the cache block containing the lock will likely cause excess bus traffic and cache fills, thus having a performance impact on all processors that are involved, and the buses between them. In some decomposed FORTRAN programs, refills of the cache blocks containing one or two frequently used locks can account for a third of all the bus bandwidth the program consumes.

Whenever there is almost no contention for a lock, one processor will have the lock and be using the guarded data. Under these circumstances, it might be desirable to keep the guarded data in the *same* cache block as the lock.

For the high sharing case, compilers should assume that *almost all* accesses to shared data result in cache misses all the way back to main memory, for each distinct cache block used. Such accesses will likely be a factor of 30 slower than cache hits. It is helpful to pack correlated shared data into a small number of cache blocks. It is helpful also to segregate blocks written by one processor from blocks read by others.

Therefore, accesses to shared data, including locks, should be minimized. For example, a 4-processor decomposition of some manipulation of a 1000-row array should avoid accessing lock variables every row, but instead might access a lock variable every 250 rows.

Array manipulation should be partitioned across processors so that cache blocks do not thrash between processors. Having each of 4 processors work on every fourth array element severely impairs performance on any implementation with a cache block of 4 elements or larger. The processors all contend for copies of the *same* cache blocks and use only 1/4 of the data in each block. Writes in one processor severely impair cache performance on all processors.

A better decomposition is to give each processor the largest possible contiguous chunk of data to work on (N/4 consecutive rows for 4 processors and row-major array storage; N/4 columns for column-major storage). With the possible exception of 3 cache blocks at the partition boundaries, this decomposition will result in each processor caching data that is touched by *no* other processor.

Operating-system scheduling algorithms should attempt to minimize process migration from one processor to another. Any time migration occurs, there are likely to be a large number of cache misses on the new processor.

Similarly, operating-system scheduling algorithms should attempt to enforce some affinity between a given device's interrupts and the processor on which the interrupt-handler runs. I/O control data structures and locks for different devices should be disjoint. Doing both of these allows higher cache hit rates on the corresponding I/O control data structures.

Implementors should give first priority to an efficient (low-bandwidth) way of transferring isolated lock values and other isolated, shared write data between processors.

Implementors should assume that the amount of shared data will continue to increase, so over time the need for efficient sharing implementations will also increase.

A.3.3 Avoiding Cache/TB Conflicts — Factor of 1

Occasionally, programs that run with a direct-mapped cache or TB will thrash, taking excessive cache or TB misses. With some work, thrashing can be minimized at compile time.

In a frequently executed loop, compilers could allocate the data items accessed from memory so that, on each loop iteration, all of the memory addresses accessed are either in *exactly the same* aligned 64-byte block, or differ in bits VA<10:6>. For loops that go through arrays in a common direction with a common stride, this means allocating the arrays, checking that the first-iteration addresses differ, and if not, inserting up to 64 bytes of padding *between* the arrays. This rule will avoid thrashing in small direct-mapped data caches with block sizes up to 64 bytes and total sizes of 2K bytes or more.

Example:

```
      REAL*4 A(1000),B(1000)
      DO 60 i=1,1000
  60 A(i) = f(B(i))
```

BAD allocation (A and B thrash in 8 KB direct-mapped cache):

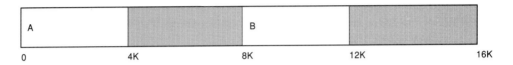

BETTER allocation (A and B offset by 64 mod 2 KB, so 16 elements of A and 16 of B can be in cache simultaneously):

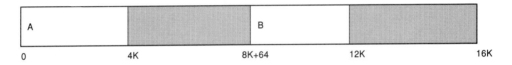

BEST allocation (A and B offset by 64 mod 2 KB, so 16 elements of A and 16 of B can be in cache simultaneously, *and* both arrays fit entirely in 8 KB or bigger cache):

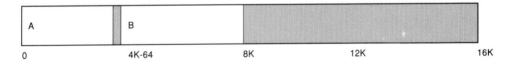

In a frequently executed loop, compilers could allocate the data items accessed from memory so that, on each loop iteration, all of the memory addresses accessed are either in *exactly the same 8 KB* page, or differ in bits VA<17:13>. For loops that go through arrays in a common direction with a common stride, this means allocating the arrays, checking that the first-iteration addresses differ, and if not, inserting up to 8K bytes of padding *between* the arrays. This rule will avoid thrashing in direct-mapped TBs and in some large direct-mapped data caches, with total sizes of 32 pages (256 KB) or more.

Usually, this padding will mean *zero* extra bytes in the executable image, just a skip in virtual address space to the next-higher page boundary.

For large caches, the rule above should be applied to the I-stream, in addition to all the D-stream references. Some implementations will have combined I-stream /D-stream large caches.

Both of the rules above can be satisfied simultaneously, thus often eliminating thrashing in all anticipated direct-mapped cache/TB implementations.

A.3.4 Sequential Read/Write — Factor of 1

All other things being equal, sequences of consecutive reads or writes should use ascending (rather than descending) memory addresses. Where possible, the memory address for a block of 2**Kbytes should be on a 2**K boundary, since this minimizes the number of different cache blocks used and minimizes the number of partially written cache blocks.

To avoid overrunning memory bandwidth, sequences of more than eight quadword Loads or Stores should be broken up with intervening instructions (if there is any useful work to be done).

For consecutive reads, implementors should give first priority to prefetching ascending cache blocks, and second priority to absorbing up to eight consecutive quadword Loads (aligned on a 64-byte boundary) without stalling.

For consecutive writes, implementors should give first priority to avoiding read overhead for fully written aligned cache blocks, and second priority to absorbing up to eight consecutive quadword Stores (aligned on a 64-byte boundary) without stalling.

A.3.5 Prefetching — Factor of 3

To use FETCH and FETCH_M effectively, software should follow this programming model:

1. Assume that at most two FETCH instructions can be outstanding at once, and that there are two prefetch address registers, PREa and PREb, to hold prefetching state. FETCH instructions alternate between loading PREa and PREb. Each FETCH instruction overwrites any previous prefetching state, thus terminating any previous prefetch that is still in progress in the register that is loaded. The order of fetching within a block and the order between PREa and PREb are UNPREDICTABLE.

> **IMPLEMENTATION NOTE**
> Implementations are encouraged to alternate at convenient intervals between PREa and PREb.

2. Assume, for maximum efficiency, that there should be about 64 unrelated memory access instructions (load or store) between a FETCH and the first actual data access to the prefetched data.

3. Assume, for instruction-scheduling purposes in a multilevel cache hierarchy, that FETCH does not prefetch data to the innermost cache level, but rather one level out. Schedule loads to bury the last level of misses.

4. Assume that FETCH is worthwhile if, on average, at least half the data in a block will be accessed. Assume that FETCH_M is worthwhile if, on average, at least half the data in a block will be modified.

5. Treat FETCH as a vector load. If a piece of code could usefully prefetch 4 operands, launch the first two prefetches, do about 128 memory references

worth of work, then launch the next two prefetches, do about 128 more memory references worth of work, then start using the 4 sets of prefetched data.

6. Treat FETCH as having the same effect on a cache as a series of 64 quadword loads. If the loads would displace useful data, so will FETCH. If two sets of loads from specific addresses will thrash in a direct-mapped cache, so will two FETCH instructions using the same pair of addresses.

IMPLEMENTATION NOTE
Hardware implementations are expected to provide either no support for FETCHx or support that closely matches this model.

A.4 Code Sequences

The following section describes code sequences.

A.4.1 Aligned Byte/Word Memory Accesses

The instruction sequences given in *Common Architecture, Chapter 4* for byte and word accesses are worst-case code. In the common case of accessing a byte or aligned word field at a known offset from a pointer that is expected to be at least longword aligned, the common-case code is much shorter.

"Expected" means that the code should run fast for a longword-aligned pointer and trap for unaligned. The trap handler may at its option fix up the unaligned reference.

For access at a known offset D from a longword-aligned pointer Rx, let D.lw be D rounded down to a multiple of 4 ((D div 4)*4), and let D.mod be D mod 4.

In the common case, the intended sequence for loading and zero-extending an aligned word is:

```
LDL     R1,D.lw(Rx)     ! Traps if unaligned
EXTWL   R1,#D.mod,R1    ! Picks up word at byte 0 or byte 2
```

In the common case, the intended sequence for loading and sign-extending an aligned word is:

```
LDL     R1,D.lw(Rx)       ! Traps if unaligned
SLL     R1,#48-8*D.mod,R1 ! Aligns word at high end of R1
SRA     R1,#48,R1         ! SEXT to low end of R1
```

NOTE
The shifts often can be combined with shifts that might surround subsequent arithmetic operations (for example, to produce word overflow from the high end of a register).

In the common case, the intended sequence for loading and zero-extending a byte is:

```
LDL     R1,D.lw(Rx)     !
EXTBL   R1,#D.mod,R1    !
```

In the common case, the intended sequence for loading and sign-extending a byte is:

```
LDL     R1,D.lw(Rx)          !
SLL     R1,#56-8*D.mod,R1 !
SRA     R1,#56,R1            !
```

In the common case, the intended sequence for storing an aligned word R5 is:

```
LDL     R1,D.lw(Rx)       !
INSWL   R5,#D.mod,R3      !
MSKWL   R1,#D.mod,R1      !
BIS     R3,R1,R1          !
STL     R1,D.lw(Rx)       !
```

In the common case, the intended sequence for storing a byte R5 is:

```
LDL     R1,D.lw(Rx)       !
INSBL   R5,#D.mod,R3      !
MSKBL   R1,#D.mod,R1      !
BIS     R3,R1,R1          !
STL     R1,D.lw(Rx)       !
```

A.4.2 Division

In all implementations, floating-point division is likely to have a substantially longer result latency than floating-point multiply; in addition, in many implementations multiplies will be pipelined and divides will not.

Thus, any division by a constant power of two should be compiled as a multiply by the exact reciprocal, if it is representable without overflow or underflow. If language rules or surrounding context allow, other divisions by constants can be closely approximated via multiplication by the reciprocal.

Integer division does not exist as a hardware opcode. Division by a constant can always be done via UMULH of another appropriate constant, followed by a right shift. General quadword division by true variables can be done via a subroutine. The subroutine could test for small divisors (less than about 1000 in absolute value) and for those, do a table lookup on the exact constant and shift count for an UMULH /shift sequence. For the remaining cases, a table lookup on about a 1000-entry table and a multiply can give a linear approximation to 1/divisor that is accurate to 16 bits. Using this approximation, a multiply and a back-multiply and a subtract can generate one 16-bit quotient "digit" plus a 48-bit new partial dividend. Three more such steps can generate the full quotient. Having prior knowledge of the possible sizes of the divisor and dividend, normalizing away leading bytes of zeros, and performing an early-out test can reduce the average number of multiplies to about 5 (compared to a best case of 1 and a worst case of 9).

A.4.3 Stylized Code Forms

Using the same stylized code form for a common operation makes compiler output a little more readable and makes it more likely that an implementation will speed up the stylized form.

A.4.3.1 NOP

The standard NOP forms are:

```
NOP             ==      BIS     R31,R31,R31
FNOP            ==      CPYS    F31,F31,F31
```

These generate no exceptions. In most implementations, they should encounter no operand issue delays, no destination issue delay, and no functional unit issue delay. Implementations are free to optimize these into no action and zero execution cycles.

A.4.3.2 Clear a Register

The standard clear register forms are:

```
CLR             ==      BIS     R31,R31,Rx
FCLR            ==      CPYS    F31,F31,Fx
```

These generate no exceptions. In most implementations, they should encounter no operand issue delays, and no functional unit issue delay.

A.4.3.3 Load Literal

The standard load integer literal (ZEXT 8-bit) form is:

```
MOV #lit8,Ry     ==     BIS R31, lit8, Ry
```

The Alpha literal construct in Operate instructions creates a canonical longword constant for values 0..255.

A longword constant stored in an Alpha 64-bit register is in canonical form when bits <63:32>=bit <31>.

A canonical 32-bit literal can usually be generated with one or two instructions, but sometimes three instructions are needed. Use the following procedure to determine the offset fields of the instructions:

```
val  = <sign-extended, 32-bit value>

low  = val<15:0>
tmp1 = val - SEXT(low)  ! Account for LDA instruction

high = tmp1<31:16>
tmp2 = tmp1 - SHIFT_LEFT( SEXT(high,16) )

if tmp2 NE 0 then
    ! original val was in range 7FFF8000₁₆..7FFFFFFF₁₆
            extra = 4000₁₆
            tmp1 = tmp1 - 40000000₁₆
            high = tmp1<31:16>
else
    extra = 0
endif
```

The general sequence is:

```
LDA  Rdst, low(R31)
LDAH Rdst, extra(Rdst)   ! Omit if extra=0
LDAH Rdst, high(Rdst)    ! Omit if high=0
```

A.4.3.4 Register-to-Register Move

The standard register move forms are:

```
MOV RX,RY  ==  BIS   RX,RX,RY
FMOV FX,FY ==  CPYS  FX,FX,FY
```

These generate no exceptions. In most implementations, these should encounter no functional unit issue delay.

A.4.3.5 Negate

The standard register negate forms are:

```
NEGz Rx,Ry   ==   SUBz   R31,Rx,Ry   ! z = L or Q
NEGz Fx,Fy   ==   SUBz   F31,Fx,Fy   ! z = F G S or T
FNEGz Fx,Fy  ==   CPYSN  Fx,Fx,Fy    ! z = F G S or T
```

The integer subtract generates no Integer Overflow trap if Rx contains the largest negative number (SUBz/V would trap). The floating subtract generates a floating-point exception for a non-finite value in Fx. The CPYSN form generates no exceptions.

A.4.3.6 NOT

The standard integer register NOT form is:

```
NOT Rx,Ry    ==    ORNOT   R31,Rx,Ry
```

This generates no exceptions. In most implementations, this should encounter no functional unit issue delay.

A.4.3.7 Booleans

The standard alternative to BIS is:

```
OR Rx,Ry,Rz    ==    BIS    Rx,Ry,Rz
```

The standard alternative to BIC is:

```
ANDNOT Rx,Ry,Rz ==   BIC    Rx,Ry,Rz
```

The standard alternative to EQV is:

```
XORNOT Rx,Ry,Rz ==   EQV    Rx,Ry,Rz
```

A.4.4 Trap Barrier

The TRAPB instruction guarantees that following instructions do not issue until all possible preceding traps have been signaled. This does not mean that all preceding instructions have necessarily run to completion (for example, a Load instruction may have passed all the fault checks but not yet delivered data from a cache miss).

A.4.5 Pseudo-Operations (Stylized Code Forms)

This section summarizes the pseudo-operations for the Alpha architecture that may be used by various software components in an Alpha system. Most of these forms are discussed in preceding sections.

In the context of this section, pseudo-operations all represent a single underlying machine instruction. Each pseudo-operation represents a particular instruction with either replicated fields (such as FMOV), or hard-coded zero fields. Since the pattern is distinct, these pseudo-operations can be decoded by instruction decode mechanisms.

In Table A–1, the pseudo-operation codes can be viewed as macros with parameters. The formal form is listed in the left column, and the expansion in the code stream listed in the right column.

Some instruction mnemonics have synonyms. These are different from pseudo-operations in that each synonym represents the same underlying instruction with no special encoding of operand fields. As a result, synonyms cannot be distinguished from each other. They are not listed in the table that follows. Examples of synonyms are: BIC/ANDNOT, BIS/OR, and EQV/XORNOT.

Table A–1: Decodable Pseudo-Operations (Stylized Code Forms)

Pseudo-Operation in Listing		Actual Instruction Encoding	
No-exception generic floating absolute value:			
FABS	Fx, Fy	CPYS	F31, Fx, Fy
Branch to target (21-bit signed displacement):			
BR	target	BR	R31, target
Clear integer register:			
CLR	Rx	BIS	R31, R31, Rx
Clear a floating-point register:			
FCLR	Fx	CPYS	F31, F31, Fx
Floating-point move:			
FMOV	Fx, Fy	CPYS	Fx, Fx, Fy
No-exception generic floating negation:			
FNEG	Fx, Fy	CPYSN	Fx, Fx, Fy
Floating-point no-op:			
FNOP		CPYS	F31, F31, F31
Move Rx/8-bit zero-extended literal to Ry:			
MOV	{Rx/Lit8}, Ry	BIS	R31, {Rx/Lit8}, Ry
Move 16-bit sign-extended literal to Rx:			
MOV	Lit, Rx	LDA	Rx, lit(R31)

Table A–1 (Cont.): Decodable Pseudo-Operations (Stylized Code Forms)

Pseudo-Operation in Listing	Actual Instruction Encoding
Move to FPCR: MT_FPCR Fx	MT_FPCR Fx, Fx, Fx
Move from FPCR: MF_FPCR Fx	MF_FPCR Fx, Fx, Fx
Negate F_floating: NEGF Fx, Fy	SUBF F31, Fx, Fy
Negate F_floating, semi-precise: NEGF/S Fx, Fy	SUBF/S F31, Fx, Fy
Negate G_floating: NEGG Fx, Fy	SUBG F31, Fx, Fy
Negate G_floating, semi-precise: NEGG/S Fx, Fy	SUBG/S F31, Fx, Fy
Negate longword: NEGL {Rx/Lit8}, Ry	SUBL R31, {Rx/Lit}, Ry
Negate longword with overflow detection: NEGL/V {Rx/Lit8}, Ry	SUBL/V R31, {Rx/Lit}, Ry
Negate quadword: NEGQ {Rx/Lit8}, Ry	SUBQ R31, {Rx/Lit}, Ry
Negate quadword with overflow detection: NEGQ/V {Rx/Lit8}, Ry	SUBQ/V R31, {Rx/Lit}, Ry
Negate S_floating: NEGS Fx, Fy	SUBS F31, Fx, Fy
Negate S_floating, software with underflow detection: NEGS/SU Fx, Fy	SUBS/SU F31, Fx, Fy
Negate S_floating, software with underflow and inexact result detection: NEGS/SUI Fx, Fy	SUBS/SUI F31, Fx, Fy
Negate T_floating: NEGT Fx, Fy	SUBT F31, Fx, Fy

Table A–1 (Cont.): Decodable Pseudo-Operations (Stylized Code Forms)

Pseudo-Operation in Listing	Actual Instruction Encoding	
Negate T_floating, software with underflow detection: NEGT/SU Fx, Fy	SUBT/SU	F31, Fx, Fy
Negate T_floating, software with underflow and inexact result detection: NEGT/SUI	SUBT/SUI	F31, Fx, Fy
Integer no-op: NOP	BIS	R31, R31, R31
Logical NOT of Rx/8-bit zero-extended literal storing results in Ry: NOT {Rx/Lit8}, Ry	ORNOT	R31, {Rx/Lit}, Ry
Longword sign-extension of Rx storing results in Ry: SEXTL {Rx/Lit8}, Ry	ADDL	R31, {Rx/Lit}, Ry

A.5 Timing Considerations: Atomic Sequences

A sufficiently long instruction sequence between LDx_L and STx_C will never complete, because periodic timer interrupts will always occur before the sequence completes. The following rules describe sequences that will eventually complete in all Alpha implementations:

1. At most 40 operate or conditional-branch (not taken) instructions executed in the sequence between LDx_L and STx_C.

2. At most two I-stream TB-miss faults. Sequential instruction execution guarantees this.

3. No other exceptions triggered during the last execution of the sequence.

IMPLEMENTATION NOTE

On all expected implementations, this allows for about 50 μsec of execution time, even with 100 percent cache misses. This should satisfy any requirement for a 1 msec timer interrupt rate.

IEEE Floating-Point Conformance

A subset of IEEE Standard for Binary Floating-Point Arithmetic (754-1985) is provided in the Alpha floating-point instructions. This appendix describes how to construct a complete IEEE implementation.

The order of presentation parallels the order of the IEEE specification.

B.1 Alpha Choices for IEEE Options

Alpha supports IEEE single and double formats. Optional extended double is not supported.

Alpha hardware supports normal and chopped IEEE rounding modes. IEEE plus infinity and minus infinity rounding modes can be implemented in hardware or software.

Alpha hardware does not support optional IEEE software trap enable/disable modes; see the following discussion about software support.

Alpha hardware supports add, subtract, multiply, divide, convert between floating formats, convert between floating and integer formats, and compare. Software routines support square root, remainder, round to integer in floating-point format, and convert binary to/from decimal.

In the Alpha architecture, copying without change of format is not considered an operation. (LDx, CPYSx, and STx do not check for non-finite numbers; an operation would.) Compilers may generate ADDx F31,Fx,Fy to get the opposite effect.

Optional operations for differing formats are not provided.

The Alpha choice is that the accuracy provided will meet or exceed IEEE standard requirements. It is implementation-dependent whether the software binary/decimal conversions beyond 9 or 17 digits treat any excess digits as zeros.

Overflow and underflow, NaNs, and infinities encountered during software binary to decimal conversion return strings that specify the conditions. Such strings can be truncated to their shortest unambiguous length.

Alpha hardware supports comparisons of same-format numbers. Software supports comparisons of different-format numbers.

In the Alpha architecture, results are true-false in response to a predicate.

Alpha hardware supports the required six predicates and the optional unordered predicate. The other 19 optional predicates can be constructed from sequences of two comparisons and two branches.

Alpha hardware supports infinity arithmetic only by trapping when an infinity operand is encountered and when an infinity is to be created from finite operands by overflow or division by zero. A software trap handler (interposed between the hardware and the IEEE user) provides correct infinity arithmetic.

Alpha hardware supports NaNs only by trapping when a NaN operand is encountered and when a NaN is to be created. A software trap handler (interposed between the hardware and the IEEE user) provides correct Signaling and Quiet NaN behavior.

In the Alpha architecture, Quiet NaNs do not afford retrospective diagnostic information.

In the Alpha architecture, copying a Signaling NaN without a change of format does not signal an invalid exception (LDx, CPYSx, and STx do not check for non-finite numbers). Compilers may generate ADDx F31,Fx,Fy to get the opposite effect.

Alpha hardware fully supports negative zero operands, and follows the IEEE rules for creating negative zero results.

Alpha hardware does not supply IEEE exception trap behavior; the hardware traps are a superset of the IEEE-required conditions. A software trap handler (interposed between the hardware and the IEEE user) provides correct IEEE exception behavior.

In the Alpha architecture, tininess is detected by hardware after rounding, and loss of accuracy is detected by software as an inexact result.

In the Alpha architecture, user trap handlers will be supported by compilers and a software trap handler (interposed between the hardware and the IEEE user), as described in the next section.

B.2 Alpha Hardware Support of Software Exception Handlers

In Alpha instructions, hardware trap behavior is determined only at compile time; short of recompiling, there are no dynamic facilities for changing hardware trap behavior.

There is an essential disparity between the Alpha design goal of fast execution and the IEEE design goal of exact trap behavior. The Alpha hardware architecture provides means for users to choose various degrees of IEEE compliance, at appropriate performance cost.

Instructions compiled without the /Software modifier cannot produce IEEE-compliant trap behavior, nor can they provide IEEE-compliant non-finite arithmetic. Trapping and stopping on non-finite operands or results (rather than the IEEE default of continuing with NaNs propagated) is an Alpha value-added behavior that some users prefer.

Instructions compiled without the /Underflow hardware trap enable modifier cannot produce IEEE-compliant underflow trap behavior, nor can they provide IEEE-compliant denormal results. They are fast and provide true zero (not minus zero) results whenever underflow occurs. This is an Alpha value-added behavior that some users prefer.

Instructions compiled without the /Inexact hardware trap enable modifier cannot produce IEEE-compliant inexact trap behavior. Trapping on Inexact will be painfully slow; few users appear to prefer this, but they can get it if they really want it.

IEEE floating-point instructions compiled with the /Software modifier produce hardware traps and unpredictable values; a software trap handler may then produce all IEEE-required behavior.

IEEE floating-point instructions compiled with the /Underflow enable modifier produce hardware traps and true zero values for underflow; a software trap handler may then produce all IEEE-required behavior.

IEEE floating-point instructions compiled with the /Inexact enable modifier produce hardware traps that allow a software trap handler to produce all IEEE-required behavior.

Thus, to get full IEEE compliance of all the required features of the standard, users must compile with all three options enabled.

To get the optional full IEEE user trap handler behavior, a software trap handler must be provided that implements the five exception flags, dynamic user trap handler disabling, handler saving and restoring, default behavior for disabled user trap handlers, and linkages that allow a user handler to return a substitute result.

Also, users must insert a TRAPB in every basic block with a floating operation that can potentially trap, so that a software handler has an opportunity to scale the true result by 2**192 or 2**1536, as appropriate for enabled user trap handlers; and to supply the default +/− infinity, +/−MAX, +/−MIN, denormal, or zero as appropriate for disabled user trap handlers.

B.3 Mapping to IEEE Standard

There are five IEEE exceptions, each of which can be "IEEE software trap-enabled" or disabled (the default condition). Implementing the IEEE software trap-enabled mode is optional in the IEEE standard.

Our assumption, therefore, is that the only access to IEEE-specified software trap-enabled results will be generated in assembly language code. The following design allows this, but *only* if such assembly language code has TRAPB instructions after each floating-point instruction, and generates the IEEE-specified scaled result in a trap handler by emulating the instruction that was trapped by hardware overflow /underflow detection, using the original operands.

There is a set of detailed IEEE-specified result values, both for operations that are specified to raise IEEE traps and those that do not. This behavior is created on Alpha by four layers of hardware, PALcode, the operating-system trap handler, and the user IEEE trap handler, as shown in Figure B–1.

Figure B–1: IEEE Trap Handling Behavior

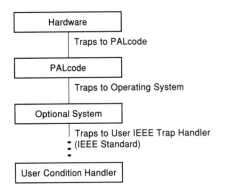

The IEEE-specified trap behavior occurs *only* with respect to the user IEEE trap handler (the last layer in Figure B–1); any trap-and-fixup behavior in the first three layers is outside the scope of the IEEE standard.

The IEEE number system is divided into finite and non-finite numbers:

- The finites are normal numbers:

  –MAX..–MIN, –0, 0, +MIN..+MAX

- The non-finites are:

  Denormals, +/– Infinity, Signaling NaN, Quiet NaN

Alpha hardware must treat minus zero operands and results as special cases, as required by the IEEE standard.

Table B–1 specifies, for the IEEE /Software modes, which layer does each piece of trap handling. See *Common Architecture, Chapter 4* for more detail on the hardware instruction descriptions.

Table B–1: IEEE Floating-Point Trap Handling

Alpha Instructions	Hardware	PAL	OS Trap Handler	User Software Handler
FBEQ FBNE FBLT FBLE FBGT FBGE	Bits Only—No Exceptions			
LDS LDT	Bits Only—No Exceptions			
STS STT	Bits Only—No Exceptions			
CPYS CPYSN	Bits Only—No Exceptions			
FCMOVx	Bits Only—No Exceptions			
ADDx SUBx INPUT Exceptions				
Denormal operand	Trap	Trap	Supply sum	–
+/-Inf operand	Trap	Trap	Supply sum	–
QNaN operand	Trap	Trap	Supply QNaN	–
SNaN operand	Trap	Trap	Supply QNaN	[Invalid Op]
+Inf + –Inf	Trap	Trap	Supply QNaN	[Invalid Op]
ADDx SUBx OUTPUT Exceptions				
Exponent overflow	Trap	Trap	Supply +/–Inf +/–MAX	[Overflow] Scale by 2**Alpha
Exponent underflow and disabled	Supply +0	–	–	–[1]
Exponent underflow and enabled	Supply +0 and trap	Trap	Supply +/–MIN denorm +/–0	[Underflow] Scale by 2**Alpha
Inexact and disabled in the instruction	–	–	–	–
Inexact and enabled in the instruction	Trap	Trap	–	[Inexact]

[1]An implementation could choose instead to trap to PALcode and have the PALcode supply a zero result on all underflows.

Table B–1 (Cont.): IEEE Floating-Point Trap Handling

Alpha Instructions	Hardware	PAL	OS Trap Handler	User Software Handler
MULx INPUT Exceptions				
Denormal operand	Trap	Trap	Supply prod.	–
+/-Inf operand	Trap	Trap	Supply prod.	–
QNaN operand	Trap	Trap	Supply QNaN	–
SNaN operand	Trap	Trap	Supply QNaN	[Invalid Op]
0 * Inf	Trap	Trap	Supply QNaN	[Invalid Op]
MULx OUTPUT Exceptions				
Exponent overflow	Trap	Trap	Supply +/–Inf +/–MAX	[Overflow] Scale by 2**Alpha
Exponent underflow and disabled	Supply +0	–	–	–
Exponent underflow and enabled	Supply +0 and Trap	Trap	Supply +/–MIN denorm +/–0	[Underflow] Scale by 2**Alpha
Inexact and disabled	–	–	–	–
Inexact and enabled	Trap	Trap	–	[Inexact]
DIVx INPUT Exceptions				
Denormal operand	Trap	Trap	Supply quot.	–
+/-Inf operand	Trap	Trap	Supply quot.	–
QNaN operand	Trap	Trap	Supply QNaN	–
SNaN operand	Trap	Trap	Supply QNaN	[Invalid Op]
0/0 or Inf/Inf	Trap	Trap	Supply QNaN	[Invalid Op]

Alpha Instructions	Hardware	PAL	OS Trap Handler	User Software Handler
DIVx INPUT Exceptions				
A/0	Trap	Trap	Supply +/-Inf	[Div. Zero]
DIVx OUTPUT Exceptions				
Exponent overflow	Trap	Trap	Supply +/-Inf +/-MAX	[Overflow] Scale by 2**Alpha
Exponent underflow and disabled	Supply +0	-	-	-
Exponent underflow and enabled	Supply +0 and trap	Trap	Supply +/-MIN denorm +/-0	[Underflow] Scale by 2**Alpha
Inexact and disabled	-	-	-	-
Inexact and enabled	Trap	Trap	-	[Inexact]
CMPTEQ CMPTUN INPUT Exceptions				
Denormal operand	Trap	Trap	Supply (=)	-
QNaN operand	Trap	Trap	Supply False for EQ, True for UN	-
SNaN operand	Trap	Trap	Supply False/ True	[Invalid Op]
CMPTLT CMPTLE INPUT Exceptions				
Denormal operand	Trap	Trap	Supply (=)	-
QNaN operand	Trap	Trap	Supply False	[Invalid Op]
SNaN operand	Trap	Trap	Supply False	[Invalid Op]

Table B–1 (Cont.): IEEE Floating-Point Trap Handling

Alpha Instructions	Hardware	PAL	OS Trap Handler	User Software Handler
CVTFi INPUT Exceptions				
Denormal operand	Trap	Trap	Supply Cvt	–
+/-Inf operand	Trap	Trap	Supply Cvt	[Invalid Op]
QNaN operand	Trap	Trap	Supply QNaN	–
SNaN operand	Trap	Trap	Supply QNaN	[Invalid Op]
CVTFi OUTPUT Exceptions				
Inexact and disabled	–	–	–	–
Inexact and enabled	Trap	Trap	–	[Inexact]
Integer overflow	Supply Trunc. result and trap if enabled	Trap	–	[Invalid Op][2]
CVTif OUTPUT Exceptions				
Inexact and disabled	–	–	–	–
Inexact and enabled	Trap	Trap	–	[Inexact]
CVTff INPUT Exceptions				
Denormal operand	Trap	Trap	Supply Cvt	–
+/-Inf operand	Trap	Trap	Supply Cvt	–
QNaN operand	Trap	Trap	Supply QNaN	–
SNaN operand	Trap	Trap	Supply QNaN	[Invalid Op]

---

[2]An implementation could choose instead to trap to PALcode on extreme values and have the PALcode supply a truncated result on all overflows.

Table B–1 (Cont.): IEEE Floating-Point Trap Handling

Alpha Instructions	Hardware	PAL	OS Trap Handler	User Software Handler
CVTff OUTPUT Exceptions				
Exponent overflow	Trap	Trap	Supply +/–Inf +/–MAX	[Overflow] Scale by 2**Alpha
Exponent underflow and disabled	Supply +0	–	–	–
Exponent underflow and enabled	Supply +0 and trap	Trap	Supply +/–MIN denorm +/–0	[Underflow] Scale by 2**Alpha
Inexact and disabled	–	–	–	–
Inexact and enabled	Trap	Trap	–	[Inexact]

Other IEEE operations (software subroutines or sequences of instructions), are listed here for completeness:

   Remainder
   SQRT
   Round float to integer-valued float
   Convert binary to/from decimal
   Compare, other combinations than the four above

Table B–2 shows the IEEE standard charts.

Table B–2: IEEE Standard Charts

Exception	IEEE Software TRAP Disabled (IEEE Default)	IEEE Software TRAP Enabled (Optional)
Invalid Operation		
(1) Input signaling NaN	Quiet NaN	
(2) Mag. subtract Inf.	Quiet NaN	
(3) 0 * Inf.	Quiet NaN	
(4) 0/0 or Inf/Inf	Quiet NaN	
(5) x REM 0 or Inf REM y	Quiet NaN	
(6) SQRT(negative non-zero)	Quiet NaN	
(7) Cvt to int(ovfl, Inf, NaN)	Quiet NaN	
(8) Compare unordered	Quiet NaN	
Division by Zero		
x/0, x finite <>0	+/–Inf	
Overflow		
Round nearest	+/–Inf.	Res/2**192 or 1536
Round to zero	+/–MAX	Res/2**192 or 1536
Round to –Inf	+MAX/–Inf	Res/2**192 or 1536
Round to +Inf	+Inf/–MAX	Res/2**192 or 1536
Underflow	0/denorm/+ –MIN	Res*2**192 or 1536
Inexact	Rounded/ovfl	Res

IEEE software trap handler requirements are as follows:

Result is unpredictable unless supplied by trap handler.
Determine which exceptions occurred.
Determine the kind of operation.
Determine the destination format.
Overflow/underflow/inexact: the correctly rounded result, including parts that do not fit in the format.
Invalid and divzero: the operand values.

Instruction Encodings

The encodings for the Alpha instruction set are given in the following sections. There is one section for each instruction format, followed by a summary of all the instruction opcodes in a single table.

C.1 Memory Format Instructions

Table C–1 lists the hexadecimal values of the 6-bit opcode field for the Memory format instructions.

Table C–1: Memory Format Instruction Opcodes

Mnemonic		Mnemonic		Mnemonic	
LDA	08	LDAH	09	LDF	20
LDG	21	LDL	28	LDL_L	2A
LDQ	29	LDQ_L	2B	LDQ_U	0B
LDS	22	LDT	23	STF	24
STG	25	STL	2C	STL_C	2E
STQ	2D	STQ_C	2F	STQ_U	0F
STS	26	STT	27		

Table C–2 lists the hexadecimal values of the 6-bit opcode field and the 16-bit displacement field for the Memory format instructions that use the displacement field as a function code. The notation used is oo.ffff, where *oo* is the 6-bit opcode and the *ffff* is the 16-bit displacement field.

Table C–2: Memory Format Instructions with a Function Code

Mnemonic		Mnemonic		Mnemonic	
FETCH	18.8000	FETCH_M	18.A000	MB	18.4000
RC	18.E000	RPCC	18.C000	RS	18.F000
TRAPB	18.0000				

PROGRAMMING NOTE
The code points 18.4400, 18.4800, and 18.4C00 must operate as Memory Barrier instructions (MB 18.4000). Software will currently only use the 18.4000 code point for MB. This allows a weaker memory barrier to be added.

Table C–3 lists the hexadecimal values of the high-order two bits of the displacement field for the Memory format branch instructions. The notation used is oo.h, where *oo* is the 6-bit opcode and the *h* is the high-order two bits of the displacement field.

Table C–3: Memory Format Branch Instruction Opcodes

Mnemonic		Mnemonic		Mnemonic	
JMP	1A.0	JSR	1A.1	JSR_COROUTINE	1A.3
RET	1A.2				

C.2 Branch Format Instructions

Table C–4 lists the hexadecimal values of the 6-bit opcode field for the Branch format instructions.

Table C–4: Branch Format instruction Opcodes

Mnemonic		Mnemonic		Mnemonic	
BR	30	FBEQ	31	FBLT	32
FBLE	33	BSR	34	FBNE	35
FBGE	36	FBGT	37	BLBC	38
BEQ	39	BLT	3A	BLE	3B
BLBS	3C	BNE	3D	BGE	3E
BGT	3F				

C.3 Operate Format Instructions

Table C–5 lists the hexadecimal values of the 6-bit opcode field and the 7-bit function code field for the Operate format instructions. The notation used is oo.ff, where *oo* is the 6-bit opcode and the *ff* is the 7-bit function code field.

Table C–5: Operate Format Instruction Opcodes and Function Codes

Mnemonic		Mnemonic		Mnemonic	
ADDL	10.00	ADDL/V	10.40	ADDQ	10.20
ADDQ/V	10.60	CMPBGE	10.0F	CMPEQ	10.2D
CMPLE	10.6D	CMPLT	10.4D	CMPULE	10.3D
CMPULT	10.1D	SUBL	10.09	SUBL/V	10.49
SUBQ	10.29	SUBQ/V	10.69		
S4ADDL	10.02	S4ADDQ	10.22	S4SUBL	10.0B
S4SUBQ	10.2B	S8ADDL	10.12	S8ADDQ	10.32
S8SUBL	10.1B	S8SUBQ	10.3B		
AND	11.00	BIC	11.08	BIS	11.20
CMOVEQ	11.24	CMOVLBC	11.16	CMOVLBS	11.14

Table C–5 (Cont.): Operate Format Instruction Opcodes and Function Codes

Mnemonic		Mnemonic		Mnemonic	
CMOVGE	11.46	CMOVGT	11.66	CMOVLE	11.64
CMOVLT	11.44	CMOVNE	11.26	EQV	11.48
ORNOT	11.28	XOR	11.40		
EXTBL	12.06	EXTLH	12.6A	EXTLL	12.26
EXTQH	12.7A	EXTQL	12.36	EXTWH	12.5A
EXTWL	12.16	INSBL	12.0B	INSLH	12.67
INSLL	12.2B	INSQH	12.77	INSQL	12.3B
INSWH	12.57	INSWL	12.1B	MSKBL	12.02
MSKLH	12.62	MSKLL	12.22	MSKQH	12.72
MSKQL	12.32	MSKWH	12.52	MSKWL	12.12
SLL	12.39	SRA	12.3C	SRL	12.34
ZAP	12.30	ZAPNOT	12.31		
MULL	13.00	MULL/V	13.40	MULQ	13.20
MULQ/V	13.60	UMULH	13.30		

C.4 Floating-Point Operate Format

Table C–6 lists the hexadecimal values of the 11-bit function code field for the Floating-point Operate format instructions that are data type independent. The 6-bit opcode for these instructions is 17_{16}.

Table C–6: Function Codes for Floating Data Type Independent Operations

Mnemonic		Mnemonic		Mnemonic	
CPYS	020	CPYSE	022	CPYSN	021
CVTLQ	010	CVTQL	030	CVTQL/SV	530
CVTQL/V	130				
FCMOVEQ	02A	FCMOVGE	02D	FCMOVGT	02F
FCMOVLE	02E	FCMOVLT	02C	FCMOVNE	02B
MF_FPCR	025	MT_FPCR	024		

C.4.1 IEEE Floating-Point Instructions

Table C–7 lists the hexadecimal value of the 11-bit function code field for the IEEE floating-point instructions, with and without qualifiers. The opcode for these instructions is 16_{16}.

Table C–7: IEEE Floating-Point Instruction Function Codes

	None	/C	/M	/D	/U	/UC	/UM	/UD
ADDS	080	000	040	0C0	180	100	140	1C0
ADDT	0A0	020	060	0E0	1A0	120	160	1E0
CMPTEQ	0A5							
CMPTLT	0A6							
CMPTLE	0A7							
CMPTUN	0A4							
CVTQS	0BC	03C	07C	0FC				
CVTQT	0BE	03E	07E	0FE				
CVTTS	0AC	02C	06C	0EC	1AC	12C	16C	1EC
DIVS	083	003	043	0C3	183	103	143	1C3
DIVT	0A3	023	063	0E3	1A3	123	163	1E3
MULS	082	002	042	0C2	182	102	142	1C2
MULT	0A2	022	062	0E2	1A2	122	162	1E2
SUBS	081	001	041	0C1	181	101	141	1C1
SUBT	0A1	021	061	0E1	1A1	121	161	1E1

	/SU	/SUC	/SUM	/SUD	/SUI	/SUIC	/SUIM	/SUID
ADDS	580	500	540	5C0	780	700	740	7C0
ADDT	5A0	520	560	5E0	7A0	720	760	7E0
CMPTEQ	5A5							
CMPTLT	5A6							
CMPTLE	5A7							
CMPTUN	5A4							
CVTQS					7BC	73C	77C	7FC
CVTQT					7BE	73E	77E	7FE
CVTTS	5AC	52C	56C	5EC	7AC	72C	76C	7EC
DIVS	583	503	543	5C3	783	703	743	7C3
DIVT	5A3	523	563	5E3	7A3	723	763	7E3
MULS	582	502	542	5C2	782	702	742	7C2
MULT	5A2	522	562	5E2	7A2	722	762	7E2
SUBS	581	501	541	5C1	781	701	741	7C1
SUBT	5A1	521	561	5E1	7A1	721	761	7E1

	None	/C	/V	/VC	/SV	/SVC	/SVI	/SVIC
CVTTQ	0AF	02F	1AF	12F	5AF	52F	7AF	72F

Table C–7 (Cont.): IEEE Floating-Point Instruction Function Codes

	D	/VD	/SVD	/SVID	/M	/VM	/SVM	/SVIM
CVTTQ	0EF	1EF	5EF	7EF	06F	16F	56F	76F

PROGRAMMING NOTE

Since underflow cannot occur for CMPTxx, there is no difference in function or performance between CMPTxx /S and CMPTxx/SU. It is intended that software generate CMPTxx/SU in place of CMPTxx/S.

C.4.2 VAX Floating-Point Instructions

Table C–8 lists the hexadecimal value of the 11-bit function code field for the VAX floating-point instructions. The opcode for these instructions is 15_{16}.

Table C–8: VAX Floating-Point Instruction Function Codes

	None	/C	/U	/UC	/S	/SC	/SU	/SUC
ADDF	080	000	180	100	480	400	580	500
CVTDG	09E	01E	19E	11E	49E	41E	59E	51E
ADDG	0A0	020	1A0	120	4A0	420	5A0	520
CMPGEQ	0A5				4A5			
CMPGLT	0A6				4A6			
CMPGLE	0A7				4A7			
CVTGF	0AC	02C	1AC	12C	4AC	42C	5AC	52C
CVTGD	0AD	02D	1AD	12D	4AD	42D	5AD	52D
CVTQF	0BC	03C						
CVTQG	0BE	03E						
DIVF	083	003	183	103	483	403	583	503
DIVG	0A3	023	1A3	123	4A3	423	5A3	523
MULF	082	002	182	102	482	402	582	502
MULG	0A2	022	1A2	122	4A2	422	5A2	522
SUBF	081	001	181	101	481	401	581	501
SUBG	0A1	021	1A1	121	4A1	421	5A1	521

	None	/C	/V	/VC	/S	/SC	/SV	/SVC
CVTGQ	0AF	02F	1AF	12F	4AF	42F	5AF	52F

C.5 Opcode Summary

Table C–9 lists all Alpha opcodes from 00 (CALL_PALL) through 3F (BGT). In the table, the column headings appearing over the instructions have a granularity of 8_{16}. The rows beneath the leftmost column supply the individual hex number to resolve that granularity.

If an instruction column has a 0 in the right (low) hex digit, replace that 0 with the number to the left of the backslash in the leftmost column on the instruction's row. If an instruction column has an 8 in the right (low) hexadecimal digit, replace that 8 with the number to the right of the backslash in the leftmost column.

For example, the third row (2/A) under the 10_{16} column contains the symbol INTS*, representing the all integer subtract instructions. The opcode for those instructions would then be 12_{16} because the 0 in 10 is replaced by the 2 in the leftmost column. Likewise, the third row under the 18_{16} column contains the symbol JSR*, representing all jump instructions. The opcode for those instructions is 1A because the 8 in the heading is replaced by the number to the right of the backslash in the leftmost column.

The instruction format is listed under the instruction symbol.

The symbols in Table C–9 are explained in Table C–10.

Table C–9: Opcode Summary

	00	08	10	18	20	28	30	38
0/8	PAL* (pal)	LDA (mem)	INTA* (op)	MISC* (mem)	LDF (mem)	LDL (mem)	BR (br)	BLBC (br)
1/9	Res	LDAH (mem)	INTL* (op)	\PAL\	LDG (mem)	LDQ (mem)	FBEQ (br)	BEQ (br)
2/A	Res	Res	INTS* (op)	JSR* (mem)	LDS (mem)	LDL_L (mem)	FBLT (br)	BLT (br)
3/B	Res	LDQ_U (mem)	INTM* (op)	\PAL\	LDT (mem)	LDQ_L (mem)	FBLE (br)	BLE (br)
4/C	Res	Res	Res	Res	STF (mem)	STL (mem)	BSR (br)	BLBS (br)
5/D	Res	Res	FLTV* (op)	\PAL\	STG (mem)	STQ (mem)	FBNE (br)	BNE (br)
6/E	Res	Res	FLTI* (op)	\PAL\	STS (mem)	STL_C (mem)	FBGE (br)	BGE (br)
7/F	Res	STQ_U (mem)	FLTL* (op)	\PAL\	STT (mem)	STQ_C (mem)	FBGT (br)	BGT (br)

Table C–10: Key to Opcode Summary (Table C–9)

Symbol	Meaning
FLTI*	IEEE floating-point instruction opcodes
FLTL*	Floating-point Operate instruction opcodes
FLTV*	VAX floating-point instruction opcodes
INTA*	Integer arithmetic instruction opcodes
INTL*	Integer logical instruction opcodes
INTM*	Integer multiply instruction opcodes
INTS*	Integer subtract instruction opcodes
JSR*	Jump instruction opcodes
MISC*	Miscellaneous instruction opcodes
PAL*	PALcode instruction (CALL_PAL) opcodes
\PAL\	Reserved for PALcode
Res	Reserved for Digital

C.6 OpenVMS PALcode Format Instructions

Sections C.6.1 and C.6.2 list the OpenVMS Alpha unprivileged and privileged PALcode function codes.

C.6.1 Unprivileged OpenVMS PALcode Function Codes

Table C–11 lists the hexadecimal values of the 26-bit function code field for the unprivileged OpenVMS PALcode format instructions. The 6-bit opcode for the PALcode instructions is zero.

Table C–11:   Unprivileged OpenVMS PALcode Function codes

Mnemonic		Mnemonic		Mnemonic	
AMOVRM	00A1	AMOVRR	00A0	BPT	0080
BUGCHK	0081	CHME	0082	CHMK	0083
CHMS	0084	CHMU	0085	GENTRAP	00AA
IMB	0086	INSQHIL	0087	INSQHILR	00A2
INSQHIQ	0089	INSQHIQR	00A4	INSQTIL	0088
INSQTILR	00A3	INSQTIQ	008A	INSQTIQR	00A5
INSQUEL	008B	INSQUEL/D	008D	INSQUEQ	008C
INSQUEQ/D	008E	PROBER	008F	PROBEW	0090
RD_PS	0091	READ_UNQ	009E	REI	0092
REMQHIL	0093	REMQHILR	00A6	REMQHIQ	0095
REMQHIQR	00A8	REMQTIL	0094	REMQTILR	00A7
REMQTIQ	0096	REMQTIQR	00A9	REMQUEL	0097
REMQUEL/D	0099	REMQUEQ	0098	REMQUEQ/D	009A
RSCC	009D	SWASTEN	009B	WRITE_UNQ	009F
WR_PS_SW	009C				

C.6.2 Privileged OpenVMS PALcode Function Codes

Table C–12 lists the hexadecimal values of the 26-bit function code field for the privileged OpenVMS PALcode format instructions. The 6-bit opcode for the PALcode instructions is zero.

Table C–12:   Privileged OpenVMS PALcode Function Codes

Mnemonic		Mnemonic		Mnemonic	
CFLUSH	0001	DRAINA	0002	HALT	0000
LDQP	0003				
MFPR_ASN	0006	MFPR_ASTEN	0026	MFPR_ASTSR	0027
MFPR_ESP	001E	MFPR_FEN	000B	MFPR_IPL	000E
MFPR_MCES	0010	MFPR_PCBB	0012	MFPR_PRBR	0013
MFPR_PTBR	0015	MFPR_SCBB	0016	MFPR_SISR	0019
MFPR_SSP	0020	MFPR_TBCHK	001A	MFPR_USP	0022
MFPR_VPTB	0029	MFPR_WHAMI	003F		

Table C–12 (Cont.): Privileged OpenVMS PALcode Function Codes

Mnemonic		Mnemonic		Mnemonic	
MTPR_ASTEN	0007	MTPR_ASTSR	0008	MTPR_DATFX	002E
MTPR_ESP	001F	MTPR_FEN	000C	MTPR_IPIR	000D
MTPR_IPL	000F	MTPR_MCES	0011	MTPR_PERFMON	002B
MTPR_PRBR	0014	MTPR_SCBB	0017	MTPR_SIRR	0018
MTPR_SSP	0021	MTPR_TBIA	001B	MTPR_TBIAP	001C
MTPR_TBIS	001D	MTPR_TBISD	0024	MTPR_TBISI	0025
MTPR_USP	0023	MTPR_VPTB	002A		
STQP	0004	SWPCTX	0005	unused	0009
unused	000A				

C.7 Unprivileged OSF/1 PALcode Function Codes

Table C–13 lists lists the hexadecimal values of the 26-bit function code field for the unprivileged OSF/1 PALcode instructions. The 6-bit opcode for the PALcode instructions is zero.

Table C–13: Unprivileged OSF/1 PALcode Function Codes

Mnemonic		Mnemonic		Mnemonic	
bpt	0080	bugchk	0081	callsys	0083
gentrap	00AA	imb	0086	rdunique	009E
wrunique	009F				

C.8 Privileged OSF/1 PALcode function codes

Table C–14 lists lists the hexadecimal values of the 26-bit function code field for the unprivileged OSF/1 PALcode instructions. The 6-bit opcode for the PALcode instructions is zero.

Table C–14: Privileged OSF/1 PALcode Function Codes

Mnemonic		Mnemonic		Mnemonic	
halt	0000	rdps	0036	rdusp	003A
rdval	0032	retsys	003D	rti	003F
swpctx	0030	swpipl	0035	tbi	0033
whami	003C	wrent	0034	wrfen	002B
wrkgp	0037	wrusp	0038	wrval	0031
wrvptptr	002D				

C.9 Required PALcode Function Codes

The opcodes listed in Table C–15 are required for all Alpha implementations. The notation used is oo.ffff, where *oo* is the hexadecimal 6-bit opcode and *ffff* is the hexadecimal 26-bit function code.

Table C–15:   Required PALcode Function Codes

Mnemonic	Type	Function Code
DRAINA	Privileged	00.0002
HALT	Privileged	00.0000
IMB	Unprivileged	00.0086

C.10 Opcodes Reserved to PALcode

The opcodes listed in Table C–16 are reserved for use in implementing PALcode.

Table C–16:   Opcodes Reserved for PALcode

Mnemonic		Mnemonic		Mnemonic	
PAL19	19	PAL1B	1B	PAL1D	1D
PAL1E	1E	PAL1F	1F		

C.11 Opcodes Reserved to Digital

The opcodes listed in Table C–17 are reserved to Digital.

Table C–17:   Opcodes Reserved for Digital

Mnemonic		Mnemonic		Mnemonic	
OPC01	01	OPC02	02	OPC03	03
OPC04	04	OPC05	05	OPC06	06
OPC07	07	OPC0A	0A	OPC0C	0C
OPC0D	0D	OPC0E	0E	OPC14	14
OPC1C	1C				

A

Aborts, forcing, *(I)*, 6–5
Absolute longword queue, *(II)*, 2–21
Absolute quadword queue, *(II)*, 2–25
Access control violation (ACV) fault, *(II)*, 6–10
  has precedence, *(II)*, 3–13
  memory protection, *(II)*, 3–8
  service routine entry point, *(II)*, 6–26
Access-violation fault, *(III)*, 3–10
ADDF instruction, *(I)*, 4–88
ADDG instruction, *(I)*, 4–88
Add instructions
  See also Floating-point operate
  add longword, *(I)*, 4–23
  add quadword, *(I)*, 4–25
  add scaled longword, *(I)*, 4–24
  add scaled quadword, *(I)*, 4–26
ADDL instruction, *(I)*, 4–23
ADDQ instruction, *(I)*, 4–25
Address space match (ASM)
  bit in PTE, *(II)*, 3–4; *(III)*, 3–4
  TBIAP register uses, *(II)*, 5–25
  virtual cache coherency, *(I)*, 5–4
Address space number (ASN)
  defined, *(III)*, 1–2
  described, *(III)*, 3–8
  in HWPCB, *(II)*, 4–2
  privileged context, *(II)*, 2–91
  range supported, *(II)*, 3–12
  TBCHK register uses, *(II)*, 5–22
  TBIS register uses, *(II)*, 5–26
  translation buffer with, *(II)*, 3–11
  virtual cache coherency, *(I)*, 5–4
Address space number (ASN) register, *(II)*, 5–4
Address translation
  algorithm to perform, *(II)*, 3–9
  page frame number (PFN), *(II)*, 3–9
  page table structure, *(II)*, 3–8
  performance enhancements, *(II)*, 3–10
  translation buffer with, *(II)*, 3–11
  virtual address segment fields, *(II)*, 3–9
ADDS instruction, *(I)*, 4–89
ADDT instruction, *(I)*, 4–89
Aligned byte/word memory accesses, A–11

ALIGNED data objects, *(I)*, 1–9
Alignment
  atomic longword, *(I)*, 5–2
  atomic quadword, *(I)*, 5–2
  D_floating, *(I)*, 2–7
  data alignment trap, *(II)*, 6–16
  data considerations, A–6
  double-width data paths, A–1
  F_floating, *(I)*, 2–5
  G_floating, *(I)*, 2–6
  instruction, A–2
  longword, *(I)*, 2–2
  longword integer, *(I)*, 2–11
  memory accesses, A–11
  program counter (PC), *(II)*, 6–6
  quadword, *(I)*, 2–3
  quadword integer, *(I)*, 2–11
  S_floating, *(I)*, 2–8
  stack, *(II)*, 6–31
  T_floating, *(I)*, 2–10
  when data is unaligned, *(II)*, 6–27
Alpha architecture
  See also Conventions
  addressing, *(I)*, 2–1
  overview, *(I)*, 1–1
  porting operating systems to, *(I)*, 1–1
  programming implications, *(I)*, 5–1
  registers, *(I)*, 3–1
  security, *(I)*, 1–7
Alpha privileged architecture library
  See PALcode
AMOVRM (PALcode) instruction, *(II)*, 2–76
AMOVRR (PALcode) instruction, *(II)*, 2–76
AND instruction, *(I)*, 4–37
Arithmetic exceptions
  See Arithmetic traps
Arithmetic instructions, *(I)*, 4–22
  See also specific arithmetic instructions
Arithmetic left shift instruction, *(I)*, 4–36
Arithmetic trap entry (entArith) register, *(III)*, 1–2, 5–3, 5–4
Arithmetic traps
  defined, *(II)*, 6–9; *(III)*, 5–1
  described, *(II)*, 6–12

Arithmetic traps (cont'd)
   division by zero, *(I)*, 4–63; *(II)*, 6–14; *(III)*,
     5–5
   F31 as destination, *(II)*, 6–12
   inexact result, *(I)*, 4–64; *(II)*, 6–15; *(III)*,
     5–5
   integer overflow, *(I)*, 4–64; *(II)*, 6–15;
     (III), 5–5
   invalid operation, *(I)*, 4–63; *(II)*, 6–14;
     (III), 5–5
   overflow, *(I)*, 4–63; *(II)*, 6–15; *(III)*, 5–5
   program counter (PC) value, *(II)*, 6–14
   programming implications for, *(I)*, 5–21
   R31 as destination, *(II)*, 6–12
   recorded for software, *(II)*, 6–13
   REI instruction with, *(II)*, 6–9
   service routine entry point, *(II)*, 6–27
   system entry for, *(III)*, 5–3, 5–4
   TRAPB instruction with, *(I)*, 4–120
   underflow, *(I)*, 4–63; *(II)*, 6–15; *(III)*, 5–5
   when registers affected by, *(II)*, 6–13
AST enable (ASTEN) register
   changing access modes in, *(II)*, 4–3
   described, *(II)*, 5–5
   in HWPCB, *(II)*, 4–2
   interrupt arbitration, *(II)*, 6–35
   operation (with ASTs), *(II)*, 4–3
   privileged context, *(II)*, 2–91
   SWASTEN instruction with, *(II)*, 2–19
AST summary (ASTSR) register
   described, *(II)*, 5–7
   indicates pending ASTs, *(II)*, 4–3
   in HWPCB, *(II)*, 4–2
   interrupt arbitration, *(II)*, 6–34
   privileged context, *(II)*, 2–91
Asynchronous system traps (AST)
   ASTEN/ASTSR registers with, *(II)*, 4–3
   initiating, *(II)*, 4–3
   interrupt, defined, *(II)*, 6–20
   service routine entry point, *(II)*, 6–27
   with PS register, *(II)*, 4–3
Atomic access, *(I)*, 5–2
Atomic move operations, *(II)*, 2–76
Atomic operations
   accessing longword datum, *(I)*, 5–2
   accessing quadword datum, *(I)*, 5–2
   modifying page table entry, *(II)*, 3–7
   updating shared data structures, *(I)*, 5–6
   using load locked and store conditional, *(I)*,
     5–7
Atomic sequences, A–17

B

Barrier instructions
   shared data structures and, *(I)*, 8–10

Barrier instructions (cont'd)
   use in I/O space read/write ordering, *(I)*,
     8–2, 8–8
BEQ instruction, *(I)*, 4–17
B field (mailbox), *(I)*, 8–5
BGE instruction, *(I)*, 4–17
BGT instruction, *(I)*, 4–17
BIC instruction, *(I)*, 4–37
BIS instruction, *(I)*, 4–37
BLBC instruction, *(I)*, 4–17
BLBS instruction, *(I)*, 4–17
BLE instruction, *(I)*, 4–17
BLT instruction, *(I)*, 4–17
BNE instruction, *(I)*, 4–17
Boolean instructions, *(I)*, 4–36
   logical functions, *(I)*, 4–37
Boolean stylized code forms, A–14
bpt (PALcode) instruction, *(III)*, 2–2
   required recognition of, *(I)*, 6–4
BPT (PALcode) instruction, *(II)*, 2–4
   required recognition of, *(I)*, 6–4
   service routine entry point, *(II)*, 6–28
   trap information, *(II)*, 6–16
Branch instruction format, *(I)*, 3–10
Branch instructions, *(I)*, 4–16
   See also Control instructions
   backward conditional, *(I)*, 4–17
   conditional branch, *(I)*, 4–17
   displacement, *(I)*, 4–17
   floating-point, summarized, *(I)*, 4–77
   forward conditional, *(I)*, 4–17
   opcodes for, C–2
   unconditional branch, *(I)*, 4–19
Branch prediction model, *(I)*, 4–15
Branch prediction stack, with BSR
    instruction, *(I)*, 4–19
Breakpoint exception, initiating, *(II)*, 2–4
Bridge
   defined, *(I)*, 8–1
   MBPR DON bit with, *(I)*, 8–6
   prefetch interrupts, *(I)*, 8–12
   with I/O space granularity, *(I)*, 8–7
BR instruction, *(I)*, 4–19
BSR instruction, *(I)*, 4–19
Bugcheck exception, initiating, *(II)*, 2–5
bugchk (PALcode) instruction, *(III)*, 2–3
   required recognition of, *(I)*, 6–4
BUGCHK (PALcode) instruction, *(II)*, 2–5
   required recognition of, *(I)*, 6–4
   service routine entry point, *(II)*, 6–28
   trap information, *(II)*, 6–16
Byte_within_page field, *(II)*, 3–2; *(III)*, 3–2
Byte data type, *(I)*, 2–1
Byte manipulation instructions, *(I)*, 4–42

Byte manipulation instructions (cont'd)
See also Extract instructions; Insert
instructions; Mask instructions

C

Cache coherency
barrier instructions for, *(I)*, 5–20
defined, *(I)*, 5–1
I/O space access, *(I)*, 8–2
in multiprocessor environment, *(I)*, 5–5
with DMA, *(I)*, 8–10
Caches
design considerations, A–1
flushing physical page from, *(II)*, 2–84
I-stream considerations, A–5
MB and IMB instructions with, *(I)*, 5–20
requirements for, *(I)*, 5–4
translation buffer conflicts, A–8
with powerfail/recovery, *(I)*, 5–4
CALL_PAL (call privileged architecture
library) instruction, *(I)*, 4–114
callsys (PALcode) instruction, *(III)*, 2–4
entSys with, *(III)*, 5–8
stack frames for, *(III)*, 5–3
Canonical form, *(I)*, 4–64
CFLUSH (PALcode) instruction, *(II)*, 2–84
with powerfail, *(II)*, 6–22
Changed datum, *(I)*, 5–5
CHME (PALcode) instruction, *(II)*, 2–6
service routine entry point, *(II)*, 6–28
trap initiation, *(II)*, 6–17
CHMK (PALcode) instruction, *(II)*, 2–7
service routine entry point, *(II)*, 6–28
trap initiation, *(II)*, 6–17
CHMS (PALcode) instruction, *(II)*, 2–8
service routine entry point, *(II)*, 6–28
trap initiation, *(II)*, 6–17
CHMU (PALcode) instruction, *(II)*, 2–9
service routine entry point, *(II)*, 6–28
trap initiation, *(II)*, 6–17
Clear a register, A–13
CMD field (mailbox), *(I)*, 8–5
CMOVEQ instruction, *(I)*, 4–38
CMOVGE instruction, *(I)*, 4–38
CMOVGT instruction, *(I)*, 4–38
CMOVLBC instruction, *(I)*, 4–38
CMOVLBS instruction, *(I)*, 4–38
CMOVLE instruction, *(I)*, 4–38
CMOVLT instruction, *(I)*, 4–38
CMOVNE instruction, *(I)*, 4–38
CMPBGE instruction, *(I)*, 4–44
CMPEQ instruction, *(I)*, 4–27
CMPGEQ instruction, *(I)*, 4–91
CMPGLE instruction, *(I)*, 4–91

CMPGLT instruction, *(I)*, 4–91
CMPLE instruction, *(I)*, 4–27
CMPLT instruction, *(I)*, 4–27
CMPTEQ instruction, *(I)*, 4–92
CMPTLE instruction, *(I)*, 4–92
CMPTLT instruction, *(I)*, 4–92
CMPTUN instruction, *(I)*, 4–92
CMPULE instruction, *(I)*, 4–28
CMPULT instruction, *(I)*, 4–28
Code forms, stylized, A–12
Boolean, A–14
load literal, A–13
negate, A–14
NOP, A–13
NOT, A–14
register, clear, A–13
register-to-register move, A–14
Code sequences, A–11
Coherency, cache, *(I)*, 5–1
Compare instructions
See also Floating-point operate
compare byte, *(I)*, 4–44
compare integer signed, *(I)*, 4–27
compare integer unsigned, *(I)*, 4–28
Conditional move instructions, *(I)*, 4–38
See also Floating-point operate
Console, overview, *(I)*, 7–1
Context switching
See also Hardware; Process
defined, *(II)*, 4–1
hardware, *(II)*, 4–2
initiating, *(II)*, 2–90
raising IPL while, *(II)*, 4–4
software, *(II)*, 4–2
Control instructions, *(I)*, 4–15
Control stream DMA, *(I)*, 8–11
Conventions
code examples, *(I)*, 1–10
extents, *(I)*, 1–8
figures, *(I)*, 1–9
instruction format, *(I)*, 3–8
notation, *(I)*, 3–8
numbering, *(I)*, 1–7
ranges, *(I)*, 1–8
/C opcode qualifier
IEEE floating-point, *(I)*, 4–60
VAX floating-point, *(I)*, 4–60
Corrected error interrupts, logout area for,
(II), 6–24
CPSY instruction, *(I)*, 4–83
CPSYN instruction, *(I)*, 4–83
CPYSE instruction, *(I)*, 4–83
Current mode field, in PS register, *(II)*, 6–6

Current PC, *(II)*, 6–2
CVTDG instruction, *(I)*, 4–96
CVTGD instruction, *(I)*, 4–96
CVTGF instruction, *(I)*, 4–96
CVTGQ instruction, *(I)*, 4–94
CVTLQ instruction, *(I)*, 4–84
CVTQF instruction, *(I)*, 4–95
CVTQG instruction, *(I)*, 4–95
CVTQL instruction, *(I)*, 4–84
CVTQS instruction, *(I)*, 4–99
CVTQT instruction, *(I)*, 4–99
CVTTQ instruction, *(I)*, 4–98
CVTTS instruction, *(I)*, 4–100

D

D_floating data type, *(I)*, 2–6
  alignment of, *(I)*, 2–7
  mapping, *(I)*, 2–6
  restricted, *(I)*, 2–7
Data alignment, A–6
Data alignment trap, *(II)*, 6–15
Data alignment trap fixup (DAT) bit, in
  HWPCB, *(II)*, 4–2
Data alignment trap fixup (DATFX) register,
  (II), 5–9
Data alignment traps
  memory management, *(II)*, 6–16
  registers used, *(II)*, 6–16; *(III)*, 5–4
  service routine entry point, *(II)*, 6–27
  system entry for, *(III)*, 5–8
Data format, overview, *(I)*, 1–3
Data sharing (multiprocessor), A–7
  synchonization requirement, *(I)*, 5–5
Data stream considerations, A–6
Data stream DMA, *(I)*, 8–11
Data structures, shared, *(I)*, 5–5
Data types
  byte, *(I)*, 2–1
  IEEE floating-point, *(I)*, 2–7
  longword, *(I)*, 2–2
  longword integer, *(I)*, 2–10
  quadword, *(I)*, 2–2
  quadword integer, *(I)*, 2–11
  unsupported in hardware, *(I)*, 2–12
  VAX floating-point, *(I)*, 2–3
  word, *(I)*, 2–1
Denormal, *(I)*, 4–58
Devices
  local, *(I)*, 8–1
  remote, *(I)*, 8–1
  shared data structures and, *(I)*, 8–10
Dirty zero, *(I)*, 4–58
DIVF instruction, *(I)*, 4–102

DIVG instruction, *(I)*, 4–102
Division
  integer, A–12
  performance impact of, A–12
Division by zero trap, *(II)*, 6–14; *(III)*, 5–5
DIVS instruction, *(I)*, 4–104
DIVT instruction, *(I)*, 4–104
DMA, *(I)*, 8–10
  atomic, *(I)*, 8–10
  control stream, *(I)*, 8–11
  data stream, *(I)*, 8–11
  defined, *(I)*, 8–2
  interrupts with, *(I)*, 8–12
DON field (mailbox), *(I)*, 8–6
/D opcode qualifier
  FPCR (floating-point control register), *(I)*,
    4–64
  IEEE floating-point, *(I)*, 4–60
draina (PALcode) instruction, *(I)*, 6–5
DRAINA (PALcode) instruction, *(I)*, 6–5
Dual-issue instruction considerations, A–2
DZE bit
  exception summary parameter, *(II)*, 6–13
  exception summary register, *(III)*, 5–5

E

entArith
  See Arithmetic trap entry
entIF
  See Instruction fault entry
entInt
  See Interrupt entry
entMM
  See Memory-management fault entry
entSys
  See System call entry
EQV instruction, *(I)*, 4–37
ERR field (mailbox), *(I)*, 8–6
Error checking, *(I)*, 8–6
Errors, processor
  corrected, *(II)*, 6–23
  uncorrected, *(II)*, 6–23
Errors, system
  corrected, *(II)*, 6–22
  uncorrected, *(II)*, 6–22
Exceptional events
  actions, summarized, *(II)*, 6–2
  defined, *(II)*, 6–1
Exception handlers, B–2
  TRAPB instruction with, *(I)*, 4–120
Exception register write mask, *(III)*, 5–6

Exceptions
   See also Arithmetic traps; Faults;
      Synchronous traps
   actions, summarized, *(II)*, 6–2
   defined, *(III)*, 5–1
   initiated before interrupts, *(II)*, 6–18
   initiated by PALcode, *(II)*, 6–31
   introduced, *(II)*, 6–8
   processor state transitions, *(II)*, 6–36
   stack frames, *(II)*, 6–7
   stack frames for, *(III)*, 5–3
Exception service routines
   entry point, *(II)*, 6–26
   introduced, *(II)*, 6–8
Exception summary parameter, *(II)*, 6–13
Exception summary register, *(III)*, 5–2, 5–6
   format of, *(III)*, 5–4
Executive read enable (ERE), bit in PTE, *(II)*,
   3–5
Executive stack pointer (ESP)
   as internal processor register, *(II)*, 5–1
   in HWPCB, *(II)*, 4–2
Executive stack pointer (ESP) register, *(II)*,
   5–27
Executive write enable (EWE), bit in PTE,
   (II), 3–6
EXTBL instruction, *(I)*, 4–46
EXTLH instruction, *(I)*, 4–46
EXTLL instruction, *(I)*, 4–46
EXTQH instruction, *(I)*, 4–46
EXTQL instruction, *(I)*, 4–46
Extract instructions (list), *(I)*, 4–46
EXTWH instruction, *(I)*, 4–46
EXTWL instruction, *(I)*, 4–46

F

F_floating data type, *(I)*, 2–3
   alignment of, *(I)*, 2–5
   compared to IEEE S_floating, *(I)*, 2–8
   MAX/MIN, *(I)*, 4–58
   operations, *(I)*, 4–64
   when data is unaligned, *(II)*, 6–27
Fault on execute (FOE), *(II)*, 6–12
   bit in PTE, *(II)*, 3–4; *(III)*, 3–4
   service routine entry point, *(II)*, 6–26
   software usage of, *(II)*, 6–12
Fault-on-execute fault, *(III)*, 3–10
Fault on read (FOR), *(II)*, 6–10
   bit in PTE, *(II)*, 3–4; *(III)*, 3–5
   service routine entry point, *(II)*, 6–26
   software usage of, *(II)*, 6–10
Fault-on-read fault, *(III)*, 3–10
Fault on write (FOW), *(II)*, 6–11
   bit in PTE, *(II)*, 3–4; *(III)*, 3–5
   service routine entry point, *(II)*, 6–26

Fault on write (FOW) (cont'd)
   software usage of, *(II)*, 6–11
Fault-on-write fault, *(III)*, 3–10
Faults
   access control violation, *(II)*, 6–10
   defined, *(II)*, 6–8; *(III)*, 5–1
   fault on execute, *(II)*, 6–12
   fault on read, *(II)*, 6–10
   fault on write, *(II)*, 6–11
   floating-point disabled, *(II)*, 6–10
   memory management, *(III)*, 3–9
   MM flag, *(II)*, 6–10
   program counter (PC) value, *(II)*, 6–8
   REI instruction with, *(II)*, 6–8
   translation not valid, *(II)*, 6–10
FBEQ instruction, *(I)*, 4–78
FBGE instruction, *(I)*, 4–78
FBGT instruction, *(I)*, 4–78
FBLE instruction, *(I)*, 4–78
FBLT instruction, *(I)*, 4–78
FBNE instruction, *(I)*, 4–78
FCMOVEQ instruction, *(I)*, 4–85
FCMOVGE instruction, *(I)*, 4–85
FCMOVGT instruction, *(I)*, 4–85
FCMOVLE instruction, *(I)*, 4–85
FCMOVLT instruction, *(I)*, 4–85
FCMOVNE instruction, *(I)*, 4–85
FETCH (prefetch data) instruction, *(I)*, 4–115
   performance optimization, A–10
FETCH_M (prefetch data, modify intent)
   instruction, *(I)*, 4–115
   performance optimization, A–10
Finite number, Alpha, contrasted with VAX,
   (I), 4–57
Floating-point branch instructions, *(I)*, 4–77
Floating-point control register (FPCR), *(I)*,
   4–64
   accessing, *(I)*, 4–66
   at processor initialization, *(I)*, 4–67
   bit descriptions, *(I)*, 4–65
   instructions to read/write, *(I)*, 4–87
   operate instructions that use, *(I)*, 4–80
   saving and restoring, *(I)*, 4–67
Floating-point convert instructions, *(I)*, 3–12
Floating-point disabled fault, *(II)*, 6–10
   service routine entry point, *(II)*, 6–26
Floating-point division, performance impact
   of, A–12
Floating-point enable (FEN) register
   defined, *(III)*, 1–3
   described, *(II)*, 5–10
   in HWPCB, *(II)*, 4–2
   privileged context, *(II)*, 2–91

Floating-point format, number representation (encodings), *(I)*, 4–58
Floating-point instructions
  branch (list), *(I)*, 4–77
  faults, *(I)*, 4–56
  introduced, *(I)*, 4–56
  memory format (list), *(I)*, 4–68
  operate (list), *(I)*, 4–80
  rounding modes, *(I)*, 4–59
  terminology, *(I)*, 4–57
  trapping modes, *(I)*, 4–60
  traps, *(I)*, 4–56
Floating-point load instructions, *(I)*, 4–68
  load F_floating, *(I)*, 4–69
  load G_floating, *(I)*, 4–70
  load S_floating, *(I)*, 4–71
  load T_floating, *(I)*, 4–72
  with nonfinite values, *(I)*, 4–68
Floating-point operate instructions, *(I)*, 4–80
  add (IEEE), *(I)*, 4–89
  add (VAX), *(I)*, 4–88
  compare (IEEE), *(I)*, 4–92
  compare (VAX), *(I)*, 4–91
  conditional move, *(I)*, 4–85
  convert IEEE floating to IEEE floating, *(I)*, 4–100
  convert IEEE floating to integer, *(I)*, 4–98
  convert integer to IEEE floating, *(I)*, 4–99
  convert integer to integer, *(I)*, 4–84
  convert integer to VAX floating, *(I)*, 4–95
  convert VAX floating to integer, *(I)*, 4–94
  convert VAX floating to VAX floating, *(I)*, 4–96
  copy sign, *(I)*, 4–83
  divide (IEEE), *(I)*, 4–104
  divide (VAX), *(I)*, 4–102
  format of, *(I)*, 3–11
  move from/to FPCR, *(I)*, 4–87
  multiply (IEEE), *(I)*, 4–107
  multiply (VAX), *(I)*, 4–106
  opcodes for, C–3
  subtract (IEEE), *(I)*, 4–111
  subtract (VAX), *(I)*, 4–109
Floating-point registers, *(I)*, 3–2
Floating-point rounding modes
  IEEE, *(I)*, 4–59
  VAX, *(I)*, 4–59
Floating-point single-precision operations, *(I)*, 4–64
Floating-point store instructions, *(I)*, 4–68
  store F_floating, *(I)*, 4–73
  store G_floating, *(I)*, 4–74
  store S_floating, *(I)*, 4–75
  store T_floating, *(I)*, 4–76
  with nonfinite values, *(I)*, 4–68

Floating-point support
  FPCR (floating-point control register), *(I)*, 4–64
  IEEE, *(I)*, 2–7
  IEEE standard 754-1985, *(I)*, 4–67
  instruction overview, *(I)*, 4–56
  longword integer, *(I)*, 2–10
  operate instructions, *(I)*, 4–80
  optional with Alpha, *(I)*, 4–2
  quadword integer, *(I)*, 2–11
  rounding modes, *(I)*, 4–59
  single-precision operations, *(I)*, 4–64
  trap modes, *(I)*, 4–60
  VAX, *(I)*, 2–3
Floating-point trapping modes, *(I)*, 4–60
  See also Arithmetic traps
  imprecision from pipelining, *(I)*, 4–62
FOE
  See Fault on execute
FOR
  See Fault on read
FOW
  See Fault on write
FPCR (floating-point control register)
  See Floating-point control register (FPCR)
Frame pointer (FP), register linkage for, *(III)*, 1–1

G

G_floating data type, *(I)*, 2–5
  alignment of, *(I)*, 2–6
  mapping, *(I)*, 2–5
  MAX/MIN, *(I)*, 4–58
  when data is unaligned, *(II)*, 6–27
gentrap (PALcode) instruction, *(III)*, 2–5
  required recognition of, *(I)*, 6–4
GENTRAP (PALcode) instruction, *(II)*, 2–10
  required recognition of, *(I)*, 6–4
  trap information, *(II)*, 6–17
Global pointer (GP), register linkage for, *(III)*, 1–1
Granularity hint (GH)
  bits in PTE, *(II)*, 3–5; *(III)*, 3–4

H

halt (PALcode) instruction, *(I)*, 6–6
HALT (PALcode) instruction, *(I)*, 6–6
Hardware context, *(III)*, 4–1
Hardware interrupts
  interprocessor, *(II)*, 6–21
  interval clock, *(II)*, 6–20
  powerfail, *(II)*, 6–22
  servicing, *(III)*, 5–6

Hardware nonprivileged context, *(II)*, 4–3
Hardware privileged context, *(II)*, 4–2
  switching, *(II)*, 4–2
Hardware privileged context block (HWPCB)
  format, *(II)*, 4–2
  original built by HWRPB, *(II)*, 4–4
  PCBB register, *(II)*, 5–16
  process unique value in, *(II)*, 2–80
  specified by PCBB, *(II)*, 4–2
  swapping ownership, *(II)*, 2–90
  writing to, *(II)*, 4–3
Hardware restart parameter block (HWRPB)
  interval clock interrupt, *(II)*, 6–20
  logout area, *(II)*, 6–24
Hose, *(I)*, 8–1
HOSE field (mailbox), *(I)*, 8–5
HWPCB
  See Hardware privileged context block
HWRPB
  See Hardware restart parameter block

I

I/O access granularity, *(I)*, 8–2
I/O bus, tightly coupled, *(I)*, 8–1
I/O device interrupts, *(II)*, 6–20
I/O devices, service routine entry points, *(II)*,
  6–29
I/O implementation dependencies, *(I)*, 8–13
I/O space, local, *(I)*, 8–2
I/O space, remote, *(I)*, 8–2
I/O space read/write ordering, *(I)*, 8–2, 8–7
I/O subsystem design, implementation
  considerations, *(I)*, 8–13
IEEE convert-to-integer trap mode,
  instruction notation for, *(I)*, 4–61
IEEE floating-point
  See also Floating-point instructions
  exception handlers, B–2
  format, *(I)*, 2–7
  FPCR (floating-point control register), *(I)*,
    4–64
  hardware support, B–1
  NaN, *(I)*, 2–8
  options, B–1
  S_floating, *(I)*, 2–8
  standard, mapping to, B–3
  standard charts, B–10
  T_floating, *(I)*, 2–9
  trap handling, B–4
  trap modes, *(I)*, 4–62
IEEE floating-point instructions
  add instructions, *(I)*, 4–89
  compare instructions, *(I)*, 4–92
  convert from integer instructions, *(I)*, 4–99

IEEE floating-point instructions (cont'd)
  convert IEEE floating format instructions,
    (I), 4–100
  convert to integer instructions, *(I)*, 4–98
  divide instructions, *(I)*, 4–104
  multiply instructions, *(I)*, 4–107
  opcodes for, C–4
  operate instructions, *(I)*, 4–80
  qualifiers, summarized, C–4
  subtract instructions, *(I)*, 4–111
IEEE rounding modes, *(I)*, 4–59
IEEE standard
  conformance to, B–1
  mapping to, B–3
  support for, *(I)*, 4–67
IEEE trap modes, required instruction
  notation, *(I)*, 4–61
IGN (ignore), *(I)*, 1–9
Illegal instruction trap, *(II)*, 6–16
  service routine entry point, *(II)*, 6–28
Illegal operand trap, service routine entry
  point, *(II)*, 6–28
Illegal PALcode operand trap, *(II)*, 6–17
imb (PALcode) instruction, *(I)*, 6–7
IMB (PALcode) instruction, *(I)*, 5–17, 6–7
  virtual I-cache coherency, *(I)*, 5–5
IMP (implementation dependent), *(I)*, 1–9
INE bit
  exception summary parameter, *(II)*, 6–13
  exception summary register, *(III)*, 5–5
Inexact result trap, *(II)*, 6–15; *(III)*, 5–5
Infinity, *(I)*, 4–57
Input/output interrupts, *(II)*, 6–22
INSBL instruction, *(I)*, 4–50
Insert instructions (list), *(I)*, 4–50
Insert into queue PALcode instructions
  longword at head interlocked, *(II)*, 2–31
  longword at head interlocked resident, *(II)*,
    2–33, 2–48
  longword at tail interlocked, *(II)*, 2–39
  longword at tail interlocked resident, *(II)*,
    2–42, 2–50
  quadword at head interlocked, *(II)*, 2–35
  quadword at head interlocked resident,
    (II), 2–37
  quadword at tail interlocked, *(II)*, 2–44
  quadword at tail interlocked resident, *(II)*,
    2–46
INSLH instruction, *(I)*, 4–50
INSLL instruction, *(I)*, 4–50
INSQHIL (PALcode) instruction, *(II)*, 2–31
INSQHILR (PALcode) instruction, *(II)*, 2–33
INSQH instruction, *(I)*, 4–50
INSQHIQ (PALcode) instruction, *(II)*, 2–35

INSQHIQR (PALcode) instruction, *(II)*, 2–37
INSQL instruction, *(I)*, 4–50
INSQTIL (PALcode) instruction, *(II)*, 2–39
INSQTILR (PALcode) instruction, *(II)*, 2–42
INSQTIQ (PALcode) instruction, *(II)*, 2–44
INSQTIQR (PALcode) instruction, *(II)*, 2–46
INSQUEL (PALcode) instruction, *(II)*, 2–48
INSQUEL/D (PALcode) instruction, *(II)*, 2–48
INSQUEQ (PALcode) instruction, *(II)*, 2–50
INSQUEQ/D (PALcode) instruction, *(II)*, 2–50
Instruction encodings
    floating-point format, C–3
    summarized, C–1
Instruction fault, system entry for, *(III)*, 5–3
Instruction fault entry (entIF) register, *(III)*,
        1–2, 5–3, 5–6
Instruction formats
    branch, *(I)*, 3–10
    conventions, *(I)*, 3–8
    floating-point convert, *(I)*, 3–12
    floating-point operate, *(I)*, 3–11
    illegal trap, *(II)*, 6–16
    memory, *(I)*, 3–9
    memory jump, *(I)*, 3–10
    operands, *(I)*, 3–8
    operand values, *(I)*, 3–8
    operate, *(I)*, 3–10
    operators, *(I)*, 3–5
    overview, *(I)*, 1–4
    PALcode, *(I)*, 3–13
    registers, *(I)*, 3–1
Instructions, overview, *(I)*, 1–5
Instruction set
    See also Floating-point instructions;
            PALcode instructions
    access type field, *(I)*, 3–4
    Boolean (list), *(I)*, 4–36
    branch (list), *(I)*, 4–16
    byte (list), *(I)*, 4–42
    conditional move (integer), *(I)*, 4–38
    data type field, *(I)*, 3–5
    extract (list), *(I)*, 4–42
    floating-point subsetting, *(I)*, 4–2
    insert (list), *(I)*, 4–42
    integer arithmetic (list), *(I)*, 4–22
    introduced, *(I)*, 1–6
    jump (list), *(I)*, 4–16
    load memory integer (list), *(I)*, 4–4
    mask (list), *(I)*, 4–42
    miscellaneous (list), *(I)*, 4–113
    name field, *(I)*, 3–4
    opcode qualifiers, *(I)*, 4–3
    operand notation, *(I)*, 3–4
    overview, *(I)*, 4–1
    shift, arithmetic, *(I)*, 4–41

Instruction set (cont'd)
    shift, logical, *(I)*, 4–40
    software emulation rules, *(I)*, 4–2
    store memory integer (list), *(I)*, 4–4
    VAX compatibility, *(I)*, 4–121
Instruction stream
    See I-stream
INSWH instruction, *(I)*, 4–50
INSWL instruction, *(I)*, 4–50
Integer arithmetic instructions
    See Arithmetic instructions
Integer division, A–12
Integer overflow trap, *(II)*, 6–15; *(III)*, 5–5
Integer registers
    defined, *(I)*, 3–1
    R31 restrictions, *(I)*, 3–1
    usage, *(III)*, 1–1
Internal processor registers (IPR)
    address space number (ASN), *(II)*, 5–4
    AST enable (ASTEN), *(II)*, 5–5
    AST summary (ASTSR), *(II)*, 5–7
    CALL_PAL MFPR with, *(II)*, 5–1
    CALL_PAL MTPR with, *(II)*, 5–1
    data alignment trap fixup (DATFX), *(II)*,
        5–9
    defined, *(II)*, 1–1
    executive stack pointer (ESP), *(II)*, 5–27
    floating-point enable (FEN), *(II)*, 5–10
    interprocessor interrupt request (IPIR)
        register, *(II)*, 5–11
    interrupt priority level (IPL), *(II)*, 5–12
    kernel mode with, *(II)*, 5–1
    machine check error summary (MCES),
        (II), 5–13
    MFPR instruction with, *(II)*, 2–86
    MTPR instruction with, *(II)*, 2–87
    page table base (PTBR), *(II)*, 5–18
    performance monitoring (PERFMON), *(II)*,
        5–15
    privileged context block base (PCBB), *(II)*,
        5–16
    processor base (PRBR), *(II)*, 5–17
    software interrupt request (SIRR), *(II)*,
        5–20
    software interrupt summary (SISR), *(II)*,
        5–21
    stack pointer, *(II)*, 5–1
    summarized, *(II)*, 5–2
    supervisor stack pointer (SSP), *(II)*, 5–28
    system control block base (SCBB), *(II)*,
        5–19
    translation buffer check (TBCHK), *(II)*,
        5–22
    translation buffer invalidate all (TBIA),
        (II), 5–24

Internal processor registers (IPR) (cont'd)
  translation buffer invalidate all process
    (TBIAP), *(II)*, 5–25
  translation buffer invalidate single (TBIS),
    (II), 5–26
  user stack pointer (USP), *(II)*, 5–29
  virtual page base (VPTB), *(II)*, 5–30
  Who-Am-I (WHAMI), *(II)*, 5–31
Interprocessor interrupt, *(II)*, 6–21
  protocol for, *(II)*, 6–21
  service routine entry point, *(II)*, 6–29
Interprocessor interrupt request (IPIR)
    register
  described, *(II)*, 5–11
  protocol for, *(II)*, 6–21
Interrupt entry (entInt) register, *(III)*, 1–2,
    5–4, 5–6
Interrupt priority level (IPL)
  See also Interrupt priority level (IPL)
    register
  events associated with, *(II)*, 6–18
  field in PS register, *(II)*, 6–6
  hardware levels, *(II)*, 6–7
  kernel mode software with, *(II)*, 6–18
  operation of, *(II)*, 6–17
  PS with, *(III)*, 5–2
  recording pending software (SISR register),
    (II), 5–21
  requesting software (SIRR register), *(II)*,
    5–20
  service routine entry points, *(II)*, 6–29
  software interrupts, *(II)*, 6–19
  software levels, *(II)*, 6–7
Interrupt priority level (IPL) register
  See also Interrupt priority level (IPL)
  described, *(II)*, 5–12
  interrupt arbitration, *(II)*, 6–35
Interrupts
  actions, summarized, *(II)*, 6–2
  from I/O devices, *(I)*, 8–12
  hardware arbitration, *(II)*, 6–34
  I/O device, *(II)*, 6–20
  initiated by PALcode, *(II)*, 6–31
  initiation, *(II)*, 6–18
  input/output, *(II)*, 6–22
  instruction completion, *(II)*, 6–17
  interprocessor, *(II)*, 6–21
  introduced, *(II)*, 6–17
  PALcode arbitration, *(II)*, 6–34
  passive release, *(II)*, 6–20
  powerfail, *(II)*, 6–22
  processor state transitions, *(II)*, 6–36
  program counter value, *(II)*, 6–2
  software, *(II)*, 6–19
  sources for, *(III)*, 5–2

Interrupts (cont'd)
  stack frames, *(II)*, 6–7
  stack frames for, *(III)*, 5–3
  system entry for, *(III)*, 5–4
  vectors, *(I)*, 8–12
Interrupt service routines
  entry point, *(II)*, 6–26
  in each process, *(II)*, 6–18
  introduced, *(II)*, 6–17
Interval clock interrupt, *(II)*, 6–20
  service routine entry point, *(II)*, 6–29
Invalid operation trap, *(II)*, 6–14; *(III)*, 5–5
INV bit
  exception summary parameter, *(II)*, 6–13
  exception summary register, *(III)*, 5–5
/I opcode qualifier, IEEE floating-point, *(I)*,
    4–61
IOV bit
  exception summary parameter, *(II)*, 6–14
  exception summary register, *(III)*, 5–5
IPR
  See Internal processor registers (IPR)
IPR_KSP (internal processor register kernel
    stack pointer), *(II)*, 5–1
I-stream
  coherency, *(I)*, 6–7
  design considerations, A–2
  modifying physical, *(I)*, 5–5
  modifying virtual, *(I)*, 5–5
  PALcode with, *(I)*, 6–2
  with caches, *(I)*, 5–5

J

JMP instruction, *(I)*, 4–20
JSR_COROUTINE instruction, *(I)*, 4–20
JSR instruction, *(I)*, 4–20
Jump instructions, *(I)*, 4–16, 4–20
  See also Control instructions
  branch prediction logic, *(I)*, 4–21
  coroutine linkage, *(I)*, 4–21
  return from subroutine, *(I)*, 4–20
  unconditional long jump, *(I)*, 4–21

K

Kernel global pointer (KGP), *(III)*, 1–3
Kernel mode, protection code with, *(III)*, 3–6
Kernel read enable (KRE)
  bit in PTE, *(II)*, 3–5; *(III)*, 3–4
  with access control violation (ACV) fault,
    (II), 3–13
Kernel stack, PALcode access to, *(II)*, 6–31
Kernel stack pointer (KSP)
  defined, *(III)*, 1–3
  in HWPCB, *(II)*, 4–2

Kernel write enable (KWE)
  bit in PTE, *(II)*, 3–6; *(III)*, 3–4
Kseg
  format of, *(III)*, 3–2
  mapping of, *(III)*, 3–1
  physical space with, *(III)*, 3–3

L

LDAH instruction, *(I)*, 4–5
LDA instruction, *(I)*, 4–5
LDF instruction, *(I)*, 4–69
  when data is unaligned, *(II)*, 6–27
LDG instruction, *(I)*, 4–70
  when data is unaligned, *(II)*, 6–27
LDL_L instruction, *(I)*, 4–8
  restrictions, *(I)*, 4–9
  when data is unaligned, *(II)*, 6–27
  with processor lock register/flag, *(I)*, 4–8
  with STx_C instruction, *(I)*, 4–8
LDL instruction, *(I)*, 4–6
  when data is unaligned, *(II)*, 6–27
LDQ_L instruction, *(I)*, 4–8
  restrictions, *(I)*, 4–9
  when data is unaligned, *(II)*, 6–27
  with processor lock register/flag, *(I)*, 4–8
  with STx_C instruction, *(I)*, 4–8
LDQ_U instruction, *(I)*, 4–7
LDQ instruction, *(I)*, 4–6
  when data is unaligned, *(II)*, 6–27
LDQP (PALcode) instruction, *(II)*, 2–85
LDS instruction, *(I)*, 4–71
  when data is unaligned, *(II)*, 6–27
LDT instruction, *(I)*, 4–72
  when data is unaligned, *(II)*, 6–27
Literals, operand notation, *(I)*, 3–4
Load instructions
  See also Floating-point load instructions
  emulation of, *(I)*, 4–2
  FETCH instruction, *(I)*, 4–115
  load address, *(I)*, 4–5
  load address high, *(I)*, 4–5
  load quadword, *(I)*, 4–6
  load quadword locked, *(I)*, 4–8
  load sign-extended longword, *(I)*, 4–6
  load sign-extended longword locked, *(I)*,
    4–8
  load unaligned quadword, *(I)*, 4–7
  multiprocessor environment, *(I)*, 5–5
  serialization, *(I)*, 4–117
  when data is unaligned, *(II)*, 6–27
Load literal, A–13
Load memory integer instructions (list), *(I)*,
  4–4

Local devices, *(I)*, 8–1
Local I/O space, *(I)*, 8–2
Local side, *(I)*, 8–1
Location, *(I)*, 5–10
Location access order
  defined, *(I)*, 5–11
  with processor issue order, *(I)*, 5–11
Lock flag, per-processor
  defined, *(I)*, 3–2
  with load locked instructions, *(I)*, 4–8
  with store conditional instructions, *(I)*,
    4–11
Lockout, *(I)*, 8–3
Lock registers, per-processor
  defined, *(I)*, 3–2
  with load locked instructions, *(I)*, 4–8
  with store conditional instructions, *(I)*,
    4–11
Lock_flag register, *(III)*, 1–3
Logical instructions
  See Boolean instructions
Logout area, *(II)*, 6–24; *(III)*, 5–7
Longword data type, *(I)*, 2–2
  alignment of, *(I)*, 2–11
  atomic access of, *(I)*, 5–2
  integer floating-point format, *(I)*, 2–10
LSB (least significant bit), defined for
  floating-point, *(I)*, 4–57

M

Machine check error summary (MCES)
    register
  described, *(II)*, 5–13
  using, *(II)*, 6–24
Machine checks, *(II)*, 6–22; *(III)*, 5–6
  actions, summarized, *(II)*, 6–2
  initiated by PALcode, *(II)*, 6–31
  introduced, *(II)*, 6–22
  logout area, *(II)*, 6–24
  masking, *(II)*, 6–23
  no disabling of, *(II)*, 6–24
  one per error, *(II)*, 6–24
  processor correctable, *(II)*, 6–23
  program counter (PC) value, *(II)*, 6–23
  REI instruction with, *(II)*, 6–23
  retry flag, *(II)*, 6–24
  service routine entry points, *(II)*, 6–29
  stack frames, *(II)*, 6–7
  system correctable, *(II)*, 6–23
Mailbox
  address alignment, *(I)*, 8–4
  bus-specific implementations for, *(I)*, 8–12
  CMD field checking, *(I)*, 8–13
  error reporting, *(I)*, 8–8

Mailbox (cont'd)
  field checking, *(I)*, 8–12
  modification by host, *(I)*, 8–6
  operational definition, *(I)*, 8–2
  posting, *(I)*, 8–2
  posting software with, *(I)*, 8–6
  remote reads, *(I)*, 8–6, 8–8
  remote writes, *(I)*, 8–6, 8–9
  static, *(I)*, 8–6
  structure, *(I)*, 8–5
  use of STQ_C lock_flag, *(I)*, 8–3, 8–8
  WHO_ARE_YOU command, *(I)*, 8–13
  with I/O space granularity, *(I)*, 8–7
Mailbox pointer (MBPR) register, *(I)*, 8–4
  defined, *(I)*, 8–2
  ordering, *(I)*, 8–7
MASK field (mailbox), *(I)*, 8–5
Masking, machine checks with, *(II)*, 6–23
Mask instructions (list), *(I)*, 4–52
MAX, defined for floating-point, *(I)*, 4–59
maxCPU, *(III)*, 1–2
MB (memory barrier) instruction, *(I)*, 4–117
  See also IMB
  multiprocessors only, *(I)*, 4–117
  using, *(I)*, 5–18
  with DMA I/O, *(I)*, 5–17
  with multiprocessor D-stream, *(I)*, 5–17
MBPR
  See Mailbox pointer (MBPR) register
MBZ (must be zero), *(I)*, 1–9
Memory, unrecoverable errors with, *(II)*, 6–22
Memory access
  aligned byte/word, A–11
  coherency of, *(I)*, 5–1
  granularity of, *(I)*, 5–2
  width of, *(I)*, 5–2
Memory access sequence, *(I)*, 5–11
Memory alignment, requirement for, *(I)*, 5–2
Memory format instructions
  function codes, summarized, C–1
  opcodes for, C–1
Memory instruction format, *(I)*, 3–9
  with function code, *(I)*, 3–9
Memory jump instruction format, *(I)*, 3–10
Memory-like behavior, *(I)*, 5–3
Memory management
  See also Address translation; Pages;
    Processor modes; Virtual address
    space
  address translation, *(II)*, 3–8
  always enabled, *(II)*, 3–3
  control of, *(III)*, 3–3
  faults, *(II)*, 3–13, 6–9; *(III)*, 3–9
  introduced, *(II)*, 3–1
  page frame number (PFN), *(II)*, 3–6

Memory management (cont'd)
  page table entry (PTE), *(II)*, 3–3
  protection code, *(II)*, 3–8
  protection of individual pages, *(II)*, 3–7
  PTE modified by software, *(II)*, 3–7
  support in PALcode, *(I)*, 6–2
  translation buffer with, *(II)*, 3–11
  unrecoverable error, *(II)*, 6–22
  with interrupts, *(II)*, 6–18
  with multiprocessors, *(II)*, 3–7
  with process context, *(II)*, 4–1
Memory-management fault entry (entMM)
  register, *(III)*, 1–2, 5–4, 5–7
Memory management faults
  registers used, *(II)*, 6–10
  system entry for, *(III)*, 5–4
  types, *(III)*, 3–9
  with unaligned data, *(II)*, 6–16
Memory prefetch registers, A–10
  defined, *(I)*, 3–2
Memory protection, *(III)*, 3–5
MF_FPCR instruction, *(I)*, 4–87
MFPR_IPR_name (PALcode) instruction,
  (II), 2–86
MIN, defined for floating-point, *(I)*, 4–58
Miscellaneous instructions (list), *(I)*, 4–113
MMCSR, *(III)*, 5–7
MMCSR code, *(III)*, 3–9
/M opcode qualifier, IEEE floating-point, *(I)*,
  4–60
Move, register-to-register, A–14
Move instructions (conditional)
  See Conditional move instructions
MSKBL instruction, *(I)*, 4–52
MSKLH instruction, *(I)*, 4–52
MSKLL instruction, *(I)*, 4–52
MSKQL instruction, *(I)*, 4–52
MSKWH instruction, *(I)*, 4–52
MSKWL instruction, *(I)*, 4–52
MT_FPCR instruction, *(I)*, 4–87
  synchronization requirement, *(I)*, 4–66
MTPR_IPR_name (PALcode) instruction,
  (II), 2–87
MULF instruction, *(I)*, 4–106
MULG instruction, *(I)*, 4–106
MULL instruction, *(I)*, 4–29
  with MULQ, *(I)*, 4–29
MULQ instruction, *(I)*, 4–30
  with MULL, *(I)*, 4–29
  with UMULH, *(I)*, 4–30
MULS instruction, *(I)*, 4–107
MULT instruction, *(I)*, 4–107
Multiple instruction issue, A–2
Multiply instructions
  See also Floating-point operate

Multiply instructions (cont'd)
    multiply longword, *(I)*, 4–29
    multiply quadword, *(I)*, 4–30
    multiply unsigned quadward high, *(I)*, 4–31
Multiprocessor environment
    See also Data sharing
    cache coherency in, *(I)*, 5–5
    context switching, *(I)*, 5–18
    interprocessor interrupt, *(II)*, 6–21
    I-stream reliability, *(I)*, 5–17
    MB instruction with, *(I)*, 5–17
    memory faults, *(II)*, 6–10
    memory management in, *(II)*, 3–7
    move operations in, *(II)*, 2–76
    no implied barriers, *(I)*, 5–16
    read/write ordering, *(I)*, 5–9
    serialization requirements in, *(I)*, 4–117
    shared data, *(I)*, 5–5, A–7
Multiprocessors
    I/O with, *(I)*, 8–3
    interrupts with, *(I)*, 8–12
Multithread implementation, *(II)*, 2–80

N

NaN (Not-a-Number)
    defined, *(I)*, 2–8
    Quiet, *(I)*, 4–57
    Signaling, *(I)*, 4–57
NATURALLY ALIGNED data objects, *(I)*, 1–9
Negate stylized code form, A–14
Next PC, *(II)*, 6–2
    defined for arithmetic traps, *(II)*, 6–14
Nonmemory-like behavior, *(I)*, 5–3
NOP, A–13
NOT instruction, ORNOT with zero, *(I)*, 4–37
NOT stylized code form, A–14

O

Opcode qualifiers
    See also specific qualifiers
    default values, *(I)*, 4–3
    notation (list), *(I)*, 4–3
Opcodes
    DEC OSF/1, C–9
    OpenVMS, C–8
    reserved, C–10
    summarized, C–6
opDec, *(III)*, 1–4
OpenVMS PALcode instruction opcodes, C–8
OpenVMS PALcode instructions (list), *(II)*,
    2–2
Operand expressions, *(I)*, 3–3
Operand notation
    defined, *(I)*, 3–3

Operand notation (cont'd)
    from VAX architecture standard, *(I)*, 3–4
Operand values, *(I)*, 3–3
Operate format instructions, opcodes for, C–2
Operate instruction format, *(I)*, 3–10
    floating-point, *(I)*, 3–11
    floating-point convert, *(I)*, 3–12
Operators, instruction format, *(I)*, 3–5
Optimization
    See Performance optimizations
ORNOT instruction, *(I)*, 4–37
OSF/1 PALcode instruction opcodes, C–9
Overflow trap, *(II)*, 6–15; *(III)*, 5–5
OVF bit
    exception summary parameter, *(II)*, 6–13
    exception summary register, *(III)*, 5–5

P

Page frame number (PFN)
    bits in PTE, *(II)*, 3–6; *(III)*, 3–3
    determining validitation, *(II)*, 3–4
    finding for SCB, *(II)*, 5–19
    PTBR register, *(II)*, 5–18
    with address translation, *(II)*, 3–9
    with hardware context switching, *(II)*, 4–3
Pages
    collecting statistics on, *(II)*, 6–11
    individual protection of, *(II)*, 3–7
    max address size from, *(II)*, 3–3
    possible sizes for, *(II)*, 3–2
    size range of, *(III)*, 3–1
    virtual address space from, *(II)*, 3–2
pageSize, *(III)*, 1–2
Page sizes, *(III)*, 3–2
Page table base (PTBR) register, *(II)*, 5–18
    defined, *(III)*, 1–3
    in HWPCB, *(II)*, 4–2
    privileged context, *(II)*, 2–91
    with address translation, *(II)*, 3–9
Page table entry (PTE), *(II)*, 3–3
    atomic modification of, *(II)*, 3–7
    bits, summarized, *(III)*, 3–3
    changing and managing, *(III)*, 3–5
    format of, *(III)*, 3–3
    modified by software, *(II)*, 3–7
    page protection, *(II)*, 3–8
    physical access of, *(III)*, 3–6
    virtual access of, *(III)*, 3–7
    with multiprocessors, *(II)*, 3–7
PALcode
    See also Queues, support for
    access to kernel stack, *(II)*, 6–31
    barriers with, *(I)*, 5–16
    CALL_PAL instruction, *(I)*, 4–114

PALcode (cont'd)
  compared to hardware instructions, *(I)*, 6–1
  defined for OpenVMS, *(II)*, 2–1
  illegal operand trap, *(II)*, 6–17
  implementation-specific, *(I)*, 6–2
  instead of microcode, *(I)*, 6–1
  instruction format, *(I)*, 3–13
  memory management requirements, *(II)*, 3–3
  OSF/1 support for, *(III)*, 5–8
  overview, *(I)*, 6–1
  processor state transitions, *(II)*, 6–36
  queue data type support, *(II)*, 2–21
  recognized instructions, *(I)*, 6–4
  replacing, *(I)*, 6–3
  required function support, *(I)*, 6–2
  required instructions, *(I)*, 6–4
  running environment, *(I)*, 6–2
  special functions, *(I)*, 6–2
PALcode instructions
  OpenVMS (list), *(II)*, 2–2
  privileged OpenVMS (list), *(II)*, 2–83
  privileged OSF/1 (list), *(III)*, 2–8
  required, opcodes for, C–10
  reserved, opcodes for, C–10
  thread OpenVMS, *(II)*, 2–80
  unprivileged general (list), *(II)*, 2–3
  unprivileged OSF/1 (list), *(III)*, 2–1
PALcode instructions, privileged

  See also individual instructions
  cache flush, *(II)*, 2–84
  drain aborts, *(I)*, 6–5
  halt processor, *(I)*, 6–6
  load quadword physical, *(II)*, 2–85
  move from processor register, *(II)*, 2–86
  move to processor register, *(II)*, 2–87
  read processor status, *(III)*, 2–9
  read system value, *(III)*, 2–11
  read user stack pointer, *(III)*, 2–10
  return from system call, *(III)*, 2–12
  return from trap, fault, or interrupt, *(III)*, 2–13
  store quadword physical, *(II)*, 2–88
  swap IPL, *(III)*, 2–16
  swap privileged context, *(II)*, 2–89
  swap process context, *(III)*, 2–14
  TB (translation buffer) invalidate, *(III)*, 2–17
  who am I, *(III)*, 2–18
  write floating-point enable, *(III)*, 2–21
  write kernel global pointer, *(III)*, 2–22
  write system entry address, *(III)*, 2–19
  write system value, *(III)*, 2–24
  write user stack pointer, *(III)*, 2–23
  write virtual page table pointer, *(III)*, 2–25

PALcode instructions, thread, *(II)*, 2–80
  read unique context, *(II)*, 2–81
  write unique context, *(II)*, 2–82
PALcode instructions, unprivileged
  See also individual instructions
  breakpoint, *(II)*, 2–4; *(III)*, 2–2
  bugcheck, *(II)*, 2–5; *(III)*, 2–3
  change to executive mode, *(II)*, 2–6
  change to kernel mode, *(II)*, 2–7
  change to supervisor mode, *(II)*, 2–8
  change to user mode, *(II)*, 2–9
  generate software trap, *(II)*, 2–10
  generate trap, *(III)*, 2–5
  insert into queue (list), *(II)*, 2–30
  I-stream memory barrier, *(I)*, 6–7
  probe for read access, *(II)*, 2–11
  probe for write access, *(II)*, 2–11
  read processor status, *(II)*, 2–13
  read system cycle counter, *(II)*, 2–17
  read unique value, *(III)*, 2–6
  remove from queue (list), *(II)*, 2–30
  return from exception or interrupt, *(II)*, 2–14
  swap AST enable, *(II)*, 2–19
  system call, *(III)*, 2–4
  write PS software field, *(II)*, 2–20
  write unique value, *(III)*, 2–7
PALcode instructions, unprivileged general (list), *(II)*, 2–3
PALRES0, *(I)*, 6–2
PALRES1, *(I)*, 6–2
PALRES2, *(I)*, 6–2
PALRES3, *(I)*, 6–2
PALRES4, *(I)*, 6–2
Passive release interrupt entry point, *(II)*, 6–29
Passive release interrupts, *(II)*, 6–20
PC
  See program counter register
PCC
  See Process cycle counter
Performance monitoring register (PERF-MON), *(II)*, 5–15
Performance monitor interrupt entry point, *(II)*, 6–29
Performance optimizations
  branch prediction, A–3
  code sequences, A–11
  data stream, A–6
  for frequently executed code, A–1
  for I-streams, A–2
  instruction alignment, A–2
  instruction scheduling, A–5
  I-stream density, A–5

Performance optimizations (cont'd)
   multiple instruction issue, A–2
   shared data, A–7
PFN
   See Page frame number
Physical address translation, *(II)*, 3–9
Physical space, *(III)*, 3–3
PME, bit in HWPCB, *(II)*, 4–2
PMI bus, *(I)*, 8–1
   uncorrected protocol errors, *(II)*, 6–22
Powerfail, CFLUSH PALcode instruction
   with, *(II)*, 6–22
Powerfail interrupt, *(II)*, 6–22
   service routine entry point, *(II)*, 6–29
Prefetch data (FETCH instruction), *(I)*, 4–115
Prefetch data registers, A–10
Prefetching data, considerations, A–10
Privileged Architecture Library
   See PALcode
Privileged context, *(II)*, 2–90
Privileged context block base (PCBB) register,
   (II), 5–16
Privileged PALcode instructions (list), *(II)*,
   2–83; *(III)*, 2–8
PROBER (PALcode) instruction, *(II)*, 2–11
PROBEW (PALcode) instruction, *(II)*, 2–11
Process, *(II)*, 4–1
   context switching the, *(II)*, 4–4
Process context, *(III)*, 4–1
Process control block (PCB), *(III)*, 4–1
   structure, *(III)*, 4–2
Process control block base (PCBB) register,
   (III), 1–3
Process cycle counter (PCC)
   in HWPCB, *(II)*, 4–2
   privileged context, *(II)*, 2–91
   RPCC instruction with, *(I)*, 4–118
   system cycle counter with, *(II)*, 2–17
Processor base (PRBR) register, *(II)*, 5–17
Processor issue order
   defined, *(I)*, 5–11
   with location access order, *(I)*, 5–11
Processor issue sequence, *(I)*, 5–10
Processor memory interconnect
   See PMI bus
Processor modes
   AST pending state, *(II)*, 5–7
   change to executive, *(II)*, 2–6
   change to kernel, *(II)*, 2–7
   change to supervisor, *(II)*, 2–8
   change to user, *(II)*, 2–9
   controlling memory access, *(II)*, 3–8
   enabling executive mode reads, *(II)*, 3–5
   enabling executive mode writes, *(II)*, 3–6

Processor modes (cont'd)
   enabling kernel mode reads, *(II)*, 3–5
   enabling supervisor mode reads, *(II)*, 3–6
   enabling supervisor mode writes, *(II)*, 3–6
   enabling user mode reads, *(II)*, 3–6
   enabling user mode writes, *(II)*, 3–6
   page access with, *(II)*, 3–1
   PALcode state transitions, *(II)*, 6–36
Processor number, reading, *(II)*, 5–31
Processor state, defined, *(II)*, 6–5
Processor state transitions, *(II)*, 6–36
Processor status (PS) register
   bit meanings for, *(III)*, 5–2
   bootstrap values in, *(II)*, 6–6
   current, *(II)*, 6–5
   current mode field, *(II)*, 6–6
   defined, *(II)*, 1–1; *(III)*, 1–3
   explicit reading of, *(II)*, 6–5
   in processor state, *(II)*, 6–5
   interrupt priority level (IPL) field, *(II)*, 6–6
   saved on stack, *(II)*, 6–5
   saved on stack frame, *(II)*, 6–7
   software (SW) field, *(II)*, 6–6
   stack alignment field, *(II)*, 6–6
   virtual machine monitor bit, *(II)*, 6–6
   WR_PS_SW instruction, *(II)*, 2–20
Process unique value (unique) register, *(III)*,
   1–4
Program counter (PC) register, *(I)*, 3–1
   alignment, *(II)*, 6–6
   current PC defined, *(II)*, 6–2
   defined, *(III)*, 1–3
   explicit reading of, *(II)*, 6–6
   in processor state, *(II)*, 6–5
   next PC defined, *(II)*, 6–14
   saved on stack frame, *(II)*, 6–7
   with arithmetic traps, *(II)*, 6–14; *(III)*, 5–1
   with faults, *(II)*, 6–8
   with interrupts, *(II)*, 6–2
   with machine checks, *(II)*, 6–23
   with synchronous traps, *(II)*, 6–15
Protection code, *(II)*, 3–8; *(III)*, 3–6
Protection modes, *(II)*, 6–7
PS<SP_ALIGN> field, *(II)*, 2–13
Pseudo-ops, A–14
PTE
   See Page table entry

Q

Quadword data type, *(I)*, 2–2
   alignment of, *(I)*, 2–3, 2–11
   atomic access of, *(I)*, 5–2
   integer floating-point format, *(I)*, 2–11
   loading in physical memory, *(II)*, 2–85

Quadword data type (cont'd)
    storing to physical memory, *(II)*, 2–88
    T_floating with, *(I)*, 2–11
Queues, support for
    absolute longword, *(II)*, 2–21
    absolute quadword, *(II)*, 2–25
    PALcode instructions (list), *(II)*, 2–30
    self-relative longword, *(II)*, 2–21
    self-relative quadword, *(II)*, 2–26

R

R31
    restrictions, *(I)*, 3–1
    with arithmetic traps, *(II)*, 6–12
RAZ (read as zero), *(I)*, 1–9
RBADR field (mailbox), *(I)*, 8–5
RC (read and clear) instruction, *(I)*, 4–122
RD_PS (PALcode) instruction, *(II)*, 2–13
RDATA field (mailbox), *(I)*, 8–6
rdps (PALcode) instruction, *(III)*, 2–9
rdunique (PALcode) instruction, *(III)*, 2–6
    PCB with, *(III)*, 4–1
    required recognition of, *(I)*, 6–4
RDUNIQUE (PALcode) instruction
    required recognition of, *(I)*, 6–4
rdusp (PALcode) instruction, *(III)*, 2–10
    PCB with, *(III)*, 4–1
rdval (PALcode) instruction, *(III)*, 2–11
READ_UNQ (PALcode) instruction, *(II)*,
    2–81
Read/write, sequential, A–10
Read/write ordering (multiprocessor), *(I)*, 5–9
    determining requirements, *(I)*, 5–9
    memory location defined, *(I)*, 5–10
Registers, *(I)*, 3–1
    See also specific registers
    floating-point, *(I)*, 3–2
    integer, *(I)*, 3–1
    lock, *(I)*, 3–2
    memory prefetch, *(I)*, 3–2
    optional, *(I)*, 3–2
    program counter (PC), *(I)*, 3–1
    value when unused, *(I)*, 3–8
    VAX compatibility, *(I)*, 3–2
    with IPRs, *(II)*, 5–1
Register-to-register move, A–14
Register write mask, with arithmetic traps,
    (II), 6–14
REI (PALcode) instruction, *(II)*, 2–14
    arithmetic traps, *(II)*, 6–9
    faults, *(II)*, 6–8
    interrupt arbitration, *(II)*, 6–35
    interrupts, *(II)*, 6–2
    machine checks, *(II)*, 6–23

REI (PALcode) instruction (cont'd)
    synchronous traps, *(II)*, 6–15
Remote devices
    defined, *(I)*, 8–1
    interrupts with, *(I)*, 8–12
    with DMA, *(I)*, 8–10
Remote I/O space, *(I)*, 8–2
    accessing, *(I)*, 8–2, 8–8
    flow control, *(I)*, 8–3
    read/write ordering, *(I)*, 8–9
Remote writes (mailbox), *(I)*, 8–5
Remove from queue PALcode instructions
    longword, *(II)*, 2–72
    longword at head interlocked, *(II)*, 2–52
    longword at head interlocked resident, *(II)*,
      2–55
    longword at tail interlocked, *(II)*, 2–62
    longword at tail interlocked resident, *(II)*,
      2–65
    quadword, *(II)*, 2–74
    quadword at head interlocked, *(II)*, 2–57
    quadword at head interlocked resident,
      (II), 2–60
    quadword at tail interlocked, *(II)*, 2–67
    quadword at tail interlocked resident, *(II)*,
      2–70
REMQHIL (PALcode) instruction, *(II)*, 2–52
REMQHILR (PALcode) instruction, *(II)*, 2–55
REMQHIQ (PALcode) instruction, *(II)*, 2–57
REMQHIQR (PALcode) instruction, *(II)*, 2–60
REMQTIL (PALcode) instruction, *(II)*, 2–62
REMQTILR (PALcode) instruction, *(II)*, 2–65
REMQTIQ (PALcode) instruction, *(II)*, 2–67
REMQTIQR (PALcode) instruction, *(II)*, 2–70
REMQUEL (PALcode) instruction, *(II)*, 2–72
REMQUEL/D (PALcode) instruction, *(II)*,
    2–72
REMQUEQ (PALcode) instruction, *(II)*, 2–74
REMQUEQ/D (PALcode) instruction, *(II)*,
    2–74
Representative result, *(I)*, 4–57
Reserved instructions, opcodes for, C–10
Reserved operand, *(I)*, 4–58
Result latency, A–5
RET instruction, *(I)*, 4–20
retsys (PALcode) instruction, *(III)*, 2–12
    PS with, *(III)*, 5–2
Rounding modes
    See Floating-point rounding modes
RPCC (read process cycle counter) instruction,
    (I), 4–118
    RSCC instruction with, *(II)*, 2–18
RS (read and set) instruction, *(I)*, 4–122
RSCC (PALcode) instruction, *(II)*, 2–17
    RPCC instruction with, *(II)*, 2–18

rti (PALcode) instruction, *(III)*, 2–13
  PS with, *(III)*, 5–2
  with exceptions, *(III)*, 5–1

S

S4ADDL instruction, *(I)*, 4–24
S4ADDQ instruction, *(I)*, 4–26
S4SUBL instruction, *(I)*, 4–33
S4SUBQ instruction, *(I)*, 4–35
S8ADDL instruction, *(I)*, 4–24
S8ADDQ instruction, *(I)*, 4–26
S8SUBL instruction, *(I)*, 4–33
S8SUBQ instruction, *(I)*, 4–35
S_floating data type
  alignment of, *(I)*, 2–8
  compared to F_floating, *(I)*, 2–8
  exceptions, *(I)*, 2–8
  format, *(I)*, 2–8
  mapping, *(I)*, 2–8
  MAX/MIN, *(I)*, 4–58
  operations, *(I)*, 4–64
  when data is unaligned, *(II)*, 6–27
SBZ (should be zero), *(I)*, 1–9
SCC
  See System cycle counter
Security holes, *(I)*, 1–7
  with UNPREDICTABLE results, *(I)*, 1–8
Seg0, mapping of, *(III)*, 3–1
Seg1, mapping of, *(III)*, 3–1
Segment number fields, *(II)*, 3–2
Self-relative longword queue, *(II)*, 2–21
Self-relative quadword queue, *(II)*, 2–26
Sequential read/write, A–10
Serialization, MB instruction with, *(I)*, 4–117
Shared data (multiprocessor), A–7
  changed vs. updated datum, *(I)*, 5–5
Shared data structures
  atomic update, *(I)*, 5–6
  ordering considerations, *(I)*, 5–7
  using memory barrier (MB) instruction, *(I)*,
    5–8
Shared memory
  accessing, *(I)*, 5–10
  access sequence, *(I)*, 5–10
  defined, *(I)*, 5–9
  issue sequence, *(I)*, 5–10
Shift arithmetic instructions, *(I)*, 4–41
Shift logical instructions, *(I)*, 4–40
Single-precision floating-point, *(I)*, 4–64
SLL instruction, *(I)*, 4–40
Software (SW) field, in PS register, *(II)*, 6–6
Software completion bit, *(II)*, 6–13
Software considerations, A–1
  See also Performance optimizations

Software interrupt request (SIRR) register
  described, *(II)*, 5–20
  interrupt arbitration, *(II)*, 6–35
  protocol for, *(II)*, 6–19
  with interrupts, *(II)*, 6–19
Software interrupts, *(II)*, 6–19
  asynchronous system traps (AST), *(II)*,
    6–20
  protocol between summary and request,
    (II), 6–19
  recording pending state of, *(II)*, 5–21
  request (SIRR) register, *(II)*, 6–19
  requesting, *(II)*, 5–20
  service routine entry points, *(II)*, 6–28
  summary (SISR) register, *(II)*, 6–19
  supported levels of, *(II)*, 5–20
Software interrupt summary (SISR) register
  described, *(II)*, 5–21
  protocol for, *(II)*, 6–19
  with interrupts, *(II)*, 6–19
Software traps, generating, *(II)*, 2–10
/S opcode qualifier
  IEEE floating-point, *(I)*, 4–61
  VAX floating-point, *(I)*, 4–61
SP
  See Stack pointer
SRA instruction, *(I)*, 4–41
SRL instruction, *(I)*, 4–40
Stack alignment, *(II)*, 6–31
Stack alignment (SP_ALIGN), field in saved
  PS, *(II)*, 6–6
Stack frames, *(II)*, 6–7; *(III)*, 5–3
Stack pointer (SP)
  defined, *(II)*, 1–1; *(III)*, 1–4
  register linkage for, *(III)*, 1–1
Stack pointer internal processor registers,
  (II), 5–1
Starvation, *(I)*, 8–4
STATUS field (mailbox), *(I)*, 8–6
STF instruction, *(I)*, 4–73
  when data is unaligned, *(II)*, 6–27
STG instruction, *(I)*, 4–74
  when data is unaligned, *(II)*, 6–27
STL_C instruction, *(I)*, 4–11
  when data is unaligned, *(II)*, 6–27
  with LDx_L instruction, *(I)*, 4–11
  with processor lock register/flag, *(I)*, 4–11
STL instruction, *(I)*, 4–13
  when data is unaligned, *(II)*, 6–27
Store instructions
  See also Floating-point store instructions
  emulation of, *(I)*, 4–2
  FETCH instruction, *(I)*, 4–115
  multiprocessor environment, *(I)*, 5–5
  serialization, *(I)*, 4–117

Store instructions (cont'd)
  store longword, *(I)*, 4–13
  store longword conditional, *(I)*, 4–11
  store quadword, *(I)*, 4–13
  store quadword conditional, *(I)*, 4–11
  store unaligned quadword, *(I)*, 4–14
  when data is unaligned, *(II)*, 6–27
Store memory integer instructions (list), *(I)*,
  4–4
STQ_C instruction, *(I)*, 4–11
  use in accessing MBPR, *(I)*, 8–3
  with LDx_L inst., *(I)*, 4–11
  with processor lock register/flag, *(I)*, 4–11
STQ_L instruction
  when data is unaligned, *(II)*, 6–27
STQ_U instruction, *(I)*, 4–14
STQ instruction, *(I)*, 4–13
  when data is unaligned, *(II)*, 6–27
STQP (PALcode) instruction, *(II)*, 2–88
STS instruction, *(I)*, 4–75
  when data is unaligned, *(II)*, 6–27
STT instruction, *(I)*, 4–76
  when data is unaligned, *(II)*, 6–27
SUBF instruction, *(I)*, 4–109
SUBG instruction, *(I)*, 4–109
SUBL instruction, *(I)*, 4–32
SUBQ instruction, *(I)*, 4–34
SUBS instruction, *(I)*, 4–111
SUBT instruction, *(I)*, 4–111
Subtract instructions
  See also Floating-point operate
  subtract longword, *(I)*, 4–32
  subtract quadword, *(I)*, 4–34
  subtract scaled longword, *(I)*, 4–33
  subtract scaled quadword, *(I)*, 4–35
Supervisor read enable (SRE), bit in PTE,
  (II), 3–6
Supervisor stack pointer (SSP)
  as internal processor register, *(II)*, 5–1
  in HWPCB, *(II)*, 4–2
Supervisor stack pointer (SSP) register, *(II)*,
  5–28
Supervisor write enable (SWE), bit in PTE,
  (II), 3–6
SWASTEN (PALcode) instruction, *(II)*, 2–19
  interrupt arbitration, *(II)*, 6–36
  with ASTEN register, *(II)*, 5–6
SWC bit
  exception summary parameter, *(II)*, 6–13
  exception summary register, *(III)*, 5–2, 5–4
swpctx (PALcode) instruction, *(III)*, 2–14
  PCB with, *(III)*, 4–1
  with ASNs, *(III)*, 3–8
SWPCTX (PALcode) instruction, *(II)*, 2–89
  with ASTSR register, *(II)*, 5–8

swpipl (PALcode) instruction, *(III)*, 2–16
  PS with, *(III)*, 5–2
Synchronous traps, *(III)*, 5–2
  data alignment, *(II)*, 6–15
  defined, *(II)*, 6–9
  program counter (PC) value, *(II)*, 6–15
  REI instruction with, *(II)*, 6–15
System call entry (entSys) register, *(III)*, 1–3,
  5–4, 5–8
System control block (SCB)
  arithmetic trap entry points, *(II)*, 6–27
  fault entry points, *(II)*, 6–26
  finding PFN, *(II)*, 5–19
  saved on stack frame, *(II)*, 6–7
  structure of, *(II)*, 6–25
  with memory management faults, *(II)*,
    3–14
System control block base (SCBB) register,
  (II), 5–19
System cycle counter (SCC), reading, *(II)*,
  2–17
System entry addresses, *(III)*, 5–3
System value (sysvalue) register, *(III)*, 1–4

T

T_floating data type
  alignment of, *(I)*, 2–10
  exceptions, *(I)*, 2–10
  format, *(I)*, 2–9
  MAX/MIN, *(I)*, 4–59
  when data is unaligned, *(II)*, 6–27
TB
  See Translation buffer
tbi (PALcode) instruction, *(III)*, 2–17
  with TBs, *(III)*, 3–8
Tightly coupled I/O bus, *(I)*, 8–1
Timeout, *(I)*, 8–4
Timing considerations, atomic sequences,
  A–17
Translation
  physical, *(III)*, 3–6
  virtual, *(III)*, 3–7
Translation buffer (TB), *(III)*, 3–8
  address space number with, *(II)*, 3–11
  fault on execute, *(II)*, 6–12
  fault on read, *(II)*, 6–11
  fault on write, *(II)*, 6–11
  granularity hint in PTE, *(II)*, 3–5
  with invalid PTEs, *(II)*, 3–12
Translation buffer check (TBCHK) register
  described, *(II)*, 5–22
  with translation buffer, *(II)*, 3–12

Translation buffer invalidate all (TBIA) register
  described, *(II)*, 5–24
  with translation buffer, *(II)*, 3–12
Translation buffer invalidate all process (TBIAP) register
  described, *(II)*, 5–25
  with translation buffer, *(II)*, 3–12
Translation buffer invalidate single (TBIS) register, *(II)*, 5–26
Translation not valid fault, *(II)*, 6–10
  service routine entry point, *(II)*, 6–26
Translation-not-valid fault, *(III)*, 3–9
TRAPB (trap barrier) instruction, A–14
  described, *(I)*, 4–120
  with MT_FPCR, *(I)*, 4–66
  with trap shadow, *(I)*, 4–62
Trap handler, with non-finite arithmetic operands, *(I)*, 4–63
Trap handling, IEEE floating-point, B–4
Trap modes
  floating-point, *(I)*, 4–60
  IEEE, *(I)*, 4–61
  IEEE convert-to-integer, *(I)*, 4–61
  VAX, *(I)*, 4–60
  VAX convert-to-integer, *(I)*, 4–61
Traps
  See Arithmetic traps
Trap shadow, *(III)*, 5–2
  defined, *(I)*, 4–62
  defined for floating-point, *(I)*, 4–58
  trap handler requirement for, *(I)*, 4–62
Trigger instruction, *(III)*, 5–2
True result, *(I)*, 4–57
True zero, *(I)*, 4–57

U

UMULH instruction, *(I)*, 4–31
  with MULQ, *(I)*, 4–30
Unaligned access fault
  system entry for, *(III)*, 5–4
UNALIGNED data objects, *(I)*, 1–9
Unaligned fault entry (entUna) register, *(III)*, 1–3, 5–8
Unconditional long jump, *(I)*, 4–21
UNDEFINED operations, *(I)*, 1–7
Underflow trap, *(II)*, 6–15; *(III)*, 5–5
UNF bit
  exception summary parameter, *(II)*, 6–13
  exception summary register, *(III)*, 5–5
UNORDERED memory references, *(I)*, 5–9
UNPREDICTABLE results, *(I)*, 1–7

Unprivileged PALcode instructions (list), *(III)*, 2–1
Unprivileged PALcode instructions, VAX compatibility, *(II)*, 2–75
/U opcode qualifier
  IEEE floating-point, *(I)*, 4–61
  VAX floating-point, *(I)*, 4–61
Updated datum, *(I)*, 5–5
User mode, protection code with, *(III)*, 3–6
User read enable (URE)
  bit in PTE, *(II)*, 3–6; *(III)*, 3–4
User stack pointer (USP)
  defined, *(III)*, 1–4
  in HWPCB, *(II)*, 4–2
  internal processor register, *(II)*, 5–1
User stack pointer (USP) register, *(II)*, 5–29
User write enable (UWE)
  bit in PTE, *(II)*, 3–6; *(III)*, 3–4

V

Valid (V)
  bit in PTE, *(II)*, 3–4; *(III)*, 3–5
vaSize, *(III)*, 1–2
VAX compatibility instructions, restrictions for, *(I)*, 4–121
VAX compatibility register, *(I)*, 3–2
VAX convert-to-integer trap mode, *(I)*, 4–61
VAX floating-point
  See also Floating-point instructions
  D_floating, *(I)*, 2–6
  F_floating, *(I)*, 2–3
  G_floating, *(I)*, 2–5
  trap modes, *(I)*, 4–62
VAX floating-point instructions
  add instructions, *(I)*, 4–88
  compare instructions, *(I)*, 4–91
  convert from integer instructions, *(I)*, 4–95
  convert to integer instructions, *(I)*, 4–94
  convert VAX floating format instructions, *(I)*, 4–96
  divide instructions, *(I)*, 4–102
  multiply instructions, *(I)*, 4–106
  opcodes for, C–5
  operate instructions, *(I)*, 4–80
  qualifiers, summarized, C–5
  subtract instructions, *(I)*, 4–109
VAX rounding modes, *(I)*, 4–59
VAX trap modes, required instruction notation, *(I)*, 4–61
Virtual address format, *(II)*, 3–2
  segment number fields, *(II)*, 3–2
Virtual address space
  minimum and maximum, *(II)*, 3–2
  page size with, *(II)*, 3–1

Virtual address spaces, *(III)*, 3–1
Virtual address translation, *(II)*, 3–10
Virtual D-cache, *(I)*, 5–3
  maintaining coherency of, *(I)*, 5–3
Virtual format, *(III)*, 3–1
Virtual I-cache, *(I)*, 5–3
  maintaining coherency of, *(I)*, 5–5
Virtual machine monitor (VMM), bit in PS
    register, *(II)*, 6–6
Virtual page base (VPTB) register, *(II)*, 5–30
Virtual page table pointer (VPTPTR), *(III)*,
    1–4
/V opcode qualifier
  IEEE floating-point, *(I)*, 4–61
  VAX floating-point, *(I)*, 4–61

W

Watchpoints
  with fault on read, *(II)*, 6–11
  with fault on write, *(II)*, 6–11
WDATA field (mailbox), *(I)*, 8–6
W field (mailbox), *(I)*, 8–5
Whami, *(III)*, 1–4
whami (PALcode) instruction, *(III)*, 2–18
WHO_ARE_YOU command, *(I)*, 8–13
Who-Am-I (WHAMI) register, *(II)*, 5–31
Word data type, *(I)*, 2–1
WR_PS_SW (PALcode) instruction, *(II)*,
    2–20
wrent (PALcode) instruction, *(III)*, 2–19
wrfen (PALcode) instruction, *(III)*, 2–21
WRITE_UNQ (PALcode) instruction, *(II)*,
    2–82
Write-back caches, requirements for, *(I)*, 5–4
Write buffers, requirements for, *(I)*, 5–4
wrkgp (PALcode) instruction, *(III)*, 2–22
wrunique (PALcode) instruction, *(III)*, 2–7
  PCB with, *(III)*, 4–1
  required recognition of, *(I)*, 6–4
WRUNIQUE (PALcode) instruction
  required recognition of, *(I)*, 6–4
wrusp (PALcode) instruction, *(III)*, 2–23
  PCB with, *(III)*, 4–1
wrval (PALcode) instruction, *(III)*, 2–24
wrvptptr (PALcode) instruction, *(III)*, 2–25

X

XOR instruction, *(I)*, 4–37

Z

ZAP instruction, *(I)*, 4–55
ZAPNOT instruction, *(I)*, 4–55

Zero byte instructions (list), *(I)*, 4–55